BA'AL BUSTERS
PRIESTCRAFT: BEYOND BABYLON

Unimaginable Evil and our Duty to Stop It

Book 1: Giving a Name to "THEY." A Historical Look at the Themes of ancient cult Mystery Schools, and how their themes manifest in Science, Medicine, Religion, Government, Banking, and more

Table of Contents

This book is dedicated to my daughter, my grandfather, my father, Mr. Milton William Cooper, his girls Dorothy and Allison, wife Annie, and to the Constitutional Republic that was envisioned by our Founders.

It is through inexhaustible reading, research, and analysis of those before me brave enough to utter the TRUTH and relay FACTS in this the *Age of Deception,* that I am able to write this book.

Although this is not nearly a full list of Brave and Honorable People, I would like to thank the following, some living, some passed on:

(It's typical to italicize book titles, and it's typical of me to do things my way)

William "Bill" Cooper – Author of **Behold a Pale Horse**, and Voice of **Hour of the Time** radio broadcast

Eustace Mullins – Author of **Secrets of the Federal Reserve**, **Murder By Injection**, and others

Thomas Paine – Author of **Common Sense** and **Age of Reason**

Stefan Verstappen – Author of several books incl **The Art of Urban Survival** and **The Master's Guide to the Way of the Warrior**

Robert Sepehr – "Most Dangerous Anthropologist" and Author of multiple books including **1666: Redemption Through Sin**

Michael S. King – Banned from Amazon, Author of several fast-paced books including **The Bad War**, **Planet Rothschild I & II**, **St. Joseph of Wisconsin**, **Andrew the Great**, and many more.

Donald Jeffries – Author of **Hidden History**, and **Crimes and Cover-ups in American Politics**

Freeman – Creator of the Freeman Perspective, Radio Freeman, and Freeman TV

Kevin Annett – Author of **Murder By Decree**, dozens other books, and a true noble warrior

Johnny Cirucci – for his book **Illuminati Unmasked** regarding the Jesuits

Introduction
(Typically Found in the Beginning)

"Almost all people of all eras are hypnotics. Their beliefs are induced beliefs. The proper authorities sought to it that the proper beliefs should be induced, and people believed properly." -Charles Hoy Fort (1874-1932)

"Ladies and gentlemen, I would like to preface the rest of this broadcast with this little statement. A lot of what you're going to hear me say today is going to make some of you very angry. Because some of you are caught up in some of these deceptions that I'm going to talk about and you have no idea what you're involved in, or what the symbology of the ceremonies in which you participate really mean. And I want to tell you this, that I am not telling you this information… I am not giving you these revelations to make you angry or to hurt you. For if you're an American, I love you. And that's the truth and that's why I've devoted my life to service to this country, and to the American People. That's why my family and I go without an awful lot of things a lot of you enjoy everyday in order to do the research and create this radio station, newspaper… all of the things that we have done to educate the American People and bring them out of deception. I want you to understand that I'm going to be bringing you this information, these revelations, if you will, in order to help you see the Truth. To find the Truth. And whether you decide to do that or not is your business because I believe wholeheartedly in Freedom. And your right to make your choice, to believe whatever you want and belong to whatever organizations you wish, to adhere to whatever religion you wish, worship on whatever alter of your choice… But I believe in order to make that choice you need to have information. You need to know the Truth about some things. And I know that many of you will resent that because you don't like to know you've been deceived. Because that makes us feel stupid when that happens. Makes us feel little and insignificant and of course we fight that. And we practice denial, and we put off any kind of Truth that tends to make us feel in that way. And I hope that we can learn... not to resist the Truth, not to fight the Truth, but to look for it and to accept it, and embrace it lovingly. For it is the Truth that sets us free. It is the Truth that will make the future… If we learn it!

If we choose to stay in the old deceptions, live the lies, practice the manipulations & all of the bad things the human race is known for throughout its history, then the future will always be full of strife and conflict & murder, rape, & all of the bad things we would like to see disappear. Or at least some of us. I choose to think the majority of us would like to see that happen.

So I want you to know that I care about each and every one of you deeply. I care about this nation…"

-Milton William Cooper, ***The Hour of the Time*** radio broadcast Episode #1078 *Stone of Foundation* Originally aired March 18th, 1997

We're embarking on a historical journey together. I'm presenting to you the patterns of behavior and a common philosophy [patter recognition] I see from reading the works of the organizations determining our path now, and draw direct connections to the Cult of Baal in Ugarit, the Alumbrato, Jesuits, Sabbatean-Frankists, Freemasons, Bolsheviks, Rothschild and Rockefellers, and the present day tyrannical despots like the UN, NATO, WHO, and the WEF. This book was originally called Most Noble Cause because once we establish an understanding of who these culprits are, and their history of behavior, objectives, and beliefs, it reveals their constants. And one of the most despicable and evil constant threads, or themes, running throughout all of these manifestations is their brutal, wicked assault on babies and innocent children. It is a well documented, and not at all hidden initiative and incorporates sneaky Eugenics. Adults, we are not without faults and poor actions. But to target the children is the greatest offense against the Creator, whomever you perceive that Creator to be, and to family. These High Priests in high places must be recognized by their actions, seen for what they are, acknowledged as to their objective, and stopped at all costs to protect not only our natural rights, but also the lives of the innocent. What more noble cause than that is there?

2

What you are about to read in the proceeding chapters should not be misconstrued as a condemnation of anyone else's beliefs, nor is it an opinion piece. It's an analysis and a conclusion as to what the facts, and the various echoing statements made by esteemed members of these fraternal orders and movements means. An "opinion" implies judgment atop of an observation; a snap decision, or preconceived biased notion. Except where there is no sensible argument such as, Murder is Bad, for instance, the opinions or judgments will be rather scarce. Be aware, a fact that's unknown to many is commonly misidentified as an opinion, and worse it's perceived as apophenia by those lacking the same devotion to analysis and research. Countless hours of study over the past ten years have gone into these pages. If one isn't dedicated to the TRUTH, and they don't bother to fully research, all they can have is an uniformed, biased opinion, and they're dealing in smug emotions, not facts. Someone who presumes to be an expert on a topic I cover because they remember something they heard that sounded good to them, is in effect spreading unverified information, ie a rumor. Instead of verifying their data, they chose to lead with their mouth. The popularity of a rumor or a belief doesn't graduate it into the status of a Fact no matter how much it's bandied about. I will present my findings, how I see it relating to other facets of our culture and human experience, both past and present, and deliver my understanding of it. What I'm seeing when I read the works and study the deeds of particular secret organizations, AKA the Mysteries, or Mystery Schools, the Invisible College, etc. is a common thread, or multitude of threads, as in common themes. After awhile they become a signature, a fingerprint impression left across the pages of time. Even with all the efforts to mask the true meaning in symbols, various degrees of exoteric, or common surface-level appearance, allegorical layers, code language, and cryptic gematria, the picture does come into focus, and it cuts through all the filters of deception.

There will not be a glossary of terms at the back of this book. It is important to explain these right now. The terms **esoteric** and **occult** simply mean "hidden." Many extrapolate and take liberties when applying a negative connotation to the terms. Even modern dictionaries have slipped away from objectivity in their slanted opinion of definitions as they attempt to mold our minds, and make us more impulsive. Yes, even definitions have suffered the effects of truth-by-consensus, or democratic, meaning Mob, rule. The programming of our culture and the inadequate, or absence of education on Thinking has led us to accept popular preconceived notions. These are called prejudices and they tie into the laundry list of logical fallacies running a muck in all present, media-driven societies. One could argue Esoteric and Occult could be finer detailed by saying Esoteric is the layer beneath the common or superficial outer appearance, and that which is Occult is communicated only to the initiated, or out of reach of ordinary, controlled knowledge. But it's saying the same thing. The info is being hidden, it's coveted by a powerful few. It isn't just that it's not obvious a distant glance. There's an active effort to supply false information in its place.

The other term that's branded with a proverbial scarlet letter is the word "CULT." Ooo, it even looks scary in all capital letters like that, doesn't it? That's the embedded programming within us sounding off the alarm. Media and government for the past 60 years or so have been increasingly using this term with the implication that once something is labeled with it, it's evil, must be evil, and there's no need to think any further, or even consider that group of people as being human anymore. It's called **demonization**, and governments and rulers since the beginning of time would arouse suspicion and doubt within the minds of people with tales, true or not, about their political opponents, or detractors, dissenters, and resistance groups. They knew with enough hypnotic repetition, and the more damning the accusations, a fire would ignite within them, or at least a mob-consensus, and the people would uniformly support whatever measures their "trusted sources" suggested for dealing with the "problem." Whether the problem was real or fabricated in the ruler's imagination, notwithstanding. These words-with-weight are first cultivated until they have a universal influence, a reflexive response, and then they are implemented quite deliberately to inspire the desired emotion within us. The word Cult doesn't organically imply anything evil or bad. When you really start to examine your own assumptions and presumptions, you will start to ask, "Evil to whom? Relative to what type of person is this (insert topic here) considered evil?" Oxford's first listed definition is the only honest one, *"a system of religious veneration and devotion directed toward a particular figure or object."* That still seems to be a slippery way to imply idolatry, and that's not always the case. For there was a time Christianity was a mere cult, and occult, for it was dangerous to practice in public. You see, any practice outside of the dominating religion, or so-called family of religious sects, is technically a cult because the word relates to the size of the following. The Open Friendly Society, or Christianity, had to be covert so as to survive the scrutiny and persecution of the ruling class who saw them as a threat to their state religion(s) and control mechanism, but I repeat myself. It was a cult for its size, and occult for its members needed to practice in secrecy to preserve their very lives.

In an effort to lay the groundwork, we turn now to Mr. William Cooper, the creator of Veritas (meaning Truth) newspaper, and the host of the classic short-wave radio broadcast, *The Hour of the Time*. On his 9-year running broadcast from May 4th 1992 until November 5th, 2001, he covered a great many topics few were aware of, let alone discussing. Numerous episodes were devoted to uncovering the motives, and identifying the true nature of what we see being acted out on the world theater today, and most especially he focused on the happenings right here in the United States. His 42 episode dive into what he called the *Mystery Babylon series* will be occasioned in this book as well. Throughout this journey we will be checking in with Bill, and seeing what he had to say on these topics going back sometimes 30 years.

This excerpt was transcribed from episode 0986, originally broadcast November 4th, 1996, the title, *Secret Societies and Psychological Warfare pt 1:*

"...In John H Towsen's *Clowns* he says this, quote, "As the mountebank delivered his harangue, the clown would repeatedly poke his head out from behind the curtain, making fun of everything his master said, parodying his patter and twisting the meaning of his words. The mountebank meanwhile played the perfect straight man. Here he was, trying so hard to hawk his wares, and his own assistant was doing everything possible to undermine sales. The merriment was of course intentional. While the clown seemingly encouraged the public not the proffered merchandise, the mountebank knew full well that the bystanders would easily be converted into customers as soon as they forgot that they were, in fact, supposed to be buying. Once the audience had been effectively **hypnotized**, once its judgment and willpower had been weakened, the real sales pitch could begin…" And in the *Encyclopedia of Freemasonry*, Dr. Albert Mackey, 33rd degree, defines *hoodwinked* as quote, "A symbol of the secrecy, silence, and darkness in which the mysteries of our art should be preserved from the unhallowed gaze of the profane." end quote. In a study, ladies and gentlemen, of mind control and psychological warfare, it is not enough to simply review the latest technology of coercion, the latest gadgetry and techno-junk littering the hardware and supply depots of governments and so-called "cults." You see, far more dangerous than these appliances is the praxis behind them: [the] **Ages-old underground current** which informs the modern project and this modern era. You see for life in our modern era is little more than life in an open air laboratory where a form of human **alchemy** has emerged to transform the mass of targeted percipients, the lead, targeted merely by their virtue of being urban dwellers plugged into the electronic and digital pageantry of the establishment's system of things… into the perfect human zombie, gold to those who practice this ancient science that has never meant what any of you have ever thought. At first many people ridicule alchemy as being absolutely impossible to transform base elements, but you see that's not what it was ever about. Not ever! In those days the church and kings ruled with an iron hand and anyone who did anything that was not politically correct, or religiously correct were swiftly and most terribly punished. So they disguised their true intent and their true teachings, the esoteric, with a system of exoteric descriptions. [And] to the profane would mean one thing, and to the initiate or the adept would mean quite another. But that was then. This is now. What sort of creature inhabits the modern domain? Who is the Modern Man? Well, the puppet masters say he is the smartest, most advanced individual to ever strut the planet, the most relatively liberated being in history. But Louis Ferdinand-Celine said it well, quote, "What does the modern public want? It wants to go down on it's knees before money and before crap," end quote.

`You see the public had been trained to do this by two principal methods: direct speaking archetypal messages of pure terror, psychic driving as the CIA's Dr Ewan Cameron termed it, encoded in massively publicized lone nut mass murders, and the sinister flattery heaped upon them by their masters in the cult of "civilization," and "progress." The acid test of a human being's freedom and will to protect the quality of his life lies in a person's attitude toward his oppressor. What is Modern Man's attitude… toward Wall St, and the Bankers, the elite, that body of adepts known as the Secret College, that combined are known as the Illuminati, or the Order? What is modern man's attitude toward Dan Rather, and the ignorance-bestowing media, and the advertising man? Toward Lincoln and Truman? Franklin Delanor Roosevelt and Reagan, George Bush, Johnny Carson, Exxon and Monsanto and William Clinton? Well, as one writer has observed and I quote, "The most amazing thing about the American people is that they are constantly defending their worst betrayers," end quote. So I ask you again, who then is the Modern Man? Well if you've listened to this broadcast long enough you know my interpretation. He is a mind-bombed patsy, an ignorant, apathetic twit who gets his marching orders from Twilight Language, keywords sprinkled throughout *his* news and current events, and even as he dances to the tune of the elite managers of human behavior, provoked by buzzwords, he scoffs with great derision at the idea of the existence and operation of a technology of a mass mind control emanating from the media and government. And that is most unfortunate…

Modern Man believes that he is much too smart to believe anything as superstitious as that. But the truth is, ladies and gentlemen, modern man is the ideal hypnotic subject. Puffed up on the idea that he is the crown of creation, he vehemently denies the power of the hypnotist's control over him even as his head bobs up and down on the string. Anyone who believes what anyone else writes or says without thoroughly researching it and making sure it is absolutely true is a puppet on a string, and when the puppet master calls the tune, he will dance. What we observe in the population today are the three destructive symptoms of persons whose minds are controlled by alien forces, and I DO NOT mean from Mars. These forces are amnesia, in effect loss of memory. The second is abulia, or loss of Will. The third is apathy, loss of interest in events vital to one's own health and survival. Amnesia, abulia, and apathy are nearly universal among us today and gaining a greater foothold with every passing day.

A Japanese philosopher, George Osawa stated that there was only one incurable sickness, Arrogance. If a patient does not regard himself as sick, he cannot submit to a cure. That's why I've urged you, ladies and gentlemen, if you want to see what is wrong with America today, go into the bathroom and look into the mirror. You will find the problem staring at you. And at that point when you make that realization you must admit to yourself, "I have been stupid. I am stupid. I am ignorant. I am apathetic, and I must change." And if you do not, nothing, Nothing will change. Nothing will become better. Nothing at all.

The Arrogant Man does not need to see. (chuckles) He already sees almost everything, and what he thinks is [what] you have to learn the experts will one day show him. And who are these experts? They're not really doctors of the soul, ladies and gentlemen. They do not have the Man's interest at heart. They are, in fact, his worst enemies. His most cunning manipulators who lead him to do their bidding like any other slave master since Egypt. Why then? Why then does modern man revere them? Well very simply, because ladies and gentlemen they flatter him! And that's why you don't get any flattery from me ever. You never have. I call the shots as they are, I tell you the truth no matter who it hurts or helps, even if it hurts me. And oh, how you hate it. Oh, how you hate to hear the truth. A man who tells the truth is universally disliked by every person. Because every person has an agenda, and is hiding behind a fantasy which the truth penetrates like an arrow, and leaves him stripped naked before the whole universe. And he does not like that. But yet it must be for a great man once said, my leader once said, "Seek ye the truth, and the truth will make you free." Nothing else will. And without the truth no man or woman is free, can be free, or ever will be free. But the truth hurts. The truth strips all away and stands golden before all men. Yet how many of you trade that gold of the Truth for the lead of the fantasy and the lies? How many of you are going backward in the alchemical process?

Modern Man reveres his puppet masters, his overseers because they flatter him. This is the very first secret of mass mind control and can be observed as the foundation stone of virtually every single false religion, party, cult, philosophy, system, training, and great organized church. How can modern man free himself when he is told that he is already a demigod? That the problem lies in only finding the pure-enough economic or political system worthy of his high-minded brilliance? If we look closely we will see, ladies and gentlemen, that this mind control principle is so simple and basic. It is almost stupidly so to the point that we marvel at anyone who could be seduced by it. But it's only a matter of attention, as we saw in the parable of the mountebank and the clown. You see arrogant hypno-patsies have been told by their masters that they are demigods, and demigods are never deceived or distracted. They're too smart. And by their arrogant self-satisfaction they blind themselves to the simplicity of the device that ensnares them, and that is when The Real Sales Pitch Begins…

You see, what the alchemical managers have bred over a millennia is a human race of the most retched stupidity and ignorance unrivaled in thousands of years. These blind slaves are told they are FREE and highly educated, and they believe it, even as they march behind signs that would cause any medieval peasant to run screaming from them in panic-stricken terror. The symbols that modern man embraces with the naive trust of an infant would be tantamount to billboards reading, quote, "This Way To Your Death and Enslavement," end quote, to the understanding of a traditional peasant from antiquity. It was their world, they understood it perfectly. I doubt seriously any medieval man would have much difficulty in feeling a sense of overwhelming foreboding in the face of the Soviet hammer and sickle symbol. Yet, obviously most modern people don't know a thing about what that symbol actually represents except on the most profane level as the (mocking tone) implements of the farmer and worker. (laughs) You really believe that? The sickle, ladies and gentlemen, symbolizes Saturn, also known as Kronos. Saturn, or as the Greek called it Demiurgos, the operating engineer of the universe, as opposed to the Creator of that universe. Satan, Lucifer. In the ring of Saturn we see exorbitant building and modeling activities and this is reflected in the Masonic reference to their god who is big builder or Architect, and their nickname, the Builders… This [Masonic Saturnian edifice] is building against the grain, against nature. What's wrong with that? Well, stick with me and you'll see…"

If this book is your first experience with the work of Milton William Cooper, I encourage you to seek out the archives of the *Hour of the Time* broadcast on billcooper.joshwho.net and the Hour of the Time channel on BitChute. Hearing his deep baritone voice brings his words to dramatic life, for he was a master orator.

3

Who am I? What is Ba'al Busters Broadcast? Why should you want to defend your natural born rights? Who is this "They" oppressing us? How long has this been going on? What institutions have "They" infiltrated, and how far along into their agenda are we?

Through the course of this book I will answer those questions to the best of my ability based on the extensive effort and time I've put into reading, analyzing, and researching human history, and present situations.

If I could be light and humorous this whole book I would, but to accurately discuss the topics of Oppression, Tyranny, and Child Crimes it requires us to venture into some very dark territory. These aren't just greedy political criminals we're dealing with. At the highest level what we call "money" is worthless to these counterfeiters. They print it. It's not an object of their desire. Human suffering is their stock and trade. They may measure the amount of suffering they cause by the level of "money" and real assets they steal away from us with this debt-slavery system, but the fiat itself isn't the object. This is PURE EVIL in its most despicable and unconscionable form. We'll "circle back to that" soon enough.

Like with all truly dark subject matter, one must first understand the risks involved before venturing. To speak a name is to summon. It's a basic precept of energetic magic. To think of is to entangle. You can't read something like the dark magic grimoires, or Aleister Crowley without those powers and principalities reading you, as well. They gain access to you as you read of them. You must be solid of substance, and strong in your faith to battle that which worms its way in as you learn of it.

Who Am I?

Without lapsing into a philosophical monologue, pondering the universe and the existential, let me get to the point. I am a once-innocent child who finds himself in an ever-aging vessel made of meat and now playing the role of adult, and Dad, which I embrace as my purpose. Although I may have been self-serving in my youth, oblivious of many things into my adulthood, and insensitive on many occasions, beneath all that, I was still once that little boy who spent countless hours alone in his toy room sensing something was wrong, with an ever-present sense of foreboding, feeling that something was watching everything and that it was a mean, nasty thing. But there was something else, and it was within me. I gravitated to my imagination and by acting out dramatic plays of good and evil with my Masters of the Universe He-Man figures, trying to build a shield of protection around me by creating good stories. The Giant, played by me, would always set both groups down and have them peacefully settle their differences. I used reason and kindness, because as a child you're naive enough to think that the world is a reflection of your own heart. Nothing and no one could ever be so evil as to actually want the suffering of others, could they? I seem to have been hard-wired to my empathy. I told you of the mocking watcher, and that I was not alone with it. I felt a loving, friendly presence and from that I believe I was given the courage to deal with what, looking back, may well have been a haunted, split-level apartment building we lived in. I had frequent terrifying "dreams" there, and when I awoke the terror didn't cease. I was still seeing moving shadows and I was paralyzed. I couldn't move, and only air would escape my mouth, but no noise when I tried screaming for my mom. My eyes were open and I was seeing things moving. When they got close to the bed sometimes I'd get something equivalent to jolt where my leg would involuntarily kick up as if from electricity, like the defib paddles used in a hospital.

I was a product of a divorce at age 3. As New York would have it, I was awarded to my mother. My earliest memory is of a fight between my dad and my mom where I was subjected to a scene that no one should ever haphazardly let happen in front of their young children. They were just arguing and throwing things at one another, but it was enough trauma at that age to have erased what was already on my memory tape, and deeply record this over the top of it. I remember trying to look down at my coloring book and just connect the dots to reveal the picture. I just wanted to draw and color, and maybe if I did I could escape the eye of their emotional storm. Maybe it would stop on its own if I just acted like I wasn't noticing it. I could look down at the book, hearing everything, responding to nothing and just wait it out. It didn't work. Even at that age where I could easily be intimidated, I perceived the need to get involved. It was a powerful sense that compelled me through the fear to where I found myself now in the middle of my mom and dad begging for them to stop fighting. Parents don't remember being a child, I guess. Their empathy, or the ability to feel things as someone else firsthand, appears to dissipate with the passing of time and their exposure to social conditioning, and likely killed out of them by the series of injections we are told we need. Even if a, and I'm trying very hard not to use the word "kid," little one doesn't visibly show signs that something affects them, when we're real fresh and pure, we absorb everything in our surroundings like a sponge. If not outwardly noticeable, you best believe we're processing and attempting to make sense of things internally. So don't serve up sewer water to your most precious sponges, OK Parents?

After I was living with just-mom, I would spend a lot of time in my toy room, an extra bedroom in our Mechanicville apartment on Park Ave. No, not that Park Ave. This was Upstate New York. My grandmother and others had bought me a bunch of He-Man figures and I would act out elaborate dramas with them, as mentioned. I would often incorporate myself into the stories as a character who intervened between the two groups. I would captivate their attention and the fighting among them would stop. I'd separate them and explain that I knew what was going on and that they didn't need to continue to hate and fight with each other. They were all appreciated by me, and I knew they were reasonable and honorable. I'd explain their misunderstandings to them, and that they should become friends because there was real evil *out there* and they would need all their strength and effort to fight it. They couldn't be too busy killing each other, weakening themselves, and miss the real threat. I had some weird pointy-eared gargoyle toys from another collection I'd use for the Evil ones. Looking back at that, it was a pretty intricate and complex make-believe to have acted out as a boy no older than 7. I didn't know what I knew at that age, and that's a common theme I see in child development. Often we're convinced to let go of more than we gain in return as we're assimilating into the culture of "civilized" society. We forget more Truth on the quest to fit-in and please than we ever acquire. It's also why I know "Come as children" doesn't mean as immature or naive, but rather as untainted by the wickedness of this desensitized and disconnected world.

Was my role as benevolent guardian, as conflict resolver, somehow a ripple effect from my experiences when I witnessed my parents fighting? Maybe. Or maybe that's what I always was, and was supposed to be, because it always felt right. Maybe there was a hand guiding me through the experiences necessary to activate what parts of my character I was supposed to train and strengthen. Either way, there are a lot of parallels one could draw from then all the way to how it applies to what I do now with my videos and podcasts for Ba'al Busters.

I went to St. Paul's Assumption for kindergarten. Which is basically like saying St. Paul's hunch, St. Paul's pretty sure, anyway. The next year they closed the school, so I went to [name omitted] Elementary, a public school. I was short, mostly quiet, and shy, reserved, but I was pretty ruthless when it came to bullies. I didn't like injustice done to others or to me. I remember a boy Steven H. being extremely annoying about wanting to carry the dodge ball back to class after recess. He was acting like he was more worthy of such an honor. So after completely ignoring his threats and insults up to a point, when we were on the long staircase heading back to class, I whipped my arm out with the ball, clothes-lining him in the gut, and said, "Here!" He doubled over crying and I walked up the stairs not ever looking back. I could hear the ball bouncing down the steps. For all I know the brat didn't have a ball at his house, so this is what I mean by being insensitive. The last thing we're ever taught is how to communicate with one another properly. I mean him. He sucked. I was an anomaly of both empathy and ruthlessness, but that latter part required provocation to draw it out of me.

4

When I was about 8 years old, my father called to tell me my little brother Christian had died over night. I maybe saw him once or twice. I couldn't make sense of life or death at my age then, or now if we're being honest. I didn't know what to say. I internalized it, not knowing where to place it, but it made me feel hollow and very sad. Now that I'm a father, I can't imagine the pain my father and stepmother went and still go through. It's a sadness that quiets us like the first snowfall on a winter's night, and makes all things that come after it dulled in color, and of less importance. He was only 2 months and 2 weeks old.

I am leading to a point, I promise. There are key details of the backstory of everyone that, when they become known, speak volumes as to who the person you now see is. You can extrapolate so much by knowing what it was that built them...

By 3rd grade we moved to the adjoining Upstate small town. I had to take a school placement test of some kind. I wasn't really sure what the test was, some sort of aptitude test that involved a lot of of situational word problems. I took it thinking I didn't do that great because some parts I hadn't finished. It was timed in sections. Whatever I did, it was good enough for them to take me out of my regular reading class and put me in something called Ideas Unlimited. Apparently whatever kind of Aptitude test it was, my score was off the charts.

This isn't an autobiography, so let's skip ahead now.

My aunt Gina was a great and beautiful being. I have written about her in a screenplay-novel hybrid called **Logos: A Mock Epic** that you can find on the retailer that ate the world's website. The story is fiction, but the part about her was not. If you want to know about Post Traumatic Stress, and you think it only happens to combat soldiers, think again. Many of you reading this probably could point back to an event that made a permanent dent in your psyche, your mental health, or at least left a haunting memory. The real good ones are the kind wrapped in a layer of guilt that you never get over regardless if the feeling of guilt is reasonably valid or not. We all have our dents. Some more than others, but none of us come out of this life without getting dinged up.

This is one of the crucial components that led to my quest against all evil, all injustice, and all forms of medical deception harming our loved ones.

My aunt was a young mother of three, and I was like her unofficial first child because we were so close. After being told she had mononucleosis for a year, that explanation wasn't cutting it anymore. Then these butchers took out her gallbladder. When she was still complaining of fatigue and overall lethargy, the doctors finally decided to cash in. They gave her a diagnosis of a convenient No-See-'em cancer called leukemia. They told her hers was acute. It turns out it was so acute that it took them 2.5 years of poisoning her with chemotherapy and radiation to finally murder her, because the alleged cancer wasn't going to do it without a lot of help by the soulless doctors. This is what is called Iatrogenesis, or plague brought on by doctor/medical intervention. Whatever they tell you the leading cause of death is, which currently they say it's Heart Disease, the true leading cause of death is Iatrogenesis. It's these sorcerers whom cover their black ceremonial robes with a more modern, large white coat who are at the center of every plague man knows. They had no regard for my aunt, a loving mother who just had her first girl, when they recommended, or rather insisted she undergo their barbarous treatments. The more innocent, intelligent, and pure of heart their victim is, the better sacrifice they make. My grandparents were destroyed. Their pain manifested as declining health and a loss of will to carry on. See, we're a family of real people with compassion and love in abundance. We are very connected to one another. I could write a whole book on my aunt, and maybe someday I will. Maybe I should co-write it with my cousins in an effort to never again let what happened to our family, or to yours. Just remember the term **Iatrogenesis**, because it's bound to come up in other chapters of this book. At an early age, just before puberty, when it could be the most devastating, I had to witness the slow, torturous decline of someone I loved very much. Then one day she was taken away. And now, at 43, roughly 30 years later, I am no stronger when I think about it. As I write this, it may as well be happening right now. The pain is ageless. The loss, eternal.

I had a head start on the rest of the world. They're just now getting an up close view, the taste of sour realization that the medical industry is a cold, uncaring, and murderous collection of demons. Pull up a seat, I knew you'd get here eventually. I've been expecting you.

It's most certainly an industry, a for-profit business, but worse, at its core it was a Rothschild-Rockefeller design for control over how we, the "profane," and common view the world, and our health. It was, and is fueled and funded by some of the most active and wealthy names behind Eugenics. If you read the history of the AMA, Rockefeller & Rothchild's-driven method of Allopathy was never an honest system focused on the health of the people. It was always a trade of charlatans, tricksters, and those whose malice for mankind outweighed any motivations of greed. One of their symbols is that of Hermes, the Trickster god of merchants and thieves.

It's natural to recognize and resist attacks on your persons until they condition you to accept it as how they do things down here in this world. I was always offended by injustice, and even though I dealt with more than my share of bullies, I was reflexive whenever I saw someone else getting similar treatment. I'd fly into action with either my fists or verbally. I got real good at ostracizing and making people look as stupid as they truly were. I bullied the bullies in a sense because I'd say things to them no one else would dare to. I had a sharp enough wit to stun them with confusion, as well. Once you made them the object of ridicule and they felt the eyes of the other students in the halls staring at them, the tables were turned, and I gave them a taste of what they normally do to others.

5

After about a year of college, I went into the US Coast Guard. This was before they came under the unconstitutional umbrella of Homeland Security. At that point we were Department of Transportation. I went in thinking I was going to be a Telephone Technician (TT) so like an IT, but the recruiter lied to me because he was trying to fill spots needed for Telecommunications Specialists (TC) and he told me the one was the other. Instead of coming out able to work with my dad who was an IT, I ended up as a TC or what was once called a Radioman, ironically. I had to get Top Secret Clearance in order to carry out my functions in the radio room on the boat. I remember my stepfather's family describing a visit from government agents who were conducting an in-person background check on me. There's a lot I could discuss on the Coast Guard topic, like us spotting boats that were identified in our intel binder as being dirty, or drug smuggling vessels. When we requested permission from command, JTAF West, to pursue and board the drug boats we were often denied with no explanation as to why. I was the one who would send the message requests. The sentiment among the crew was, "Then why are we wasting time out here away from our families?" The sentiment with you should be more like, "Then what are my taxes paying for?"

I was in Cabo San Lucas, MX in a Best Western with my shipmates the morning of the 9/11 attacks. One of the guys who I would occasionally hang out with outside the boat knocked on our door. He came right in without saying a word and went right to the

TV, turned on the news, and just sat there. It was still early. Other people started showing up and our room got a bit crowded. He had put on the news coverage of the smoldering tower. We all watched the "impact" as what we saw as a plane hit the second World Trade Center tower. Everyone freaked out, and I had that quiet, internalization type of response I usually get from traumatic events. It doesn't show much on the outside, but inside it's an overwhelming sense of despair. I can't remember if we were still watching as the towers fell. We were still waking up, and were now being ordered back onboard the ship after less than 10 hours of a planned 3 day port call. Everyone was likely hung over, but shaken sober by the images we had seen. Some of us may have been more than hung over. It was Mexico, after all.

Back onboard, I was in the radio room handling Z-rated message traffic for the first time. Straight from that communist-socialist source itself, Wikipedia, this is what it says about it:

*"**FLASH (Z)** is reserved for initial enemy contact messages or operational combat messages of extreme urgency. Brevity is mandatory. FLASH messages are to be handled as fast as humanly possible, ahead of all other messages, with in-station handling time not to exceed 10 minutes. Messages of lower precedence are interrupted on all circuits involved until the handling of the FLASH message is completed."*

The term "Al-Qaeda" was used extensively in the messages. These were printed and securely hand-delivered to the captain on the bridge as quickly as they came over. That was one of the interesting things about being a TC. I got to report directly to the Captain and the Officer of the Watch. If you want to read more about my experiences in the US Coast Guard, from the Rave scene of San Fran-sicko in the years 1999-2000, where I saved 4 student coast guardsmen from driving off the Golden Gate Bridge, to my time in Astoria, on patrol in Baja California, my time on Pier 1 in Seattle, and my middle finger in-the-air goodbye to the service, then ask for it in another book. It's not the topic of this one.

In happier times I earned the TSTA MVP for the Ops department. TSTA is a month-long Naval evaluation of shipboard operations conducted by the "tans." NAVY wears tan colored uniforms, or khaki, if you prefer. I got the award for being able to troubleshoot the systems they intentionally sabotaged. They send you out of the radio room for a couple minutes while they change your settings, pull out plug cables, patch them incorrectly like mischievous Gremlins, and then call you back in. As a test you have to get comms back online. You're timed. If you can establish comms again on all systems that's a successful completion of the first part of the test. Then they say, "OK you did it, but can you explain what you did?" I was able to draw diagrams of every comms system and illustrate how it's supposed to work. Then I showed them what was hooked up wrong or not hooked up at all. I impressed the two NAVY guys running this drill, so I got the MVP. I remember the TC2 (Petty Officer 2nd Class) was ridiculing me days prior when I was practicing drawing my diagrams the way they taught us in TC training. He said that it was a waste of time and it didn't mean I knew what I was doing. Funny that he wasn't made the MVP of the radio room with all that profound wisdom. I was 2 ranks below him, had less experience by years, and I beat him and I beat Brian, our class valedictorian who was also assigned the same duty station as me, the USCGC Alert, after class ended in Petaluma.

Backstory almost done! I went back to college after the Coast Guard, got my AA that I never bothered to go to graduation to actually be handed, and continued doing stupid jobs like before. I finished with a 3.7 GPA. While in college the first time, I became the Creative Editor of the college paper and once or twice filled in for the guy operating the college radio station. To get a sense of my previous self, I wasn't very fair as a creative editor. I published a lot of my own writing and didn't really put a lot of time into the paper after class like I should have. I had a high school friend attending the same college, and I drove her home. She was very attractive, had a huge chest, and modeled see-through lingerie for me on days I took her home. Extracurricular activities took a distant 2nd place to that.

The Coast Guard experience had matured me a little, but I still had a lot to learn.

If you want to know how my 5 years as a mortgage consultant went, you can read *Divided Highway: the Quest to Save the American Dream.* Don't get the audiobook. The guy who did it, was new, and he omitted things that change the whole feel of the book. Get the paperback or Kindle version.

For the past 9 years I have been in business for myself. Just before that I was a Union (IBEW) Electrician's Apprentice for 5 years. The 5th year you become a journeyman, but I had other plans that didn't involve being barked at by lazy men who complain like women, act like primadonnas, and don't show you how to do anything. I am NOT a soulless, self-centered Communist-Socialist, so I wasn't really meshing well at the Union Hall's mandatory brainwashing sessions they call "meetings," anyway.

In 2013 I decided I wanted to explore my passion for cooking and product making. When I was younger my mother and stepfather owned an Italian restaurant in Upstate, NY and for awhile we lived in a finished basement apartment in the restaurant. My grandmother was a great cook, and her and my mom handled the kitchen duties. My aunt hadn't gotten sick yet, and my brother Steven was just a newborn. The experience represented happy times, when the family was its closest. It was that magic that prompted me to take a chance on myself, and so I got the permits needed to make and sell handcrafted artisan hot sauces at farmers markets. The bureaucracy of permits is a catch-22 nightmare, by the way. I was living in San Diego at that time, and farmers markets ran all year round. Quite quickly I was seeing I really had something with my particular spicy food condiment. I had a lot to learn still, but the product itself was of great quality.

Time went on and the business grew, and so did the varieties of the hot sauces I made. Eventually I left the IBEW all together to work for myself. That was the last time I worked for anyone. That was 2014.

I met Rebecca and our first official date was on Friday, June 13th 2014. Look it up. It was a rare lunar event called a Honey Moon. Here's what the National Geographic article had to say about it:

"...having the combination of a honey moon and Friday the 13th is rare, last occurring on June 13, 1919, according to the popular astronomy site, Universe Today. We'll have to wait until June 13, 2098, for the next one.."

That wasn't planned, at least not by us. We spent that evening at a campsite in the Malibu Creek State Park watching the moon and getting acquainted. We were unofficial guests because I couldn't find anyone to pay, so we just drove to an empty lot and it happened to be number **33**. That wasn't planned either. I just pulled into that parking space and back then those sort of things didn't mean much to me.

Four years later I would learn that that same campground had become a crime scene. A chemist, Tristan Beaudette, who was working on a clean vaccine that didn't have dead baby parts and poison metals in it had been killed. He was shot in the head in his tent with his two young daughters looking on. In retrospect, he was the first Bing Liu style casualty. No one ever was arrested for the murder. I recommend catching my videos to learn more details on topics such as this.

6

I said all that to get to this point. Rebecca and I got offered a store in San Diego in 2015. We accepted, and moved from farmers markets to a storefront. Exactly one year to the day we first opened the doors for business, our daughter was born. Shortly after that I had been at my daughter's 2-month checkup at the pediatrician with Rebecca. There was a young guy in the office with the doctor. He was in a short-sleeved dress shirt and tie, and had a clip board. I associated his short trimmed, well groomed facial hair to that of a professional salesman like I encountered in my days selling mortgages. Rebecca had already been researching vaccines several months before giving birth, and showing me all the very alarming information she was discovering. We went in there knowing we weren't subjecting our daughter to this dangerous, archaic practice. When the doctor said it was time for the you-know-whats, Rebecca and I both said we weren't going to be allowing that, and that he wasn't going to be doing it.

In fact, we had a notarized birth plan that we made the hospital staff agree to before doing anything when Rebecca was delivering. No poison injections, delayed cut-of-chord, and so on.

The fact that the pediatrician was so arrogant to think we would just cave in to his pressure 2 month's later was astounding to us. The demeanor of the doctor changed like a horror film. He went from this happy old man with buttons and a flare on his hat to amuse the children, to a seething demon. It was as if the muscles in his face changed his appearance the way a cuttlefish or octopus can. He argued with us a bit and I got very protective. It turns out the quiet guy with a clipboard was a ghoul for a pharmaceutical company. He was there that day to personally witness the injection. He was ensuring the shot went into all the doctor's tiny victims. Mind you this was September of 2016. These practices have been sinister long before mRNA was ever part of the equation. I recommend everyone find and read ***Murder by Injection*** by Eustace Mullins. At that time I had not read the book yet. I had however read all the stacks of computer paper Rebecca had printed out regarding vaccine injuries, drug company Whistle Blowers, murdered Whistle Blowers, ingredient lists which should just be called poison lists, and supporting documentation. It was clear that before the introduction of this dark age of compulsory inoculation, things like cancer, heart disease (number one killer, remember) juvenile cancers, diabetes, etc, were hardly even heard of. SIDS is a reaction, not a disease. After having read and listened to Rebecca it started to dawn on me that my first brother was a little over 2 months old when he stopped breathing in his sleep. They said it was SIDS. That's not something that just happens to children. More recently I had this confirmed by my longest standing guest to Ba'al Busters, Dr Bryan Ardis, DC. He said one of two things cause SIDS: a misaligned Atlas vertebrae from the childbirth process, or neurotoxic poisoning in the form of vaccines. The neurotoxin effects the part of the brain responsible for controlling the respiratory system. The takeaway here for you expecting parents, is to have a good chiropractor in the room with you when your child is born who can make adjustments, if necessary, right away. The misaligned Atlas can pinch nerves responsible for sending the messages to your baby's respiratory system. These doctors aren't always gentle when pulling out a new life.

For months on end I kept obsessively contemplating my family's safety. We were one family of semi-aware people in a huge state full of heavy-handed socialist politics, and conditioned, programmed minds. If we kept going to these ridiculous "wellness checks," aka excuses to put needles in your child's arm we'd always be subjecting our daughter to these sick individuals who don't care what they're plunging into little babies. There's a Pharma kick-back bonus for doctors who maintain a certain percentage of fully-poisoned patients.

The pediatrician threatened us that day with the statement, "Eventually she'll have to have them all or she can't go to school." I don't know what I look like to other people, but I'm not a pushover, and I don't cower to false authority. I don't think, "Oh, then I best conform." Instead I think, "If you want to fight, let's go." I told him in a firm voice, "Then we'll home school," and his face got even more contorted and red.

7

I did a little research on the next state over, and learned they weren't as insistent on poisoning infants and toddlers as California was. Arizona at that time had tremendous promise. They don't have a helmet law here, there was no forced vaccination agenda at the time, 2A is as strong in this state as it can hope to be in a Socialist UN-run country, more on that later, and the opportunities for our daughter to grow up in a more sane, less predatory environment inspired me to start looking for a new place to live.

We had a 4-year head start on getting the hell away from California. We did it even before it became the cool thing to do in 2020-present. I had a very successful store providing for our family. The decision to move was a simple one. What it meant wasn't so simple or easy, however. It meant I was going to have to pay a lot more in labor costs because employees would need to cover most of the week. I wouldn't be right around the corner anymore. It meant a lot of driving, 3 hours one-way, 6 hours in total each time I had to go restock the store with more of our handcrafted products. I would make that drive one or two times every single week, sometimes 3 times a week if my employees were unreliable.

I didn't care. I made a **Dad Decision**. No more bad decisions. Rebecca and I both gave up drinking and stupid little things when we found out she was pregnant. It's been 8 years since I drank alcohol, and there was a time when the only thing in my refrigerator was different varieties of beer. These decisions to break routine have been instant and easy whenever it had to do with my daughter. Her birth activated whatever I was supposed to be all along. Before then it didn't matter. It was down time. I had gotten a lifetime of Stupid out of my system before having to turn that page and start the real story.

Next Question:

What is Ba'al Busters?

Quick Answer: Ba'al Busters is my 2x BANNED and Deleted YouTube channel, hacked and deleted BrandNewTube channel, my banned Patreon account, my permanently suspended Twitter, almost suspended Instagram account, and currently attacked Rumble channel, RokuTV channel, radio show, JoshWhoTV, # 1 Shoutcast Talk Show, Odysee, and BitChute channels. I'm back on YouTube as "Disguise the Limits" and had to use a new, encrypted email address to set it up so YouTube would approve it.

Becoming a father activated me, like I mentioned. I am now an independent researcher and historian. I felt there was a clear need for a historical preservationist with my knack for finding the little details and patterns others may not. It's almost like historical forensics because no one wants you to learn this stuff, and it's most certainly an ongoing crime of omission being perpetrated on all of mankind.

The more I researched into the unusual suspects; the Jesuits, the secret societies, the Frankists, their affiliations, the still-present and cloaked Roman Catholic World Empire, the ongoing Counter-Reformation War we find ourselves in, the Banking role in human misery and the founding of a Terrorist state in disputed "Holy land," the practices and patterns of these wicked, indifferent psychopaths operating key roles seemingly everywhere, I couldn't help but see a direct connection to the dark, ancient cult of Ba'al. The rites and rituals carry on today and are embedded in organizations such as the Freemasons, and even in the quiet inter-workings of the Roman Catholic Empire, the Vatican, Knights of Malta, CIA, etc. Some of it is encrypted within the Tanakh, or Old Testament, as well, but that would take some time to explain, and a great deal of time for some to accept. Mystery Babylon and the hand of the Maccabean Priest Kings found its way into the Old Testament, for the short answer.

I have been interested in writing, photography, and cinema my whole life. One of the first works of fiction I read that wasn't required by school was Stephen King's **The Dark Tower, The Gunslinger**. It was customary for me to read a bunch, then have to stop and write my own short story to get all the ideas out that the reading had inspired.

There's a part toward the end of the book where the Man in Black is sitting with Roland, the Gunslinger, at a campfire while Roland has a sort of magic-induced vision. I would equate the experience to a hefty amount of psilocybin. Don't you worry about how I know that. The Man in Black is imparting these visions into Roland's psyche and says, *"You are surrounded by your own romantic aura, you lie cheek and jowl daily with the arcane. Yet now you approach the limits—not of belief, but of comprehension. You face reverse entropy of the soul."* Very much in alignment with the attitude of the Mystery Schools, Stephen King reveals a lot of himself in this book series.

That's what this strange journey seems to constantly be pushing at the borders of. The egg is not all of reality, for when cracked, light comes in and we see infinitely more as we make our way out into the "world." Infinite births into infinite worlds, each encompassing all of the previous within it.

As time went on, I never lost that overwhelming need to write my own thoughts and ideas out whenever I saw a good movie, or read something that stimulated my mind.

Life is life. Spoil Alert: I didn't go to Hollywood and become the next Quentin Tarantino. I had no idea about the true nature of these people back when I daydreamed about being what they were. Now you couldn't get me near any of these "people," or whatever they really are, without me sensing their slithery, despicable hidden nature. Like I said, I was stupid. I got brought to life with Purpose when my daughter was born.

The awareness was more of an ever-present sense of danger that got stronger over time. Not fear, but recognition of something I couldn't quite place, but sensed. Through researching and some other key events that forced me into realization, it got harder and harder for me to write off that sense I was feeling as just "social anxiety" and my own "awkwardness." That was part of it, but not nearly all of it. No. It's because most of us are born able to sense this evil, but then we are convinced, conditioned, and programmed into rejecting and ignoring that trait within us. And just for good measure, they'll also inject you with poison to scramble your brain and erase the purpose God installed in you when you were created. Now imagine if you evaded all that, and instead you valued, cultivated, trained, and exercised that ability. Imagine what would happen if instead of rejecting it as a weirdness or flaw, you embraced it and gave it a voice, gave it a chance to alert you and help guide you through situations. You're not imagining. I told you to imagine, damn it. Now imagine the monsters among us creating more and more elaborate vaccines, poisons in food, and suppressive electromagnetic grids of frequency and radiation around us to kill or disconnect that thing within you that alerts you of the dangers these monsters pose… A silent weapon for a quiet, spiritual, and mental war.

About 5 years ago I started making videos inspired by ebooks I had been reading while on my elliptical. Like before, I would be inspired to express my thoughts, share what I read, and elaborate on it with extra insights, dots I connected, and similarities I found from other things I had read. I was noticing seemingly unalike details had similarities when putting them together. At first I thought it was coincidence and a tangential byproduct of the creative process, itself. Later I learned the term "Pattern Recognition" and saw these similarities as having more substance.

The more I read, the more patterns I recognized. I kept at it, and kept making videos reading from books and doing commentary. The hobby became a passion the deeper I got into the true history of things that many people are unaware of, and most would never accept.

As I progressed, my channel name changed a couple times, and finally I decided on Ba'al Busters. It had to do with what I had discovered about ancient cults that are NOT buried in the past, but rather they are thriving in secret, and practiced by those whom claim authority over mankind in present day. The one commonality that runs through them all is a series of dark, insidious traits from this ancient cult, and a beyond horrific [EVIL] indifference to human suffering.

I'm a New Yorker, remember. I'm a movie fan, as I mentioned. The name Ba'al Busters taken phonetically has a New Yorker flare to it. The logo I created was a parody of the Ghostbusters logo. And realizing how little I really knew about the world, and how many people still do not, I made it my mission to share this information and point out the wicked hands at work in things. In other words I was Busting them by reporting on their deeds throughout history. And why is history my focus? Because too many people are deeply subverted as Yuri Besmenov pointed out, conditioned at birth to trust certain figures such as doctors, officers, the media, movies about war, and government figures. But if I show a long track record of very evil behavior by these people, their affiliation with a handful of societies with a particularly sinister agenda they have stuck to throughout the ages, then maybe it's easier to accept that it's more than possible these trusted members of society could be capable of some very bad things. Scrutiny toward certain professions and positions is shunned or forbidden by the culture they have manufactured for us. They get to us early through educational conditioning and social programming, just as the Jesuits have commented on in the past.

I soon realized that this hobby was important. It was necessary. I understood why I was drawn to it. I was instinctively aware that if I was to protect my little family from this world that I would need help. I would need a well informed community. If I could be that catalyst that sparked their curiosity, or pissed them off enough to motivate them to do their own research, then mankind may have a fighting chance. When I say "pissed off," I make no distinction between being upset to learn what I'm revealing, or angry with me for challenging their beliefs. The latter happens most often, but if that inspires them to prove me wrong, and they find out I'm not lying in the process, well now they've been shoved in the water and have to swim. They've inadvertently taken the first step down the path that cuts through the surface deceptions. "*...because strait is the gate, and narrow is the way, which leadeth unto life, and few there be that find it.*"

Ba'al Busters has become a video preservation of the real historical record. While History is being erased, taken down, banned, censored, omitted, and rewritten in mainstream institutions, Ba'al Busters, and a few other honest People that are not corporatized or commercialized have done, and are doing the good work. Real patriots that know what their natural, inborn, Creator-given rights are, are in a battle for the hearts of men. This is an ancient fight of Good vs Evil, make no mistake about it.

The Goal of the Ba'al Busters Projects are to inspire and rebuild the strength of community values through information. We have to unite and stand together against this perverse wickedness that is coming for us all, and that preys on our most precious and innocent.

To put it plainly, the objective of Ba'al Busters is to Create a World where Child Killers run for their lives instead of for office.

That only happens if the community isn't in ignorant denial of the true dangers, or aren't themselves afflicted with this dark perversion. If you see the value and necessity of defending your community and thereby defending your own family from this darkness rising, this Storm god's posse of perverts, then start by reading your constitution, and Bill of Rights. They separate them, but they are NOT separate. The People would not accept the document until specific provisions were outlined detailing their rights, and limiting the public servants so they would not become tyrannical. The Bill of Rights, isn't just the first 10 Amendments of the Constitution. It IS the Constitution. Learn the Bill of Rights, teach them to your children and neighbors. Hold them as high as you would the 10 Commandments.

Read these words and then read them again: We have to start Now. We have to take responsibility. No one else but that person you see in the mirror is going to do a damned thing about this horrible state of affairs we find ourselves spiraling deeper and deeper into. Take a stand and be involved before it flushes you and your children into the abyss. Smells down there. You won't like it.

Read these coming chapters with an open mind, and then do what Bill Cooper said to do almost every episode of the Hour of the Time, "Listen to everyone, Read everything, Believe NOTHING until you yourself can prove it with your own research."

Too often people just hear things. They like what they heard from one fella or another, and you're saying something different, and so you must be wrong, or a liar, or someone who doesn't know anything because you're not parroting the same rhetoric as the other guy or gal they like. Truth and Facts aren't in a popularity contest. There is no such thing as Truth by consensus. The level of human acceptance of a Fact has no bearing on how factual it is. If you think you're doing research just by listening to other people telling you something, you will never stop being manipulated and misled. Do the research yourself, then open your mouth. You don't get to skip that crucial step. Otherwise you're putting your faith in man instead of in what you perceive to be above that, ie, your perception of GOD. You're choosing believing over knowing, and therefore have made subjective reality into religion with patriot broadcasters as your cult leaders. That's you doing that by being lazy. Remember whose responsibility this is, whose responsibility your safety, your property, and your loved ones is. It's your responsibility to Know, not just to Believe. Save that faith for God. Man can't be trusted, even if he doesn't know it. With so much bad information out there, he could be under the impression he's telling the truth when he or she isn't. And you'll believe it, because you didn't know either. You just heard what he said and it sounded nice. It seemed reasonable. It fit your biases, and pleased your ear. I would add, consider your sources and resources, before you trust those references either.

As for the rest of the questions I began this introduction with, I will answer those throughout the coming chapters.

Since I cannot reach out to the spiritual world for something as superficial as
a request that Bill Cooper collaborate with this book,
the next best thing is to honor his memory by keeping it alive, and
introducing his work to a generation that never got to know him.
Few know that Bill had intended to write a sequel to Behold a Pale Horse, and
he was writing the *Cua Viet* book about his time
as a river boat captain in Vietnam.

The following is an excerpt of an Hour of the Time transcript, Bill's radio show.

Hour of the Time
Episode: 0956
Original Broadcast: September 20th 1996

Darkness
(Mystery Babylon)

Tonight's episode, ladies and gentlemen, is entitled "**Darkness**." There is no study so intriguing and yet so mysterious as that of the early religions of mankind to trace back the worship of god to its simple origin to mark the gradual process of those degrading superstitions and hollowed rights which darkened and finally extinguished his presence in the ancient world.

At first, men enjoyed the blessings of nature as children do in an age of innocence. Without inquiring into causes, it was in fact sufficient for them that the Earth gave them. Herbs, the trees bore them fruit; that the stream quenched their thirst. They were happy and every moment though unconsciously they offered a prayer of gratitude to him whom as yet they did not know.

And then a system of theology arose amongst them. Vague and indefinite as the waters of the boundless sea, they taught each other that the sun, the earth, the moon, and the stars were moved, and *illumined* by a great soul which was the source of all life which caused the birds to sing the brooks to murmur and the sea to heave. It was a sacred fire which shone in the firmament and in mighty flames. It was a strange being which animated the souls of men at which when the bodies died, returned unto itself again. Ancient man silently adored this great soul in the beginning, and spoke of him with reverence and sometimes they raised their eyes timidly to his glittering dwelling place on high and soon they learned to pray.

When those whom they loved lay dying they uttered wild lamentations and flung their arms despairingly toward the mysterious soul. For in times of trouble the human mind so imbecile, so helpless always clings back to something that is much stronger than itself. As yet, in that time, they worshiped only the sun, the moon, and the stars... And not as gods, but as visions of that divine essence which alone ruled and pervaded the Earth, the sky, and the sea. They adored him, kneeling with their hands clasped and their eyes raised. They offered Him no sacrifices. They built him no temples. You see, they were content to offer him their hearts which were full of awe in his own temple which was full of the grandeur of nature. For the god they worshiped was indeed nature's god... And it is said by some that there are yet some barbarous islands where men have no churches, nor ceremonies, and where they still worship God reflected in the work of his uncountable hands, and the mystery in the balance the perfection of nature.

But you see they were not long content with this simple service. There were those amongst them who learned how to subvert and twist so that they could control the others around them. Prayer, which had first been an inspiration, suddenly fell into a system and men already grown wicked, prayed the deity to give them abundance of wild beast skins, and to destroy their enemies. They ascended eminences, mountain tops... They built towers as if hoping that thus their being near God he would prefer their prayers to those of their rivals. Those who controlled those eminences became powerful. Such is the origin of that superstitious reverence for high places which was universal throughout the whole entire heathen world.

Then it is clear in the ancient annals that someone came forth. Orpheus was born, and he invented instruments which to his touch unto his lips gave forth notes of surpassing sweetness. And with these melodies he enticed the wandering innocent savages into the recesses of the forest. And there their Orpheus taught them precepts of obedience to the great soul and of loving kindness toward each other in harmonious words. And he became the high Priest. And so they devoted groves and forests to the worship of the deity. There were men who had watched Orpheus and who had seen and envied his power over the herd who surrounded him. For even then there were Sheeple.

They resolved to imitate him, and having studied these barbarians, they banded together and called themselves their priests. Religion is divine, but its ministers after all, are men. The idea from the beginning that imperfect men could rule over imperfect men is flawed. For alas, sometimes they are demons with the faces and wings of angels. You see the simplicity of men, and the cunning of their priests has destroyed or corrupted all the religions of the world bar none. For these Priests, ladies and gentlemen, taught the people to sacrifice the choicest herbs and flowers. They taught them formulas of prayer, and made them make so many obeisances to the sun and to worship those flowers which opened their leaves when he rose and which closed them as he set. For the great ball of fire that makes its way from dawn to dusk across the sky was seen as the savior to those who huddled in the cold darkness surrounded by wild beasts. They'll pray, and it was to that sun that they directed their worship as the great symbol in the heaven, of the power of god, and the source of all life on this earth. For remember, theirs was a worship of nature's god.

They composed the language of symbols, which was perhaps necessary in those times since letters had not been invented, but which perplexed the people and perverted them from the worship of the one god. Those symbols are still used upon the sheeple of the world today. To the great herd thus the sun represented the great doctrine of this religion. The moon represented the church reflecting the pure light of the sun, and the sun and the moon were worshiped as emblems of god, and fire by the philosophers of fire, as an emblem of the sun. Water as an emblem of the moon, which by faith reflected the pure light of its master. The **serpent** represented the full body of the priesthood, the initiates was to be worshiped as an emblem of wisdom, and eternal youth since it renews its skin every year. Thus it periodically casts off all symptoms of old age and begins anew, reborn if you will. And the bull, the most vigorous of animals, and whose horns resemble those of the crescent moon was also worshiped.

The priests observed the ability with which the barbarians adored these symbols and increased them. It was a time of great mystery and little understanding of any that was seen around them. To ancient man the sun was seen to die. The darkness descended around them. It was a time of great danger and cold. And then, as if by magic, the sun was reborn each morning and made its way across the sky where it became old, and then died again. And they began to measure their world by the seasons of the sun and their religion reflected all of this. And religions today, even though denying any connection with this ancient paganism, still reflects this exact religion in its ceremonies and in its holy days. Even to the layout of its churches. To worship the visible is a disease of the soul inherent to all mankind, and the disease which these men could have healed. Instead they pandered to it. It's true that the first generation of men might have looked upon these merely as the empty symbols of a divine being, but it is also certain that in time, the vulgar forgot the God in the emblem and worshiped that which their fathers had only honored. And therefore the symbol became the God.

Egypt was the fountainhead of these idolatries. And it was in Egypt that the priests first applied real attributes to the sun, and to the moon, whom they called his wife, and sister, and mother. And the son became Osiris. The moon became Isis. Brother and sister, Mother and son, Husband and wife.

It may... It may perhaps for those of you who have not heard, and maybe have not been listening to this broadcast for a great period of time, it may perhaps interest you to listen to the first, the very first fable of the world:

From the midst of Chaos was born Nimrod, and at his birth a voice was heard proclaiming the ruler of all the earth is born. And from the same dark and troubled womb were born Semiramis, the queen of light, and the spirit of darkness. This Nimrod traveled over the whole world, and civilized its inhabitants, and taught them the art of agriculture. And his wife Semiramis built the first fortified city's walls. But on his return, the jealous darkness laid a stratagem for him. And in the midst of a banquet, had him slain. He was nailed down in his prison, which cast into the river, floated into the sea which even in that ancient time was never mentioned but with marks of detestation. And when Semiramis learned this sad news she cut off a lock of her hair, and put it on her morning robes and wandered through the whole country in search of the dead body of her husband.

Eventually she found it by casting a magic spell... A magical intercourse was obtained between Semiramis and the dead Nimrod from which a child emerged. The child was Tammuz. And Semiramis fed the infant with her finger instead of with her breast, and put him every night into fire to render him immortal.

Let me read you a later story of the same myth only with different names. And I have to depart from my narration here and read this to you:

From the midst of chaos was born Osiris, and at his birth a voice was heard proclaiming, "the ruler of all the earth is born!" And from the same dark and troubled womb were born Isis, the queen of light, and Typhon the spirit of darkness. This Osiris moved over the whole world and civilized its inhabitants, and talked in the art of agriculture, brought them together in societies for their mutual benefit and protection. But on his return to Egypt, the jealous Typhon laid a stratagem for him. And in the midst of a banquet had him shut up in a chest which exactly fitted his body. He was nailed down in his prison which cast into the Nile, floated down to the sea by the mouth which even in the time of Plutarch was never mentioned by an Egyptian except with disdain and loathing. When Isis heard the news, she cut off a lock of her hair and put on her morning robes, and wandered through the whole country in search of the chest which contained the dead body of her husband. At length she learnt that the chest had been carried by the waves to the shore of Byblos, and had there lodged in the branches of the tamarisk bush which quickly shot up and became a large and beautiful tree growing around the chest so that it could not be seen. The king of the country amazed at the vast size the tree had so speedily acquired, ordered it to be cut down, to be hewn into a pillar to support the roof of his palace, the chest being still concealed in the trunk. The voice which had spoken from heaven at the birth of Osiris made known these things to poor Isis who then went to the shore of Byblos, and sat down silently by a fountain to weep. The damsels of the queen met her, and accosted her, and the queen appointed her to be nurse to her child. And Isis fed the infant with her finger instead of with her breast, and put him every night into fire to render him immortal. While transforming herself into a swallow, she hovered around the pillar which was her husband's tomb, and bemoaned her unhappy fate. It happened that the queen thus discovered her and shrieked when she saw her child surrounded by flames. And by that cry she broke the charm and deprived him of immortality. By that cry Isis was summoned back to her goddess form, and stood before the awestruck queen. Shining with light and defusing sweet fragrances around, she cut open the pillar and took the coffin with her and opened it in a desert. There she embraced the cold corpse of Osiris, and wept bitterly.

Isis returned to Egypt and hid the coffin in a remote place, where Typhon hunting by moonlight chanced to find it and divided the corpse into 14 pieces. Again Isis set out on her weary search throughout the whole land. Sailing over the fenny parts in a boat made of papyrus, she recovered all the fragments except one which had been thrown into the sea. Each of these she buried in the place where she found it which explains why in Egypt there are so many tombs of Osiris. And instead of the limb which was lost she gave the phallus to the Egyptians. The disgusting worship of which was thence carried into Italy, into Greece, and into all the countries of the East. And today people pay obeisance to this phallus when they stand in awe of the Washington monument, or when they attend SPIKE training. For truly... For truly it is the shaft.

When Isis died she was buried in a grove near Memphis. Over her grave was raised a statue covered from head to foot with a black veil and underneath was engraved these divine words, quote, "I am all that has been, that is, that shall be, and none among mortals has yet dared to raise my veil." End quote. Beneath this veil, ladies and gentlemen, are concealed all the mysteries and learning of the past. A young scholar, his fingers covered with the dust of venerable folios, his eyes weary and reddened by nightly toil, will now attempt to lift a corner of this mysterious and sacred covering... The folios are the old books that I have discovered in used bookstores across the country and around the world, and truly in some of those dark and dim corners and shelves that have never been touched. I have been literally covered with the dust of years that has settled upon these ancient volumes. Those that I could afford found their way into my library where they still serve today. You see, these two deities, Isis and Osiris were the parents of all the gods and goddesses of the heathens or were indeed those gods themselves worshiped under many different names. Nimrod, Semiramis, Isis Osiris, Diana and Dionysus... The fable itself was received into the mythologies of the Hindus, and the Romans. Sarah is said to have mutilated the Brahma as Typhon did Osiris. And Venus to have lamented her slain Adonis as Isis wept for her husband, god, brother, son. And as yet the sun and moon alone were worshiped under these two names.

And as we have seen besides these twin beneficial spirits men who had begun to recognize sin in their hearts, and had created an evil one who struggled with the power of life and fought with them for the souls of men. I must tell you that in my studies I find that it has been natural through all history for man to fabricate something that is worse than himself rather than take the responsibility upon his own shoulders. And even in the theology of the American Indians which is the purest of the modern world there is found a Matantu, or dark spirit.

Osiris, or the sun, was now worshiped throughout the whole world though under different names. He was the Mithra of the Persians, the Brahma of India, the **Ba'al** or Adonis of the Phoenicians. He was the Apollo of the Greeks, the Odin of Scandinavia, the Hue of the Britons on the byway of the Laplanders. Isis, ladies and gentlemen also received the name of [portion unclear], Rhea, Venus, Vesta, Cybele, Epione, Melissa, Nehalennia in the north, Isi, with the indians, Puja among the Chinese, and Cerridwen among the ancient Britons.

The Egyptians were sublime philosophers who had dictated theology to the world. And then in Chaldea arose the first astrologers to watch the heavenly bodies with curiosity as well as with awe, and who made divine discoveries, and who called themselves the Interpreters of God. And to each star they gave a name. And to each day in the year they gave a star. And the Greeks and Romans who were poets, read these names into legends. Each name was a person, and each person was a god. From these stories of the stars originated the angels of the Jews, the Genie of the Arabs, the Heroes of the Greeks, and the Saints of the Romish church.

And then corruption grew upon corruption, and superstition flung black and hideous veal over the doctrines of religion. You see, a religion ladies and gentlemen, is lost, utterly lost as soon as it loses its simplicity. **Truth has no mysteries**. It is deceit alone that lurks in obscurity. It is only the lie that is hidden behind a door! Men multiplied God into a thousand names and created Him always in their own image. Him too whom they had once deemed unworthy of any temple less noble than the floor of the earth and the vast dome of the sky which he had created. They worshiped in caves and then in temples which were made of the trunks of trees rudely sculptured and arranged in rows to imitate groves of trees and with other trunks placed upon them traversely to form the cross that is seen when you hold up your son behind some obstacle, a streak across the sky. These were the first buildings of worship erected by man from no reverence for the deity, for god, but only to display that which they conceived to be a stupendous effort in art and to display their knowledge and power so as to more adequately rule and subjugate the herd-the sheeple, the profane. Humanity that had not a clue, and still doesn't, by the way. It may be necessary to remind some of you that a superior being, God if you will, must view the elegant temples of the Romans, the gorgeous pagodas of India, and the Gothic cathedrals of the western world with feelings similar to those with which we might contemplate the rude efforts of the early heathens; are a hill of ants who deemed God unworthy of the fruits and flowers which He Himself had made and offered to Him the entrails of beasts and the hearts of human beings! Can you imagine the audacity?! The arrogance of such a thing?!

We can compare, ladies and gentlemen, an ancient and fallen religion to the ship of the Argonauts which the Greeks, desiring to preserve to posterity, repairing in so many different ways that at length there did not remain a fragment of the original vessel which had borne to caucus the conqueror of the golden fleece. So let's pass over a lapse of many many year, centuries if you will, and then contemplate the condition of the nations in whom religion had been first born. We find the Egyptians adoring the most common of plants, the most contemptible of beasts, the most hideous of reptiles. The solemnity and pomp of their absurd ceremonies held them up to the ridicule of the whole wide world Clement of Alexandria describes one of their temples the thusly. Quote, "The walls shine with gold and silver, and with amber, and sparkle with the gems of India and Ethiopia, and the recesses are concealed by splendid curtains, but if you enter the penetralia, and inquire for the image of God for whose sake the fame was built, one of the pastor fori, or some other attendant from the temple approaches with a solemn mysterious face and putting aside the veil suffers you to obtain a glimpse of the divinity. And there upon an altar you behold a snake or a crocodile or a cat or some other beast. A [unclear] inhabitant of a cavern or a [unclear] of a temple, or a giant penis, the phallus of Osiris." Which Isis had substituted upon the altar of Egypt.

The priests of Egypt were always impostors. The once so celebrated had degenerated into a race of jugglers, a circus, if you will. Also the Chaldeans lived upon the fame of their fathers and upon their own base trickeries. **No one was honest anymore**. No one could point to God. No one understood that all the symbols of the universe and nature represented the power of an unseen God that the first men worshiped. The Brahmans whose priests of India once so virtuous and celebrated as being so wise, they too had fallen. Once they had forbidden the shedding of so much as an insect's blood. One day in the year alone at the feast of Jagan they were authorized to sacrifice the flesh of a beast and from this many had refrained from attending unable to conquer their feelings of abhorrence, but now they've learned from the fierce Scythians and from the Phoenicians who traded on their coast to sacrifice the wife upon her husband's pier to appease the gentle Brahma with the blood of men. And that ceremony continues to this day. The angels who presided over them became savage demons who scourged them onto cruel penances even to lifetimes of suffering and famine. And in the sacred groves where once the Brahman fathers had taught their precepts of love, men emaciated, terror-worn, even dying, wondered sadly waiting for death as tortured prisoners wait for their liberty. But worse still, these wicked priests sought through the land for the most beautiful young women and trained them to dance in the temples and to entice the devotees to their arms with lustful attitudes and languishing looks, and with their voices which mingled harmoniously with the golden bells suspended on their feet. They became prostitutes for the priesthood. They sang hymns to the gods in public and in private enriched the treasuries of the pagoda with their infamous earnings. And thus a pure, very simple religion was debased by the avarice and lewdness of its priests till the temples became a den of thieves. So prostitution set enthroned upon the altars of the gods and today it continues although prostitution in a different way.

Most religious meetings today are spiritual consumerism. It begins with a problem and when the hour is over the problem has been solved and the coffers of the priest, the minister, have been filled in the process. Greece and Rome buried in sloth and luxury did not escape the general contamination. The emblem of generation, the phallus which Isis had bestowed upon the Egyptians which they had held in abstract reverence, had now obtained a permanent place in the festivals of these nations. And did the lingam and those of the Hindus. And it was openly paraded in possessions, before guests in the home, and processions in the streets. It was worn by Roman nations in bracelets upon their arms. It adorns our nation's capital as the Washington monument, and stands mocking us in Dealey Plaza in Dallas, Texas. The sacred festivals and mysteries which they had received from the Egyptians and for which the women had been want to prepare themselves by continence and the men by fasting, were now mere vehicles for all the depravities and deceptions of the very lowest kind. Men were permitted to join the women in their worship of Bacchus or Adonis, of the Bona Dea and even of Priapus. And so dissolute did the Dionysia become, ladies and gentlemen, that the civil powers were compelled, yea forced to interfere with those of religion and the Bacchanalia were abolished by a decree of the Roman senate. But it was too late for Rome's fate had been sealed.

And the Jews, the "chosen people" of God, had not their religion changed? Had not God, weary with their sins, yielded them to captivity? Scourged them with sorrow? Menaced them with curses? And isn't the State of Israel more a secular state than a religious state, today despite the claims of Zionism? They worshiped **Ba'al**, [unclear] the Priapus of Assyria. they sacrificed their children to Moloch. They had dancing girls in the holy temple. This corruption spared no race, no people, no religion, and no one can point to any other and say truthfully that they are more guilty than they. For all are guilty. All people, all religions, all nations all over this world have destroyed the simple precepts of all of the different religions of the world. And none resemble even slightly what they began to be.

And I'm not going to go deeper into particulars that are so degrading to human nature. I can see you squirming from your seats as it is already, so i will have mercy. I will instead invite you to follow me by steadily listening to the Hour of the Time to a corner where you may begin to more readily understand where we are at, and where we are going. For there are many who have traveled this route before. And the history of the world it is enacted in cycles and those who ignore history are doomed to repeat it!

William Cooper:
a Father, a Husband, a son, and a True American Patriot

He was shot at his home on November 5th, 2001.

These Evil Bastards took a loving dad away from his two beautiful little girls, and wife.

They robbed the rest of us of a friend.

Let it not be in vain.

Love to Pooh (Dorothy), Allison, and Annie

If you girls are out there somewhere, you have a friend in me you have yet to meet.

Edmond Ronayne

1

Before we get into just who and what Ba'al is in greater detail, let's Cliff Note it in simple form:

Ba'al is a name meaning "Lord" when used generically. As in Baalzebub, meaning "Lord of the Flies." That sort of reveals the crypto-symbolic meaning of that book you pretended you read for school, doesn't it? It was also the name of one specific, predominant deity, Ba'al in the Ugaritic texts. He was a Canaanite, or perhaps pre-Canaanite god of fertility, and the first Geoengineer for he was also credited as being the Storm god. Some will pipe up and say, "No! It was a Philistine deity." That exposes the level of confusion even among scholars. Look above. Baalzebub, or the "Fly Lord" was the Philistine deity. Ba'al and Baalzebub aren't necessarily the same thing, given the generic application of the term. They didn't have a lot of money back then, so they couldn't afford a lot of words, apparently. They therefore had to give what words they had multiple applications to cover for the scarcity. As you continue reading, it'll be easier to identify when I'm using humor and sarcasm.

Unlike most other significant gods in the Ugaritic texts, Ba'al was not an offspring of EL, the "benevolent" one. He was instead the son of Dagon, another fertility god whose name means "Grain." Was it Ba'al himself, or the worshipers who were wickedly corrupt, the Priestcraft who influenced them, or all three? After all it was man and woman who willfully brought their children to the alter, the furnace of Moloch, to be horrifically burned alive in sacrifice to Ba'al. Was it not the hands of the Canaanites themselves who crafted such a furnace in the first place? As mentioned in the Bill Cooper section, there were priests in those days as are now, that convinced the people of their time of a great many wild and dramatic tales and explanations of things. Always of course, putting themselves at the center of importance, making for them a secure role as an Authority whom should guide, rule, and "protect" the people. Just do what they tell you, don't ask questions, and everything will be alright. Obey us as you would the gods, and behave. Give of yourself what is demanded by the gods so as not to anger um… *them*.

To fully understand the impact of the ancient Ba'al Cult on modern times, we need to discuss its prevalence in current organizations. Is there any remnant of this presumably dead practice, as according to scholars who claim it to have been eradicated? Child sacrifice seems to be the predominant theme within the Cult of Ba'al, as are cannibalistic ceremonies and habits that accompanied the rituals. Do we not still see this practice carried out with political encouragement in modern guises such as abortion and infanticide? In child trafficking's all too often end result, and Satanic Ritual Abuse (SRA)? Perhaps the Sabbatean-Frankists' stated duties of child torture, sacrifice, blood-drinking and cannibalism is derived from the Cult of Ba'al where there seems to be many well-defined parallels between their deeds dating back to Nimrod, and maybe further. Does our conditioned society not only support abortion, but even viciously defend it as a right? Does that sicken anyone else? Eugenicist Nurse Margaret Sanger brought Planned Parenthood into being, and is that not just another altar of sacrifice and butchery remnant of olde?

When I recently spoke to Scott Schara on my show, the father of Grace, his loving daughter who was murdered by modern plague doctors with COVID NIH protocols, he said a staggering 67% of prenatal infants expected to have Down's Syndrome are aborted. It's been culturally programmed into societies around the world as a reflexive response to such a prognosis. I say prognosis rather than diagnosis, because they're projecting future complications. We rarely question or even request verification of any claim a person in a modern magician's white coat makes. We just accept the diagnosis as fact, because why would they lie, right? Why would they want to trick us into killing our babies, like Loki? Oh wait, why would the Priests in Canaan have wanted to trick the desperate, superstitious, and corrupt into killing their babies?

That's just the prenatal infants with Down's Syndrome. They are hardly the only group of purely innocent life targeted for swift eradication by the white coated sorcerer priests. They have many unnatural methods to reach the same gruesome ends. Whether it's a living sacrifice through medically maiming your child, like with vaccines, or the resulting outcome of said injections such as juvenile cancers, autism, paralysis, or a life-shortening illness of the heart or other vital organs, and neurological damage. What of the foods we have advertised, the air we breathe, the water we drink, bathe, and water our gardens and animals with?

Let's have a look at the most widely familiar, and maybe one of the oldest depending upon who you ask, secret fraternal orders and see what we can learn about its connections to the ancient priestcraft.

2

Edmund Ronayne was a highly respected, trusted, and regarded member of the fraternal order we recognize as the Freemasons, or Free and Accepted Masons. He was Master Keystone of Lodge 639 in Chicago. Interesting lodge numbers, too when you think of vortex math and the writings of Nikola Tesla. Ronayne claims he left the Order after which he published ***Mah Hah Bone***, alternately called, ***The Master's Carpet***, in 1879. 1879 is also the year Margaret Sanger was born, incidentally. Although I find a great deal of this book to be essential reading, we're going to focus primarily on the "mysteries" regarding a dark deception, or the secrets you learn in time as a member, if ever it is revealed at all. If you wish to more deeply understand the nature Freemasonry, you can find a free pdf of ***Mah Hah Bone*** online quite easily. The passages regarding the Freemasonic link to Babylon, the ancient priestcraft, and Ba'al idolization are what we're going to focus on here.

Edmund Ronayne was greatly admired by his peers all throughout masonry, for it was he who had researched their own history and cataloged it for preservation. Upon being unanimously elected Senior Warden in a meeting in December of 1871, he took to holding weekly schools of instruction meetings for the benefit of the members. The school taught the customs, the meanings of symbols, and secrets of the order, etc. He ran the school with guests of high insight such as Grand Examiners from nearby lodges all the way up until June 24th of 1874. Scholarly minded, he developed official handbooks at first intended only for the members, detailing the ceremonies and rituals, the gestures, the pantomimes and hand signals of proper, true masonry. You can find a stripped down version of Ronayne's handbook of Freemasonry right on the abysmal Amazon.

If I may tangent here, Abner Doubleday, the man accredited posthumously for the invention of baseball, was a president of the Theosophical Society later in his life. He also fired the first shot at Fort Sumter. However the man who codified the game, added the diamond layout, and really put forth a structured game was a Freemason by the name of Alexander Joy Cartwright. It's not surprising there's a complicated system of secret hand signals both between Freemasons and the between teammates in baseball. I actually lived in Ballston Spa, NY, the birthplace of Doubleday. I digress…

It's said that through Edmond Ronayne's scholarly quest to restore the fading or lost information of Freemasonry's rites and rituals, he came across some information that shattered his enthusiasm to the point he abandoned the fraternal order all together, and then set out to reveal their darkest secrets.

Evident from the writings in **Mah Hah Bone,** which itself was a secret term to which there is scarcely a handful of people who know the true meaning, something dramatically affected Ronayne to the point of reverse-inspiration. The same passion he had once put into his devotion to the Order, he had now redirected against them. But specifically, we can begin to get a picture of this through these passages referencing Ba'al, and the Babylonian Mystery Schools.

The very first reference right out of the gate to Ba'al is in the subtitle where he states, "Masonry and Ba'al-Worship Identical." He goes straight to task in the preface of the **The Master's Carpet/Mah Hah Bone**. Under the 4 claims known to members of the order, the 3rd lists,

*"3rd—That all ceremonies, symbols, and the celebrated legend of Hiram in the Master Mason's degree, were directly borrowed from the '**Ancient Mysteries**' or the secret worship of **Baal**, Osiris, or Tammuz..."*

The next reference to Ba'al comes from the 11th page of the book. It's of great importance in understanding the nature Freemasonry and gives us a better idea as to the hidden loyalties and obligations of all those whom are members of these societies. They are either willfully or unwittingly entering into servitude. Whether enticed and charmed with vague promise of an edge in life, or a deliberate, driven desire to push the agenda of the order forward, all lose their individuality, their freedom. They take an oath in the lodge, and then often an oath of office to serve the People. They cannot serve 2 masters, and when it's between following the law and serving the People, or carrying out orders handed down by the brotherhood, the people will always come in second place, if not looked down upon with disdain and disgust all together.

"Freemasonry is far too serious a matter for any man to assume its villainous obligations without due reflection; for, once you have crossed the threshold of the lodge room, divested of your own clothing, and wearing the habiliments of the order, and when once you become, as it were, bound by the **cable tow of Satan to the alter of BAAL,** *'there is no place for after repentance,' though like Esau of old, you may 'seek it carefully with tears.' Living or dead, Freemasonry will never give you up. The law of Romanism is, 'once a priest, always a priest,' and so it is in Masonry; 'once a Mason, always a Mason.'*

There are 55 references to Ba'al in total in ***The Master's Carpet***. This particular passage is in reference to the Roman Catholic Church and Freemasonry.

...But the contention between them is not for truth and purity, but for power and supremacy. It is a mere conflict of authority and nothing more. The Pope, or Sovereign Pontiff, is the Pontiéx Maximus, or the Jupiter of pagan Rome, and represents the god of Romanism, while the Worshipful Master is the personification of Hiram Abiff, or Osiris, or **Baal**, *which was the name of Jupiter in Egypt and Phoenicia, whence the Masonic philosophy has come, and is the representative of the god of Masonry. But as every worshipper of the Romanism god must reveal or confess to the priest, who alone is to be the custodian of all secrets, while every worshipper of the Masonic god must* **conceal** *and* **never reveal**, *but must himself be the keeper of all secrets, and is therefore exalted above the priest, both systems cannot harmonize, and hence the bitter antagonism which arose between them in 1738.*

But notwithstanding this apparently wide gulf thus separating these two terrible powers of **despotism** *and falsehood for the present, yet, should an* **emergency** *ever arise when it would become necessary for men to array themselves on the side of righteousness and to defend the pure principles of gospel truth and the full freedom of an open Bible, untrammelled either by* **Jesuit** *cunning or lodge duplicity, it is very greatly to be feared that, forgetting their petty differences for the time being, both Romanism and Freemasonry would make common cause and stand shoulder to shoulder, the very embodiment of the works of* **Darkness**.

"Should an emergency arise," or be created artificially for such a galvanization of despotic powers worldwide, is the question. When you overlay that passage onto the landscape of the present day's global events and conditions, it would be as if it were the framework of what we are all witnessing in real time. If not a prophetic one, it is at the very least a message of warning from Ronayne.

Ronayne mentions "Jesuit cunning," and this is an element we will discuss in more detail, but for now, put a tab or a mental pin in that. What he is saying is that in time of great emergency the false authorities, the overlords of the world whom have created false monetary substance and grew wealthy on the scheme, would combine their efforts against the People of the world. As the men and women grow weary, anxious, and then resistant of the ever-growing stresses of oppression they are being subjected to they will rise, and that seems to be part of the despotic plan. The despots are already in many ways mobilized and attacking us not only through the medical establishment, but through a war of attrition, eating out our substance, as a great man once put it, and targeting the most innocent of us, the children.

On page 152 of **The Master's Carpet** we see this passage:

"The prayer as we see, is offered to the "Great Architect of the Universe," the "G.A .O.T.U," but who is this "G.A.O.T.U.? And what attributes does he possess ? It can not possibly mean the God of Heaven, because he "at sundry times, and in diverse manners spake in times past unto the fathers by the prophets," and gave man even a written law in which he has fully revealed both his name and will, but he has never styled himself an Architect."

Page 153 continues:

*"An Architect is a man who **furnishes plans** for, and **superintends** the erection of a building made from material already prepared; but God created of nothing the heavens and the earth, and all the host of them, and hence he cannot be a mere Architect, and it would be a direct insult to call him such a nick-name."*

This is in reference to the generic nature of the Masonic prayer to the Great Architect of the Universe. It implies there's an Impostor working through those in the fraternal order whom cannot create anything itself, but can only manipulate that which is already brought into creation, and "it" does so by *furnishing plans*, and guiding, or superintending those of the flesh to carry out "its" bidding. Kind of like AI? To extrapolate, it means the Masons are following a different leader than the Creator God.

Beginning on page 225 we read:

*"And while the pagan masses offered their public devotions to their myriads of senseless idols, the pagan priests and philosophers and rulers had a different worship, which they practiced only in secret, which they conducted with the **most imposing ceremonies**, and which they always celebrated in honor of the chief deity, or sun-god. This secret worship of paganism in every country was termed the "Mysteries," and is that which was revived by the "Masonic fathers" in the beginning of the eighteenth century; so that what was called the "Mysteries" of Osiris, or **Baal**, or Bacchus, or*

*Dionysius in ancient times, is to-day known as the mysteries of Masonry. On this point all our Masonic writers, as has been already mentioned, give such plain, positive, unqualified, affirmative testimony, that, if we do not believe what they say concerning their own pet philosophy, it is useless to receive human testimony on any subject. And for the purpose of illustrating this **Baal worship**, and as if to give emphasis to their teaching, the emblem of the sun, moon, stars… is found in all our lodges and manuals.*

In the "Traditions of Freemasonry," p. 232, we read:

'More pages of the writings of the ancients, that have been preserved to our times, are devoted to the MYSTERIES than to the development of empires. Hence we have better knowledge of the ceremonial and legend of many of the phases of the mysteries, than we have of the country in which they were practiced.'

This being the case then, let us now see how clearly the Masonic philosophy and Masonic institution are shown to be identical in every feature with these pagan "Mysteries."

In the "Lexicon of Freemasonry," by Mackey, p. 125 we read:

'EGYPTIAN MYSTERIES. -- Egypt was the cradle of the mysteries of paganism. At one time in possession of all the learning and religion that was to be found in the world, it extended into other nations the influence of its sacred rites, and its secret doctrines.'

And in describing the "Mysteries," Dr. Mackey again says, on p. 315:

*'This is the name given to those religious assemblies of the ancients, whose ceremonies were conducted in **secret**, whose doctrines were known only to those who had obtained the right of knowledge by a previous **initiation**, and whose members were in possession of signs and tokens, by which they were enabled to recognize each other."*

Is not this an exact description of Freemasonry? Or could any language be employed to portray the Masonic system more accurately?

But again:-

*'Warburton's definition of the 'Mysteries' was as follows. Each of the pagan gods had (besides the public and open) a **secret worship** paid unto him, to which none were admitted but **those who had been selected by preparatory ceremonies**, called INITIATION. This **secret worship** was termed the mysteries.' (Divine Legation, vol. i, p. 189.)*

*'The most important of the **mysteries** were those of **Mithras**, celebrated in Persia [and an adopted secret cult of Roman nobility]; of Osiris and Isis, celebrated in Egypt;*

of Eleusis, instituted in Greece, and the Scandinavian and Druidical rites which were confined to the Gothic and Celtic tribes."

Masonic text-book relates:
> *'Traditions of Freemasonry,' p. 233*
> *'And the mysteries throughout the world **were the same in substance**, being derived from one source and celebrated in honor of the same deities, though acknowledged under different appellations."*

I would argue Revelation of the Method, or public disclosure of lesser details, is a form of low-level initiation approved by the priestcraft for the "masses." They do this in various ways. In modern times we are provided small nuggets of insight into the machinations of a particular operation being run in opposition of mankind's benefit through such mouthpieces as highly energetic actors whom claim to be exposing the "Truth" through "Awareness." If we were to be completely oblivious to any ill intent, we who will listen to the "truth" they're making us "aware of" and entertain such notions in our own pursuit of understanding, would not know there were anything to Fear, let alone What to fear. It's this sort of MindWar that gives the deliberate impression of overwhelming odds stacked against us. We may get alarmed or even outraged at such attacks once made "aware," but it produces little more than verbal disagreement to it, and that of course is even diffused by the offering of a comment section to vent our frustrations with similar minded fellows, and even argue with those whom attack such notions and the character of those who do believe in it. The war then, is fought in cyberspace, in an artificial world with no impact on the real world. But we feel like we're doing something. We Feel like we're in some noble fight, but if we're honest, we're LARPing, or Live Action Role Playing. We're participating in a game rather than taking any real action to oppose the many misdeeds of the false authorities who continue pressing forward with their objectives with little true resistance at all.

Another disclosure method, one that attracts our attention is the conducting of public rituals. That can range from the highly cryptic and symbolic, such as the Gotthard Tunnel ceremony of June 1st, 2016, near CERN in Switzerland, to something like unconstitutional agencies of the illegitimate government garnering public support, through lying-media manipulation, to murder 77 or more innocent lives, 25 of which were children and infants, in Waco, Texas.

The first example piques our curiosity with no true compass for what everything means as a whole, so we watch in distrustful wonder, as we become satellites projecting our energy into such a ceremony. On the internal, spiritual, and ancient DNA memory level, we have a sense of connection, and faint familiarity to it all. Meanwhile they are extracting our energy remotely, like cyber thieves.

In the second example we are guided by reporters from "trusted" news networks who are handed lies to tell the viewers. They spin a tale, such as in times of military conflict, that demonize the target of government hostility. To cover up their own, completely unjust misdeeds against an innocent group of people who minded their own business, they told us David or Vernon, whichever you prefer, was holding his flock hostage, that he was guilty of everything from polygamy to child abuse, to having hellfire automatic gun triggers, to grenades, and so on. All was a complete and bald-faced lie perpetrated by government and mainstream media to turn the American people against their neighbors, fellow man, etc. The Davidians bought and sold guns at gun shows as a way to provide an income for the many members to sustain a peaceful existence and practice their faith. There were no missing paperwork for the guns as claimed by the ATF. Previous to the standoff, David was attempting to clear up any misunderstanding on this very issue when agents visited a gun store where the Davidians did some business. He was called by the owner and the owner got David on the phone and attempted to hand the phone to the lead agent. The agent refused to speak or even go near the phone. He chose to approach the situation covertly and sneakily, rather than resolve the matter simply. I could write an entire book just on the three topics of Randy and Vicky Weaver at Ruby Ridge, the Waco mass murder, and the Alfred P. Murrah building self-attack carried out by our police state thugs.

These are all forms of public rituals, and in the case of Waco and the Gotthard Tunnel ceremony, both were abundant in symbolism. The Gotthard being the blatant, displayed openly, however without explanation save those on media and alt media giving you their impressions of it. It was a "pagan mass" as Ronayne's passage coined it, made for public consumption and bewilderment while something far more cryptic was going on beneath the surface most wouldn't or didn't see, mainly because we weren't shown. That which we did see was the theater, the drama, the circus, or distraction. Our energy and our attention was being pulled there for a purpose unseen to us.

Now let's test this. After reading of these two events, the Gotthard Tunnel having been described in far less detail, which of those would you have identified as a ritual before I put that suggestion into your thoughts? If you're not familiar with the Tunnel ceremony, take a moment now to search for a video online so you can see it for yourself. There are several out there easy to find. Now look up "Waco The Big Lie" by Linda Thompson. You may even come across my reposting of it on BitChute. Please really do that, otherwise this point will have less impact.

In one we have blatant, in your face depictions of pagan symbolism right down to a man dressed as a goat depicting either Pan, Baphomet, or Bacchus. There's more sinister depictions of what appear to be uncovered dimensional portals, zombified mine workers, an orgy or two, the Pope in sunglasses, even Celtic symbols of the 3 witches.

In Waco we see everyday imagery of a dwelling, a regular looking building. Just a home. It's surrounded by tanks, choppers, armed thug agents, and police vehicles, but no obvious symbols or ritual acts visible.

But which one involved a real sacrifice of human lives? We can only speculate what went on before or after the Tunnel ceremony, but we are certain of the blood sacrifice at Waco, and just to remind you, 25 of them were children and infants! None of 80 or so people inside posed any threat to the agents whom were the sole aggressors. Would it surprise you to learn a majority of the Davidians were from Great Britain, and were black? Oh… They didn't tell you that, did they? I encourage you to look up another video, Waco the Last Will and Testament. I reproduced it on on my Rumble channel along with Waco: A New Revelation during the 30 year anniversary of the tragedy. The Last Will and Testament was filmed by the people inside. The families speak. Everyone on that tape was murdered except for one woman. There's children and babies on that tape. You can see their faces. You can start to understand the true EVIL of that April 19th ritual blood sacrifice right at the kickoff of the Festival of Moloch. The Tunnel ceremony was a cartoon by comparison. It was art school level weirdness and play acting. The Festival of Moloch, Moloch being the name of the **sacrificial furnace** into which babies were carried during the fertility rituals in honor of Ba'al, is recognized from April 19th-21st. Do you recall a fire at Waco?

Once seen, once we are drawn into the ritual as spectators, and our consent given over to such wicked acts, we are low-level initiates into their mystery school cult. For we have entered into their makeshift symbolic temple upon our "Own Free Will, and Accord." Were we really tricked into it, or were some of us all too willing and eager to be part of the social gathering, cheering, "Get those weird Branch Davidians?" We're so starved of our natural need for tribal, or community belonging, that we leap without looking into whatever opportunity the mass manipulators present us. And once we do, we cease to be innocent. We have crossed a threshold, stepped over the seal on the tiled floor, and made our commitment to the Order.

"…for, once you have crossed the threshold of the lodge room, divested of your own clothing, and wearing the habiliments of the order, and when once you become, as it were, bound by the **cable tow of Satan to the alter of BAAL,** *'there is no place for after repentance…"* -Ronayne

Fear for our own well-being should we stand in defiance to the EVIL within our own government, or more superficially, the fear of being ostracized by the group cheering and championing the wickedness, results in ignorance. Not unawareness, deliberate ignorance. Selfishness is fertile soil for Cowardice. We wouldn't want to be that nail that sticks up when the hammer comes around, now would we? We slip then into a subjective reality, rather than an objective one. Truth by consensus. It's time we reminded ourselves that right is right, no matter how many fail to acknowledge it. Right and Wrong are not subject to popular vote. They are unmoving natural laws, natural constants. Rationalize how we may, we know in our hearts when we are betraying our very nature.

The Ugaritic Text and the Cult of Ba'al

From what I have come to learn from my reading on the subject, and even Hebraic tutorials, the name Ba'al is pronounced like (Bah' ahl). I get corrected a lot by those who assume they know, but haven't taken the couple seconds needed to confirm their suspicions. It's not pronounced like "Bale" of hay. And it's not spelled Bael, like the character in the Tekken video game. I tried to make it easy for people. The name Ba'al Busters hints to the fact that it sounds more like Ball than anything else! The only difference is a short pause at the '. That's a break. It's a 2-syllable word. Don't make it more difficult and convoluted than it is. Yes, I feel better, now. Ha ha. Moving on…

1

Why is history important? If we don't go back far enough we'll never truly understand the nature of this adversary, and who they the followers manifest as cannot be fully recognized without knowledge of their roots, their objective throughout the aeons, and their prime motivators. To many, they just see inept politicians making terrible, destructive, and perverse decisions. They say it's corruption and that big money is buying their policy. They see an agenda, maybe, but you hear things like "follow the money" echoed repeatedly across so-called Truth-minded and Patriot social media influencers' channels, and I'm here to tell you that's a very superficial layer to all of this. It's a remedial perception of a much more deliberate, malicious, and hostile objective. It's so remedial, in fact, that I question whether or not it's a deliberate effort to keep viewers on an island using compelling, dramatic deliveries, distracting, erroneous data, and flat-out misinformation to keep people chasing their tails while the agenda the social media personalities claim to oppose moves ever forward. The influencers on the Patriot and Truth channels are doing their part to keep people occupied chasing many leads that go nowhere, endlessly. I worked as a Senior Mortgage Consultant for 5 years. I know what a bad lead is. We had a Leads Dept. full of Albany thug kids doing the same hustle on the phones as they did in the street.

There is a MindWar going on, as Michael Aquino coined, and it's not exclusive to one socially engineered cultural philosophy or another. It's all daggers pointing inward to the middle. Like the symbol for Walmart, or the peacock feathers of NBC, or what appear to be magnetron wrist-watches on the ancient Sumerian carvings of their gods. Evil doesn't sleep, and We the People of the world are not fully awake. To be so would be a living hell, not a Gaia TV Yoga session. It's not carefree, it's daunting when everything, and I mean everything around you still looks familiar, but you now sense a nightmarish dark mockery to it all. It's as if the ordinary is now embodied with a sense of despair. It's seeing the people of the world paralyzed as if bitten by a poisonous viper, or under a spell. There's a surreal presence in your surroundings you never noticed before. As foreign as it may feel, the realization that comes over you is that it's always been there. You just never were able to pick up on it before. You're tuned into a whole other station, or dialed between two stations. You sense a presence and it's as if you are seeing into the abyss, but what's more it can see you. Whatever defensive, natural, and maybe even spiritual cloak you once wore has been cast aside, stripped away, and you are no longer camouflaged. You're Daniel in the lion's den, and the lions just recognized you're not one of them. As they peer at you curious and amused at first, you have this thought form in your mind, the law of nature, "If you run, you're food." If you show fear, you're weak. If you behave as prey, you will be treated as prey. Like encounters with false authorities we call police, if you run at the sight of them, they will chase you. They may not know what you did, but you must have done something if you're running from them. They'll figure out what that is later. Keep your cool, even if you find yourself surrounded by vipers. True awakening isn't pleasant. You see things you can't unsee. Often what you experience will be baffling, lacking any familiar frame of reference. There's far more to this realm than meets the eye. It's as if other layers, other realms are all right within this one. You needn't venture to the great beyond. It's right here. It's as if it's invisible, and immaterial, meaning we typically probably pass right through it and it passes through us none the wiser. But if you turn that dial, increase or decrease your frequency, your vibration, you tune yourself to a different station and can sense these other realms, this other presence, even if only in the mind. It's like being a newborn in a scary, foreign environment. Things may look the same, but something dwells within it. Until you have this experience, what I am describing probably doesn't make a lot of sense. Trust me, it doesn't make a bit more sense after you've experienced it, either. You'll just know that something happened, it was very unsettling, and you wanted it to be over, but at the same time you felt like you had to do it, and wonder if it was some kind of a test. Were you tapped for some greater purpose? I can tell you this, if it does happen to you one thing will become abundantly clear. Faith is very important. Knowing is the most important. There is no question a battle is waging for the hearts and souls of men and women, and it's happening more dramatically in the realm in which you were allowed a glimpse.

I'm telling you this to get you thinking and wondering what may have made men like the priestcraft described in the Bill Cooper Darkness segment of this book in the first place. Did they see or sense something? Did it corrupt them rather than test their faith successfully? Were they seduced or too weak, too cowardly, not to bring a passenger back with them? Something that now works through them and determines their behavior? And is it that dark passenger's goal to infect all souls, all vessels of our realm with more of their own kind? Could this be the true motivator of these ancient cult practitioners, and is the modern day push for Transhumanism indicative of this objective?

2

We already learned Ba'al can simply mean "Lord," and therefore a guy like Lord Jacob Rothschild, could be seen as Ba'al Rothschild. It needn't be any more specific as the term Czar, Caesar, or King. The Ba'al we're concerned with, however, is that of the ancient Canaanite-Phoenecian cult known for orgiastic fertility rituals, which in themselves sound like a lot of fun. So long as we're talking consenting adults, that is. Heck, what better way to get to know your cute neighbors? I'm an Italian male. You can't fault me for my nature, here.

Here's where it gets repulsive, and unconscionable. The orgy wasn't the whole of the ritual. There was more to it than that. Guided by their Priestcraft who claimed they had favor with the gods, and would often demonstrate some slight of hand parlor trick to convince those of their community of their magical powers, the people willfully carried their own infants to a fiery furnace at the behest of the Priests leading the ceremony. In some literature it is said these babies were conceived at the previous orgy, and therefore a product of the former, and a worthy sacrifice for the current. The notion being the life created wasn't made out of love, but rather it was made for disposal. Before I continue, is this mentality beginning to sound a little familiar? It's like the night club and Spring Break culture where responsibility for choices made is avoided simply by disposing of the product of such hasty, drunken, or drugged decisions. Rather than an abortion murder, however, we're talking about infanticide. This type of party culture is glorified on MTV shows, and other television, movies, music, especially rap, and the money movers behind all these things promote the most graphic of it. Cardi B comes to mind. I'm sure everyone was thrilled to see the illegitimate Leader of the "Free" World sitting down with a woman who raps about her Wet Ass Pxssy.

If burning their own babies alive wasn't heartless and despicable enough, the word "cannibal" comes from combining "Canaan" and "Ba'al." They often cannibalized the burnt offerings. Can you imagine the level of inhumanity required to do such a thing with your own child? And one you held onto and cared for, that trusted and bonded with you for months before you betray it in the most horrific way imaginable, by burning it alive? What favor, and from what kind of a god are you expecting from such karmatically devastating actions as these? Did they really do all that for a little rain and a good crop yield? How can the whole of a culture be whipped into such a frenzy, such a dissociative trance as this? What sort of drugs and alcohol were they potentially using so long ago that may have helped obliterate their inhibitions? Belief is a very powerful thing, and the Priestcraft since the dawn of time have manipulated the many into their promoted belief systems with compelling public displays and magician's trickery.

It's an evidenced fact that rampant child sacrifice took place in the Hinnom Valley region, and was tied to the Rite of Molech, or Moloch. It is the valley surrounding the old city of Jerusalem, and the adjacent Mount Zion from the west and south. The KJV Bible translates Hinnom to be Hell. In Hebrew it is known as Gehinnom. The

Phoenician settlement of Carthage, modern day Tunisia, is the site of one Tophet, another term for Hell according to online dictionaries, where vast piles of bones of children were discovered by the conquering Romans. The ceremony was the same. Child sacrifice by passing a child through fire was the common method. At a particular time in history the Priestcraft of Sicily, Sardinia, and Malta also widely practiced child murder in an effort to gain favor with their gods. Notice it's never the Priestcraft practitioner jumping into the flames, but rather they expected other devotees to give up their children to please the gods.

I am highly suspicious of accounts and translations by modern day, agenda-serving scholars, and likely through biblical manipulation, they already have some of us unwittingly paying homage to their Ugaritic or Babylonian deities. I don't personally speak or read any ancient, dead languages, so I cannot translate cuneiform, ancient Greek, or Hebrew to get a direct answer from the past on this topic. We turn now to the translations of the multitude of tablets discovered in Ugarit for potential insights into the culture and rituals of people with such indifference in their hearts. A seemingly soulless group they were.

3

Before we do that however, be forewarned this tale of mankind's past, or at least we're told they were human, however inhumane they may have been, is not complete without a closer look at the Biblical translations. This may run the risk of offending some, and that is not the intent. It's simply an analysis of everything and I mean everything we take for granted as having a particular meaning and value. As is with the deception of the Allopathic [Allo-pathetic] Medical Monopoly, all things should be examined to see whether what they claim is in fact what we can discover ourselves. Don't take anyone's word for anything. Our presumptions and impressions of things have been molded a particular way so that it would seem unnatural and perhaps offensive to even suggest we question something. We have certain sacred cows that are off-limits to scrutiny. Well, that's where manipulators would do the most manipulation. In the metaphoric Gun-Free Zones, where questions dare not challenge. I'm referring to the use of the words Lord and Ba'al in the Tanakh, or Old Testament. No distinction is made as to who they are referring to, and we have already established that Ba'al can simply mean "lord."

It could be argued that there may have been multiple "Lords" being referenced in a single passage with no effort made to clarify it to the reader. Therefore we could have a misunderstanding as to the particular traits attributed to the one we think they're talking about when they translate the word as "Lord." I wonder if some other presence was influencing the people of the time and that it was mixed into the overarching term "Lord," incorrectly. I ask this not to challenge God or the Bible, but rather in Defense of the one I call the Benevolent Creator. I cannot bring myself to accept some of the commands given by *God* in the Old Testament as being from the same Benevolent Creator I have come to know.

Consider these instances from the Tanakh, AKA Old Testament, cataloged on a site called badnewsaboutchristianity.com I don't pick the names. Don't place the blame on me:

"The God of the Old Testament takes an active part in battle. On occasion he kills more of the enemy than the Jews themselves (Joshua 10:11). He killed 185,000 Assyrians in a single night (2 Kings 19:35). He encouraged murder and even genocide. In Numbers 31 for example, Midianite married women and male children were slaughtered in accordance with his wishes. Helpless captives, they were killed on the orders of Moses, acting on God's instructions. God arranged for Joshua to kill all that lived in the city of Ai, 12,000 men and women (Joshua 8:1-29). Earlier, he had arranged for Joshua to take Jericho, and on this occasion had wanted absolutely everything destroyed. Joshua therefore killed men and women, young and old, cattle, sheep and donkeys (Joshua 6:15-21). At Dabir, Joshua "utterly destroyed all that breathed, as the Lord God of Israel commanded" (Joshua 10:40). Generally, when a city was taken, God wanted all the men killed and the women, children, and animals taken as plunder, but in the case of the Hittites, Amorites, Canaanites, Perizzites, Hivites and Jesubites everything that breathed had to be destroyed completely (Deuteronomy 20:10-17)."

This site is indirectly making a case for potential misinterpretations in translation, or perhaps deliberate ones. Translations that mix deeds of more than one "Lord" together as one. If God, the Benevolent Creator, the source of Love, was in fact actively participating in the lives of mankind at some point in our history, it bears to question whether it was because another, or several other deities were here as well, and perhaps He was intervening. So when a culture records their previously only oral tradition, it may be that by the time it was written the cultural memory had morphed, or simply that the modern translators think in modern terms of the past. They may assume if a culture is discussing God, or Lord, that it implies the God we more commonly recognize these days. These cultures may have had different influences either in the form of God, or of exalted priests or even something more foreign and yet identified that they would have perceived as their god.

The site continues:

*"God often forbids his followers to show pity or mercy (e.g. Deuteronomy 7:2, Ezekiel 9:5-6). Sometimes, God undertakes the mass killing of children himself (Exodus 12:29). Indeed, children have a particularly hard time of it. Not only are they punished for the crimes of their ancestors, but they are also victims of **family cannibalism**. To people who fail to meet God's requirements he promises that, amongst many other tribulations, **they will have to eat their own children** (Leviticus 26:29 and Deuteronomy 28:53)."*

Leviticus 26:29 reads: *You will eat the flesh of your own sons and daughters.*

Deuteronomy 28:53 the "Lord" threatens: *And thou shalt eat the fruit of thine own body, the flesh of thy sons and of thy daughters, which the* **Lord** *thy God hath given thee, in the siege, and in the straitness, wherewith thine enemies shall distress thee*

Note: vaccines have fetal tissue in them. In recent decades they have been using human remains in fertilizers, using the bones of the dead, calling it calcium, and adding it to an array of food products including supplements, and it's been found in the water.

The verses in Deuteronomy as many other places in the Bible are a laundry list of vicious threats. It makes you wonder if this "God' is the infallible, Benevolent one, then how is it that he continues to have to annihilate His own Creation, cutting down whole swaths of people? Couldn't he have just made them correctly to begin with?

The cannibalistic component here seems to suggest more of a Ba'al Lord than that of the Benevolent Creator "Lord" God. Could it be perhaps there was a mix-up here? Are they possibly following the commands of Ba'al as spoken through their manipulative Dark Priests rather than God Himself? It seems to follow more closely the modus operandi of the various cults devoted to Ba'al. Is it possible that an opposing so-called deity was interwoven with the Creator by way of mistranslation?

What of the early desire of the "Lord" for routine blood sacrifices? That he preferred animal over agricultural sacrifices was confirmed by the tale of Cain and Abel. But as a Socratic, I have to stop on this and ask, if He made these things, why does He need them back? Has the Creator not the power Create what He wants? Why does he insist on blood sacrifices of people and animals in the Tanakh? It's no less EVIL to murder your baby, and sometimes eat it, just because "God" told you it would please Him. That's when you have to question the nature of this "God" which they're referring to.

On blood sacrifices that site also states:

"As in many primitive religions, God wanted blood. **Blood** *was far more important than the flesh. It was the life force, the seat of life itself (Genesis 9:4, Leviticus 17:11). Anyone might eat the flesh but* **the blood belonged to God** *himself.* Leviticus 17:11 reads: For the life of the flesh is in the blood, and I have given it for you on the altar to make atonement for your souls, for it is the blood that makes atonement by the life.

According to the book of Judges, Jephthah killed his only child in fulfillment of a promise made to God (Judges 11:29-40). As the narrative points out God was taking a personal interest in Jephthah at the time, yet he did not attempt to stop him. Nor was Jephthah regarded as acting excessively. He was well regarded as a judge and was mentioned with approval in the New Testament."

God repeatedly makes the point that this [animal sacrifice] must be done in front of him, and that he likes the smell of the burned flesh. Referring to Noah's mass animal sacrifice, Genesis 8:20-22 tells us that he Lord smelled the pleasing odour"

In front of Him, pleasing Odor? That would give human, living attributes to the one they call "Lord." This is all too confusing and why I have a difficulty with reading the Book. The impression I have of the God I know is in opposition to the one described in the Tanakh. While in my view there is nothing wrong with the warrior attributes when destruction of EVIL is the goal, it's all together different to take pleasure in harming, or even threatening children, let alone targeting them specifically as a punishment to their parents. The blood obsession seems to point more toward the cult of Ba'al, and later day adrenochrome applications.

Another site, this time a Ministry called Come and Reason posted an article in May of 2020 with this passage:

Two Kinds of Laws

God is the Creator, who built all reality, and His laws are the laws upon which reality operates. When one breaks God's laws, one takes themselves out of harmony with God, with life itself, and the sure, natural result is ruin and death. As the Bible teaches, "The one who sows to please his sinful nature, from that nature will reap destruction" (Galatians 6:8 NIV84).

*But false gods, like **Baal, do not create**; they impose. Their laws are imperial, rules designed to **control others**. Breaking the imposed rules that created beings make up doesn't cause damage to the breaker of the rules; it results in the ruling authority **inflicting punishment**. This is the root of all false systems of worship, a **false law** construct, which leads to a false god construct in which the deity is the **enforcer of punishment**, one that **requires appeasement and payment**.*

After having read the previous passages from the Tanakh, which of these two separate entities or deities do the Old Testament describe better? It's just something to think about. If there is interest in further analysis on this, it may be a topic for a future Ba'al Busters book. But for now let me say it's my suspicion those like the influential and conquering Warrior Priesthood known as the Maccabees were guilty of perceiving God in archaic ways that justified, and even glorified their own brutality, and therefore were dusting off old deities such as Ba'al when contributing to the OT. They simply polished off Ba'al and gave him other names. I said polished their Ba'als, ha ha.

4

As previously mentioned, Ba'al is the son of Dagon, a name meaning "Grain." Like his father he possesses the attributes of a fertility god, when in reference to agriculture, and possibly more. Other titles are given to him as we read in this passage from https://www.phoenicia.org/ethnlang.html :

*Baal also bears the titles "Rider of the Clouds," "Almighty," and "Lord of the Earth." He is the **god of the thunderstorm**, the most vigorous and aggressive of the gods, the one on whom mortals most immediately depend. Baal resides on Mount Zaphon, north of Ugarit, and is usually **depicted holding a thunderbolt**. He is the protagonist of a cycle of myths from Ugarit. These tell of a challenge from Yamm ("Sea"), to which Baal responds. Armed with magical weapons made by the craftsman god, Kothar, Baal manages to overcome Yamm.*

El was the gray-bearded elder, father to most other gods, to humankind, and supreme deity in the time of Ba'al's rise. He was the lead figure in the pantheon. There were more than 234 deities in the Ugaritc texts. The stories are spread across many cuneiform tablets, and interior wall engravings in temple ruins. Many tablets telling the tale of the Ba'al cycle are badly damaged and therefore incomplete in their transcription. El was said to be the Creator God, although the attributes ascribed to him, and whether or not they live up to that of a Benevolent Creator is still something scholars are in hot debate over. While the Met Museum website claims he was the Creator god, and a good natured being, there exist no creation story in the Ugaritic writings. Perhaps things always were, and ever will be, with no beginning nor end. El had a wife, Asherah, so for those who say El is the God of the Bible, he had a female counterpart. An Asherah pole is a sacred tree or pole to honor this mother goddess. Whether sacrifices of children were conducted around these sacred trees is unclear. It may interest you to know Yahweh had his beginnings as one of the many Canaanite deities, and he was the god of metallurgy.

The Ba'al tales, although interesting, and expansive poems, are not going to be discussed in great detail here. What we need to get a better look at is the culture that produced the cult.

Scholars give the impression that the cult of Ba'al drifted away from El in favor of the more aggressive, and somewhat defiant deity whom the humans needed favor of to get the much needed rain for their crops. Ba'al challenged Yamm (sea) and Mot (death.) Ba'al, in their culture was given the title of Prince Lord of the Earth, & Lord of the Rain and Dew according to the Encyclopedia Britannica. The people felt he determined the safety of sea voyages because he controlled the storms, and defeated the Sea. Over time the Priest class warped this into the notion that the people best appease him, or they may not survive in the ocean. It wasn't presented so much that he was a patron of the seas, but that Ba'al would potentially kill you if you didn't give him something. In Phoenician he was Ba'al Shamen, the Lord of the Heavens. That's likely a reference to the Storm God motif, than the more Christian-minded would perceive as the Heavenly Father.

Ba'al was actually a respectable and even noble, chivalrous, fearless, and heroic character in the Ugaritic texts, at least in the first saga, or Ba'al Cycle. By the 2nd Ba'al Cycle, with Anath by his side who avenged and smote his enemies, taking great pleasure in the bloody carnage she caused on humans perceived as enemies of Ba'al, or loyalists to Yamm/Yammu, one may say, "things got a little weird." Did they though? Think about it for a moment. If you were protecting say a king, would you allow yourself to ignore an insurgence group brewing and building against your leader? The method she dispatched them aside, or however amount of pleasure taken in the deed, the functionality of such a security measure makes logical sense. Same with the modern day threats to our families, I see nothing wicked in the annihilation of the Wicked. I often say, "I would love to go all Vlad the Impaler" on these child predators and global alliances against humanity. Be honest, would you shed a tear if the United Nations, UNESCO, NATO, WHO, the Council on Foreign Relations, the Bank of International Settlements, IMF, City of London Banksters, the Members of the World Economic Forum, all High level Child Predators, the Vatican, but I repeat myself, several CEOs, lots of judges, lawyers, death doctors, homicidal lying scientists, and ALL Politcians-period were at once thrown into a Fargo-style wood chipper, or impaled on a 20ft spike? I think the public Impaling method serves as pretty powerful warning to others inflicting harm on good people. It makes for one hell of a deterrent. Anyone who would clean up the threats to the innocent should be regarded as heroes, and shown gratitude. I don't think people who do what needs to be done, and are brave, driven warriors are sinful in any way. Who then would pull the weeds choking the garden? If you are waiting for God's intervention, um… YOU are it. He sent his warriors already; they are us. Stop looking around or up. We were sent here with purpose-forgotten, probably vaccinated out of us at birth and childhood. I went on a little tangent there. I'm back now.

Having limited access to the Ba'al Cycle I of the Ugaritic tablets, I turn now to https://brewminate.com/baal-ancient-canaanite-phoenician-god-of-fertility-and-weather/ Brewminate.com is a virtual coffee table discussion among fellow historians and academics where they can submit articles and treatments on their areas of study. This piece was submitted by Dr. Joshua J. Mark, Professor of Philosophy at Marist College in Poughkeepsie, New York. The title of the essay is, Ba'al: Ancient Canaanite-Phoenecian God of Fertility and Weather. He writes:

...Tales concerning Baal date back to the mid-14th and late 13th centuries BCE in written form but are understood to be much older, preserved by oral tradition until committed to writing. Excavations of the ancient city of Ugarit (modern-day Ras Shamra, Syria) beginning in 1929 CE revealed thousands of cuneiform tablets, many of them relating the tales of the gods and, specifically, Baal, who became king of the gods, replacing El...

...Baal's popularity is attested by the many copies found of the stories that make up the so-called Baal Cycle which relates how Baal conquers death and assumes the kingship of the gods. The story of Baal's descent to the underworld and return has often been cited as an early example of the dying and reviving god motif but this has been challenged as Baal does not actually die and return to life...

...A stele from the site shows him with a club in one hand and a lightning bolt in the other, identifying him as a god of storms and war. He would be primarily associated with storms and rains throughout his worship in Ugarit and later after c. 1200 BCE when Ugarit was destroyed…

…While still a thriving city, however, Ugarit participated in trade with others including the major urban centers of the Levant. Baal Hadad seems to have traveled there via trade, though precisely when is unknown. He became a central deity of the Canaanite pantheon which would inform, first, Canaanite beliefs and, later, Phoenician religion. The Phoenician city of Baalbek (in modern-day Lebanon) was his cult center where he was worshipped with his consort Astarte, goddess of love, sexuality, and war (associated with the goddess Inanna/Ishtar, among others). Even so, Astarte was the most popular deity at Sidon, even eclipsing Baal in the number of temples dedicated to her, and is equally well represented at Baalbek…

…The interpretation of the pairing of Baal and Astarte has been challenged for various reasons, among them the possibility that the goddess associated with Baal is his sister, Anat, who is thought to have informed the development of Astarte. This argument, however, seems to ignore her depiction in the Baal Cycle and other tales like *El's Drinking Party* (in which she is clearly differentiated from Anat) as well as her temples at Baalbek…

…**Three goddesses** appear regularly in the stories [about Baal] – Astarte, mentioned only in passing, Asherah, and Anat. The latter two have significant though not dominant roles in the myths, for Ugaritic theology, like Ugaritic society, was patriarchal. Asherah is El's consort and the mother of the gods. The only goddess with a vivid character is Anat. She is Baal's sister and is closely identified with him as a successful opponent of [Yamm, Mot] and other destructive powers...

…All three goddesses would come to be associated closely with Baal in the biblical narratives as Asherah is referenced as a sacred fertility pole (or possibly tree) in Deuteronomy 16:21, II Kings 21:7, II Kings 23:4, 6-7, and elsewhere. Prior to these works, however, she appears as El's consort and a central figure in the Baal Cycle…

Baal Cycle:

The Baal Cycle begins with Baal, son of Dagon [half man, half fish], confident that he will be chosen as king by El, lord of the gods. El disappoints his expectations, however, by choosing Yamm, who almost instantly subjugates the other gods and forces them to work for him. The gods complain to Asherah who agrees to intercede for them with Yamm. She offers him all kinds of treasures, but he is only interested in possessing her. She agrees but must first return to El and the divine court to inform them of their contract.

Every god in attendance supports Asherah's decision to give herself to Yamm except Baal who swears revenge on Yamm for insulting Asherah in this way and promises to kill him. His reaction is interpreted as treason by some of the other gods who are quick to inform Yamm of it, and Yamm then sends emissaries to the court demanding Baal's surrender. The other gods show the emissaries the utmost respect, but Baal refuses to bow and is disgusted by the No decision is given by the gods and so Yamm sends a second delegation who are arrogant and neglect the proper rituals due to El and the court. Baal wants to kill them for this affrontery, but he is held back by Anat and Astarte, who warn him against the sin of killing a messenger who is only acting on orders and is therefore innocent. El does not move against the messengers either but, instead, promises them that Baal will not only appear before Yamm but will bring lavish gifts.

Baal is enraged but understands he is not powerful enough to defeat Yamm in single combat. Kothar-wa-Khasis suggests a way, however, and tells Baal he can create two clubs for him, Yagrush and Aymur, which will destroy Yamm if used as instructed. Kothar-wa-Khasis makes the weapons and tells Baal how to use them, and Baal goes to meet Yamm, bearing no gifts. He strikes Yamm on the shoulders with Yagrush, but Yamm is unhurt. Baal retreats and returns to strike Yamm with Aymur between the eyes, and Yamm falls. Baal then hauls him back to the court, announces his victory, and casts Yamm back into the sea.

Baal is now king of the gods, but Mot objects to this usurpation and sends the sea monster Lotan (possibly a form of Yamm) to attack Baal, but Baal defeats and kills him. Mot is now enraged further and swears he will devour Baal. Mot is unstoppable, and Baal understands that there are no magical weapons that can defeat death. He goes into hiding, sending a double in his place to be eaten by Mot, and all the gods mourn his death. As he was the god of rain and fertility, the earth becomes barren in his absence, and **Anat**, swearing revenge, attacks and kills Mot.

As Mot is immortal, he returns to life, but Baal then emerges from hiding and subdues him, forcing him to return to his underworld home and recognize Baal as the legitimate king. He then asks for and receives permission from El and the other gods for Kothar-wa-Khasis to build him a grand palace on a mountain top (initially with no windows since it was thought Mot-as-Death entered a dwelling through a window) and begins his reign.

The story is understood as illustrating a transition in power from the elder gods to a younger set, a familiar pattern in religious works of many different cultures as noted by Coogan and Smith:

> The transfer of power from an older sky god to a younger storm god is attested in other contemporaneous eastern Mediterranean cultures. Cronus was imprisoned and succeeded by his son Zeus, Yahweh succeeded El as the god of Israel, the Hurrian god Teshub assumed kingship in heaven after having defeated his father Kumarbi, and Baal replaced El as the effective head of the Ugaritic pantheon.

> ...Baal's cult was eventually replaced by the cult of Yahweh and his name became synonymous with the enemies of the one true god. In II Kings 1, Ba'al Zebub is associated with Ekron, god of the Philistines, the people famously cast as the enemies of Israel in the Bible. Ba'al Zebub would eventually be known as Beelzebub to the New Testament scribes and linked with the Christian devil, an association that would last up through the time of the Protestant Reformation.

By that time, Baal had also come to be associated with the figure of Iblis, the devil in Islam, through passages in the Quran. Allah, in Islam, and Yahweh, in Judaism and Christianity, were recognized by their respective adherents as the only god and Baal as an aspect of chaos, darkness, and evil who threatened world order.

Initially, however, Yahweh was part of the same pantheon that embraced Baal, and the two would have been regarded as co-workers in the cause of order against the forces of chaos. Scholars J. Maxwell Miller and John H. Hayes comment:

> Archaeological evidence indicates an essentially continuous religious and cultic scene throughout Palestine during the Early Iron Age. Nothing has been discovered, in other words, that suggests any notable distinctiveness in temple layout or cultic furniture for the time and territory of the early tribes. Continuity between early Israelite religion and that of the other inhabitants of Syria-Palestine is confirmed further by parallels between the religious and cultic terminology of the biblical materials and the corresponding terminology of extrabiblical documents. Elements of Syro-Palestinian mythology, such as a divine struggle with the cosmic dragon of chaos, also appear here and there in biblical poetry. Occasional biblical

passages suggest, in fact, that Yahweh was once viewed as a member of the large pantheon ruled over by El.

In order for Yahweh to be recognized as the supreme god, however, his predecessors had to be eliminated, and Baal was demonized in accomplishing this end. In the present day, the god's reputation as a powerful protector and life-affirming agency has been revived through the Neo-Pagan and Wiccan movements who reject the biblical narratives and rely on older constructs like the Baal Cycle. Although hardly widespread, the worship of Baal continues in the present day alongside the more popular Yahweh, mirroring the similar relationship the two gods had in the ancient world.

What's inconsistent is that she's (Anat) said to be his sister. She can't be if Dagon is Ba'al's father, because El is the father of Anat(h). Many incorrectly say El is the father of all the gods including Ba'al. Scholars have indicated that regional stories vary, but that El is the father of Ba'al in the Ugaritic cuneiform tablets. I'm not a reader of cuneiform myself, and I don't think it's out of question to say neither are they. Whomever transcribed them may have taken liberties in the translations where information was missing or unclear. Without getting into this theological Maury Povich show too much, Anath was very devoted to Ba'al and even threatened to brutally murder her father, El, after he denied her request to approve the building of a suitable pantheon for Ba'al after he had himself time and again in defeating all challengers to his supremacy.

As you read that summary provided by Dr. Mark, you can't help but think, "If this is true, then Ba'al seems to have noble, even commendable qualities." He may be a hot head, but he's a gallant, chivalrous hot head. He vows to kill Yamm/Yammu (Sea) for the indignities Asherah endures. Where the hell was El in all that? Isn't that his woman? Why is Ba'al more outraged than El? You can only pull that "cultural differences" card so much before you say, no. The gods as they may be, have enough human traits in these stories to apply human nature to their responses. They weren't lions. In lion social constructs the dominant male has his choice of the females.

The treachery of the other gods who inform Yamm, the Rapist, basically, is at the level of weak-willed, back-stabbing, favor-seeking cowardice we see in corporate America, politics, and mafia of present day. It's what I call weaselly behavior. They have no true integrity, yet act offended by those who do what is right, regardless of the laws of tradition. Weaker gods as they were, complained to Asherah about Yamm, but then rush right out to tell Yamm that Ba'al is plotting revenge for the injustice against Asherah. This is a very convoluted story. With Yamm out of the picture they'd be freed of their own servitude to him. So why the treachery? Why the loyalty to Yamm? Why the modern day people's defense of the corrupt government agencies by turning in their neighbors? Cowards think they'll win favor by showing loyalty to what they perceive as the most powerful force governing their lives. Stockholm syndrome coupled with weaselitis. It's a thing.

Yahweh, who is a superficial god of metallurgy, appearing first in Canaanite lore, somehow transcends all of these prime gods and becomes the supreme, true "God." Credentials, please? That's like having a presidential race and someone who wasn't even running as a candidate winning the office. I'm being objective here. People won't like this, but this is the history as it was written long before this notion of required commitment to monotheistic concepts was ever developed.

Interestingly, Ba'al had a particular animosity toward snakes. He fought the Tannin, or Twsited Snake, the Fugitive Snake, and the Snake of Seven Heads. This ties into his conquest of Yamm, the Sea god. What's more interesting is the claim that Canaanites worshipped snakes. I don't buy it. Much of that comes from Philo who's conflating Egyptian culture with that of it's neighbors. He's a more antique example of a fake expert on social media.

The FactsandDetails.com website has this to say about the Urgaritic tales:

Following the victory, [of Ba'al over Yamm] ***Anat****, El's daughter who is also called Baal's sister, goes on a rampage and **slaughters human enemies** presumably allied against Baal. Afterward, Baal pursues the construction of a magnificent royal palace on his sacred mountain. The craftsman Kothar-wa-Hasis suggests that the palace have windows, but Baal disagrees so that Yamm/Nahar not enter stealthily. Cedars are brought from Lebanon together with silver, gold, and precious stones to adorn the palace. When the building is finished, all the deities celebrate with a great feast. Afterward, Baal defeats all of his enemies in surrounding territories in order to form an empire for himself. Now flush with victory, Baal sends a courier to Mot, son of El and ruler of the Underworld, to declare his kingship. But Mot in his reply turns the tables on his adversary and invites him to come to the Underworld. When Baal accepts and descends, he becomes trapped in the vise of death, which results in the cessation of rain. **Anat**, Baal's sister and the **goddess of hunting and war**, goes in search of him. Finding him in the realm of the dead, she confronts Mot, attacks him with a knife and winnowing fork, and burns his body, which is then eaten by birds. Now rescued, Baal resumes his place on the royal throne. But Mot revives and the two giants of the heavens battle. Finally, **Mot capitulates and declares Baal to be the rightful ruler of the cosmos**.*

In that interpretation there was no mention of a replacement being sent on Ba'al's behalf to suffer the fate for him. If these are gods, how could a body double fool them, anyway? Shouldn't they be able to sense one another's divine force, and recognize when it is absent? How else would they identify one another? I don't think Ba'al tucked his own driver's license into the pocket of the bull that became his double. What pockets?

This author has read the Ugaritic texts Ba'al Cycle II, and I stand firm that Ba'al was indeed an outsider, not of the main pantheon of El's offspring, and therefore Anat was his bat shit crazy, but loyal-to-a-fault girlfriend, not his sister, and not Both. Other mythologies are saturated so much with incest it's as if it's not even worth pointing out. That's just how they roll. Making mutants and more violent offspring each successive generation. Someone who would know the secret teachings well, H.P. Lovecraft, wrote of the Esoteric Order of the Dagon, Ba'al's father, which he strangely called the "Fish-god," and not the fertility god of grain, and harvest.

So what do we know from Ugarit, itself, and Not just from outsiders looking in with some religio-politcal agenda, such as what is found in the latter years? It may surprise you, or it may even enrage your sensibilities. To be fair and objective, I have to take the research where it leads. I cannot skew the evidence in favor of preconceived notions, nor to loyalty to a particular set of religious ideals. I can't be party to a clean-up operation and still consider myself any kind of student of historical pathology, and detective work.

In Dennis Pardee's research into the topic of the Ugaritic tablets, he has this to say:

...The tablets excavated so far represent the results of accidental and random preservation. Therefore, they cannot be considered a fair or complete representation of the cult. Further, the difficulty of vocabulary and syntax in these texts is compounded by the fact that they are almost entirely prescriptive. That is to say, they define aspects of what is to be offered or said in a sacrifice or ritual. They do not explain the significance of these actions or of the ceremony as a whole. This leaves many uncertainties and questions regarding the practice of religion at Ugarit. Nevertheless, the texts do say something about religion there.

The texts themselves are divided into two large groups. The first constitutes those writings that describe religious matters associated with the official sacrificial cult. These include lists of gods and goddesses, descriptions of which animals are to be sacrificed and what the officiates are to do during various holy days, mortuary offerings, texts about divination, and one or two prayers. Some texts even reveal a form of check marks in the left margin of the tablet. Placed beside each deity's name, they indicate that the appropriate sacrifice was made. A second group of texts examine religious practice outside the cult. This includes incantations and recipes for **snakes***, a hangover, sexual dysfunction, and other problems. It also may include rituals involving the dead as well as other texts describing administrative taxation and the distribution of goods for religious purposes.*

...Most significantly are the few prayers that are preserved. This indicates the different type of literature that has been discovered at Ugarit more than it suggests the amount of praying that the citizens of Ugarit did. One of the prayers preserved **exhorts the reader to invoke Baal when attacked by an enemy***. The supplicant promises to visit Baal's temple and to offer sacrifices in a manner not unlike some of the lament psalms of the Bible (Psa. 17:9; 18:3; 66:15; etc.). Another text, sometimes called the Ugaritic Day of Atonement ritual, is described by Pardee as a ritual of national unity. Nevertheless, a sense of confession and forgiveness seems to be involved.*

*….In his conclusion, Pardee helpfully provides his list of similarities and contrasts between Ugaritic religious practice and that found in the Bible. Among the former he lists vocabulary such as altar, peace offering, burnt offering, and the house of the deity. Mostly, he notes a similarity in terms of what is absent. Both **do not mention the sacrifice of children, pigs, and wild animals; nor do they record a New Year's festival or a fertility cult**. In terms of contrasts there are differences of genres between the two collections of literature. Ugaritic sacrificial texts do not mention expiation, sin, atonement, blood, and fat. There is a text describing a donkey sacrifice and there is **more emphasis on offerings of wine and of textiles**. Distinct personnel and their roles are not mentioned much at Ugarit.*

In light of the more recent publication of the thirteenth century B.C. Emar religious texts from this north Syrian city, it would have been useful to note comparisons and contrasts between the three groups. Emar has priestly installation, festival, and cultic calendar texts that much more closely resemble the genres found in the Bible than those from Ugarit…

That write-up can be found at: https://denverseminary.edu/the-denver-journal-article/ritual-and-cult-at-ugarit/ Denver Seminary website.

So where is the child sacrifice mentioned, if not in the as-close-to-original texts we have surrounding Ba'al? If you think this journey I'm taking you through is disproving this element of the ancient practices, it's actually making it. For my understanding is not that Ba'al himself was the progenitor of such a concept, but rather the priesthood(s) who would claim to be constituents of Ba'al. The longer the practice of the Ba'al Cult carried on, and was transported to other neighboring cultures and interpreted, the more it was morphed and manipulated by the priests who claimed authority over all knowledge of the gods. Opportunists have always existed, as was the desire for ultimate power. This desire to control was satiated best not by being a king or a ruler, but by being the trusted advisors of said rulers. For example, if you look at the ancient Egyptian culture, it was ultimately the priestcraft that influenced the decisions and superstitions of the Pharaohs. To have the highest of all nobility looking to them for guidance left rulers susceptible to the whims and personal objectives of the priests. If someone or some group of people refused to acknowledge and pay homage to the priests, they could drum up lies and propaganda about them. Having the ear of the rulers meant they could whisper thoughts of doubt or of mutiny and manipulate the highest lawful authority to execute individuals, or wipe out whole settlements. If you had the king, you had their army. Religions, as we will explore, have always been fertile soil for corruption. For even if you thought something was amiss, you dare not question the teachings of the holy ones, lest you suffer the wrath of the gods themselves for your insolence. This power to dictate at will gave way to the lowest and most despicable of acts to be carried out in the name of their gods, but really it was in the name of the morally bankrupt and wicked sorcerers of the priesthood. The people, taking the lead from the rulers and their warlock-like priests would be worked up into great frenzies, orgiastic rituals, and dark ceremonies in an effort to please the gods and be blessed with protection from invasion, good crop yield, and health and prosperity within their community.

The belief that the sacrifice of the first born is the highest, ultimate form of worship would have some sick logic to it if you were a loving parent, but if you were a loving parent, how could you? If you were an unloving parent, as when the infant was the product of a ritual orgy, how was it much of a gesture at all? This idea of immolating (it means sacrificing, especially by burning) infants and toddlers seems to have been transmitted by the practitioners of the dark priests of the time. Meaning they suggested such a sacrifice would please the god(s) and bring blessings upon the people. Philo writes:

Philo of Byblos [where we get the word "Bible" after the papyrus] *((A.D. 4th century, Porphyry): "It is the custom among the ancients, in times of great calamity, in order to prevent the ruin of all, for the rulers of the city or nation to sacrifice to the avenging deities the most beloved of their children."*

That's a whitewashing if you ask me. They did this as a matter of routine, and what say of the orgy component? Was that what you do in "times of great calamity?" You throw a huge party? You consume all what you do have in one evening? And just for kicks, you, as the parent of the child walk it to the furnace yourself and betray it? You eat what you once held in your hands? You live on after such an act? How? How could you think you deserve to? A parent's sole purpose in life is to love, raise, and protect their children. They would have annihilated their primary reason for continued existence. What for? Some misguided sense of a higher responsibility to a community, driven by vague superstition? What empty shells they must be afterward! I wish I had suicide rate statistics for that time period in Hinnom, Sidon, etc. I think Philo did much of his "worldly observations" from conditions of isolation. It seems like he spread cultures across borders like an artist mixing colors of paint. Who verified his claims?

To lend a little bit of credence to Philo, it would depend on the specific region of the practicing Ba'al Cult as to the particularities. We read from the Italian website, La Sicilia in Rete (lasiciliainrete.it) of such a variation of the practice in Sicily, Sardinia, and Marsala:

"An embodiment of natural forces, Baal was linked to agriculture. The deity, also known by the name of Baal Hammon, was already known in the East in the XNUMXth century BC, and the Carthaginians spread the cult among other peoples of the Mediterranean. Later, with the Romanization of the Mediterranean, the cult of Baal was identified by the Romans with that of Saturn and by the Greeks with that of Kronos…

*When Phenicia came under the hegemony of the Jews, the god of the pre-Israelite peoples was associated with the devil, as hostile to the deity worshiped by the Jews. The name **Baal Zebub**, meaning "lord of the flies," was replaced first, in the contemptuous form of **Baal-Zebul** which meant "lord of the dung" and finally in **Beelzebub**, name used to indicate the lord of the devils. He was also called by the Jews "**Molech**," Which in Hebrew means "king of ignominy,"* [shame and disgrace] *due to the human sacrifices that were offered to him and which saw children as innocent victims.*

*The sacrifice took place in open and enclosed shrines called "**Tofet**", where the urns containing the remains of cremated children were buried. Tofet have been found in Carthage, in Punic Africa, in Sicily a Mozia, and also in Sardinia.*

*The sacrifice concerned the **first-born of the noblest families**, even if, often, subterfuges were used to spare them: in fact, the even more barbaric habit of buying or kidnapping **foreign children who were fed and then sacrificed in place of children** was not rare, true.*

*Diodorus Siculus (lib. XX.14) tells us that during the siege of Carthage, which occurred by Agatocles in 310 BC, the Carthaginians reproached themselves for having abandoned the tradition by sacrificing foreign children and, seeing the enemy at the gates, hastened **to ask forgiveness from the gods by sacrificing two hundred children** chosen from the most prominent families in the city.*

"To explain the significance of this type of sacrifice it has been hypothesized that it served to renew divine energy through the blood of the best children. The fire, then, would give a new divine life to the sacrificed children, thus alleviating the pain of the parents."

From the passage we see the connection between that of Ba'al and the furnace depiction, Molech, or Moloch, the king of shame and disgrace.

I hope you picked up on the early, if not the very origins of child trafficking here. The demand for kidnapped foreign infants, as in unknown to, and outside of their community was high among the **ruling class** [elite] of these peoples. They would **buy**, or **kidnap** them for the purpose of ritual sacrifice! Take a long, objective look at Child "Protective" Services, Department of Child "Safety," and tell me that's not kidnapping and child-trafficking, often with the very same end result, if not purpose. These ancient traditions are carried on in modern guises at official capacity!

Although referred to as the "nobility," there's certainly nothing noble about their despicable acts. When faced with an opposing army their response was to start murdering their own first-born, and I would argue if they told themselves it was to appease a god, what they were really doing is being absolute cowards and scum (opinion). It was a desperate act, and one deserving of whatever fate awaited them when the army broke through their defenses. This hypothesized rationalization for killing children of good stock is insulting to read. That was no doubt proposed by some detached apologist with no children, or no loved children, of their own. Thinking this act would imbue them with some sort of divine energy is counterintuitive. What sort of deity that would ask of you such a sacrifice as destroying the most innocent, murdering your own children, could have any divinity within them to offer anyone else? They couldn't possibly be under the impression Ba'al was a benevolent Creator God. Why would God want you to destroy the masterpiece of his Creation, and give it back to Him? If that was the intent, why would He give you children in the first place? It's a destructive assault on his blessings. How does that produce a positive return? See, I suspect that much like today with government handouts leading to obedience to Statism, these people knew very well they were worshipping a god that was not the Creator, but that of materialism. The selfish tendencies took them away from God in favor of someone who would toss them crumbs when they pleased him. How undignified, and yet incredibly selfish! They care more about the personal gain than for the lives of their own children. If they wanted to give up something, why not just fast for a few days, and give something up themselves? Because some group among them was filling their heads with superstitious nonsense. The sorcerers, or priests leading the communities here, were the ultimate manipulators, living Loki figures tricking the most powerful in their tribes to kill their own children. And they did it. They did it in hopes to spare themselves, like the cowards they were, and are today. Even those who send their children off to fight wars for the New World Order, and ignorantly perceive it as patriotic, are guilty of this cowardice. It's not your sacrifice if it isn't YOU descending into the fiery furnace. It's you dodging a true sacrifice by offering up a replacement. Ponder that for awhile. It's an atonement ritual like that of Yum Kippur where the chicken is the hapless stand-in for the sinful person, as it is cursed, ritualistically killed, and then fed to the poor of the community thus contaminating "lesser people" with the sins of another.

5

What were the fate of the Canaanites? Apparently they may not have been eradicated as the Old Testament/Tanakh had said. This from Science.org:

*"...the Bible's Old Testament, which suggests a grisly end for many Canaanites: After the Israelites' exodus from Egypt, God ordered them to destroy Canaan and its people (though other passages suggest that some Canaanites may have survived). But did that really happen? Archaeological data suggests that Canaanite cities were **never destroyed or abandoned**. Now, ancient DNA recovered from five Canaanite skeletons suggests that these people survived to contribute their genes to millions of people living today.*

*The new samples come from Sidon a coastal city in Lebanon. Marc Haber, a geneticist at the **Wellcome Trust** Sanger Institute in Hinxton, U.K., extracted enough DNA from the ancient skeletons to sequence the whole genomes of five Canaanite individuals, all around 3700 years old.*

Sidon was a Phoenician settlement later occupied by the Templars. You noticed where the researcher is from? Klaus the Louse's Wellcome Trust Fund group. They can't even spell 'welcome' right.

Baalbek Temples of the Ancient Phoenicians (Lebanon)

Long after the origins of the Ugaritic Baal worship and tales of the Baal Cycles, the Phoenicians (meaning red, or purple-red) founded Carthage in 814 BC. As La Sicilia in Rete (lasiciliainrete.it) noted, 200 children of the most noble families were hastily sacrificed apologetically to their god(s) for having had abandoned the practice of giving up their own first born, reverting instead to victims supplied by child slave trade for stand-ins. Seeing the enemy about to overtake their city, it was a hellish, last ditch effort to appease Ba'al and save their people from certain capture.

The site, remember I don't pick the names, Climate-Policy-Watcher.org, writes:

"During the political crisis of 310 B.C., some 500 were killed. On a moonlit night, the body was placed on the arms of an effigy of Baal made of brass. The Priests lit fires that heated the effigies from its lower parts. The victims were placed on the burning hot outstretched hands. As they were burned alive they vehemently cried out. The priests beat a drum sounded flutes, lyres, and tambourines. This drowned out the cries of the anguished parents. The father could not hear the voice of his son, and his heart might not be moved...

"...Now, allow me to turn your attention to Nimrod as Baal was also known. It is important that you know that Nimrod incorporated into his worship system the grisly practice of human sacrifice and cannibalism. Our authority Hislop says, "the priests of Nimrod or Baal were necessarily required to eat of the human sacrifices; and thus it has come to pass that 'Cahna-Bal' (cahna meaning priest & Bal referring to Baal) is the established word (cannibal) in our own tongue for a devourer of human flesh."

5

What happened to the Canaanites? Recent digs conducted at Sidon seem to indicate that there was no interruption in the culture of the Canaanites as depicted in the Tanakh, or Old Testament. Geneticists from separate universities and organizations have found what they claim to be Canaanite DNA contributing to 90% of the DNA of present day Lebanese, and to some degree "hundreds of others in genetic databases." To this they say it doesn't necessarily mean that there was no great conflict between Israelites and Canaanites, but that the peoples may have been genetically quite similar, however culturally at odds with one another. The present day people of Jordan are also said to be closely tied genetically to the Canaanites.

The heads of this particular study at Sidon are funded by Klaus Schwab,

Wellcome Trust Sanger Institute. science.org/content/article/ancient-dna-reveals-fate-mysterious-canaanites

A Spider Does Not Stick To Its Own Web

1

Why is this historical trail so important? If we don't go back far enough we'll never truly understand the nature of this adversary, and who they manifest as cannot be fully recognized without knowledge of their roots, their objective throughout the aeons, and their prime motivators. To many they just see inept politicians making terrible, destructive, and perverse decisions. They say it's corruption and that big money is buying their policy. They see an agenda, maybe, but you hear things like "follow the money" echoed repeatedly across so-called Truth-minded and Patriot social media influencer channels. I'm here to tell you that's a very superficial layer to all of this. It's a remedial perception of a much more deliberate, malicious, and hostile objective. It's so remedial, in fact, that I question whether or not it's a deliberate effort to keep viewers on an island using compelling, dramatic deliveries, distracting, erroneous data, and flat-out misinformation that has many good intentioned people chasing their tails while the agenda the social media personalities claim to oppose moves ever forward.

There is a MindWar going on, as Michael Aquino coined, and it's not exclusive to one social engineered cultural philosophy or another. It's all daggers pointing inward to the middle. Like the symbol for Walmart, or the peacock feathers of NBC, or what appear to be magnetron wrist-watches on the ancient Sumerian carvings of their gods. Evil doesn't sleep, and We the People of the world are not fully awake. To be so would be a living hell, not a Gaia TV Yoga session. It's not all incense and yoga pants. Nor is it crystal rubbing and self-indulgent meditation. It's not carefree, it's daunting when everything, and I mean everything around you still looks familiar, but you now sense a nightmarish dark mockery to it all. It's as if the ordinary is now embodied with a sense of despair. As foreign as it may feel, the realization that comes over you is that it's always been there. You just never were able to pick up on it before. You're tuned into a whole new station. You sense a presence and it's as if you are seeing into the abyss, but what's more it can see you. Whatever defensive, natural, and maybe even spiritual cloak you once wore has been cast aside, stripped away, and you are no longer camouflaged. You're Daniel in the lion's den, and the lions just recognized you're not one of them. As they peer at you curious and amused at first, you have this thought form in your mind, the law of nature, "If you run, you're food." If you show fear, you're weak. If you behave as prey, you will be treated as prey. Like encounters with false authorities we call police, if you run at the sight of them, they will chase you. They may not know what you did, but you must have done something if you're running from them. They'll figure out what you did later. First, they're going to get you into custody.

While others are parroting, "Follow the money," I recommend you FOLLOW the PRIESTCRAFT. We operate on fiat, a fugazi, a fake currency system that these dark practitioners and priesthoods print at will. Money is meaningless, and worthless to those at the highest levels. It was created for control, to enslave and ensnare. A spider does not stick to its own web. They are not caught up in the system and networking they fashioned. Therefore you cannot apply the same concepts, methodology, or strategies that would suit the world we are accustomed to, and familiar with. We need to all become students of their world and learn an entirely different realm which exists within our own, a world that is in direct opposition to that which we "know."

In Murder By Injection, a book everyone should own, read, memorize, and treat like a survival guide so long as the sorcerers of Allopathy run the world, Eustace Mullins writes:

*...In "The Curse of Canaan," I wrote of the deliverance of our children up for ritual sacrifice, a practice which seemingly ended with the destruction of the **Baal cult** some five thousand years ago. Unfortunately, the Cult of Baal seems to be firmly entrenched in the present Establishment, which is often known by the sobriquet, the Brotherhood of Death. It is disturbing to see how the educationists eagerly embrace each new offense against children in our schools, railing against any mention of morality or religion, while solemnly indoctrinating six year olds in the advantages of "an alternative life style" in their sexual preferences. The present goal of the National Education Association seems to be that teachers should hand out condoms to the class before beginning each day's activities. The urgency of my vaccination was not that there was any epidemic then raging in the city of Roanoke, nor has there been one in the ensuing sixty years. The urgency was that no child shall be spared the ministrations of the **Cult of Baal**, or forego sacrifice on the **altar of the child molesters**. The Medical Monopoly cannot afford to have a single pupil escape the monetary offering to be paid for the compulsory vaccination, the tribute of the enslaved to their masters...*

He continues:

*"However, it is unlikely that the **High Priests of Modern Medicine** will be able to give up one of the Four Commandments. It will be necessary for an outraged public to bring pressure to bear to abandon the **modern ritual of sacrificing our children to Baal** in a five thousand year old ritual called, in its modern version, "compulsory immunization."*

In the book Eustace is referencing above, the **Curse of Canaan**, a book with some claims not subscribed to by this author, there are still noteworthy passages. They help to paint the picture of the mindset of the high priests and advisors of the rulers, when the rulers were, and were not the high priests, themselves.
Eustace writes on page 12 of the format I possess:

*"Not only did Nimrod kill and eat the fair-skinned descendants of Shem, in his fury and hatred he often burned them alive. The type of human sacrifice involving the **eating of the slaughtered human victims** derived its name from the combined names of his uncle, Canaan, and the demon god Baal, the two names being combined to form the word "cannibal." **Nimrod** was also known in ancient history by the names of Marduk, Bel, and Merodach. Because of his importance in its history, Babylon was known as the Land of Nimrod. Nimrod is also cited in the most ancient Masonic constitutions as the founder of **Freemasonry**."*

I am not a Biblical scholar, and certainly no expert on the Tanakh, or Old Testament. There are people far more qualified to give their interpretations than I am. But coming from someone beholden to no group, and not bound to a loyalty to said that would guide me to sanitize an analysis, I find myself with no religio-political agenda, and no motivation to hide anything I may see in my analysis. There seems to be some strong supporting evidence for the nature of Freemasonry claimed by Edmond Ronayne. I found this footnote in **The Constitutions of the Free-Masons 1734**:

** NIMROD, which signifies a Rebel, was the Name given him by the holy Family, and **by Moses** ; but among his Friends in Chaldea, his proper Name was BELUS, which signifies LORD, and afterwards was worshipped as a God by many Nations, under the Name of Bel or **Baal**, and became the Bacchus of the Ancients, or Bar Chus, the Son of CHUS.*

There's a lot of mixed accounts as to the era of the flood, both in academia, and in ancient writings. From India to Iraq, which is where Nimrod was said to have risen to power, modern day Iraq, the answers differ. If the Ice Age declined 11,000 years ago, then it would logically fall in line with a proceeding flood, I mean, if we're to apply climate change claims of today to events of the past. But when you go to writings that all came afterward, the flood is said to have been roughly 5,000 years ago. Nimrod is said to be the great grandson of Noah, and the first of "Mighty" men to arise after the flood. Many place him in the time-frame of the Bronze Age. The reason I ponder this at all is to find a beginning to this history of influence on culture as we trace the origins of the dark, bloody rituals and orgies. I want to know who initiated, and what inspired the Mystery Schools in the first place. I want to take fingerprints of the Hidden Hand. Is it a giant hand? Is it a highly advanced hand, or that of a living demon, or innerterrestrial, meaning something that dwells within the Earth? I'm too firm on my conviction of a firmament to consider "space" aliens, but maybe other-realmly is plausible.

Apart from fire-pit incineration, the slaughtering and eating of children to then throw the remains into a furnace under Nimrod, was there any other accounts of infanticide not conducted in the trance of public mob-rituals?

"Another horrible practice was what they called 'foundation sacrifice.' When a house was to be build, a child would be sacrificed and its body built into the wall, to bring good luck to the rest of the family. Many of these were found in Gezer. They have been found also at Megiddo, Jericho, and other places." -**Halley's Bible Handbook**

The parents were **forced by the priests**, or coerced by the crowd following the lead of their priests, to throw their children into the furnaces at the rituals, but this building practice was something else. The **masons** are builders so this brings up all kinds of questions. Namely, is that a practice they carry over to modern day? Was that bizarre tunnel opening ceremony in Switzerland masking a more horrific act of sacrifice? There are also known accounts of sacrificial rites taking place in caves, out of sight under cliff edges, and in groves. I can't but reflexively think of a particularly infamous modern *grove...* The way I understand it, the undesired products of orgies between the underclasses were disposed of in this more discreet manner, but still were imbued by the sense of ritual duty. It was programmed into these people by their priests. It's mentioned that even King Solomon was influenced by these priests to build a sacrificial altar to Milcom or Molech. King Solomon plays a heavy role in the origin mythos of the Freemasonic priestcraft.

2

As a side note, when I have to write about this type of subject matter it is detrimental to my being. Even as you read it it takes you to a dark place you want to push out of your head and reject before it can produce imagery you'd sooner not see. Knowing we have manifest power, but really no compass or understanding of how to control it, I fear the chance of calling this nightmare to materialize somewhere in our realm of existence. I don't want that evil to know I'm talking about its deeds. I don't want it to know me at all. I don't want the abyss to look back at me and remember my face. If you've ever seen the movie, *Sphere* you can conceptualize this very real idea of the power of manifestation, and our inability to wield such a sword without cutting ourselves. I'm sure there's probably some Zen masters out there that can control what thoughts and imagery they allow to penetrate their mind, but they would need to live a very sheltered life with very limited outward stimuli.

I balance myself with humor. My grandmother taught me there's two things that take the power from evil. Ignoring it, meaning not giving over your energy to it, and ridicule. Ridicule saps its strength, because it needs you to be afraid. You can't show fear. You must criticize it. This idea of "hate speech" and the misuse of concepts like bullying, or sensitivity training are weaponized by those serving some form of Evil. They want you to endure the assaults on your sensibilities, on your sense of Right, on logic, or common sense, and "accept."

This is why I, half joking, call myself a *Disillusioned* Bodhisattva. A bodhisattva is an individual who has reached a high sense of awareness, or gnosis, but delays getting the hell off this karmatic hamster wheel. Instead they stay in this level of existence to help others on their journey to awareness. *They devote all their power and energy to saving suffering beings in this world.* The "disillusioned" part can best be explained by my coast guard experience. Once I realized we were not really out there because Command wanted to stop drug boats, then the purpose I thought we were serving was dissolved. The illusion of doing something I perceived as somewhat noble was lost. My purpose was taken away, and I had to ask myself, then what other purpose are they using us for? Is it worth my time to serve it? Is it even noble or right? I had to find a different purpose.

I can muster up the energy and effort to do just about anything if there's a positive reason for doing it. The reason can be something as simple as the opportunity to be employed and be paid to work, learn, and improve skills. I am one of those types that is your best worker in any crew, or at least the most enthusiastic about the task at hand. I am a good morale booster for coworkers and if I don't directly inspire them, I motivate them to do better to be competitive. When I was working in the IBEW as an apprentice in New York, I had journeymen tell me to throttle down my productivity because they wanted to either milk a job, or didn't want to move as fast. I actually had grown men who were my superiors tell me to do less when I was being paid to perform. Obviously they weren't the foreman saying that.

The moment the illusion fades, however, so goes the motivation to continue. When you lose the inspiration you lose the drive. When I look around at some of the absolutely insincere and unappreciative people I deal with, or worse the low-comprehension rude ones, I ask myself, "Why am I trying to help people again?" Bill Cooper points out that a society of mostly cowards depends on the few brave leaders to carry them through tough times. But these warriors are always admonished and rejected verbally all the way. Those who carry on in spite of this resistance to their helpful nature and protect the community, or fix the problems, are rewarded with resentment. They become a living example of the weaker members' inadequacies and the weaker ones usually gather together and find ways to dispose of this warrior class when they don't feel there's anymore need for them. With a pension like that for a lifetime of selfless devoted service, what more could one ask for, right? That's why I sometimes think, what the hell am I still doing here? Pack your bags, children. We're ditching this NPC planet. To quote a Less Than Jake song, *"One hand on the wheel, the other out the window, a smile on my face, my middle finger up..."* It's a nice daydream.

I remind myself it's not the few strangers calling me names on social media, or the lazy, entitled people I come across in my daily activities that my purpose is to serve. It's my family, my friends, my God, and my memories of a love and nurture I felt from beautiful angels like my aunt and grandmother, my grandfather, that my purpose is meant to serve. As far as my show goes, it's the families that I may make aware of dangers to avoid, of charlatans and thieves, and of healthier alternatives to harmful allopathic medical practices. That motivates me. Being helpful has a reward of its own.

Those who listen or watch consistently do appreciate it. If a child is healthier because of something their parent learned from me or my guests, then it was worth every amount of effort I put into that broadcast. Forgive these free-form tangents. I think this is something we all can relate to, and this heavy subject matter we're covering merited a pause to get us recharged and refreshed.

In an effort to have this book act, in part, as a historical education tool, it's important to explore deeper into the mystery of these ancient priesthoods, priest-kings, and even earlier gods than those we find in the Ugaritic texts, or tablets. Who influenced who? And furthermore, who then, influenced them? It's almost unavoidable to find ourselves stepping into esoteric theoretical territory to find this answer.

3

Are we going back far enough to understand the origins of this notion of child sacrifice? What civilization came first? Sumer? It's tricky to gather an explanation of culture and practices much further back than that, mostly because we're told there was no written record predating the Mesopotamian settlements of Sumer (Sumeria is a term used to describe all the territory controlled by Sumer) and later, Babylon. Göbekli Tepe in modern day Urfa, Turkey, although seemingly at least twice the age of Sumer, is decorated with carvings of animals, not graffiti. One would have to have a working understanding of the culture already to accurately decipher what the symbolism of the depictions meant to them. According to researchers, the discovery of seemingly decapitated skulls have been found, in fragments, at Göbekli Tepe. Instead of specific mindsets and cultural insights, we're given generalizations as to the reasons for such a practice. One gets the impression they're guessing at best as to whether Göbekli Tepe was a true site of ritual sacrifice. Their explanations are grafted from what they know about other cultures from different eras, but of similar geographic locations. It's interesting to this author that Urfa was once known as Edessa. Ralph Ellis is a rearcher, and author of the book, **Jesus, King of Edessa** where he makes an argument that Izuz Manu of Edessa (Syria) was whom we have come to know as the Lord of Christianity. It should be mentioned that Mr. Ellis is a self-proclaimed Freemason. That said, there are a lot of interesting insights found in his pages into the history of Christianity, nonetheless. It's interesting to ponder the idea that Christianity was founded by the enemies of Jesus, and may help explain the control mechanisms set in place by the Romans in the centuries that followed as they built the Roman Catholic Empire.

Başur Höyük, also in Turkcy, is the site of a sacrificial burial dating as far back as 3100 BC. The Natural History Museum (NHM) article by Katie Pavid from June 28th, 2018 had these remarks:

"...In three graves were found the remains of at least 11 people, male and female, ranging from age 11 to young adults..."

"...Several people were buried outside the tomb with elaborate ornaments and grave goods... Brenna says, 'The burials are remarkable because of the youth of the individuals, the number that were buried and the large wealth of objects that were buried with them... There are various pieces of evidence which suggest that these young people did not die accidentally or naturally - rather they were sacrificed."

"...The ancient Near East was made up of the region that now includes modern-day Iraq, as well as parts of Turkey, Iran, Syria and Kuwait. Its history begins from about 4,000 BCE. Much of this area formed Mesopotamia, a collection of cultures bonded by their writing systems and gods. It is often thought of as the cradle of Western civilization..."

"Although researchers are unable to confirm exactly how these people died, at least two of the retainers from the outside of the tomb show evidence of sharp force trauma including stabbing and cutting wounds, suggesting unnatural deaths. In particular, one of the young adult males suffered trauma to his hip and head, and seems to have suffered a violent end, perhaps being stabbed in the hip and skull by a sharp point. The head wounds are similar to the reconstructions of skull trauma seen in the sacrificial burials at the Royal Cemetery of Ur. Brenna says, 'It is unlikely that these children and young people were killed in a massacre or conflict. The careful positioning of the bodies and the evidence of violent death suggest that these burials fit the same pattern of human sacrifice seen at other sites in the region."

4

Who were the gods of these ancient Mesopotamian people? Anu, Enlil, Enki, Ninhursag, Nanna, Utu, and Inanna are the oldest gods we have to work with, according to those who control the information we're allowed to see. If you follow the work of archaeologists, and explorers such as Brien Foerster, or researcher Michael Tellinger, those names should sound all-too-familiar. They're the names of the infamous Anunnaki. Zecharia Sitchin, and more recently Anton Parks have penned extensive controversial publications on the topic of the Anunnaki. You may have to learn á francais to read Parks' books. Not all of them have been translated into other languages as of yet. Also, I am not stating I back Sitchin. He had questionable funding sources.

While each of these topics are rich in mystery and intrigue, and worthy of their own books, if not full libraries on the subjects, the goal here in Ba'al Busters Book 1 is to establish a working knowledge of the ancient priesthoods, and their practices to find where these sacrificial practices were first introduced. From there we can better understand their influence on mankind throughout proceeding cultures all the way into present day. Know thy Enemy, in other words. As tempted as I am to delve into the gods themselves and analyze the many interesting assertions of Parks, namely that the word "paradise," as in the Garden of Eden's paradise, originally meant an enclosed park, extrapolated out to imply a pen for animals—or people, let's focus on how gods or the concept of gods gave the priests a purpose and function in societies. It's the blending of mysticism, sorcery, superstition, and yes pharmakeia that gave these influencers the appearance of having magical powers over the natural world, thus favor from the gods setting them apart. This inferred superior status and distinction among their people formed the concepts of a ruling class, and therefore a mechanism of subjugation. When the priests weren't the priest-kings themselves, as it appears Nimrod was claimed to be, they were the advisors to the man-in-front, the king. Just as then we still have a collection of advisors influencing the decisions of leaders [false authority] throughout the world today. Even dictators consult with their trusted few. If you're asking, "Then where does the real power lie?" you understand why it's important to understand these sorcerers and magicians.

We at least need some cliff notes on who these aforementioned deities were:

Enlil of the Anunnaku (Anunnaki) is, to the Sumerians, the supreme lord and exalted king of the universe. He is also described as the Blue-Eyed Earth colony commander. That's incredibly interesting for many reasons, namely that blue eyes are not at all common to that region, at least not in modern times after much migration to factor in, and yet all these gods, his daughters, etc. are depicted with that common trait. To be named Earth colony commander implies they came from somewhere other than here, and colonized or subjugated the Earth and ruled it as their colony. The *mesopotamiangods.com* site lends this chilling statement, *"...his commands are final."* We'll go over why I think we're looking the wrong direction for "visitors" and that they may be innerterrestrials, rather than extra, as this riddle unfolds. Enlil is later known as Elil which could be the root of El the Canaanite – Israelite supreme god. Not to go too far off on a tangent, but the hyphen is implying similarity, not separation.

Enki is of great interest and potentially the inspiration for Prometheus of the Greek mythos. Referencing my own knowledge base as a measurement, and avoiding the far reaching speculative (rumors, I hate rumors) I checked various references all throughout the research for this book. The same holds true for the topic of Enki. After looking at several resources, I came to settle on *historycooperative.org* for their statements on the Sumerian deity. The three consecutive dots indicate a break in the quote where I shortened it down to the more relevant details for our purposes:

*"The origins of **Enki** can be found in the Babylonian epic of creation, Enuma Elish* [translated "When Above"]

*"...Enki, later known as Ea by the Akkadians and Babylonians, was the Sumerian deity of **wisdom**, intelligence, **tricks** and **magic**, fresh water, healing, **creation**, and **fertility**. Originally, he was worshiped as the patron god of Eridu, which the Sumerians considered to be the first city created when the world began. According to myth, Enki gave birth to the Tigris and Euphrates rivers from the streams of water flowing off his body. Enki's waters are considered life-giving and his symbols are the goat and the **fish**, both of which symbolize fertility."*

I'd put a tab in that point. The fish symbolism is also used by Christians and Catholics symbolizing the savior Jesus, but here it represents fertility according to people who say things. Ha ha. We continue:

"The Sumerian 'En' translates roughly into 'lord' and 'ki' means 'earth'. Thus, the commonly accepted meaning of his name is 'Lord of the Earth.' But this might not be the exact meaning. A variation of his name is Enkig... Enki's other name is Ea. In Sumerian, the two syllables E-A put together mean 'Lord of Water...'

Water is essential to life, to crop growth, and it's therefore of the greatest importance to all living things without even having to go into the spiritual attributes of water memory, Dr. Emoto's work, and how it relates to biological harmony. All of which are very important aspects worthy of closer examination in a more metaphysically focused book.

*"...It is intriguing that Enki is known as a **Trickster** god* [but not like Loki] *by the Sumerians given that in all the myths that we come across this god, **his motivation is to actually help both human beings and other gods**. The meaning behind this is that as the **god of wisdom**, Enki works in ways that do not always make sense to anyone else. He helps to enlighten people..."*

Before Socrates there was Enki. This passage passage resonates with the idea of using methods to inspire the psyche, and guide people, and gods, into using critical thinking, and therefore navigate their own way through a given predicament. Socrates used a method whereby he would ask seemingly basic questions to get his pupils to examine that which they take for a given by the err of assumption and presumption, so that they discover their own logical fallacies in the process without Socrates having to directly identify their errors for them. It's one thing to point out a flaw. It's something else to have the patience and compassion to kindly teach others how to discover it themselves.

"This definition of trickster god is rather strange to us, being used as we are to accounts of celestial deities who make trouble for mankind to entertain themselves. [like Loki, and the many examples in Greek Mythology] *But Enki's manner of trickery appears to be for the purpose of helping humanity, albeit in a roundabout manner."*

Again we're seeing parallels to Socrates here. Where at first Socrates may appear as playing the fool, asking questions as if he knows nothing of the world or of basic concepts. You don't really know where the line of questioning is going until the process of honest examination Socrates is leading you down brings you to your Ah Ha! moment, a revelation. It's at that point you see Socrates' alchemy at work converting the unwitting student's apprehension into deep appreciation. The resulting product: Wisdom.

*"It was Enki who came up with the idea of the **creation of man**, a **servant of the gods**, made of clay and blood. He was helped in this by Ninhursag, the mother goddess. It was also Enki who gave mankind the ability to speak one language to communicate with each other...*

*Eventually, as the humans grow in number and become louder and more difficult, they cause great disturbance to Enlil, the King of the Gods. He sends down several natural disasters, **ending in a flood** to wipe out humanity. Time and time again, **Enki saves humanity from the wrath of his brother**. Finally, Enki instructs the hero Atrahasis to build a ship to save life on Earth."*

I'm sure this sounds familiar without me pointing out the Biblical flood parallels, but keep in mind the histories of Sumer, as recorded, stretch much farther back in history than the Old Testament, or Tanakh. It seems just as natural events are periodic, if not cyclical, these tales that may even originally detail a far older cataclysmic event, can be transposed and repurposed as they suit.

M   Many cultures recognize that there are multiple gods, a divine council or "council among the gods." The online encyclopedophilia, Woke-ipedia, I mean Wikipedia, notes: *"The concept of a divine assembly (or council) is attested in the archaic Sumerian, Akkadian, Old Babylonian, Ancient Egyptian, Babylonian, Canaanite, Israelite, Celtic, Ancient Greek and Ancient Roman and Nordic pantheons."*

At least they note that correctly. The point here is that also in the Abrahamic, even though mostly whitewashed and given more fitting definitions, there's mention of a council of gods, referred to as the sons of god, assembled as the supreme God was basically conducting a boardroom meeting where He was telling the shareholders He was going to create Man. Oh and by the way, they will kind of outrank you. We're then told these sons of God felt disenfranchised, sullen, ENVIOUS over being cheated out of their anticipated inheritance, then rebellious. In Enoch we're told they made a pact on Mt. Hermon, at the Summit Ardis [meaning *blooming meadow*] to swoop down on mankind from their high places and turn the world into a giant Spring Break orgy. It's said slightly different than that, but that was basically what was depicted to have transpired—basically. It may be a slight leap to say the sons of God were one-in-the-same that eventually defiled the irresistible human women. There's no mention of the "fallen" to have given one another fist-bumps between sexual conquests, but I have my suspicions. It was a time when all the lands were like that of Tijuana, Mexico, only much cleaner… And no tacos. So the Watchers went from creepy Peeping-Toms to mustering up their courage, and taking the initiative to "just go talk to her," probably regretfully, given the dramatic consequences.

If the comparison of Enki to Socrates is accepted, then Enlil may be the Sophist of the bunch. The term Sophist traditionally means a paid teacher of philosophy to the extent that they focused on matters of cunning debate, where winning was put above ethics and morality. If they could sell you on their position, they didn't care if that required deception to achieve. They were early traveling salesmen, but of a greater value to the nobility who hired them to educate their children. Their willingness to convince an audience without the regular hesitation of a guilty conscience made them invaluable teachers of future statesmen, political influencers, and those in the realm of law. Sophists were skilled in etiquette, and were known to teach music, philosophy, and mathematics, as well as rhetoric and debate. There are times when Enlil peaceably resolves conflict between other gods, but in the matter of allegedly Enki's creation, that of Man, there's little understanding or empathy afforded us.

There is mention of sacrifice to appease Enlil in the story of Atrahasis, the Biblical equivalent of Noah. HistoryCooperative.org's Rhittika Dhar writes:

"In this Babylonian flood myth, Atrahasis [also known as Zuisudra] *survives a seven day deluge and **performs sacrifices** to appease Enlil and the other gods after the flood. Enki explains his reasons for saving Atrahasis and shows what a good man he is. Pleased, the gods agree to repopulate the world with human beings but with certain conditions. Humans will never again be given the opportunity to become too populous and **the gods will make sure that they die by natural means before they run over the earth**."*

Apparently, in present day those monitoring and regulatory functions once conducted by the gods have been delegated to members of the World Economic Forum, and its partners the United Nations, World Health Organization, mainstream scientists, and the monopolistic allopathic medical industry. That's not just said in jest, although it may seem ridiculous or humorous on its surface. Wait until we get into Mystery Babylon and the still active, ancient secret societies. What now seems like a joke will rather appear as an explanation for this ever-escalating assault on Mankind.

Rhittika Dhar continues:

*"Through the reign of Hammurabi, Enlil continued to be worshiped even though Marduk, the son of Enki, had become the new King of the Gods. The most important aspects of Enlil were absorbed into **Marduk** who became the **chief deity** for both the **Babylonians** and the Assyrians. Nippur remained a sacred city throughout this period, second only to Eridu. It was believed that Enlil and An had willingly handed over their powers to Marduk.*

Even as Enlil's role in Mesopotamian religion dwindled with the fall of Assyrian rule, he continued to be worshipped in the form of Marduk. It was only in 141 AC that the worship of Marduk declined and Enlil was finally forgotten, even under that name."

Although it's said Atrahasis/Zuisudra sacrifices an ox and a sheep in honor of Enlil and the other gods, this idea that sacrifices to gods will please them is established in this Epic. Enlil is quite pleased, and bestows immortality upon Zuisudra. If that's true, maybe he has a Twitter account we can reach him at to get a firsthand account and see what he's been up to these past 4,000 plus years.

Combined we just learned from the Sumerian account, *"Humans will never again be given the opportunity to become too populous and **the gods will make sure that they die by natural means before they run over the earth**,"* and that blood sacrifice, in general, pleases the gods, and may result in great rewards and favor. It takes no stretch of the imagination to see how this could escalate for various reasons. What if the priests of ancient Mesopotamia, and later Babylon, sacrificed an ox and asked the gods for protection in battle, a good crop yield, or rain for said crops, and it didn't come? That could cause the cult followers to eventually question the validity of the priesthood's favor among their gods. If they couldn't demonstrate their sway with the higher authority, that could jeopardize their political influence in the community, and maybe even endanger the priests' lives. Angry mobs might demand their king find suitable replacements for the failed sorcerers. The social control mechanisms would deteriorate. Heck, the spell the people had been under could lift, and independent, less obedient thoughts may arise. Even the king, if not counted among the priests himself, may say, "You better think of something, and you better think of it quick." What does a cunning priestcraft do under such performance pressure? Blame the sacrifice! Blame it for being subpar, deemed unsuitable to the gods for such lofty a requests as rain on-demand, or victory in war. The people then have the responsibility for the failure projected on themselves for not doing enough, or maybe they're not obedient enough so the gods are withholding gratification like an offended wife. They begin questioning themselves, and stop questioning the "Science." It's their shortcomings that are causing this. The gods are punishing them, not dissing the priest, who like an MD assures a grieving family after killing one of their loved ones, "We did everything we could…"

If not one ox, how about 2 oxen? Three? Three oxen and 4 chickens? 5 oxen, 8 chickens, and a goat? Still nothing? Since it's not the priests giving up anything, therefore it's not really their sacrifice, they huddle together… "Ready, break!" They come back on the field with a fresh game strategy as they announce the unthinkable, unconscionable, and unacceptable… Unacceptable in less desperate times, that is. They'll remind them they've seen all the other offerings fall short, and since it obviously can't be that the priests themselves are running a scam operation on the public, the fault must still fall on the people for not having done enough. What worked in the past simply isn't cutting the mustard, anymore. What is the ultimate of sacrifices, then? Oh tell us priests, we'll do whatever it takes to bring us back in favor with the gods! Wait… Do what, now?

After the follow-through and mass acceptance of something like child sacrifice once, there's no going back. A new benchmark in proper sacrifice to the gods in times of desperation is established. If the common people's children didn't bring their desired request of the gods, the next round will be the first born of the most noble of the community. And it was, as we saw in Carthage. Not to mention we discovered the early origins of a child kidnapping and trafficking demand by the nobility, or elites, that used the acquired children as stand-ins rather than sacrificing their own.

Eventually it rains, and eventually they win in battle simply because they had superior forces and will. The superstitious and scared people don't see the obvious factors, however. They see the desired results and make an erroneous correlation to their sacrificial deed for the reason why.

If you don't think the priests would abuse and manipulate people when there wasn't any real crisis, for their own personal gains… If someone offended them, they could tell the ruler that person is bringing shame on us from the gods for some reason and have them killed. They could get rid of heirs to the throne with a convenient first-born nobility sacrifice whenever they felt their power was threatened by a new generation of less superstitious offspring. They could make up never ending crises, keeping people in a constant state of fear, a state much easier to manipulate because clear thinking is slapped out of the equation. I'm not sure they had a manufacturer for M95 masks back then, but they could amuse and enrich themselves in many ways simply by playing the role of oracle and physician. Tithings aren't such a bad idea, huh? The priests, after all, being so close to the gods themselves should be honored and kept happy too, otherwise they may curse us, and bring plague to our household. They may work up the crowd against us for our impiety and let them handle our disposal. Back then the sorcerers and the physicians were the priests. That's no different than today. If they wanted to demonstrate how very real their curses were, they could simply poison your food or water, or do the same to your livestock. They could make an example of you and your family to scare the rest back in line. With no forensics, or crime scene investigators, and the priests being the town square mainstream media, their story would stick. "I warned them their waning faith would bring misfortune upon us all, and they were the first to be hit by this new deadly plague as a result. The rest of you had better repent, and do it most generously. We're not sure you're worthy of our intervention between you and the gods anymore."

Another way this desperation is said to have manifested into child sacrifice in the cultures around the world may require a certain open mind to at least a possibility there were indeed superior beings interacting in the flesh, or in some form, with Man on a daily basis in the past. This theory derived from accounts in the tribal histories of Central and South America have to do with a sense of abandonment. The gods were here, times were prosperous, although strict under their rule, and then one day they left. They left everyone to figure things out for themselves and no longer guide, nor intervene in any matters. They may have appointed lesser stand-ins, a ruling class, but the true innovators had gone. It was this sense of being incomplete, the trauma of separation that led to a loss of direction. It would deteriorate the morality of the various people, longing for their return. They would go from one extreme to another to try and get the gods' attention, again. That could mean brutal wars, and sacrificing their POWs to their gods, or children, or both. The Mayans were never a unified group of people. It was a generic term for a region in perpetual turmoil.

From a January 2nd, 2019 Associated Press "News" article we read:

"Priests worshipped Xipe Totec by skinning human victims and then donning their skins. The ritual was seen as a way to ensure fertility and regeneration. The Popolocas built the temple at a complex known as Ndachjian-Tehuacan between A.D. 1000 and 1260 and were later conquered by the Aztecs."

The Aztecs kept the practice, too. In an October 19th, 2022 CuratedTaste.com article by "Kendra" we get this:

"While the reasons behind this practice are still debated, there is no doubt that the Aztecs did, in fact, wear human skin. The most common theory for why the Aztecs wore human skin is that they believed it would bring them closer to the gods. **The Aztecs were a deeply religious people** [shit-bird apologist] *and they believed that by wearing the skin of a sacrificed human, they were honoring the gods and asking for their protection. Another theory is that the Aztecs saw human skin as a status symbol. Wearing the skin of a conquered enemy was a way to show off one's power and status. Whatever the reasons behind it, there is no doubt that the Aztecs did wear human skin. And while it may seem barbaric to us today, it was simply part of their culture and beliefs."*

You can always spot the brain dead liberal journalist by their bizarre rationalizations. Directly murdering your own offspring either in or out of the womb is somehow beyond reproach, explained away by "My body, my choice." Yet having a gas stove is an insult to all of humanity because TV said so. Yay, Church of Statism! And yes the analogy of infanticide was selected because of it's correlation the with child sacrifice practices we've been talking about. In the vacuous mind-void of someone like that, we should expect such statements as the Aztecs flayed the skin off other human beings and WORE them because they "were a deeply religious people" trying to get closer to their gods by wearing human roadkill.

Then right after that, it reads in paraphrase: or they just felt like it, and thought it looked cool, like the Fonze in his leather jacket. These are about as different of reasons one could give for an explanation. It reveals they have no idea and are just guessing. What's necessary for us to all begin to understand is that all the important claims of medicine, science, and politics are just as made-up, and spewed from just as clueless people. The "experts" are Frauds and con artists running a deadly deception.

"...While it may seem barbaric to us today, it was simply part of their culture and beliefs." Wow. Infinite understanding for and acceptance of a whole society of Buffalo Bill serial killers… What if owning firearms, and NOT exposing our children to sexual predators in thick makeup, or teachers pushing gender reassignment, is simply part of *our* culture? Where's the live-and-let-live fluidity of tolerance and respect, now?

The article continues:

The Aztec **priest***, or shaman, was a key figure in the Aztec religion and society. The shaman would wear the skin of a jaguar or other powerful animal to channel the animal's spirit and power. The shaman would also use the skin to communicate with the spirit world and to* **heal the sick***.* [Results may vary]

During the Aztec year's second ritual month, Tlacaxipehualiztli ("Flaying of Men"), the **priests killed their victims by cutting their hearts in half***. They then glued* *the skins to the bodies, which were dyed yellow and referred to as teocuitlaquemitl ("golden clothes")…*

…Human sacrifice was considered significant and even necessary to Aztec rituals…

*…The sacrifice of humans was offered by Xipe Totec's **priests** during Tlacaxipehualiztli (meaning "Flaying of Men"), an event that symbolizes the sacrificing of men to appease god. War captives who are sacrificed would usually perish as a result of having their hearts removed. It was also possible to sacrifice the victim by tying him to a frame and shooting him in the head with an arrow…"*

The lesson: don't get captured by an Aztec. The outlook isn't promising.

Any charlatan promising they could accomplish a reunion of the departed gods with the people could step into a position of influence, and manipulate these people simply by playing the role of a far-out, charismatic medicine man. Kind of like what Fauci has done ever since his the cytotoxic marine sea sponge poison called AZT. It was deemed too deadly for continued use as a chemotherapy drug, so after being shelved for over a decade, Jesuit Anthony Fauci and his "advisors" repurposed it in healthy people, and infants, who came up positive for HIV using a PCR test that can't diagnose anything. That sounds like a familiar scenario for some reason… Full blown AIDS was a result of the drug AZT. There was not a natural progression from HIV (not a virus, not contagious) to AIDS, if left untreated (not poisoned.)

If you loyally, continuously go to the same people for answers, and their status and/or wealth depends on them providing you that answer, they will come up with an answer. That doesn't mean it's an actual solution. They are more often than not lying about the ultimate goal, masking their true intent as they continue making up new lies as they go along. In their delicate threading of deceptions one thing has proven certain. A Spider does not stick to its own web. At least not yet.

Babylon and the Mystery Schools

1

There's no clear path to writing about the Mystery Religions, or Mystery Schools. Putting a bead on pre-flood, or antedeluvian, or what I may suspect as a past RESET event is difficult in terms of dates. After all, the goal of elimination is to erase the knowledge and the memory of the previous era, as well as the people who possess it. This would be crucial for a dominant class who's history of offenses would prevent them from garnering trust for a new round of deception. Steve Falconer of Spacebusters had some interesting comments to make on my Ba'al Busters show regarding the origin of God myths, and even of giants. His research has brought him to the conclusion that those who wound up in Sumeria, and were treated as gods, were mortals, and highly advanced survivors or culprits of a Reset-like event. He notes a Celtic origin of the people whom would later become the Emperors of Rome.

If there were a cyclical, deliberate wiping out of life here, and I say "here" rather than just calling this realm "Earth," because I am not confident in anything we're taught to accept, then it would only be natural that some group, or some-thing did it. Unless they were suicidal as well as homicidal, they would be the ones leftover to build anew on the Phoenix-like ashes of the previous era. Let's consider possible natural events, or God's intervention, as well as manufactured destruction brought on by physical beings as being causes that may bring about such devastation that few remain to tell the tale.

I'm certain the peoples given credit in our history books for building impossible structures were later inhabitants of the newer civilizations that built up around these awe-inspiring feats of architecture. They may have lived there, but they didn't build it. Their technological abilities do not match their accredited achievements. Case in point: we can live in a house without having been the ones who built it. Either we're lied to about the technology of these studied civilizations, or we're looking at architectural relics from a lost and forgotten era. It could be that most people lived extremely primitively, while the rulers coveted the technology. To some degree that is definitely true, but I stand firm that most architectural feats attributed to the Romans, the wonders of Egypt, the Kailasa Temple, aka Ellora Caves, for example, were already there long before the inhabitants we accredit for their construction ever showed up. That holds true in South America, as well. In the case of the Kailasa temple, the whole thing looks like it was 3D printed from the same, single piece of mountain rock. Where the heck did that technology fit into the fairy tale historical depiction of our ancient past? These sites are glaringly indicating a cyclical progression of mankind, where something happened, and knowledge was lost, sending us back to the mercy of the elements to start anew.

If nearly everyone, at least in certain locations, were annihilated, who would be left but a few who carried the knowledge of their history and understanding of their technologies? If you needed me to build you a cellphone right now, I wouldn't know where to start. If techies didn't survive, then there would be no more new cell phones.

In 40 years, or two generations, there wouldn't be many people who even knew the old ways because they grew up in a world where it was already becoming lost to time. Without the people who kept the infrastructure going, it would be gone. The very identities of the people would become a mystery to them, and the struggle for basic necessities would take priority over anything of a fanciful nature. Not everyone in the past knew how to build a pyramid, even then. Just like I can't build a smart phone, nor a communications system that would make it useful.

These days we build structures with disposable, flimsy, and degradable components that wouldn't last more than 200 years, let alone 2,000. They have us creating a disposable world that will leave no trace of itself. Wood planks, drywall, and paper versus the lost era of immortal stone...

Agriculture would be of the utmost importance to survival, and a new cycle would begin of primitive man, in stark contrast to the mysteriously advanced structures left behind. They wouldn't know what they were for, how to use them, or who built them. All that knowledge would have been washed away leaving only wonder and superstition in its wake.

With mankind again dependent on the natural world, it starts to make sense so many "first civilizations" had fertility gods, some with names that directly translate to "Grain," like that of Dagon. We look back to this time thinking there is a linear progression of mankind, and that here must be the beginning, because they were primitive then, working fields, worshiping natural and celestial objects, using crude tools, and creating crude pottery and artwork. Most of us don't stop and wonder whether or not this was a regression, that maybe the story of life thus far is more cyclical than linear, and that our collective history may stretch back much farther than we're told.

So rather than saying the Sumerians were the first to develop a form of writing, could it be, like their myths say, that the "gods" taught them their form of writing, and perhaps those people taught by the so-called "gods" had lost their own form of writing and technologies long ago? These more advanced throwbacks from a lost era, the "gods" taught them Their society, and gifted them with the knowledge of agriculture and animal raising, in basics of life, because they needed these primitive people to build a society that would suit the lifestyle of the "gods," and furnish their needs. Like setting up a base camp, they instructed the underlings in what they needed to know to put together an outpost for the "gods." If they came from somewhere else by sailing vessel or whatever, they went seeking a new home. They stumbled upon a ripe group of adoring fans who willfully subjugated themselves, exhausted from the toil of doing things the hard way. Remember, the best and brightest were likely the first to be executed in the last phase, so the bumbling idiots that weren't worth the effort were survivors by default, having to figure things out.

These new arrivals were in fact introducing a class system, where they were on top, and all the locals were expected to serve. There was a sense of obligation. After all, they did seemingly miraculous things, and did help raise the level of quality of their lives. Even if it was more or less job-training for a life of servitude. If they helped, they must be friends of man, right? Maybe even one (or two) of the top gods who was delegating most things to other gods could be perceived as benevolent. After all, it was his/her will that the people should be taught such useful wonders. Someone whom possesses seemingly far superior ability and appears as a nurturer, guide, and authority would of course be interpreted as a "Father." Heck, maybe even an almighty one. That was always a curious adjective to me because it's comparative in nature. God or Father is sufficient in distinguishing It from Man. "Almighty" seems to indicate multiple "gods" of which He/She is the Most Exalted. "Most High" is also used… Are multiple "gods" explained away by this designation of "angel?"

It's difficult to read these ancient depictions of gods and not notice the very many human characteristics and attributes they possessed. Is that a tell in itself? There's passages in the Tanakh or Old Testament of God smelling something and being pleased by it… None of the ancient gods were perfect. Many were bloodthirsty. Jumping forward in time to Canaan again, Anat was said to have brutally slaughtered all of Ba'al's human enemies who were plotting against him in favor of Yamm. And getting back to the many gods themselves, it was as if they were a crew dispatched to train people in a variety of skills that would serve the gods better. Yahweh first pops onto the scene as a superficial god of metallurgy, a tradesman of sorts, and then becomes more important through the Bronze [Copper] Age.

2

It's just Turtles all the way down. There. I solved the mystery in the same tongue-in-cheek fashion others have. Epistemology, or the study of knowledge, philosophy, and metaphysics, seems to be a bit of an Ouroboros at a certain point. Whether it's because of our Reset induced amnesia, or the natural limitations of our mind, you get so far before the information seems to double-back on itself and consumes what you previously had thought you knew. Maybe we're asking the wrong question. Maybe we're looking for a beginning to the infinite, and therefore reach a point of unraveling and reassembly. What holds up the turtle that holds up the World you ask? What is World? What is Turtle?

I'm tempted to copy and paste the entire Babylonian Genesis story, known as the Enuma Elis(h) here. It's on a series of seven tablets, and the form is that of a repetitive poem that has rhythm, but no rhyme. That holds true for the other Semitic tablets that make up the Ugaritic texts previously discussed. Tiamat and Apsu are the two beings of first creation in this tale. Apsu the male figure, Tiamat his wife or consort, created the first gods and were quickly displeased by their creation. They couldn't take the disruption and noise. Apsu gets pissy and wants to kill them. Tiamat, a little *salty*, but not batshit crazy yet, pleads with Apsu not to do this. I say "salty" because in the beginning there was a chaos of swirling waters until finally they separated into Apsu the fresh water, and Tiamat the salt water.

Ea, or Enki, yes the one from the Sumerian story, is warned by Tiamat his mother that Apsu intends to shut them all up for good. Ea-Enki then lulls Apsu back to sleep and murders him to save the rest of his siblings. The real hero in the eyes of the Babylonians however is Marduk, who comes to the aid of the gods on the next round when Tiamat herself and Kingu attempt to seek vengeance for the murder of her first love, Apsu. Ea-Enki is the father of Marduk, and through a series of dealings becomes the most exalted of the gods before putting an end to Tiamat with an arrow. He then captures and imprisons the ranks that stood with Kingu and Tiamat. Marduk is awarded the 50 names that become important in later grimoires or books of spells that were of interest to many of the secret societies, including Aleister Crowley.

Earlier people of the same region of the Tigris and Euphrates tell the tale of Oannes, and his brethren. Berosus, a priest of Bel-Marduk, and historian at the time of Alexander the Great, says that Oannes came out of the sea to find a lawless Chaldean culture. He, Oannes, was "destitute of reason," whose whole body was a fish, but with legs and a second head underneath the fish head. This, to me, sounds a lot like the Canaanite deity, Dagon, the father of Ba'al, and the one who HP Lovecraft referenced. It also could be a primitive interpretation of a man in some sort of diving suit or SCUBA type gear. It's said he took no food, and gave insight into letters, sciences, and arts of every kind. He taught them architecture and building of cities, founding of temples, how to compile laws, and explained geometry. He taught them agriculture, and helped install "civilization" to the region. He improved their quality of life. At sunset, Oannes would return, or "retire" to the sea. When I read curious things like this I see them as potential clues or insights into another interpretation.

Oannes is said to have told this tale, however it's unclear if this is paraphrased or not:

"There was a time in which there existed nothing but darkness and an abyss of waters, wherein resided most hideous beings, which were produced of a two-fold principle. There appeared men, some of whom were furnished with two wings, others with four, and with two faces [See Janus, and Hermaphrodite]. *They had one body but two heads: the one that of a man, the other of a woman: and likewise in their several organs both male and female. Other human figures were to be seen with the legs and horns of goats: some had horses' feet: while others united the hind quarters of a horse with the body of a man, resembling in shape the hippocentaurs. Bulls likewise were bred there with the heads of men; and dogs with fourfold bodies, terminated in their extremities with the tails of fishes: horses also with the heads of dogs: men too and other animals, with the heads and bodies of horses and the tails of fishes. In short, there were creatures in which were combined the limbs of every species of animals. In addition to these, fishes, reptiles, serpents, with other monstrous animals, which assumed each other's shape and countenance."*

Is this description of chimeras evidence of a lost ancient, high society where genetic experimentation ran wild in the face of the true Creator? Could there have been an Island of Dr Moreau component to our past? Was the cataclysm an effort to wipe out these hideous abominations? If so, by whom? Man himself, or a divine force? Although Oannes says there was only the Abysmal Waters and darkness, there must too have been land. These creatures described must have stood upon something, rested, ate, and resided. Was man even directly responsible for these creatures, or had AI manufactured them possibly in an effort to destroy mankind, and corrupt the blood? Are vaccines not just another form of corruption of the blood? Have you noticed the popularity of the chimera theme in children's toys in recent years? Whether this tale of Oannes is fantasy, metaphor, or a very foreign type of reality, perhaps in a time without separation of dimensions, it appears to be a theme honored in the present day culture, and of course, aimed most directly at the psyche of our children.

One final note, the tale of Oannes coming from the sea seem very similar to the folklore of the Dogon in Mali, West Africa. There seems to be an amphibious group of hideous abominations, beings that appeared to be mermen and mermaids in Babylonian, Akkadian, and Sumerian mythos. That's not a topic for this book, nor is the incredibly advanced knowledge of Sirius A and Sirius B by the Dogon that they claim was taught to them by these ugly Nommos.

Isn't that always the way? You're going about your day, minding your business, doing your work, and all of the sudden a bunch of Nommos show up, and complicate things. Like Pride Month.

3

It's interesting to note the Priest caste, or Akkadi, were the interpreters of the Law in Babylon. The language of the Akkadi was a privilege of the priestly caste, who were assigned a book given to them in the palace schools. In it were found magic formulas in which they "pretended" to exercise supernatural powers. To me that resonates with the modern system of Latinized allopathic medicine. Most can't understand Latin, and the two main things the priests controlled then were the law and the magic. Those are both encrypted by a double-language barrier of Latin, and legalese, today. Legalese simply refers to words having different meaning in the law than in common use, thereby causing you to unwittingly state something you didn't intend to by the legal interpretation. They covet the information. The Allopathic medical industry is in many regards a cult of its own, comprised of sorcerers or priests, indoctrinated by the book or curriculum, and its practitioners pretend to perform supernatural feats of healing, assuming control over life and death. They fashioned themselves as gods, both then and now. None dare challenge their decree, and they have the power of social and political coercion on their side. It's a wonder where the borders of the cult are drawn, for it is the law that empowers the tyranny of medicine and most politicians are lawyers practicing in the Latin tongue. Don't take this as a slander against a language, but rather I'm pointing out the means by which they covet their practice and encrypt it against the uninitiated. With neither a full understanding of law nor medicine accessible to the common person, it is thereby weaponized against them.

3

"Let his high priesthood be supreme…" -a tablet in the Enuma Elish, line 106, regarding the Priests of Marduk.

For those of you interested there were three in total, Enlil, Ea (Enki), and Anu (Akkaidian name), the Sky God which made up the Triad of deities.

It's written in the Enuma Elish that Enki was the father of Marduk whom had conquered Tiamat, and freed the Anunaki of compulsory servitude. Together they are said to have co-created mankind. But to what end? If the Anunnaki were no longer working, was Man created to take their place as servants to the gods? It's not an uncommon theme. Regardless of the religion, all pose the notion that we are subservient to whatever god or gods of that religion. But there's a fine line between pleasing God by doing Him proud in a father-to-son/daughter relationship, and being a worker bee expected to toil endlessly for a master.

Scholars claim the Enuma Elish portrayal of Marduk's conquest over Tiamat is a reworking of an older tale of Ninurta and Anzu. Ninurta was the Sumerian and Akkaidian god-supreme.

He is described as *the Sumerian and Akkadian Lord of the Earth (Ringgren 1973). His father is* **Enlil**, *the* **storm god** *and the ruling god. Ninurta is a young god and has to prove his worth to the pantheon of gods (Burkert 1986). Ninurta is also responsible for the fertility of the fields by aiding in the irrigation of Sumer by the Tigris and Euphrates rivers.* -http://people.uncw.edu/deagona/herakles/ninurta.htm

It's interesting that Ninurta would be Enlil's son, and Marduk, Enki's. When Marduk's arrow strikes Tiamat it splits her in two, and it's said to have resulted in the Tigris and Euphrates Rivers, which in a more understandable manner, Ninurta irrigated fields with. So in one depiction, the rivers are already there, and Ninurta whose story allegedly came before Enuma Elish, was putting them to use.

According to the Labors that Ninurta went through to prove his worth in the Pantheon, one of the 12 labors to rid the world of 12 monsters, is defeating the seven-headed serpent. Do we recall the multi-headed snake from the Ugaritic text that Ba'al had defeated? It gets weirder. The tale of Marduk is similar, as is the tale of Herakles, or Hercules, if you prefer. He battles and defeats a seven-headed Lernaean Hydra as part of his 12 labors.

"Cults were also dedicated to Ninurta. These cults focused on his valiant deeds that helped rid the world of monsters. Like Herakles, Ninurta is a force for civilization

and order in a chaotic world. Healing was attributed to Ninurta through his consort Gula who was the goddess of healing (Ringgren 1973).

Ninurta differs from Herakles partly because he is the embodiment of all divine powers (Ringgren 1973) and in many other ways. Nevertheless, the association between Ninurta and Herakles is deeper than mere surface characteristics. The "get and bring" idea of their labors are the same. Their function is to make the surroundings hospitable for humans and gods. They turn nature into culture (Burkert 1986).

From ancient-origins.net/myths-legends-asia/ninurta-god-war-and-agriculture-0010909, we read:

Ninurta was a Mesopotamian deity associated with war, agriculture, and the scribal arts. He could be thought of as a defender of civilization against chaos. Ninurta was originally revered in southern Mesopotamia and later in the north under the Assyrian kings. He remained a prominent deity until the fall of the Assyrian Empire. His primary symbol was the plow...

...In another story that also takes place in primordial times before humans, Anzu, a giant lion-headed bird monster from the mountains, steals the Tablet of Destinies from Enlil, the chief of the gods. Possession of the tablet gives Anzu supreme power over the universe. The gods, terrified, turn to Ninurta, the mighty warrior and the son of Enlil. Ninurta sets out to defeat Anzu, retrieve the Tablet of Destinies, and restore order to the cosmos. Ninurta is successful in slaying Anzu and returning the Tablet of Destinies to his father...

It should be mentioned Ninurta, although it's said the plow is his symbol, he is often depicted with a bow and a club in is 12 labors. He, as Dagon, was an agricultural deity.

If this soap opera of characters hasn't made your head spin yet, this could go on forever if I deprived no detail or deity of a mention. For all of our sanity, let's get back on track as to the mysteries, Marduk, Babylon, demons, and magic(k).

5

"You wanna get nuts? C'mon, Let's get nuts!" -Michael Keaton, Batman

You ready to get dark? Let's get dark. Remember my warning. You can't study this stuff without it studying you. There's no barrier but your own inner strength and will. This stuff will bond with your psyche, and try to mesh with it. It will crawl up your inner framework and bond to your DNA. Be careful if you decide to study these topics on your own, because many who do, become lost in the search, or come back with more than they bargained for; a new "friend," a dark passenger.

Just so you, the reader, understand what we're dealing with here, and appreciate my warnings, Michael W. Ford, a self proclaimed Luciferian, writes in the opening of his grimoire, ***MASKIM HUL Babylonian Magick***,

This living or 'dead' grimoire Maskim Hul is a gate to not only the Ilu Limnu, or 'Evil Gods,' yet also [to] all of the Gods of the Babylonian-Assyrian Pantheon…

I can attest the Gods and Demons do adapt just as you, for consider that each individual is a temple and gateway to life for them, so there is a "give and take" involved. All worthwhile relationships are "give and take" although many have such with more on one side than the other.

As inviting, and lovely as that may sound to the unhinged Marxist psychopath, chances are most people would read that and tread lightly, if at all into these topics. Fear not. For I am not taking you into a pit, nor a ceremonial circle. I don't want to go there either. We're simply the flies on the wall, gleaning from a distance.

First we must understand "Luciferian" is a much older concept with a more modern name. There were no mention of Lucifer, or Satan uttered in the world or scribbled by a scribe, for the practice predating Abrahamic religions. It later found more shape and identity in the framework of opposites and similarities that Judaism and Christianity provided, and therefore a far more ancient practice was assigned a moniker relating to the popular, recognizable religion. It's important to grasp that to understand how Luciferianism, which utilizes Theurgy, or *the ritual practices associated with the invocation, or evocation of the presence of one or more deities, especially with the goal of achieving henosis (uniting with the divine) and **perfecting** oneself,* (Wikipedia; Theurgy), could have passed along from Sumer and Akkad, been forged and refined in the Mystery Schools of ancient Babylon, practiced by the Assyrians, Chaldeans, Egyptians, Canaanites, Hitties, and so on, without any of them ever knowing it by that name.

As we explore and track this priestcraft throughout history, pay close attention to recurring themes and objectives such as the perfected man, the utilization of common sigils and symbols, and just where these efforts have steered mankind throughout history.

In Sumer the high priests were the Ensí, Lugal, or gala, if they were the priests of the goddess, Inanna. In Akkad, the priests of Inanna were the kalú. Some of the attributes of Inanna's later form as Ishtar include oracle goddess, warrior goddess, and mistress who bathed in the blood of her enemies, like Elizabeth Bathory. This transition from Inanna to Ishtar seems to have come about as a result of the conquest of Sargon of Akkad. Prior to that they were two distinct goddesses.

The feminine Tiamot, the salted sea waters, was known as the Dragon Serpent of Chaos, Mother of all Gods and Demons, and mother of all. It's interesting that she was polymorphic, meaning of many shapes, and as a Serpent she was attributed with being the spark of Intelligence, which seems to pair with the serpent in the garden offering knowledge. It's similar, or congruent, if not exactly the same. She took on the form of Hubur, the creating one, and her children were the eleven Monsters of Chaos, made for the task of defeating Marduk. Thus setting the 12 labors theme, with her defeat being the twelfth task of Marduk, solidifying his supremacy.

In Babylon the priests were the **ereb biti**, or the Temple enterers. The sesgallu was the temple officer in charge of reading the hymn of Enuma Elish during the Babylonian New Year's Bash ritual. I think Dick Clark may have also hosted that event. The man didn't age for thousands of years before having a stroke. The important ones who conducted the rituals were the kalú, and another fellow was the tupsarru, or the scribe.

Often these priests would merge their names with that of the gods, as the adepts in the secret societies of these Mystery Schools do today. Gog and Magog were adopted names of Bush Sr. and George W as Skull and Bones members. Words have meaning, and in the name there is power. This I would conjoin with the idea of sound resonance and frequency. There's a specific shape for every sound and it strengthens with amplification. This is probably another reason for so many ancient amphitheaters, and resonating pillars in ancient structures. They could be seen as energy devices to power other structures, or themselves, in ceremonial group chants involving a great many people. This too, is a principal of the need for public ritual. You needn't know the meaning to have it use your energy. I'm sure people were terrified and tortured en masse just to funnel their reactions into powering a ritual. Doesn't media do that in a less coherent, less focused, way by reporting things that scare, anger, or traumatize you? So-called patriot channels are no different, although that need they build inside you for a resolution is typically supplied to you in inference by a product they offer. Sigils are carved or painted signs and symbols considered to have magical powers. Well, they literally have energetic properties when they are mimicking the shapes of particular sounds. This may help in understanding how symbols can effect you without your awareness. Just as sound vibrates, and will effect you, so will the sight, for sight is light, and light is also a frequency.

The term, "Mystery Schools" is defined in modern times by New Agers, and mind you, *New Age Magazine* used to be the publication of the Scottish Rite Freemasons, as an education of self-enlightenment, **perfecting** one's self, and attaining higher understanding of nature, and reality. This seems to fit into the crystal-rubbing, patchouli and armpit scented neo-hippy archetype you'd see on a yoga mat somewhere watching Gaia TV. The stereotype exists in abundance, and that's how it becomes a stereotype. From my personal experiences living in Southern California, and having attended Contact in the Desert twice, which later I began referring to as "Communists in the Desert" after becoming aware of their agenda, it's usually those of independent wealth with all this free time to devote to hot-boxing their own flatulence and calling it divine wind. No doubt they own a Tesla, or a Pruis. In reality they're practicing a form of

Secular Humanism, where Man is God, and that is what these mystery schools ultimately teach. Incidentally, *The New Age* was also a publication inspired by the British Fabian Socialist society, and promoted the poison doctrine of Christian Socialism. Giving the New Testament teachings a paint job of socialism has continued to taint the pulpits through the National Council of Churches and other Marxist-run organizations including Christian Zionism, like the long-running Pat Robertson headed 700 Club.

Pulling out of a hat, here's what one website, incentrelondon.com, has to say in regards to what a Mystery School is:

"Mystery Schools have been in existence since ancient times. Their primary mission was to protect and preserve the ancient systems of enlightenment, healing, manifestation, transmutation and transformation so that they can be continually used by humanity for its collective progression."

Then why all the secrecy, and exclusivity if it's for the betterment of humanity? Isn't that something you'd typically share with, oh I don't know, other humans? What's the danger? If it's difficult most wouldn't do it, and if it didn't interest them they wouldn't either.

Let's talk about those "ancient times" a moment. Assyrian King, Ashurnasirpal II documented his bloody conquests, and was known for cruelty. He would stake down the arms and legs of captives, face and belly facing the ground, and flay the flesh off of all the people while they lived, and he would have all of their heads chopped off and placed in pyramidal piles. He would decorate the besieged area's buildings with the flesh of the flayed, and drape skins over the skull piles as well. Some he'd cut off their hands and feet, others he'd cut out their tongues for speaking against his gods. He got giddy talking about gouging, and sometimes ripping out, the eyes of many prisoners. He mused of tearing off their faces, and keeping a collection of their lips to bring back and show his kingdom. He left not one single thing living. He'd burn the maidens, and the children. He'd plunder or murder their livestock. He described turning roads into rivers of blood, and waters red with blood. You see, all this good, clean, Saturday afternoon fun was for a purpose. It was ritualized as a sacrifice to his gods and he fed them in blood and carnage. He was a Priest-King, and if you think any priestcraft of his kingdom was aspiring to make man enlightened, well, I guess that depends on what your definition of "enlightenment" is.

"It depends on what the meaning of the word of 'is' is." - Bill Clinton

By no means was Ashurnasirpal II unique in his treatment of a conquered tribe. The Priest-Kings of all these territories were ferocious. The Gutians, Lulubi, later Anatolian Hittites, all were legendary and infamously feared warriors. I failed to mention Ashurnasirpal II, that little Ashur-hole, also self-chronicled his many impaled victims he used to decorate the perimeter of a conquered area. He was Vlad long before there was a Vlad. If you know me from my Ba'al Busters Broadcast, you know I have spoken often of the virtues of such methods when dealing with truly evil child harmers, and those attempting to starve and poison the entire population. You can't reason with the vacant, and they wouldn't deserve such honors. Evil knows and responds to only one thing; devastation. Because most are scared weasels when directly threatened, such decorations around whatever town you wish to protect would make one heck of a deterrent. If you are rightfully defending yourself from a force with overwhelming numbers, superior weapons, and more battle experience, implementation of psychological warfare isn't only useful, it's essential. What could be more "influential" than seeing the rotting bodies of fellow scumbag Marxist military thugs sliding slowly down 20 ft spikes as the next battalion marches into the zone? It may make them reconsider, or reassess the importance of a particular objective. In the case of Vlad the Impaler, his killing fields full of Ottoman scum were hoisted up on high for their brethren to see, and when they did, they had a change of plans, and turned back. His smaller forces of no more than 20,000 repelled over 100,000 Ottomans that day without need for additional combat. See, Vlad was defending his homeland from invaders. He had a deeper drive for victory for it meant protecting his countrymen, and his kingdom.

The Ashur-hole II was a little less reserved, killing everyone and everything, children and women included. That's beyond the argument of doing it so you don't get attacked by others. That's just sick, twisted evil, and it was his pleasure to spill as much blood as possible for his deities. The more you spill, the more you tell yourself how powerful you are, and how favored you think you are among the god archetypes you think exist.

Here's some more from this frolicking-in-tall-grass website, incentrelondon.com:

"Mystery School teachings are imparted by an oral tradition. Rooted in shamanic and mystic ways of wisdom, these teachings are handed down unbroken from teacher to student in an unbroken lineage that has withstood the test of time.
It is not premised on "energetic downloads" or "channelled teachings" that create instant masters of teachers. Rather, it is the power of lineage-based physical initiations that confers the authority of the path. This has been down [I think they meant "done"] *with every Master of Light who has ever walked the earth - such as Lord Buddha, Guan Yin and **Jesus Christ**.*

*It is through the process of **initiation** that our energy structures are able to bring in more light so that we may work with it to fulfill our life's purpose. It is also through the process of initiation that we are able to retain that light and radiate it outwards like a beacon to the world.*

*The initiates are those who are known as the Guardians, the Protectors, the **Light bearers**, the Teachers, the Healers, the Record Keepers, the Magickians, and the Watchers, among many other names."*

Like how they swooped up, and grouped in Gautuma, incorrectly calling him "Lord Buddha," and Jesus Christ? They just claimed both were initiates going through training, and the implication you may not see here is that they're inferring man can, and has become as God by providing these two as examples. This is the core of Secular Humanism. They bastardized what Jesus as a man, or as a symbol, represents by claiming he is an example of becoming God, the perfected man. It's subtle, and unless you know what the New Age, which isn't anything new, and secular humanism is all about, you wouldn't be able to detect the deliberate insult and mockery being portrayed by this inverse representation. It also, in both cases, Gautama, and Jesus, reduces them to the level of student, an apprentice, not an inherent identity, but rather an acquired one granted to them by some nameless master in a mystery school. They claim it is their processes of initiation which bring "more light," and the initiation itself is the tool by which you are able to retain said light.

They also mention "Light bearers." Prometheus and Lucifer are known as the light bearer. The article spelled magic with a "k" distinguishing it as Aleister Crowley first had, as being of true power over nature and man, and not just a slight-of-hand sideshow act. From what I think I am supposed to understand from Enoch, I am not sure why the New Ager marketing material would associate themselves with what ultimately became the Fallen Ones. The Grigori were the Watchers. Grigori is also where you get the name Gregory from, as in Pope Gregory, Gregorian calendar, etc.

Apparently passing bills in congress is a form of initiation as well, where sometimes you can't read it until you pass it. Such is the way of the lodges of more recent centuries. They have a secret, lots of them, but can't tell you even what the secrets are about until after you take that plunge into the abyss with no lifeline they call an initiation. No turning back, no repentance. Even then, that's just the beginning of it. You then have to try figuring out the secrets they were coveting, or claiming to be coveting, by simply being among them, and expressing unquestioning obedience. Now be a good little slave with your fancy lodge title.

6

I'm going to provide very rough, brief history of the Babylonian Empire with approximate dates and conquests of the area. I'm doing this to galvanize all the variables between reigns of Priest Kings and peoples into one reference, and therefore when I say "Babylon" the capital city, or "Babylonia" the empire, from here on, it's generally referring to the area, not so much as who was ruling at any particular time.

To write this passage, I'm referencing a couple sources, but humorously enough, kids.britannica.com is the chief resource. Apparently Dr. Seuss never tackled the subject.

"Babylonia and Assyria were empires in ancient Mesopotamia, a region that is now part of Iraq. The Babylonian empires were centered in the city of Babylon, in southeastern Mesopotamia. The Assyrian empire was centered in Ashur, in northern Mesopotamia."

Assyria ~ Modern Syria, get it? In roughly 1900 BC, the Amorites conquered the Mesopotamian area, but adapted the culture of Sumer and Akkad within its own. It was at this time we can point to an actual Babylonia, the Empire named after its capital.

Nimrod is said to have been the Priest-King of Shinar, not technically Babylon, as some people write. There was no Babylon or Babylonia yet. He would have been in the Sumer and Akkad era. Historians have failed to find evidence to verify Nimrod's actual existence. Although, he could potentially be Naram-sin, grandson of the great Sargon of Akkad. This would also mean Nimrod certainly was NOT "the first on earth to be a mighty man," as Genesis 10:8-12 attests. I believe that is in the context of being the first mighty man post flood, which still is lacking in detail. IsraelmyGlory.org goes as far as to say Nimrod was the Egyptian Osiris, and Horus, the risen Osiris. That places him in completely different area, in a likely mismatched time period. Other Archaeologists say that Nimrod and Sargon are one in the same. Sargon being from Kish, named after Noah's grandson, and Nimrod from Cush, it's then possible to see the two origins being from the same fabled first city in Sumer to rise after the flood. If any of the tales of Nimrod's behavior are true, he may have set the cruelty standard for Ashurnasirpal II of Assyria. That's murky, too. See from my perspective, Nimrod was conscientious when it came to his people. If he did indeed unite people under one, common cause to protect their lives from a vindictive god who liked to throw temper tantrums, pose as the Creator, and drown the world when he was cranky, then the Tower of Babel wasn't in defiance to any true Creator God. It was in defiance to the random tyranny of an impostor. Can you believe it? The first union job with multiple contractors on the jobsite gets Union-Busted by some guy who thinks he's the only god. You know how much planning goes into a project like that? We're talking about 2300 BC when Sargon of Akkad founded the Akkadian Empire. The city of Babylon was founded in the same time as best as I can tell. My father uses the name Nimrod the way some people make Polack jokes. He has called people Nimrods, meaning they're idiots, ever since I was a child. When I read the Tanakh I come away thinking, "the only guy who wasn't a friggin' *Nimrod* in the Old Testament, was the one guy called Nimrod."

They say the first Babylonian Dynasty, or line of kings was where we get that 1900 BC date of the Amorite conquest from. Hammurabi was the most notable of the first dynasty, at least to the historians, and he reigned a good 500 years after the death of Sargon of Akkad. Hammurabi is known for his set of oppressive government actions known as laws. Remember, there are but 2 laws. Love your God, and love thy neighbor as yourself. If you don't like that, then stick with the natural law. You are free to do what you wish providing it doesn't harm others or damage their property. You were born to be Free. Cause No Harm is the common law, and that is way different than "Do what thou wilt," from Crowley's Book of the Law. Do what thou wilt has no stipulation for predatory behavior. Basically, if you can get away with imposing your will on others and making them victims, it's perfectly fine in the mind of Uncle Fester—Aleister Crowley.

Coming from the northern mountains, the Kassites conquered the Empire of Babylonia in about 1600 BC and reigned, quite-disputed, for about 400 years. In 1300 BC, the Assyrians broke away from the governorship of the empire, and were brutal enough and powerful enough to get away with it. They took what is now Turkey for themselves, and periodically, the Assyrians ran the whole damn empire whenever they happened to be the victors in battle. In the 2nd-ish dynasty the Arameans and Chaldeans would test the dominance of the Assyrian rule over Babylonia.

Ashurbanipal, not to be confused with the demented predecessor, Ashurnasirpal II 200 years prior, was the last King of Assyrian Babylonia. He is most known for his 38 year reign, the longest of any of the Assyrian Kings, and the creation of the first major library in the Middle East. It was located in the Austin, TX of Assyria, Nineveh. It housed a collection of knowledge from sciences to mathematics, religion, languages… You know, like a library. Although the most populous city of the Assyrian Empire, the Nineveh decimal system never really caught on. A grand and important library in a beautiful, modernized (for that time period) city… So yes, of course someone destroyed the whole city and burned it all to the ground, library included. History has patterns. You should have called that one from a mile away. House a bunch of enriching, important knowledge and human history in a centralized location, expect some asshole to come along with his Boring Company flame thrower, and torch the place. If you can't stop it, at least be the bookie for those betting against the fire. In this case it was Medes and some Babylonians with no regard for their own history that ruined it for everyone. They were the Antifa of their time.

Soon after the death of Ashurbanipal, the Chaldeans moved into control over the empire. The name you should know from their short turn as top dogs was Nebuchadnezzar II, who ruled a whopping 43 years. Let's just call him Chad. Chad conquered Syria and Palestine, the second one may have upset a few historical gatekeepers. The story goes, many Jews were forced out of the area after Chad II captured the city. Ask yourself why. So you get new management. What's making you have to vacate? Or is it something about the local practices that other cultures find offensive and unconscionable? Think Canaanite for a moment, here. Chad is most notorious for having destroyed the potentially imaginary Solomon's Temple of Jerusalem. This might be a good time to discuss the revisionist historians and their revisionist history.

I'm not saying what these book passages are about to tell us is true. I wasn't there. I don't know the truth, because how could anyone if the historical record has been altered and the evidence tampered with? The following series of excerpts come from the book, ***The Laughing Jesus: Religious Lies, and Gnostic Wisdom*** by Timothy Gandy, and Timothy Freke:

"Our earliest mention of Israel is in the so-called 'Israel Stele' of Pharaoh Merneptah, dated from 1207 BCE. It says simply: 'Israel is desolate; its seed is no more'... There is a dispute about whether the name 'Israel' refers to a people or simply a person, but it is ironic that our earliest mention of Israel tells us that Israel no longer exists!"

This is just setting the stage for the following bombshells, but understand that Nebuchadnezzar II reigned reigned from August 605 BC- 7th of October 562 BC. Remember that because allegedly there was an elaborate temple conveniently destroyed without a trace by Chad during this period. Pay close attention to that claim and how it compares to the condition the Greek conquerors of Palestine, led by Alexander the Great find Jerusalem to be in 200 years later.

"There is a further problem with the names 'Jerusalem' and 'Israel'. Their derivation tells a history that is completely at odds with the Tanakh. The word Israel means 'fighter for El' who was a Canaanite god. Jerusalem is named after another Canaanite god called Shalem. But according to the Tanakh, the Canaanites were the deadly enemies of the Israelites. What is going on here? The answer is simple but shocking. All the evidence now points to the Israelites being indigenous inhabitants of Canaan. The Biblical story that they arrived in Palestine from Egypt is a myth. The Israelites did not come from somewhere else, they were already there. This view is now widely share by scholars. One modern archaeologist states:
'The Israelites never were in Egypt. They never came from abroad. The whole chain is broken. It is not an historical one. It is a later legendary reconstruction... of a history that never happened.'
Reliefs at Karnak in Egypt do not show any distinction of hairstyle or clothing between Israelites and Canaanites, so the Egyptians clearly did not discriminate between the two."

Is the picture beginning to form in your head, yet? I read this book over 5 years ago, and it's tough to have this information that seemingly no one else you encounter has been given to process. I'm not saying accepted, but simply exposed to, so they can process it for themselves, and let them decide if truth resonates from it or not. We as mankind should be treated like adults, not protected from information. Jerusalem does NOT mean, "city of peace." Shalem/Shalim, is a Canaanite Goddess of the dusk. She is the deity representing VENUS, the Evening Star. Who claims to be the Morning Star, again? Venus is of course a Roman deity, but she's congruent with Aphrodite of the Greek. In Roman folklore Lucifer (light-bringer) was another name given to the Planet Venus. The Greek name for the same planet [wanderer] was Phosphoros which also means light-bringer, and is where we get the elemental name for phosphorus.

"The story of the Jews return from captivity in Egypt is a myth. And so is the story of their return from captivity in Babylon. Although we now consider the Jews and Israelites to be the same, in ancient times they were two distinct peoples and bitter enemies. The Israelites lived in northern Palestine and had their capital at Samaria. The Judeans (a.k.a. Jews) lived in southern Palestine and had their capital at Jerusalem. When the Assyrians invaded Palestine in 733 BCE the Israelites resisted and were ruthlessly punished. Their city of Samaria was leveled to the ground and the population taken into slavery. The Judeans, however, offered the Assyrians their support, and after Israel was liquidated Judea began to flourish as a new Assyrian province."

Mind you that 733 BC date is still over 100 years before Chad allegedly came by to loot and wreck their glorious first Temple of Solomon, which remember, was built by Solomon the sorcerer who commanded demons to do it, and maybe had some help from Hiram Abiff, and Mickey Mouse. Hiram Abiff was allegedly conscripted into the service of building the temple by King Hiram of Tyre. Where's Tyre you ask? It's Phoenician. What did we learn about the practices of the Phoenicians from our walk through of the cultures associated with Ba'al Cults? They burned their babies, and kingly noblemen would be expected, if not obligated to sacrifice their first born to the flames at the high priest's behest. That was how they petitioned for favor from the Storm and Fertility God. If Hiram of Tyre was a Phoenician leader, he was a child-killer. Plain and simple. Whether it was his own, or he was sneaky and had a stand-in kidnapped he could pawn off as his own, he was a child killer nonetheless. That's what they give us for allegory of the Temple with Hiram Abiff, so I'm just explaining what that suggests. If it's a fairy tale, then it's morbid and annoying. If it's supposed to be true, then it's despicable.

In 587, the Babylonian Empire under new management of Chad II, went to Palestine, and destroyed Jerusalem. They deported the Judeans into slavery. Judea ceased to exist, having met a similar fate as Israel previously.

So when and where was this Temple that only appears in literature after it's already been allegedly destroyed? Let's fast-forward to the next phase of relevance. In 331 BC, Alexander the Great, after a 5 year campaign, defeated the Persians who were then controlling the Babylonian Empire.

"The great scholar Bickerman described Jerusalem at the time of Alexander as 'the obscure abode of an insignificant tribe.' This explains why there is no mention of the Jews in all of the Greek texts prior to Alexander...

*After the death of Alexander in 325 BCE his general Ptolemy ruled Palestine from Egypt. The next century and a half saw momentous change in Palestine as Greek technology and customs were introduced into the region. Coinage replaced barter. Agriculture was revolutionised by artificial irrigation, waterwheels, the plough, the wine-press and other similar implements. Now Jerusalem really did become a city 'skilled in many crafts', as one of the Jewish writers of the time puts it. In this same period there was an explosion of Jewish literature. For the **first time in the history** of this region we have the beginnings of a high culture capable of creating and sustaining a **literate class**...*

From the beginning of the second century BCE Palestine produced many famous philosophers, poets, satirists and rhetoricians, some of whom even became friends and advisors to influential Roman statesmen, such as Pompey, Brutus and Cicero. The Jews had finally arrived on the world stage as a sophisticated people. But, ironically, they had only achieved this through an education that was thoroughly Greek. Almost all of the Jewish literature produced in this period is written in Greek. The Jews wrote in Greek and thought in Greek. And yet the Jews were not Greeks and never could be, no matter how hard they aspired. The Greeks had divided the whole world into two mutually exclusive categories: Greeks and barbarians. In response, the Jews divided the world into Jews and Gentiles, and produced a body of literature that proved, at least to their own satisfaction, that the Jews were not only equal to the Greeks, they were better."

Are you picking up on the implications of what they're saying? You might need a moment to absorb and process what you just read, but there are telltale giveaways in this passage. What does it mean the Jews "wrote in Greek, and thought in Greek?" This passage is the key to the whole enchilada, or bagel perhaps. What do we know specifically about Greek as a language? They have many words, or expressions that do not translate into other languages, correct? When you are native to a language, you can see a word and sense and feel its meaning is even if you can't verbally translate it into someone else's language. Such would be the case for the word, Logos, for instance. For the writers to claim, and history to prove, that the Jews wrote in Greek, and not their presumed indigenous language, is interesting enough. To then say, they Thought in Greek, is to say they were taught literacy in Greek by Greeks, and there was nothing they had before. To think in a language that complex comes from learning everything you know through that language, which displaces any idea that they were literate before the Greeks taught them. The Greeks gave them a language. They merely claimed Hebrew as their own later, but it did not originate with the Israelites. It isn't a native language to them. Hebrew is more closely related to the Phoenician and Moabite languages, and therefore said to be related to a rougher Canaanite version. But who were the Canaanites? Didn't we just read that there was no distinction between the Israelites, and the Canaanites except from the pens of more modern court historians?

Didn't we also read that the "Israelites" and the Jews were separate people that were bitter rivalries?

It could be that the first time Jews had an intellectual identity was through the Greek education. And this could be extrapolated out to explain why they identify with the Greek culture today, such as Epstein with the architecture on Little Saint James, before it was dismantled. That of course assumes a lot of things, starting with this whole business of who's really a Jew, and who's shielding themselves under the facade, and ending with, hey, it's just symbolism, man.

This is not an assault on any individual or their ethnicity. I'm simply reporting on what is being shown in historical records and how it conflicts with the story we're told. This is for your personal information, not for my judgment whatsoever. We'll discuss more on how the impostors in the Jewish community are harming their image when we get to the Sabbatean-Frankists section.

One final note from the same book that I think is important for understanding the origin of yellow journalism and revisionist history. History has been tainted ever since it was first recorded:

"THE JEWISH FANTASY FACTORY

No sooner had the Jews assimilated their Greek education than they began to give a novel [meaning false] *account of how they had come by it. They had not learnt from the Greeks. It was the other way around. In 220 BCE the Jewish writer Hermippus recorded his opinion that Pythagoras, the first man in the Greek world to be called a philosopher, had actually acquired all his wisdom from the Jews. Aristobulus, writing in the middle of the second century BCE, added that Plato had borrowed his ideas from Moses. In the first century CE Josephus claimed that 'the wisest of the Greeks', including Plato, Pythagoras, Anaxagoras and the Stoics, had 'learned their conceptions of God from principles with which Moses supplied them.' According to the Jewish writer Eupolemus, however, the Greeks even owed their knowledge of the alphabet to Moses. He had taught it first to the Jews, who then taught it to the Phoenicians, who in turn taught it to the Greeks. Artapanus, another Jewish writer, tells us that Moses acquired the name Mousaios from the Greeks, became the teacher of Orpheus and conferred a whole host of benefits upon mankind, including the invention of ships, mechanisms for stone construction, weaponry, hydraulic engines, implements of warfare and, of course, philosophy."*

Well, if you're going to tell a lie, tell a big one, I guess. But why insult and show lack of gratitude to your teachers by claiming they were insignificant in your education? I'm not talking about public school. I'm talking about Alexandria and the sharing of knowledge that occurred. The Greeks never even heard of the Jews until they acquired them through the conquest of Babylon. Pythagorus lived a good 2,000 years before that.

*"In Egypt Moses' achievements were even more spectacular. He taught hieroglyphics to the Egyptian priests, divided the nation into the thirty-six names, assigned to each the god it was to worship, and was named 'Hermes' because of his ability to interpret sacred writing*s.

    During the Hellenistic period there was no end to the Jews' delight in rewriting history and playing one-upmanship with the Greeks, Egyptians and their other powerful rivals."

Freke, Tim; Freke, Tim; Gandy, Peter. The Laughing Jesus: Religious Lies and Gnostic Wisdom (p. 37). Tim Freke Publications. Kindle Edition.

    Busy guy, that Moses. I wonder if he had a "M" on his chest like Superman's "S."

    Nebuchadnezzar II was also responsible for rebuilding the Temple of Marduk in Babylon. The Chaldeans didn't hold onto the empire long before the Persians came in and smacked them around. That brings us to the Macedonian era of Alexander the Great and Ptolemy Soter we just covered. So when I describe anything from a mystery school, I'm not going to point out or distinguish from what point in the tumultuous past of Babylon, specifically. I will however distinguish between the Babylonian and the Egyptian schools.

    One final fun trivia fact: Saddam Hussein fashioned himself the successor, if not the embodiment of, Nebuchadnezzar [II]. I tell you this to illustrate the occult themes and ceremonial attributes of what you've seen thrown in your face all your life with only your subconscious truly taking notice. If you believe in the millions of years of experience-gained information in the very makeup of human building blocks, DNA, then these ancient themes resonate within us because of past witness, and consciously forgotten linkage to our ancient ancestors. All is connected by the Godly Aetherial tapestry.

    From a source website whose symbol is a circumambulated compass or triangle, with another circle within the center of the triangle, Atlas Obscura, atlasobscura.com/articles/babylon-iraq-saddam-hussein, we read this:

"In the 1980s, during the Iran-Iraq War, Saddam Hussein became obsessed with the Babylonian ruler Nebuchadnezzar, who is notorious for waging bloody wars to seize large swaths of current-day Iran and Israel. Saddam saw himself as a modern reincarnation of Nebuchadnezzar, and to prove it, he spent millions building a massive reconstruction of Babylon...

    Notice they say "Israel" and not Palestine? Nebu… Chad II wasn't invading anyplace called "Israel." What was the name of Morpheus' ship in the movie, *The*

Matrix? The Nebuchadnezzar. What were they, in the Nebuchadnezzar, rather inversely trying to protect in the trilogy? "Zion."

Morals & Mysteries… And a Lot of Snakes

1

To get the best, uninitiated understanding of the Mysteries we turn now to Albert Pike's **Morals & Dogma of the Ancient and Accepted Scottish Rite of Freemasonry**. Please write notes as you read, and go back to the histories of the gods we've covered to see just who or what they are invoking and evoking in the rituals.

*"Certain faculties of man are directed toward the Unknown—thought, meditation, prayer. The unknown is an ocean, of which conscience is the **compass**. Thought, meditation, prayer, are the great mysterious pointings of the needle. It is a spiritual magnetism that thus connects the human soul with the Deity. These majestic irradiations of the soul pierce through the shadow toward the light."*

Pike, Albert. Morals & Dogma: Of the Ancient and Accepted Scottish Rite of Freemasonry (Annotated Version). Kindle Edition. Location. 118

This excerpt sets forth the principal ideas behind the use of magic to interact with whomever they're referring to as the "Deity" at a given time. It gives the initiate the sense of attainable insight through thought, meditation, not-exactly bedtime or Sunday morning style prayer, and ritual. As far as conscience being a compass pointing the right direction, that assumes the subject has a conscience. In the absence of a moral or ethical tether, you have a compass without a needle. Desire will steer, rather than nobility of character. Selfishness will consume. Without empathy there is no compass. The only compass one has and needs is **compass**ion. Chemically, and through vaccination, they do their best to cut that tether to the divine, or higher-self, which is really just a stepping-stone euphemism for saying God. I don't jump all over people for the terms they use. If they're more comfortable expressing it as "higher-self" why insult or scare them off the path of one day coming to terms with the realization of the term? We're not here to act superior, for it is truly inferior to behave as such. Help them on the lifeboat when they want to come aboard. Don't throw anchors and cannon balls expecting them to warm up to an idea you represent. Forgive the philosophical tangent, but it's important to examine our own actions when dealing with others, and ask ourselves how we would respond if we were the object of our own approach.

"To return to its source in the Infinite, the human soul, the ancients held, had to ascend, as it had descended, through the seven spheres. The Ladder by which it reascends, has, according to Marsilius Ficinus, in his Commentary on the Ennead of Plotinus, seven degrees or steps; and in the Mysteries of Mithras, carried to Rome under

the Emperors, the ladder, with its seven rounds, was a symbol referring to this ascent through the spheres of the seven planets...

...The Mithraic Mysteries were celebrated in caves, where gates were marked at the four equinoctial and solstitial points of the zodiac; and the seven planetary spheres were represented, which souls needs must traverse in descending from the heaven of the fixed stars to the elements that envelop the earth; and seven gates were marked, one for each planet, through which they pass, in descending or returning.

Pike, Albert. Morals & Dogma: Of the Ancient and Accepted Scottish Rite of Freemasonry (Annotated Version). Kindle Edition. L. 187-188

Let me preface this next passage by saying Pike is not without his brilliant insights. If these men were not of high intellect, there would scarcely be any threat from their plans of a "one-world totalitarian-socialist government," as Bill Cooper had often described it. It's easy to agree on the smaller points, and overlook the grander deception being played. Plus it's not so much the world they want to fashion for themselves that's the concern, but rather the world they are determined to erect around us, and control everyone else by. They're two separate spheres of existence, and the deception is somewhat a self-deception, in that, through inference, they allow others to think they will be spared the one and reside in the other if they should prove their worth and devote themselves to the "Great work."

"God makes visible to men His will in events; an obscure text, written in a mysterious language. Men make their translations of it forthwith, hasty, incorrect, full of faults, omissions, and misreadings. We see so short a way along the arc of the great circle! Few minds comprehend the Divine tongue. The most sagacious, the most calm, the most profound, decipher the hieroglyphs slowly; and when they arrive with their text, perhaps the need has long gone by; there are already twenty translations in the public square—the most incorrect being, as of course, the most accepted and popular. From each translation, a party is born; and from each misreading, a faction. Each party believes or pretends that it has the only true text, and each faction believes or pretends that it alone possesses the light."

Pike, Albert. Morals & Dogma: Of the Ancient and Accepted Scottish Rite of Freemasonry (Annotated Version). Kindle Edition. Location. 333-334

Is this not a description of the artificial, so-called "independent media" sources pulling you 100 different directions, getting you stuck in eddy currents, as the flow of tyranny marches right by you without resistance? Do we spend time on a beer company that promoted trans-politics when they're planning to enslave us all with the UN's World Health Organization, Biometrics, Biosurveillance, and a cashless society digital currency? Which is the more emanate danger to us all? Where should our energies be focused? Although Pike makes a great point here, it is his modern lodge fellows bringing about this global enslavement. Let's not lose sight of that.

"Though Masonry is identical with the ancient Mysteries, it is so only in this qualified sense: that it presents but an imperfect image of their brilliancy, the ruins only of their grandeur, and a system that has experienced progressive alterations, the fruits of social events, political circumstances, and the ambitious imbecility of its improvers. After leaving Egypt, the Mysteries were modified by the habits of the different nations among whom they were introduced, and especially by the religious systems of the countries into which they were transplanted. To maintain the established government, laws, and religion, was the obligation of the Initiate everywhere; and everywhere they were the heritage of the priests, who were nowhere willing to make the common people co-proprietors with themselves of philosophical truth."

Pike, Albert. Morals & Dogma: Of the Ancient and Accepted Scottish Rite of Freemasonry (Annotated Version). Kindle Edition. p. 384-385

Here we're told the priests coveted and sequestered the "philosophical truth(s)" from the common people. The only reason to do that is to reinforce a hierarchy among men that is dependent on secrecy to secure. If given to all to study, it would perhaps have enlightened those who pursued the information. Then the people would become more independent from the controls of the priests, kings, etc. They weren't about to allow that. Anywhere this knowledge traveled it was guarded and kept from the public eye. The assumption of course being that they possessed information of actual value, and not just a collection of demonic incantations that involved unconscionable acts of cruelty and degeneracy.

*"Eight hundred Degrees of one kind and another were invented: Infidelity and even **Jesuitry** were taught under the mask of Masonry. The rituals even of the respectable Degrees, copied and mutilated by ignorant men, became nonsensical and trivial; and the words so corrupted that it has hitherto been found impossible to recover many of them at all."*

Pike, Albert. Morals & Dogma: Of the Ancient and Accepted Scottish Rite of Freemasonry (Annotated Version). Kindle Edition. L. 5175

In the Edmund Ronayne section, I explained that he, Ronayne, endeavored to research and restore the practices and rituals of Freemasonry. He was able to develop a masonic handbook from his research that was distributed to the initiates. It was through this continued effort, where he found himself in library vaults sifting through dusty books and perhaps even scrolls, that he made his dark discoveries. Masonry has always spoken of Ba'al, but to grasp the true connections to the dark practices of the ancient cult is to realize the nature of the master each mason was serving whether they knew it or not. The lodge then is simply a temple for a dark agrigori, or energetic spirit. Grigori is also the name of the "fallen ones."

"The serpent was a familiar symbol in the Mysteries of Bakchos. The Initiates grasped them with their hands, as Orphiucus does on the celestial globe, and the Orpheo-telestes, or purifier of candidates did the same, crying, as Demosthenes taunted Æschines with doing in public at the head of the women whom his mother was to imitate, EVOI, SABOI, HYES ATTÊ, ATTÊ, HYES!"

Pike, Albert. Morals & Dogma: Of the Ancient and Accepted Scottish Rite of Freemasonry (Annotated Version). Kindle Edition. L 6692

Whether reading from Pike or Alesiter Crowley, this is the type of highfalutin language you have to endure. Basically this describes snake handling as part of a particular ritual. Ophi means being, or resembling a snake. Orphic, however, means having to do with Orpheus, the great musician of Greek mythology.

We must really absorb these next excerpts as we use the descriptions given to us by Albert Pike, the symbolism of the rites and rituals of the Mysteries, as a decoder ring in our present day. Is there something to this whole snake thing, or am I suffering from Ophidiophobia? I kind of like snakes, so if anything it's a healthy Foniasophobia.

"In the Mysteries of the bull-horned Bacchus, the officers held serpents in their hands, raised them above their heads, and cried aloud "Eva!" the generic oriental name of the serpent, and the particular name of the constellation in which the Persians placed Eve and the serpent...

...The mystic winnowing-fan, encircled by Serpents, was used in the feasts of Bacchus. In the Isiac Mysteries a basilisc twined round the handle of the mystic vase. The Ophites fed a serpent in a mysterious ark, from which they took him when they celebrated the Mysteries, and allowed him to glide among the sacred bread. The Romans kept serpents in the Temples of Bona Dea and Æsculapius. In the Mysteries of Apollo, the pursuit of Latona by the serpent Python was represented. In the Egyptian Mysteries, the dragon **Typhon** *pursued Isis...*

...The Egyptian Priests fed the sacred serpents in the temple at Thebes...

...The Phœnicians called the serpent Agathodemon [the good spirit]; and Kneph was the Serpent-God of the Egyptians...

...In the hieroglyphic characters, a snake was the letter T or DJ. It occurs many times on the Rosetta stone. The horned serpent was the hieroglyphic for a God...

...According to Eusebius, the Egyptians represented the world by a blue circle, sprinkled with flames, within which was extended a serpent with the head of a hawk. Proclus says they represented the four quarters of the world by a cross, and the soul of the world, or Kneph, by a serpent surrounding it in the form of a circle...

...The Egyptian Goddess Ken, represented standing naked on a lion, held two serpents in her hand. She is the same as the Astarte or Ashtaroth of the Assyrians. Hera, worshipped in the Great Temple at Babylon, held in her right hand a serpent by the head; and near Khea, also worshipped there, were two large silver serpents...

...The serpent of the Temple of Epidaurus was sacred to Æsculapius, the God of Medicine, and 462 years after the building of the city, was taken to Rome after a pestilence...

...The Phœnicians represented the God Nomu (Kneph or Amun-Kneph) by a serpent...

...Python, the Serpent Deity, was esteemed oracular; and the tripod at Delphi was a triple-headed serpent of gold...

...The portals of all the Egyptian Temples are decorated with the hierogram of the Circle and the Serpent...

*...The Mexican hierogram was formed by the intersecting of two great Serpents, which described the circle with their bodies, and had each a **human head** in its mouth. All the Buddhists crosses in Ireland had serpents carved upon them...*

...Wreaths of snakes are on the columns of the ancient Hindu Temple at Burwah-Sangor. Among the Egyptians, it was a symbol of Divine Wisdom, when extended at length; and, with its tail in its mouth, of Eternity. In the ritual of Zoroaster, the Serpent was a symbol of the Universe. In China, the ring between two Serpents was the symbol of the world governed by the power and wisdom of the Creator...

...The Persian Ahriman was called "The old serpent, the liar from the beginning, the Prince of Darkness, and the rover up and down..."

*...**Ophi**oneus, in the old Greek Theology, warred against Kronos, and was overcome and cast into his proper element, the sea. There he is installed as the Sea-God Oannes or Dragon, the Leviathan of the watery, half of creation, the dragon...*

This goes on for a lot longer, and there's a lot I skipped over, but the message is clear. Serpents, snakes, dragons, whatever you wish to call them, are of great significance to the Mystery Religions and their Mystery Schools. That last one, Oannes, do you recall him? Although he appears to be a jerk to the gods, he's the one talked about by the Priest of Bel Marduk, Berossus. Oannes came ashore and taught the people a great many useful things and would retire back to the sea each night, never taking any food while he was ashore. There's something about these fish-people. Forget about ancient astronauts. We need to explore Ancient SCUBA-naut possibilities, and Innerterrestrials, underground rather than "extra." There's a firmament, so… The only way anything would be coming in would be through some sort of plasma energy portal, a magnetic null point, and from where exactly are they coming? Do we not all just live in a Yellow Submarine called Earth, and the waters from the heavens, are they not just on the other side of our snow globe we call a firmament? Maybe. It's tough to believe anything the mainstream academia nuts tell us, so speculation is always fun. My ideas of this water above as below isn't directly biblical. It's based on work done by many over the years, collected and presented well by Michael Tellinger. It's also reference to a collection of admissions from the Babylonian Space Cult masquerading as "NASA." If you don't know who John Whiteside Parsons of Jet Propulsions Laboratory & AEC was, you will. One may fancy themselves a dog-lover, but I doubt they'd go as far as Jack did with it.

This Æsculapius-snake relation to even modern medicine needs to be examined. Between the adepts of all these mystery schools that Pike discussed, there's a definite, recognized, and powerful meaning in snake symbolism.

Jumping back into Michael W. Ford's ***MASKIM HUL: Babylonian Magic***, we read beginning on page 191:

"The Tree of Life to the Sumerian mythos was a bright star in the heavens, if originated as the Eastern or rising star it would be easy to associate Dumuzi and Gizzida as the Morning Star, thus a primal manifestation of the deific mask of the later visualized Lucifer of the Greeks.

Ningishzida is depicted as two coiled serpents, akin to the later Caduceus and also as a dragon with two coiled basmu."

Terms: Dimuzi, or Tammuz, was the first consort of Inanna, and seen as the shepherd god. Ningishzida, son of Ninazu, was associated with serpents and said to spend half the year in the underworld, much like Dimuzi. A **basmu** is an ancient "mythological" horned snake with forelegs (hind legs) and wings. It was, according to the sorcerers of Wikipedia, the Akkadian name for a Babylonian constellation associated with the Greek Hydra. We continue:

"Ningishzida also represents the wisdom of the hidden [Occult Mysteries], *the place of the underworld and is associated with the "Azul'ucel"-Holy Guardian Angel-Daimon which the Chaldeans called 'Personal God...'*

Ningishzida is the son of Ninazu (the Lord of Serpents) and Ningurda (who is a variant of Ereshkigal). Ningishzida is consistently the throne-bearer of Ereshkigal in many hymns and tales. In short, the serpent-god works with the desires of Ereshkigal and conducts workings for her not only in the underworld, but also on earth."

Terms: Ereshkigal is the goddess of the Underworld, said to be the older sister to Inanna. Her name translates to "Queen of the Great Below" *Ereshkigal is always represented in prayers and rituals as a formidable goddess of great power but often in stories as one who forgives an injustice or a wrong in the interests of the greater good.*

In this role, she encouraged piety in the people who should follow her example in their own lives. If Ereshkigal could suffer injustice and continue to perform her tasks in accordance with the will of the gods, then human beings should do no less. Her further significance was as the ruler of the underworld by which she was understood to reward the good and punish the evil, of course, but more importantly to keep the dead in the realm where they belonged. The seven gates of the underworld were constructed both to keep the living out and to keep everyone who belonged there in.
-worldhistory.org/Ereshkigal

Ereshkigal stood against the forces of chaos. If a soul slipped out to roam the earth, you can bet it was on special permission of Ereshkigal.

Going back to Michael W. Ford's MASKIM HUL.. :

"As a healing god, Ningishzida is symbolized as the crowned serpent, the wise one who brings fertility of the mind and body.
Ningishzida is also able to ravage the land with plague and fever as well, much like Pazuzu. His manifestations are varied, yet usually always appearing as a serpent in some way.

However, the God of War, Plague, and the Underworld who later resides with Ereshkigal for half the year, is Nergal. Probably because he gave the curator of the dead so much business.

Ningishzida Caduceus guarded by Mushussu Dragons

Irkalla is the name of the Babylonian Underworld, and is the home of many demons, monsters, and many take the form of serpents and dragons. They will at times feed on the "etheric substance" of mankind, which is best put as high intensity emotion such as fear and anxiety. They can also cause sickness and death by poison and plague. The Brotherhood of Death assumes this role, and may invoke these ancient demons in magical workings as helper agents in their eugenic culling agendas.

Pazuzu statue from the film, *The Exorcist* (1973) Notice the Snake coiled around the leg, and the erect member.

Another rendition of Pazuzu from the Pazuzu blog shows his member as the snake itself. Here he also has a scorpion tail. The venoms of both snakes and scorpions are widely used in toxic/poisonous pharmaceuticals, vaccines, (See Celtic Biotech) and crop insecticides/pesticides, including, but not limited by any means to Round-Up, which also contains glyphosate. The sex organ being the administrator of venomous poison is not unlike that of the single-fang, or syringe.

Clinton's Arkansas. Enough said.

The Baphomet child-predator here with the erect penis in the form of the Caduceus, or as some may describe it, the Allopathic Medical symbol. So either the semen of the wicked one has healing powers, like we probably have told a girl or two ourselves pertaining to our own, or they're plainly telling you they're injecting an evil seed into you and your children. The fact that he-she is erect in the presence of two children should tell you something else about Baphomet, and those who would identify with its symbol. Being that the Rod of Aesculapius had but one serpent, or snake, I believe what is actually being depicted here is the Staff of Hermes, the Trickster, and god of merchants and thieves. Mercury serves the same role as Hermes, and the Mercury aspect ties into alchemy as does Hermes. Some may argue the staff is Mercury's if you don't know the two deities are filling the same position. I would go so far as to say they are attributable to Loki, the mischievous trickster. In some of the tales, Loki got his kicks from deceiving people into murdering their own children... Maybe reconsider the vaccine schedule, and protect your children from it at all costs.

From my research, having been inspired and spurred on by my many talks with Dr Bryan Ardis, DC, I have found animal toxins as the model, or a synthesized version thereof, in multiple drugs used on the American public, and the world. The ones with the greatest death tolls have been fashioned from venoms, such as AZT, the true killer of people told they have HIV/AIDS. That drug was made from replicating a shallow sea sponge cytotoxin. Cytotoxin can be thought of simply as "Cell Death." It's not specific. It doesn't choose what to kill. It kills, period. There is an unbroken chain from ancient times to present of the use of snake venom and other poisonous animal venoms by the sorcerer-priests and what we now call in the nautical terms,"doctors." You're the vessel being docked, get it? They are docking you, so they're the doctors. Mooring lines tie a vessel to a pier just as restraints tie a patient to a gurney, and bed. We will cover unam sanctam in full, later. As far as the snake and the inference of poisonous venom, it's in their symbolism even to this day. The allopaths tucked in their dark robes, threw on a white coat and stethoscope, and everyone dropped right back on their knees to worship their mystic "superiority." They're the same snake-oil salesmen and trickster sorcerers from ancient times, still in covens of exclusivity, indoctrinated into one-mind thinking.

There is a place for God in actual science. The fact that so-called scientists and doctors reject God shows their science is a fraud. Their approach is atheistic, and assumes that life is an accident waiting to fall apart. They put man in the role of God and offer a trickster's solution. In a way they are assisting God, for they can only harm those who turn their back on nature and God in favor of the assumed knowledge of Man. They, inadvertently then are helping to expose the weak and defiant among us. Natural medicine follows natural law. Allopathic medicine defies natural law, and natural order with a blind, distasteful arrogance. You can't treat a natural being with artificial methods and expect anything but disaster. When in some miracle, the individual survives the best efforts of the doctors and hospitals, they should chalk it up to the strength of their own spirit body. They became well in-spite of, rather than because of the best efforts of the white-coated Priestcraft.

"Certainly anyone who has the power to make you believe absurdities has the power to make you commit injustices. If you do not use the intelligence with which God endowed your mind to resist believing impossibilities, you will not be able to use the sense of injustice which God planted in your heart to resist a command to do evil."
— Voltaire

Rather than see that we are being poisoned by a deliberately contaminated environment, by our food, water, air, and MEDICAL "CARE," we allow ourselves to be fooled by a germ theory, and virus Lie. Instead of considering our own life habits, or compulsory immunizations as the source of ailment, we accept this idea that there's invisible unicorns spread from person-to-person. We lose all ability to reason. Fearful, we ask the same ones responsible for our illness for the cure. It's a self-feeding system. We go to an MD who prescribes additional poisons or procedures that create new issues, adding to our decline. Then we end up going back to the MDs asking them to fix those new problems we don't realize they caused. Blind trust in an industry, the assumption that they have a code of ethics, or that they even know what they are doing, allows iatragenesis to be the True leading cause of death in this country and the world.

Are We Getting The Picture? Magick

1

You're probably asking yourself, "What have we actually learned about the Mystery Schools? What's so secret about their secret knowledge? What are they doing in those lodges, and temples through the ages?"

Gay stuff. And magic. And magical sodomy. There. Mystery solved. Happy? "What the hell, Daniel?"

That's actually quite accurate, in that there is more going on, but there is definitely a lot of ceremonial sodomy. Ask anyone signed to a record deal what they had to do to get the contract. Just as the cults of Canaan described earlier that sacrificed children, and had orgies out in the open to please their fertility god, Ba'al, similar acts were done in secrecy, in underground caverns, catacombs, caves, lodges, and in the chambers surrounding the pyramids.

There are different categories of magic(k). Crowley added the "k" to distinguish it from illusion, and slight-of-hand. There's **Ceremonial Magic**, considered "high magic" which involves intense study, preparation, adherence to strict tradition, accuracy, and intricate rituals, often with many steps. They're like the Kata of magical acts. Have you ever taken martial arts, and had to learn a kata? They're choreographed multi-step movements sometimes called a "form." As a student you learn more and more intricate katas, with more movements to memorize for each rank. Typically you must prove mastery of the kata of your rank to advance to the next rank. Ceremonial high magic is done with spiritual purpose rather than a practical one. Again, similar to the kata, which is more about memorization, concentration, and balance than it would be for practical self-defense. A great example of elaborate ceremonial magic is from the Golden Dawn. Co-founder Samuel Liddell MacGregor Mathers was into elaborate costumes, drawn-out ceremonies, and flamboyance. He liked a big spectacle. Incidentally, he also feuded with the scoundrel Aleister Crowley for many years after Crowley was entrusted with MacGregor's grimoire, his life-work, and Crowley stole it, and published it!

Folk magic, or low-magic, may be viewed as the peasantry's defensive magic. Healing, protection, etc. would be encompassed by this type of practice. Folk magic is simple in nature with a practical purpose. This may be seen as old country magic, as gypsy magic, when not done with ill intent, or the quiet coven of white magic practitioners in a village. Herbs, stones, and amulets may be implemented. You may have a grandmother or great grandmother who practices Stregheria, an Italian form of "witchcraft" rooted in folk magic, and having little resemblance to any other form of magic with that moniker. The sense I get from Stregheria, and folk magic in general, is that it isn't a disciplined study. It isn't something you'd practice 10,000 hours like playing the piano or guitar. It's more like a utensil or a tool hanging on the wall that you take down when needed, and hang back up when you're finished. The application of folk magic seems to almost solely be for the benefit of others, or a family member. If you were a practitioner, and you fell ill, it would likely be others in your village that would come lay hands on you and meditate, rather than you being able to self-heal. This form of magic was as common as farming to ancient cultures, and it made the people who practiced it prime targets for the clever deceivers we termed the Priestcraft. The people knew prayer or magic did have power, so they were susceptible to the mystical snake oil salesman.

Witchcraft as a term, is a murky one. Too often the benign, white folk magic gets lumped into this term which owes more to darker influences. When we discuss witchcraft in this book, it will be interchangeable with sorcery; imposing one's will onto others, concocting poisons, potions with ill intent, manipulating emotional and physical wellness, and causing direct harm to others. It could also be a craft that appears to do good, but at the expense of a favor to some dark force. A contract with evil to get something seemingly good typically has a stipulation, a small print detail that trips up a person in fables, and fairy tales. To the question "What goes on in the Mystery Schools," it would depend on the degree and what they're allowed to be exposed to. In the upper rank and file, you're talking anything from primitive, but effective voodoo to some of the darkest, cruelest sacrificial sorcery you can barely imagine. These human conduits for dimensional beings, energies, archetypes, and demons, are but a tool of their own making. Self-serving desire has given way transitionally to serving the desires of the dark ones. We will discuss one of the most notorious modern sorcerers, Aleister Crowley, if only in brief overview. He is a topic for a whole volume of books, and honestly, I don't wish to pay him that honor. To discuss, to think of, is to summon. Even the most level headed, logical thinker, Ken Wheeler, has recently said this in a video on his Theoria Apophasis YouTube channel. You can't play in mud and not get dirty. You get it in the fibers of your clothing. You take it home with you.

I came across something extremely deceptive when I was researching these next two terms. **Right-hand path**, and **Left-hand path**...

*"...the **right-hand path** can be thought of as one of dogma, ritual, and a belief in the community and formal structure as well as a higher power. Though each of those can also be found in left-hand path religions, there is less focus on indulging the self in the right-hand path..."* -learnreligions.com/left-hand-and-right-hand-paths-95827

So far so good. But this is the first source I came across:

*"The Right Hand Path is the orthodox path; the Left Hand Path is the heterodox path. The Right Hand Path is **typically collectivist** in nature, while the Left Hand Path strongly emphasizes more individualist approaches. One is order, one is disorder. One leads to unity; the other to disunity. One should note that both paths lead to the same place — enlightenment...*

*Of course, with Christianity, the way up and the way down are not the same. The way up leads to Heaven; the way down leads to Hell. The Right Way leads to virtue and God; the Left (Sinister) Way leads to vice and Satan. If the **right is collectivist** and the **left is individualist**, that means <u>collectivism</u> is good and <u>individualism</u> is evil. There is one way to salvation; you cannot get there by your own way. This is then a deeply Christian division."*

-medium.com/complexity-liberalism/the-right-hand-path-and-the-left-hand-path-and-the-middle-way

Stop the friggin' presses, right now. Caring for others is NOT collectivist, it's compassion. The Left-hand path isn't some kind of liberating individualism, it's excessive indulgence in **selfishness** to the point of harming others for personal pleasure and gain. You can't replace utter selfishness and indifference to the suffering you cause others with "individualism." That's deceptive, and it's detached, inhuman insanity. They make it seem to be about personal freedom, but they think releasing themselves from moral and ethical responsibility to others is what freedom is. Basically indifference or pleasure in the pain of others is liberation, is this web article author's "individualism." I'll tell you what was really expressed here. This is the inversion. This is Sabbatean-Frankist philosophy of the doctrine of inversion, or Jacob Frank's specific call to undo commandments through violation. and to commit every conceivable taboo. This included eating the flesh and drinking the blood of a child, infidelity, orgies, homosexual acts, the raping of children of both sexes, incest, torture, sacrifice, and drug use. Jacob Frank may have been a big influence on Crowley given the similarities in philosophy. Some of these Left-hand path practitioners don't stop at ritual sex magic between consenting adults. There isn't enough so-called magical energy in that. They're pushing the boundaries, and they can't help themselves.

Collectivist schemes are Communist-Socialist, or Marxist schemes concocted by enemies of mankind. The Bolsheviks deliberately starved tens of millions of people to death in two separate famines with collectivist/collectivization schemes. To label someone who is empathetic to the feeling of others and tries to cause them no harm as a collectivist is completely upside-down and backward. That's extremely alarming that someone could make a statement so opposite to reality, and to the definition of words. If someone made this statement to me in-person about the left-hand path being individualism, which is a euphemism for Satanic as hell, I might just hammer a stake in their chest or impale them in an effort to prevent them from finding victims. If they protest, I could just say, "hey, you follow 'Do what thou Wilt,' and that's dependent on the law of nature, the strongest survive. This is my will." That's what happens when they meet someone whose will is to harm them in their system. I don't typically carry large pieces of wood around with me, so the staking and impaling would probably be less likely than me just knocking them out with fists or a fart. Cause no harm, or Do what thou wilt, until only maniacs like Ashurnasirpal II are left standing? They don't get it. That Crowley philosophy wasn't setting them free of their morality. It was setting them into the wild with a bunch of stronger, savage animals who will devour them if they are of the same philosophy as them. Crowley even said might makes right, in so many words. Cowardly, despicable, perverse child harmers took that to mean they had license to prey on children because they're bigger and stronger. Crowley also felt children should witness all forms of sexual acts at a young age. These pieces of shit enrage me. Since when do we call a sick pedophile a MAP, anyway? We should have a MAP of their locations. That would be a good community building exercise all the parents in a town could take part in. MAP could then mean we splatter them all over the map. I have a strong reaction against evil. If you do not, check your pulse, and find out why the hell you don't.

I basically explained the left-hand path via comparison. It's the selfish, or self-indulgent path.

"One very large limitation of this terminology is that it is primarily used by followers of the left-hand path. Satanists commonly describe their path as that of the left-hand. However, Christians, Jews, Wiccans, Druids, and the like do not identify themselves as being of the right-hand path. As such, definitions of the right-hand path tend to be phrased in fairly derogatory terms...
...In addition, many people described as being of the right-hand path would disagree to varying degrees with the definitions commonly given."

-learnreligions.com/left-hand-and-right-hand-paths

Yeah, you really shouldn't let snide Satanists handle definitions of terms that describe those of different philosophies. It might not be the most brilliant of task assignments. Go figure.

I once received a comment on one of my YouTube videos from the now deleted channel that said, "No wonder satanists hate you." I think they meant that as an insult. I didn't take it that way, because last time I checked I wasn't trying to win anyone's admiration, least of all Satanists. My apologies to all those Satanists with hearts of gold out there… While I'm at it I may as well acknowledge all the tall pigmies, and hot-climate Eskimos, too.

The difference in the terms **Black** and **White magic** usually have to do with intent. Intending to do good, or to do harm, to serve others, or serve yourself above whom you're directing your efforts on are determining factors as to what kind of magic is being practiced. Black would be considered the more sinister, and the white the more helpful. Another way of putting it is Black magic is predatory in nature, even if righting a wrong. It's still Black or sorcery when causing justified harm, because it's invoking dark forces to do it. If you're asking dark forces to do something, and you're attempting to hold them at bay, and put the genie back in the bottle when finished, you're practicing black magic. When they ask you for a give and take and the cost of their services is blood, chances are you're not invoking the benevolent spirit of Mr. Rogers.

Now for the one the dirty little weirdos have been waiting for, **Sex Magic**. Remember the Red Hot Chili Peppers song and album of the same name, *Blood Sugar Sex Magik?* That's a strange grocery shopping list. It's a pretty crappy album as well when I looked back at it. The blood sugar part makes it sound like a diabetic looking for a miracle boner when grouped with "Sex Magik." At their ages now, that's probably accurate. Anthony "Diabetes" Kiedis [if you say it like Wilford Brimley it rhymes] aside, let's get Ba'als deep into this topic.

Astonishingly, some pretentious, emasculated shithole of a publication called Teen Vogue was addressing the topic of sex magic. I felt compelled by absurdity-magic [is that a real thing?] to share it with you. Their resident witch, and chronic masturbator, Lisa "Stardust" had this to say:

"...Did you know that orgasms can help manifest desires and bring forth dreams?
...In magic, orgasms are considered to be the ultimate magical force. In fact, occultists believe that orgasms can help cleanse the body, produce magical power, and are a vital tool in manifesting desires...
...You can attempt to cast any spell you want using sex magic, but, the first thing to remember is that magic works best when done on yourself. Using magic on others is a dangerous game — it can have unpredictable results and shouldn't be done because it's attempting to manipulate another's will. Practicing magic on others can work against you in the end. That's why the kind of sex we're trying to make magical here is the kind you have with yourself!"

"the kind you have with yourself" is hyperlinked to another multi-topic page teaching your teens how to masturbate, and one of the images is a cartoon female Baphomet at a school dance that is supposed to be seen as sexy.

Under the headers, "Techniques for Sex Magic: Art of Visualization we read this:

*"Now that you have set your intention, it's time to meditate on it through the act of visualization. Since we're focusing on magic for yourselves, let's also focus on self-pleasure. When you start to masturbate, Kristen Sollee, author of **Witches, Sluts, Feminists: Conjuring the Self Positive** suggests tuning "into the goal you have in mind and channel all of the electric energy of your orgasm into that visualization." This will allow your energy to mystically connect with your intention and give it power, potentially enabling it to come true."*

If a book called *"Witches, Sluts, Feminists: Conjuring the Self Positive"* gets published, then my book had damn well better. This is our world. The Sabbatean-Frankist-Marxist-Bolsheviks have given platform and promotion to complete and total idiots in a successful effort to discourage and destroy society. Bravo, scumbags. From the same article:

*"A **radical** approach of incorporating the lunar vibrations into your sex magic manifestation is to charge your sex toys under the moon."*

It makes for peculiar lawn decorations, but if they say so. Is that what that book, *Rules for Radicals* is about? Lunar dildo charging instructions? In magic, mockery and ridicule are energy-sapping. It takes the gale from their demonic sail, their phoenix-bird will have no wind beneath its wings, their rainbow flag will hang limp. That's why they call it hate speech when you criticize their blatant and numerous mental illness manifestations. They're energizing a public ritual. You mustn't get manipulated into feeding it with fear, or even with anger. Those reactions are exactly what they need to charge their working. Plus these weasels love attention and can't stand being ignored or belittled. It's not to make light of it. Not taking what's happening seriously is a sure ticket to a mass grave party as the guests of honor. But don't feed it, either. Starve it.

One last reminder, this was on Teen Vogue's website… This is youth-targeted perversion.

Sex Magic isn't just self-pleasure oriented as Ziggy, I mean Lisa Stardust suggested. However, there is a coffin-confessional ritual said to be conducted as part of the Skull & Bones initiation. The details vary, but some accounts say the initiates are lying naked in the coffin divulging all their sexual experiences to a bunch of other guys, and some accounts say they're required to masturbate in the coffin. In another variation of the story there's a red ribbon tied around their genitalia.

If the latter detail is truly an element, it may give some insight into the rash of forced "suicides" involving a red scarf some years back. It could be a signature, or calling card for those in-the-know. Like a warning to others with a crisis of conscience to keep their mouths shut. Red is, after all, the color associated with communism, perhaps with roots dating back to Ignacius of Loyola and the Jesuits, or perhaps much further back. The Skull & Bones have a counterpart in Harvard known as the Scroll & Key. Collectively they're known as the Brotherhood of Death, death bringers bound by death oaths.

These secret societies, bound by said death oath, are what birthed the structure of the Sicilian mafia under the guidance of Guiseppe Mazzini, a Freemason and correspondent to Albert Pike. The word MAFIA itself is a 13th century acronym for Morte Alla Francio Italia Anela, meaning "Death to the French is Italy's cry!" My Siciliano ancestors were outraged by the presence of the marauding French, and on Easter Sunday of 1282, they killed every Frenchman that didn't flee for their lives from the Island of Sicily. In 1860, Mazzini altered the words, but kept the acronym. He organized people under "Mazzini autoriza furti, incendi, avelenamenti," which means,

Mazzini Authorizes Theft, Arson, and Poisoning. If you have a look at the Jesuit oath, you will find similar methods implemented against their enemies.

Resource: mtcarmelstcristina.org/did-you-know/the-roots-of-the-mafia/

The channeling of energy from intercourse and orgasm toward a specific purpose is sex magick. It can also be an inner magick for obtaining higher insight, wisdom, and magical energy when it's transmuted, or not spilled (not spilling the cup of Hermes) such as with Tantric sex. When listening to Robert Sepehr, the anthropologist, you hear the term, "tiny death," referring to the orgasm. It's meant to imply the depletion of energy, and magical ability due to the inability to hold it in and therefore failing to energize the self, or "transmute" it. The tantric practice, along with self practice, are ways of getting oneself to the point of climax, and then using the willpower to hold it in, transmute it, and then working back to that edge of climax again, and repeating the process of abstaining from orgasm multiple times. Some practice tantra for hours, and days. Hey, why cut the good times, short?

During Sex Magick rituals, the orgasm is desired to energize a component of the ritual, to effect the desired outcome. These rituals can span from the solitary, to the consensual sex between two or multiple people in an orgiastic manner, to very dark, brutal sex acts that are sometimes still consensual, but often are not. The darker sex magic involves a victim or victims, and can involve torture, bondage, shaming, brutal rape, gang rape, and potentially murder as part of the completed ritual. The practitioners of this form do this to the same sex, the opposite sex, to children, infants, and/or animals. In the case of Jack Parsons, let's just say he really loved his mom, and his dog.

"The most important magical project of Jack's life was the Babalon working. This involved him and L. Rob Hubbard, founder of Scientology and all-round piece of shit, going into the desert and jerking each other off with the aim of summoning the Whore of Babalon (a deliberate misspelling of Babylon) to bring about the apocalypse. After finishing the lengthy ritual in 1946, Jack believed that he and Hubbard had achieved their aim. Pendle notes that "He [Parsons] believed that Babalon, in the manner of the Immaculate Conception, was due to be born to a woman somewhere on earth in nine months time." If Jack was right, this means that the Whore of Babalon would have been born in 1947. Think of the most powerful women in the world and then guess which one was born in 1947. That's right, good ol' Hillary!
Obviously, I don't believe that Hillary Clinton is the Whore of Babylon, but it turns out that I'm not the only one to have noticed the coincidence. There's

already several loopy videos and blogposts claiming that she is the Moonchild of Jack Parsons."

-nocturnalrevelries.com/2018/05/27/the-peculiar-tale-of-jack-parsons/

First off, there's no such thing as a deliberate mistake, so it's not a "misspelling" of Babylon, but an alternate spelling. L. Ron Hubbard was Naval Intelligence, and not just anyone gets into Naval Intelligence, as Bill Cooper has taught us in **Behold a Pale Horse**, and on his 9-year running radio broadcast. You're normally only selected if you're already a current, or past member of a fraternal order such as the Freemasons, their offshoots, or a member of the Mormon Church. Hubbard was also a "Special Police Officer" from 1947-1948 in Los Angeles. This time seems to overlap when he was assisting Parsons in the ritual to bring about the whore of Babalon and the Moon Child. The most evil man in the world, self-proclaimed, and the Therion (Beast) Aleister Crowley warned Jack Parsons about Hubbard. He said he was an untrustworthy scoundrel. And that's him saying that! When the world's most despicable, sinister being is appalled by someone else, that's really saying something.
On May 22 (?) Crowley wired "Suspect Ron playing confidence trick–John Parsons weak fool–obvious victim–prowling swindlers."

This was related to Jack being robbed of $10,000 by L. Ron & his stolen girlfriend, Sara (Betty.) Jack had already taken over the Thelemite OTO Agape (Love) Lodge in California at Crowley's request in 1942. He was being prepared to be Crowley's successor. Thelema is politely called polyamorous, but it's more plainly stated as being founded on ritual Sex Magick.

Another misstatement above is that crudely written line alleging the two were tugging each other's 14th part of Osiris in the desert. That's not exactly how the written account of Parsons himself put it. He was the conductor, and Hubbard was basically the scribe. That's not to say there wasn't an ingredient of sodomy in this Babalon Working, or in his other sex magic rituals, but I just think it's speculative in this particular instance to say they were cleaning each other's guns for this *working,* or multi-phase, multi-step magical act.

Sex and sacrifice are powerful tools of the dark practitioner. This should give some insight into what goes on in the mystery schools from then to now. Sex magick can also be used by healthy adults with no ill will toward anyone. The actions leading to sex itself are inherently a mating *ritual.*

Examples of sects practicing Sex Magic are fertility cults as we first covered, Thelema, and the OTO (Ordo Templi Orientis). Luciferian would tend to mix left-hand, chaos, and sex magic in practice, and really these degrees of separation between the supposed 'types' of magick are terms more utilized by the outsider looking in, for the benefit of their own comprehension. A practitioner doesn't say, "OK, I'm practicing sex magic now… Now I'm practicing Black magic…" They just go about their ritual.

Chaos magic(k) has elements of, and can be categorized as some of the aforementioned types of magick. It can involve sex magic, and often does. It can be categorized as Black magick, and witchcraft, and often is. It would certainly be considered that of the left-hand path. Or maybe even a, "Look mom, no-hand" path.

"According to chaos magick, successfully executing an act of magic is dependent on bypassing the conscious mind. To achieve this, it is necessary to enter into an altered state of consciousness in which thoughts are stilled, and awareness is held on a single point. Only then will the ritual, sigil or working flow unimpeded into the unconscious, from where it works its effects...

...Aleister Crowley had also argued that the key to magic was an altered state of consciousness, whether attained through meditation, sexual practices, or the use of drugs. However, the real breakthrough of the early chaos magicians was the realization that there are many states of exhaustion, arousal or inhibition that cause consciousness to briefly "blink", sidestepping the need for years of meditative attainment."
-en.wikipedia.org/wiki/Gnosis_(chaos_magic)

Austin Osman Spare and Peter Carroll are notable names attached with this concept of Chaos Magick. There, I noted them. Inhibitory gnosis utilizes deep meditation to reach a trance state. Ecstatic gnosis is mindlessness through sensory overload, intense sexual arousal, drumming, chanting, self-induced hyperventilation, aphrodisiacs, and hallucinogens. This to me sounds like the most primitive form of tribal dance and orgiastic ritual where the participants may be carried away by the beat, the frenzied energy of the ceremony, lose hold of their sensibilities and be compelled by the state of consciousness to even pass their own children to a furnace god for sacrifice. Indifferent vacuity is another form of mindlessness that's vague in explanation.

What does all this mean, and why is it important? It's at the heart of the unseen motivations of powerful people and the groups they're affiliated with. The occult, which means hidden, remains hidden because we don't recognize their signatures, signs, symbols, and sigils. There are very dangerous people in our world, and we have sat back and allowed them to take hold of key positions in schools, police stations, and local politics. They have created numerous agencies, assumed powers that were never given, and took charge of aspects of our lives that are no business or concern of these false authorities. The unelected, unconstitutional agencies, with their many ranks and divisions are a weaponized army against the American people, and the people of the world. We seem to have lapsed into a vegetative, reflexive passivity, or suffer from a fear driven quieting of our tongues. We are manipulated on a constant, daily basis by an onslaught of psychological ploys that give us pause, and instill a hollow sense of hopelessness and defeat into our subconscious. Electromagnetic suppression and manipulation can also effect us both physically, and mentally. There's more dishes, transmitters, cell towers, and DEW weapons we think are just satellites (Starlink may be one such network, for example) than ever before bombarding us with constant radiation, frequencies, and pulses. We don't even know what normal is anymore. No one living now has been alive prior to the telegraph, or radio. These frequencies and radiation from modern emitters, and receiving devices, can cause anxiety, discouragement, anger, rage, terror, and when directed, debilitating and even a deadly impact on our biological makeup. In addition to that, the amount of toxic food additives and pharmaceutical poisons we're subjected to cause a slumped, apathetic, and emasculated state within us, weakening our motivation through hormone destruction, and causing malaise and fatigue to replace virility and confidence. We are under attack. We are at war! These are just a few of the many silent weapons in that war.

In addition, these self-appointed judges and overlords, members of these ancient schools, are summonsing and conjuring demon archetypes to assist them in murdering mankind, and bringing back a Babylonian Gold Era that never truly existed. They resent us because they must exist and practice in secrecy. That may be less true at present than even 100 years ago. After the two World Wars, it appeared the beginning of the end was initiated, kicked-off, so to speak. These dark practitioners, these sodomites, child rapists, and murderers are flooding our realm with the demons of Assyrian Babylon. Most of the drones that prop up their system can't rub two brain cells together to make a spark, and they all seem to land government positions whether at the DMV, a citiy's department of Health, CPS, police, etc. The process is two-stage. Stage 1: use popular culture and brain & hormone damaging chemicals to create the vacant and detached shell-human.   Stage 2: implement a psychological evaluation in the application process to identify these programmable shell-humans when said apply for government work. I guess a stage 3 could be "Create the artificial concept of 'Over-Qualified' to make the superior candidate feel better about being rejected for the monkey-work."

I don't want to entangle the psyche of the reader anymore than I want to my own with too dangerous a description of spells for conjuring and binding. We may discuss powers and principalities, but we want to do so without arousing their attention.

MASONIC INITIATION: the Entered Apprentice

Beginning lightly with the initiation of the three degrees of Blue Lodge Freemasonry we can begin to form a picture of the pantomime and play-acting of a type of ritual. These are of a more traditional and symbolic nature than they are of magic. There are no invocations or, at least no discernible ones within these ceremonial reenactments. Learning of the processes which a Mason goes through helps to dispel (totally organic pun) the tendency to have your imagination run wild with rumors and slanderous disinformation. In the Scottish Rite of Freemasonry you have the notorious 33 degrees that buzz about in the truth channel rumor mills. Thirty of the thirty-three are not of a successive, higher ranking, but of a lateral nature, not superior or inferior to the others. In reality then, there still is only 3 ranked degrees of hierarchy to both the Blue

Lodge, and the Scottish Rite, and then you have additional honorary designations, and possibly secretive degrees thereafter.

I was able to find the account of a one William Morgan who served in the War of 1812, but whether he was a captain or not as he had claimed, records seem inconclusive. Morgan had a falling out with the Freemasons, and warned he would write a book exposing their hand grips, signals, rituals, and secrets. The Batavia, NY Lodge denounced Morgan, and soon Morgan found himself the target of relentless persecution. He was jailed the first time on September 11th, 1826, a day and month that should raise your eyebrow. The one form of magic yet mentioned in these pages is probably the most recognizable to the newly trained eye, and widespread in public ritual and annual ceremonies. **Sympathetic Magic(k)** is the utilization of objects, signs, and/or symbols that characterize a specific event or person over which you are attempting to harness, and direct the energy of. This is a form of hacking the imprint or impact of an event or thing on our reality and consciousness, and exploiting its energetic influence, or sometimes paying homage to it. It could be said to indirectly follow the Homeopathic medicine's model of Like Cures Like, only with sympathetic magic it's Like Produces Like. Morgan was held on allegations of theft on separate occasions, and from jail to carriage, disappeared in 1826. What's interesting is in the same year, only two short months prior, both Thomas Jefferson and John Adams died on July 4th. Two of the key founders of our Constitutional Republic were dead within hours of one another on the most curious of days, the 50 year anniversary of the congressional adoption of the Unanimous Declaration of the Thirteen United States. Was that a statement being made by the recently reinstated Jesuits, perhaps a little sympathetic magic of their own? Morgan's book, *Illustrations of Masonry, By One of the Fraternity Who was Devoted Thirty Years to the Subject,* was published in 1827, after he had already gone missing. This kidnapping and uncertain outcome of Morgan outraged people. An Anti-Masonic movement arose from it, but much like today, how organic of a movement it was is questionable. It may have just been cheapened to a tool used to demonize political opponents, as it was certainly implemented to do. Hegelian controlled opposition?

Transcribed in part, the important details from the website, ***Sacred Texts*** on page sacred-texts.com/mas/dun/dun02.htm tells us that the Master Masons conduct the first part of the meeting after instructing the Tyler to remove those brothers of lesser a degree. The Master Masons then present Due Guard, or the sign of a Master Mason to one another… By the Seventh order of business at the lodge meeting, after all other regular matters are discussed and attended to by the Master Masons, the Worshipful Master (W.M.) says:

"Brethren, if there is no further business before this Lodge of Master Masons, we will proceed to close the same, and open an Entered Apprentices' Lodge, for the purpose of initiation…"

W. M.--*"Brother Senior Warden, are you sure all present are Entered Apprentice Masons?"*

After some formal back & forth between the Senior Warden and the Worshipful Master, repetitive of the procedures of lodge meetings, the Entered Apprentices come to order upon command, and place their hands in the position of *Due Guard* of an Entered Apprentice. Mind you these are all whom have already been initiated to the First Degree assembling to kick off the business of an Entered Apprentice Lodge while the W.M. is closing the "Lodge" of the Master Masons. They refer to the business per degree as separate "lodges," but they are still in the same building, perhaps they may move to another floor or room for an initiation.

When the Master makes the sign, by drawing his hand across his throat, all follow suit; Worshipful then makes one rap with the gavel, Senior Warden one, and the Junior Warden one...

W. M.-- *"I now declare this Lodge of Master Masons closed, and an Entered Apprentice in its stead. Brother Junior Deacon, inform the Tyler; Brother Senior Deacon, attend at the altar* (which is placing both points of the compasses under the square).

Worshipful Master gives one rap, which seats the whole Lodge.

W.M.-- *"Brother Junior Deacon, you will take with you the necessary assistants (the two Stewards), repair to the ante-room, where there is a candidate in waiting* (we'll call him, Mr. Lipshitz), *for the First Degree in Masonry), and, when duly prepared, you will make it known by the usual sign.* (one rap)

...The Junior Deacon and his assistants retire to the ante-room, but before they leave the Lodge-room they step to the altar, and [m]*ake the sign of the First Degree to the Master. It is the duty of the Secretary to go out into the ante-room with them, and before the candidate is required to strip, the Secretary gets his assent* [expression of agreement] *to the following interrogations...*

Secretary-- *"Do you seriously declare, upon your honor, that, unbiassed by friends, and uninfluenced by mercenary motives, you freely and voluntarily offer yourself a candidate for the mysteries of Masonry?"*
Candidate-- *"Yes/I do."*

This is an important element to this, and all initial curiosities that lead a man to a lodge. It is important to the Freemasons that you come of your own free will, and accord. Remember those words, "I come of my own free will, and accord." No one is forcing the candidate. They make them confirm this. What else must you come to of your own free will? What must you "let in" for it to possess, or have power over you? In vampire movies, don't they usually require permission to enter a home, and they can use all forms of trickery and temptation to compel someone in the films. The inferred, or assumed promise of knowledge, stature, and importance once a member are tantalizing drivers of self-deception.

Secretary-- "*Do you seriously declare, upon your honor, that you are prompted to solicit the privileges of Masonry by a favorable opinion of the institution, a desire for knowledge, and a sincere wish of being serviceable to your* **fellow-creatures***?"*

Author's note: Interesting choice of words, there. Not fellow-masons, or fellow-man, but fellow-creatures…

Secretary-- "*Do you seriously declare, upon your honor, that you will con-form to all the ancient established usages of the Order?"*

Author's note: Typically a candidate has absolutely no idea what this means, or how it's applied. They may never learn, either. They're simply agreeing to a verbal, yet very formal contract without much thought for its implications.

The Secretary returns to the Lodge, and reports that the candidate has given his assent to the interrogations. The candidate is now requested to strip. [Dirty old men]

Junior Deacon-- "*Mr. Lipshitz, you will take oft your coat, shoes, and stockings, also your vest and cravat; and now your pantaloons; here is a pair of drawers for you. You will now slip your left arm out of your shirt-sleeve, and put it through the bosom of your shirt, that your arm and breast may be naked."*
　　The Deacon now ties a handkerchief or hoodwink over his eyes, places a slipper on his right foot, and after-wards puts a rope, called a cable-tow, once round his neck, letting it drag behind.

I love the word, pantaloons. If you do nothing else but bring that word back into popular use, you have lived a full and meaningful life. One pantaloon leg is rolled up on the same side as the bare arm. In this setting, I don't think it symbolizes that the candidate has drugs for sale. Sure, in a public park, or college campus, chances are they're open for business.

　　The Junior Deacon now takes the candidate by the arm and leads him forward to the door of the Lodge, and gives three distinct knocks, when the Senior Deacon. on the inside, rises to his feet, makes the sign of an Entered Apprentice to the Master, and says,
Senior Deacon (S.D.)-- "*Worshipful Master, there is an alarm at the inner door of our Lodge. W. M.--You will attend to the alarm, and ascertain the cause."*
(The Deacon repairs to the door, gives three distinct knocks, and then opens it.)
S.D.-- "*Who comes here?"*
J.D.-- *(who always responds for the candidate.)* "*Mr. Richard Marx Lipshitz, who has long been in darkness, and now seeks to be brought to light, and to receive a part in the rights and benefits of this worshipful Lodge, erected to God, and dedicated to the holy*

Sts. John, as all brothers and fellows [whom] *have come before."* Here it said "clone before" instead of "come before," but I, maybe incorrectly, assumed it was the site's auto-correct error.

S. D.-- *"Mr. Lipshitz, is it of your own free-will and accord?"*

Here they reaffirm he has come of his own free will. Remember, 3 times is the law.

Mr. Lipshitz.--*It is.*

S. D.--*Brother Junior Deacon, is he worthy, and well qualified?*

J. D.--*He is.*

S. D.--*Duly and truly prepared?*

J. D.--*He is.*

S. D.--*Of lawful age, and properly vouched for?*

J. D.--*He is.*

S. D.--*By what further right or benefit does he expect to gain admission?*

J. D.--*By being a man, free born, of good repute, and well recommended.*

S. D.--*Is he such?*

J. D.--*He is.*

S. D.--*Since he is in possession of all these necessary qualifications, you will wait with patience until the Worshipful Master is informed of his request, and his answer returned.*

Deacon closes the door and repairs to the altar before the Worshipful Master, raps once on the floor with his rod, which is responded to by the Master with his gavel, when the same thing is passed through with as at the door, and the Master says:

W.M.-- *"Let him enter, and be received in due form."*

The Senior Deacon takes the compasses from off the altar, re-pairs to the door, opens it, and says:

S.D.-- *"Let him enter, and be received in due form."*

Senior Deacon steps back, while the Junior Deacon, with candidate, enters the Lodge, followed by the two Stewards. As they advance they are stopped by the Senior Deacon, who presents one point of the compasses to the candidate's naked left breast, and says:

S.D.-- *"Mr. Lipshitz, on entering this Lodge for the first time, I receive you on the point of a sharp instrument pressing your naked left breast, which is to teach you, as it is a torture to your flesh, so should the recollection of it ever be to your mind and conscience, should you attempt to reveal the secrets of Masonry unlawfully."*

To which he could say, "My Lipshitz are sealed." To which they'd probably say, "Not for long..."

The Junior Deacon now leaves the candidate in the hands of the Senior Deacon, and takes his seat at the right hand of the Senior Warden in the west; while the Senior

Deacon, followed by the two Stewards, proceeds to travel once regularly around the Lodge-room, as follows, viz.: Senior Deacon takes the candidate by the right arm, advances a step or two, when the Master gives one rap with his gavel. (Deacon and candidate stop.)

The circumambulation is what that walkaround is called. This goes on and there's more little pauses and redirections of the candidate before he reaches:

Conductor (S. D.)-- *"Mr. Richard Marx Lipshitz, who has long been in darkness, and now seeks to be brought to light, and to receive a part in the rights and benefits of this Worshipful Lodge, erected to God, and dedicated to the holy St. John, as all brothers and fellows have done before."*
 J. W.-- *"Mr. Lipshitz, is it of your own free will and accord?"*
Mr. Lipshitz-- *"It is."*

Third confirmation. Three times is the Law. He stated it was of his own free will that he has come, and given himself and his fate over to the Lodge. Another round of "is he worthy" and some more hooplah and repetition occurs. He is told by the Worshipful Master that he will study with the Senior Warden, and face the East, the place of the light… Then after more ceremonial macarena, the W.M. makes him kneel on his bare knee.

W.M-- *"Mr. Lipshitz, before you can be permitted to advance any farther in Masonry, it becomes my duty to inform you, that you must take upon yourself a solemn oath or obligation, appertaining to this degree, which I, as Master of this Lodge, assure you will not materially interfere with the duty that you owe to your God, yourself, family, country, or neighbor. Are you willing to take such an oath?"*

Yeah, not materially. Just your immaterial soul. No big deal.

OBLIGATION.

"I, Richard Marx Lipshitz, of my own free will and accord, in the presence of Almighty God, and this Worshipful Lodge, erected to Him, and dedicated to the holy Sts. John, do hereby and hereon (Master presses his gavel on candidate's knuckles) most solemnly and sincerely promise and swear, that I will always hail, ever conceal, and never reveal, any of the arts, parts, or points of the hidden mysteries of Ancient Free Masonry, which may have been, or hereafter shall be, at this time, or any future period, communicated to me, as such, to any person or persons whomsoever, except it be to a true and lawful brother Mason, or in a regularly constituted Lodge of Masons; nor unto him or them until, by strict trial, due examination, or lawful information, I shall have found him, or

them, as lawfully entitled to the same as I am myself. I furthermore promise and swear that I will not print, paint, stamp, stain, cut, carve, mark, or engrave them, or cause the same to be done, on any thing movable or immovable, capable of receiving the least impression of a word, syllable, letter, or character, whereby the same may become legible or intelligible to any person under the canopy of heaven, *and the secrets of Masonry thereby unlawfully obtained through my unworthiness.*

*All this I most solemnly, sincerely promise and swear, with a firm and steadfast resolution to perform the same, without any mental reservation or secret evasion of mind whatever, binding myself under no less penalty than that of having my throat cut across, my tongue torn out by its roots, and **my body buried in the rough sands of the sea,** at low-water mark, where the tide ebbs and flows twice in twenty-four hours, should I ever knowingly violate this my Entered Apprentice obligation. So help me God, and keep me steadfast in the due performance of the same."*

And they're not effing around when it comes to the punishments. Remember Stephen King's Creepshow?

Stephen King's *Creepshow* (1982) Ted Danson, Leslie Nielsen

The initiation process goes on and on. The candidate is finally accepted as an "Obligated" Entered Apprentice, and is shown the secret hand grip of the degree, the signs: right angles, horizontals, and perpendiculars, and tokens. They demonstrate the BOAZ always spelled with A first so as to reveal impostors.

The rest of the ceremony seems noble. It teaches you to be generous and supportive, not so much to your fellow man, but to fellow travelers. Remember, as a member there's an air of superiority, and a sense of importance instilled within to guard secrets from the common, uninitiated man, or the profane, as everyone else is referred to. The attitude being, "If you aren't one of us, you're nothing." Sounds awfully Christian, indeed. (sarcasm)

The Second Degree is called the Fellow Craft, and the Third is the Master Mason's Degree, otherwise described as the ritual play-act of the tale of Hiram Abiff. Some also refer to it as the Death & Resurrection Ritual.

The WIDOW'S SON: The MASONIC ACCOUNT of HIRAM ABIFF

Returning to the descriptions laid out by William Morgan, as preserved and presented by sacred-texts.com, I must compress this ceremony to its key points. There is a lot of repetition from the previous degrees, an order of operations of the lodge as it transitions between orders of business, and the way meetings are conducted, and the ever-present sense of a pantomime, or theatrical performance to initiation rituals and that which leads in and back out of said rituals. Not all the details are important if you're not studying for your own upcoming advance to Master Mason.

Beginning right after the formal method knocking, or rapping, and the Fellow Craftsman enters, once again prepared with rolled up pantaloon leg, hoodwinked (blindfolded) a noose around the neck, and one arm, and one breast bare, the Junoir Deacon declares:

J.D-- *"Let him enter this worshipful lodge, in the name of the Lord, and take heed on what he enters."*

In entering, both points of the compass are pressed against his naked right and left breasts, when the Junior Deacon stops the candidate and says,

J.D.-- *"Brother, when you first entered this lodge, you were received on the point of the compass, pressing your naked left breast, which was then explained to you; when you entered it the second time you were received on the angle of the square, which was also explained to you; on entering now you are received on the two extreme points of the compass, pressing your right and left breasts, which are thus explained: As the most vital parts of man are contained between the two breasts, so are the most valuable tenets of Masonry contained between the two extreme points of the compass, which are virtue, morality, and brotherly love."*

Author's Note: The type of "brotherly love" you continually need to reemphasize with physical assault, and implied threats of murder should you reveal a secret.

"The Senior Deacon then conducts the candidate three times regularly round the lodge. [I wish the reader to observe, that on this, as well as every other degree, that the Junior Warden is the first of the three principal officers that the candidate passes, traveling with the sun when he starts round the lodge, and that as he passes the Junior Warden, Senior Warden and Master, the first time going round, they each give one rap, the second time two raps, and third time three raps each. The number of raps given on those occasions are the same as the number of the degree, except the first degree, on which

three are given, I always thought improperly.] During the time the candidate is traveling round the room, the Master reads the following passages of Scripture, the conductor and candidate traveling and the Master reading so that the traveling and reading terminate at the same time:

W. M.-- *"Remember now thy Creator in the days of thy youth, while the evil days come not, nor the years draw nigh when thou shalt say, I have no pleasure in them while the sun or the light, or the moon, or the stars be not darkened, nor the clouds return after the rain; in the day when the keepers of the house shall tremble, and the strong men shall bow themselves, and the grinders shall cease because they are few, and those that look out of the windows be darkened, and the doors shall be shut in the streets; when the sound of the grinding is low, and he shall rise up at the voice of the bird, and all the daughters of music shall be brought low. Also, when they shall be afraid of that which is high, and fears shall be in the way, and the almond tree shall flourish, and the grasshopper shall be a burden, and desire shall fail; because man goeth to his long home, and the mourners go about the streets; or ever the silver cord be loosed, or the golden bowl be broken, or the pitcher be broken at the fountain, or the wheel at the cistern. Then shall the dust return to the earth as it was; and the spirit shall return unto God who gave it."*

The others ask the question as before in previous initiations, Where did he come from and where is he traveling. I am including this element of the ceremony because masonic themes are often used in films, musical performances, and TV in augmented form or straight-forward. If you are ever asked a seemingly odd question by so-called authorities, it may not be a bad idea to attempt a little Spy Craft, and use these formal expressions and postures to give off the appearance that you're one of them, if they are in fact in the order. You can be a ***cowan***, or a pretender, briefly if it helps you out of a situation. Jesus wasn't above spy craft. He wanted you to use your head and adapt to situations.

So when asked where you are going and why at say, a checkpoint or roadblock, maybe it would be helpful to answer:

Candidate-- *"From the west, and traveling to the east."*

W.M.--   *"Why do you leave the west, and travel to the east?"*

Candidate-- *"In search of more light."*

Like before the Worshipful Master instructs the Senior Deacon to point the blindfolded man in the proper direction and then a very interesting oath is recited by the prospect that I highly recommend reading at least twice, and writing down any mythological, symbolic, or unusual mentions within it for your own additional study. Why are these elements appearing in Freemasonry, and what is their significance? What insights could they possibly give us into the mysteries?

W.M.-- *"Brother, you are now placed in a proper position [the lecture explains it] to take upon you the solemn oath or obligation of a Master Mason, which I assure you, as before, is neither to affect your religion or politics. If you are willing to take it, repeat your name and say after me:"*

Candidate-- *"I, Richard Marx Lipshitz, of my own free will and accord* [contractual language], *in the presence of Almighty God, and this worshipful lodge of Master Masons, dedicated to God, and held forth to the holy order of St. John, do hereby and hereon most solemnly and sincerely promise and swear, in addition to my former obligations, that I will not give the degree of a Master Mason to any of an inferior degree, nor to any other being in the known world, except it be to a true and lawful brother or brethren Master Masons, within the body of a just and lawfully constituted lodge of such; and not unto him nor unto them whom I shall hear so to be, but unto him and them only whom I shall find so to be, after strict trial and due examination, or lawful information received. Furthermore do I promise and swear, that I will not give the Master's word which I shall hereafter receive, neither in the lodge nor out of it, except it be on the five points of fellowship, and then not above my breath. Furthermore do I promise and swear, that I will not give the grand hailing sign of distress except I am in real distress, or for the benefit of the Craft when at work; and should I ever see that sign given or the word accompanying it, and the person who gave it appearing to be in distress I will fly to his relief at the risk of my life, should there be a greater probability of saving his life than losing my own. Furthermore do I promise and swear that I will not wrong this lodge, nor a brother of this degree to the value of one cent, knowingly, myself, or suffer it to be done by others, if in my power to prevent it. Furthermore do I promise and swear, that I will not be at the initiating, passing and raising a candidate at one communication, without a regular dispensation from the Grand Lodge for the same.*

*Furthermore do I promise and swear that I will not be at the initiating, passing, or raising a candidate in a clandestine lodge, I knowing it to be such. Furthermore do I promise and swear that I will not be at the initiating of an old man in dotage, a young man in nonage, an Atheist, irreligious libertine, idiot, mad-man, **hermaphrodite**, or woman. Furthermore do I promise and swear that I will not speak evil of a brother Master Mason, neither behind his back nor before his face, but will apprise him of all approaching danger, if in my power. Furthermore do I promise and swear that I will not violate the chastity of a Master Mason's wife, mother, sister, or daughter. I knowing them to be such, nor suffer it to be done by others, if in my power to prevent it. Furthermore do I promise and swear that I will support the constitution of the Grand Lodge of the state of* [New York], *under which the lodge is held, and conform to all the by-laws, rules, and regulations of this or any other lodge of which I may at any time hereafter become a member.*

Furthermore do I promise and swear that I will obey all regular signs, summonses, or tokens given, handed, sent, or thrown to me from the hand of a brother Master Mason, or from the body of a just and lawfully constituted lodge of such, provided it be within the length of my cable-tow [noose around the neck, also what a necktie loosely represents.]

 *Furthermore do I promise and swear that a Master Mason's secrets, given to me in charge as such, and I knowing them to be such, shall remain as secure and inviolable in my breast as in his own, when communicated to me, **murder and treason excepted**; and they left to my own election."*

Author's Note: It is revealed in further, honorary degrees, and in the Scottish Rite, that this oath changes once you reach a particular level. At that point you must swear to secrecy and assistance of a Mason even if Murder and Treason are divulged. Bill Cooper had affirmed this in more than one broadcast of ***The Hour of the Time*** throughout its nine year run. The Candidate for Master Mason continues:

Candidate-- *"Furthermore do I promise and swear that I will go on a Master Mason's errand whenever required, even should I have to go bare-foot and bare-headed, if within the length of my cable-tow."* If within the length of his leash, basically. -D.K.

Candidate-- *"Furthermore do I promise and swear that I will always remember a brother Master Mason when on my knees offering up my devotions to Almighty God."* That may not be the only time he'll find himself on his knees around his Celestial Sodomite brothers. -D.K.

Candidate-- *"Furthermore do I promise and swear that I will be aiding and assisting all poor, indigent Master Masons, their wives and orphans, wheresoever disposed around the globe, as far as in my power, without injuring myself or family materially.*

 Furthermore do I promise and swear that if any part of my solemn oath or obligation be omitted at this time, that I will hold myself amenable thereto whenever informed. To all which I do most sincerely promise and swear, with a fixed and steady purpose of mind in me to keep and perform the same, binding myself under no less penalty than to have my body severed in two in the midst, and divided to the north and south, my bowels burnt to ashes in the center, and the ashes scattered before the four winds of heaven, that there might not the least track or trace of remembrance remain among men. or Masons, of so vile and perjured a wretch at should be, were I ever to prove willfully guilty of violating any part of this my solemn oath or obligation of a Master Mason. So help me God, and keep me steadfast in the due performance of the same."

W.M-- *"What do you most desire?"*

Candidate-- *"More light."* An expression of more knowledge, more secrets revealed, as in Lucifer (or Prometheus), the Light-Bearer, bringing the gift of intellect, often depicted as fire, to Man. -D.K.

At this point the text is confusing. It says a bandage that was around the head of the candidate is loosened and put over his eyes, as he's "brought to light." This could just be a symbolic case of inversion where dark is light, or the text is potentially corrupted. It's in this next passage where they finally mention Hiram Abiff and set the stage for what may be considered the next act of this ritual-drama. The W.M. tells the Candidate:

W.M.-- *"You first discover, as before, three great lights in Masonry, by the assistance of three lesser, with this difference: both points of the compass are elevated above the square, which denotes to you that you are about to receive all the light that can be conferred on you in a Master's lodge."*

The W.M. demonstrates the sign and dueguard of a Master Mason, and shows the universal sign of a Mason in distress, which should be accompanied with the words, *"O Lord, my God! is there no help for the widow's son?"*

Grand Hailing Sign of Distress.

The pass-grip is given by pressing the thumb between the joints of the second and third fingers where they join the hand; the word or name is "TUBAL CAIN." It is the pass-word to the Master's degree. The Master, after giving the candidate the pass-grip and word, bids him rise and salute the Junior and Senior Wardens, and convince them that he is an obligated Master Mason, and is in possession of the pass-grip and word. While the Wardens are examining the candidate, the Master returns to the east and gets an apron, and, as he returns to the candidate, one of the Wardens (sometimes both) says to the Master:

Wardens-- *"Worshipful. we are satisfied that Bro. [R. M. Lipshitz] is an obligated Master Mason."*

W.M.-- *"Brother, I now have the honor to present you with a lamb-skin or white apron, as before, which I hope you will continue to wear, with credit to yourself and satisfaction and advantage to the brethren; you will please carry it to the Senior Warden in the west, who will teach you how to wear it as a Master Mason."*

If you are curious as to what that apron looks like, pull up the image icon for GMail. This apron is the cultic piece of clothing, the identifying marker of a Master Mason which gives them all their identity, as far as visible status within the walls of the Lodges. Dr Ardis had mentioned one thematic element used by cults being a garment they make their members wear and express great and sacred importance in. With the Mormans, it's a type of underwear. With the Masons, it's an apron, or wearing your underwear on the outside, I suppose. The apron dates back to Egypt and even Babylonia (the Empire.) Your pseudo-corporate, mostly governmental, under the auspices of

"Alphabet, Inc.," email service provider uses Mystery Religion iconography thousands of years old, but kept fresh as a daisy-filled jockstrap in the Masonic Lodges. The fact that pop-culture calls weaponized clandestine and a semi-public organizations "Alphabet Agencies," did they really try very hard to conceal the true point and purpose of Alphabet, Inc., and Google, as its recognized extension? YouTube is an intestinal water slide to the Abyss, where Lamia will gladly greet you.

The Worshipful Master continues:

W.M.-- *"Brother, I perceive you are dressed, it is of course necessary you should have tools to work with. I will now present you with the working tools of the Master Mason, and explain their use to you. The working tools of a Master Mason are all the implements of Masonry indiscriminately, but more especially the trowel. The trowel is an instrument made use of by operative masons to spread the cement which unites a building into one mass, but we, as Free and Accepted Masons, are taught to make use of it for the more noble and glorious purpose of spreading the cement of brotherly love and affection; that cement which unites us into one sacred band or society of friends and brothers, among whom no contention should ever exist but that noble contention, or, rather, emulation, of who can best work or best agree. I also present you with three precious jewels; their names are* **Humanity**, **Friendship**, *and* **Brotherly Love**.

Forgive me, but "spreading the cement of brotherly love" seems like something you'd see in the Castro District of San Francisco if you stumbled into a club on a given night. It appears to suggest this newly apron'ed Master Mason's efforts for acceptance have just begun…

W.M.- *"Brother, you are not invested with all the secrets of this degree, nor do I know whether you ever will be until I know how you withstand the amazing trials and dangers that await you."*

This is the first allusion to another drama about to unfold within the ceremony.

W.M-- *"You are now about to travel, to give us a* **specimen** *of your fortitude, perseverance, and fidelity in the preservation of what you have already received. Fare you well, and may the Lord be with you and support you through all your trials and difficulties."*

The candidate is then conducted out of the lodge, clothed, and returns; as he enters the door his conductor says to him:

C.-- *"Brother, we are now in a place representing the sanctum sanctorum, or holy of holies, of King Solomon's temple. It was the custom of our Grand Master, Hiram Abiff, every day at high twelve, when the Crafts were from labor to refreshment, to enter into the sanctum sanctorum, and offer up his devotions to the ever living God. Let us, in imitation of him, kneel and pray."* It's at this point the newly adorned Master Mason transitions into the role of Hiram Abiff. -D.K.

After a long prayer, they rise and the action begins.

C-- *"Brother, in further imitation of our Grand Master, Hiram Abiff, let us retire at the south gate."*

They then advance to the Junior Warden [who represents Jubela, one of the ruffians], who exclaims,

Jubela-- *"Who comes here?" [The room is dark, or the candidate hoodwinked.] The conductor answers,*

C-- *"Grand Master, Hiram Abiff."*

Jubela-- *"Our Grand Master, Hiram Abiff! He is the very man I wanted to see." Seizing the candidate by the throat at the same time, and jerking him about with violence. "Give me the Master Mason's word or I'll take your life!"*

Conductor (C)-- *"I cannot give it now, but if you will wait till the Grand Lodge assembles at Jerusalem, if you are found worthy, you shall then receive it, otherwise you cannot."*

The ruffian then gives the candidate a blow with the twenty-four inch gauge across the throat, on which he fled to the west gate, where he was accosted by the second ruffian, Jubelo, with more violence, and on his refusal to comply with his request, he gave him a severe blow with the square across his breast, on which he attempted to make his escape at the east gate, where he was accosted by the third ruffian, Jubelum, with still more violence, and on refusing to comply with his request, the ruffian gave him a violent blow with the common gavel on the forehead, which brought him to the floor; on which one of them exclaimed:

Jubelum-- *"What shall we do? We have killed our Grand Master, Hiram Abiff!"*

The dramatic play continues, and the W.M. plays the role of King Solomon conducting an investigation into the missing Grand Master, interrogations, and getting confessions from the three ruffians, whom all contain the word 'Bel' in their name, which is another spelling for Ba'al. The three are sent to execution in the manners described by their own tongues, which were the masonic penalties for betraying the brothers and the lodge.

First, Jubela—*"O that my throat had been cut across, my tongue torn out, and my body burled in the rough sands of the sea, at low water mark, where the tide ebbs and flows twice in twenty-four hours, ere I had been accessory to the death of so good a man as our Grand Master, Hiram Abiff!"*

The second, Jubelo—*"O that my left breast had been torn open and my heart and vitals taken from thence and thrown over my left shoulder, carried into the valley of*

Jehosaphat, and there to become a prey to the wild beasts of the field and vultures of the air, ere I had conspired the death of so good a man as our Grand Master, Hiram Abiff!"

The third, Jubelum—*"O that my body had been severed in two in the midst, and divided to the north and south, my bowels burnt to ashes in the center, and the ashes scattered by the four winds of heaven, that there might not the least track or remembrance remain among men, or Masons, of so vile and perjured a wretch as I am; ah, Jubela and Jubelo, it was I that struck him harder than you both. It was I that gave him the fatal blow; it was I that killed him outright…*

Having found the body of Hiram (Candidate) the lodge members of the lower degrees attempt to raise him from the dead, each with their degree-level grip or dueguard, and they fail. The Master then attempts with the "lion's paw," or master's grip. Utilizing the grip, the five-points of fellowship, and the secret word *Mah Hah Bone*, the W.M. is able to raise Hiram/Candidate from the dead, and we have a death and resurrection ritual conducted to completion.

There's a lot more long dialogues that follow that are meant to impress upon and reinforce in the new Master Mason the sense of importance in loyalty, and in the sacred traditions of the Lodge.

BILL COOPER'S MYSTERY BABYLON SERIES hr. 9 (February 24th 1993)
Initiation

The following transcript is from over 30 years ago at the time these words are being typed. Mr. William Cooper had presented 42 broadcasts dedicated specifically to his Mystery Babylon series on his ***The Hour of the Time*** shortwave radio broadcast. Having listened myself to probably well over 1,000 hours of is shows, there are even more episodes than the 42 designated that would easily fit under the same header.

I am manually transcribing this while listening to it, so forgive any minor discrepancies.

From Tinker Bell to Artie Shaw, to George Bush's thousand points of light, America has been mesmerized by stardust since its very inception. And Now America is beginning to learn what all these references to the star, the Morning Star, to wish upon a star, and stardust really is about. There was something very strange about the classical mysteries. Something which attracted people to them, and having attracted them, made their initiates with very few exceptions, permanent devotees.

In Egypt, Greece, India, Rome, and a dozen other places and countries, sacred initiations took place in specially prepared sanctuaries, usually in a cave or underground. Priests of the Mysteries enjoyed the profound respect of the masses as well as that of Kings and councilors. And in those days there was nothing really sacred about it except the initiation rites, and the knowledge which they retained for themselves, giving only the exoteric to the people.

What were the Mysteries? Until relatively recently, and relying upon comparatively scattered fragments such as Apuleius's Golden Ass, historians and religious writers had formed an opinion of them which has been shown to be extremely naive, if not outright false. They knew that at the ceremonies symbolical teaching took place, and hints inferred that the mysteries were a relic of the times when academic knowledge was guarded by the very few. And scientific truths such as Pythagorean theorems were given only, and only to the elect. They knew also that orgiastic drumming and dancing formed a part of many of the rituals and therefore told their readers that this was a degenerate form of religion, or a mere excuse for licentiousness. They found that stories of ancient gods and heroes were recited and were sure that the Mysteries constituted little more than an underground survival of prehistoric religion, magic, or tribal initiation. Or maybe that's exactly what they wanted us to believe, knowing full-well that it was false. And of course if those who did the writing were members of the Mysteries, they would never have allowed the secrets to be revealed to the profane.

But times have changed, folks. The study of brainwashing and mind-control, and conditioning the mind within the past decade or so has helped to lay bare the essence of the Mysteries, and has answered the riddles which surrounded them. You see, in this process, those who had tried to keep the celebration of the Mysteries alive, who tried to revive them, have been shown up as relying upon the symbolic interpretation alone. And this revelation has been, in its own way, one of the most startling developments of contemporary religion. You see, for almost anyone for instance can get away with telling anyone else that he was an Egyptian priest in a former incarnation because there's so very little verifiable material available to prove the reverse. It becomes obvious though when you attend a party populated by these nuts when six people introduce themselves as having been Abraham Lincoln in a past life. But let anyone attempt to celebrate any of the ancient mystery cults' rituals, and unless he has a sound idea of how the human mind works he is likely to escape the criticism of those physiologists who now see in the Mysteries an almost open book. So let us return to a sketch of the conventional knowledge about the mysteries and those of Eleusis [*Eleusinian Mysteries*] celebrated in Greece.

The candidate had to undergo fasting, or abstinence from certain foods. There were processions with sacred statues carried from Athens to Eleusis. Those who were to be initiated went for long periods of time outside the hall in the temple where the rites were to be held… Building up a tremendous tension of suspense. Eventually a torchbearer led them within the precincts, usually underground.

The ceremonies included a ritualistic meal, one or two dramas, the exhibition of sacred objects, the giving of the word, an address by the Heirophant [*High Priest*], and oddly enough, closure with the Sanskrit words, Kansha umpaksha [*spelling reliant on hearing the pronunciation*]. The elements included the clashing of symbols, tension, and a certain degree of debilitation, eating something, plus conditions which were awe-inspiring, strange. The candidate was in the hands of, and guided by the priesthood. Other factors were drinking a soporific draught, symbolic sentence of death, whirling around a circle. Initiation ceremonies of secret cults, the Mystery type invariably involved tests, sometimes most severe ones. The effect of certain experiences was a carefully worked program of mind training which is familiar in modern times as that which is employed by certain totalitarian states to condition or reshape the thinking of an individual. Are you listening to me, all you Freemasons out there who think that you're so smart? Well, you're not.

This process produces a state in which the mind is pliant enough to have certain ideas implanted. Ideas which resist a great deal of counter-influence. This was the secret of the Mysteries. This, and nothing else. Echoes of such training are to be seen in the rituals of certain secret societies without mystical pretensions which survive to this day. Trials, terror, expectancy, drinking, and the rest. That this fact was known in the past, is evidenced by the words of Aristotle who was exiled because he was said to have revealed something about the Mysteries... And he said this, quote, "Those who are being initiated do not-so-much learn anything, as experience certain emotions, and are thrown into a special state of mind," unquote. Well what was this "special state of mind?" Folks, it was a plasticity in order that the conditioning might take permanent root.

The psychologist, William Sargent, the greatest authority on the subject, says in his classic, "*Battle for the Mind*," quote, "It seems therefore there are common, final paths which all individual animals, though initial temperamental responses to imposed stresses vary greatly, must finally take, if only stresses are continued long enough. This is probably the same in human beings, and if so, may help to explain why excitatory drumming, dancing, and continued bodily movement are so much used in such a number of primitive religious groups. The efforts and excitement of keeping the dance in-progress for many hours on end should wear down, and if need be, finally subdue even the strongest, and most stubborn temperament. Such as might be able to survive the frightening and exciting talk alone for days or weeks," unquote. Now... Understanding what I just read to you in this quote I just read to you from "Battle for the Mind," by William Sargent, can you still say that music plays no part in the conditioning of the mind? That the words in the music is not being entrapped by the subconscious by those young people who dance for hours listening to this music? If so, I think you'd better rethink that position, for it is a form of Mind Control—brainwashing.

Dr Sargent notes that Chinese experiments in mass excitation, breaking down, and reconditioning, are based on the same psychological principles as religious conversion, and also group, and individual psychotherapy treatments. Folks, these include the application of tension, fear, anxiety, conflict... to the point where the subjects are uncertain. And in this state suggestibility is increased and the old pattern of behavior is disrupted. The fact that the devotees of the Mysteries were thoroughly conditioned to them, and felt that they were important in their lives as seen in much historical evidence. Even in the fourth century Christian era the Greeks were insisting that they quote, "Would consider life unbearable if they were not allowed to celebrate those most sacred Mysteries which unites the human race," unquote.

Now the work of those who have pointed out the function of the Mysteries as mind-training and conditioning has, of course, evoked no answer from those who still think that the rituals are mere symbolic representations of knowledge or facts, and indeed they cannot admit this simply because they would be admitting their own foolishness and stupidity in the process. So they will resist at all costs and continue to go to their meetings for, to do otherwise, would be to confront their own fallibility. And in human nature that is one of the most difficult things for any individual to do. We all realize that. It's interesting to note, folks, that the ecstasy which is produced by excitatory methods, and is followed by manipulation of the mind is still sought by members of many cults who are aware of the scientific explanation. You see irregardless, even when they know this they still seek it out because for them it fulfills some terrible need way down deep inside their gut. The reaction is that the experience may well be induced by physical methods, but in spite of that, and this is what they say, quote, "It is nothing less than actual, spiritual communion with a supernatural power," unquote. This is the point at which scientists and mystics cannot agree. The mystic feels sure that he has experienced something sublime, and who is to say that they haven't? For if you have not experienced it, you have no basis upon which to make a decision. But to experience it is to put yourself in a position to be controlled by others. So we are in a quandary now. How do we explore this? The scientist tells the mystic that it is an illusion. He just simply will not believe it. The situation reminds one of the time when someone produced the soul of a departed relative to tell a spiritualist that there was no life after death. (Bill laughs) Although this is alleged to have happened in Ireland, one can visualize it taking place easily enough in the mutually heated atmosphere of scientist versus mystic anywhere in the world.

The orgiastic side of the Mysteries also has a place in the sphere of psychology. The catharsis, or the cleansing of the mind, which the secret cult of the Kothari experienced after ecstasy is paralleled by the modern therapist procedure in bringing his patient to a state of excitement, and then collapse, before implanting what he considers more suitable ideas in the mind.

Christianity, of course, has not been behind in its use of the Mystery system for initiates. For it was not until AD 692 that every believer was ordered to be admitted to the worship of the Christians following the period when it was thought advisable to celebrate certain parts of worship in secret. You see Christianity, in the beginning, was a secret society itself, and the correct name for it was the Friendly Open Secret Society. Although in the beginning, there was nothing open about it. Traces of this survive in such customs as the Greek Orthodox Church where the priest celebrates divine worship behind a curtain which is only taken away during the elevation of the host. "Since at that moment the worshipers prostate themselves and are not supposed to see the Holy Sacrament." The reason given for the secrecy of the practice of the Christian cult gives a clue in explaining that the celebrant must be prepared by expectation. St. Augustine laid down that secrecy was essential because the Mysteries of Christianity were incomprehensible to human intellect and should not be derided by the uninitiated. Secondly, because this secret produced greater veneration for the rites. Thirdly, that the holy curiosity of those to be initiated into the experience of Christianity should be increased in order that they might attain to a perfect knowledge of the faith. And to tell you quite frankly, folks, in my study of mind control the Christian Church would swell well beyond any conception or imagination of what their numbers could be if they had continued their secrecy. St. Basil De Spiritu Sancto… That's a writing, folks, tells how the Fathers of the Church quote, "were well instructed to preserve the veneer of the Mysteries in silence for how could it be proper publicly to proclaim in writing the doctrine of those things no unbaptized person may so much as look upon," unquote. Now this all sounds silly to us today, but believe me folks, there is nothing silly about it. And if it were practiced today as it was then the Christian Church would be more powerful than you could possibly conceive. Now remember this is the results of our research. I, myself, consider myself to be a Christian in that I follow the teachings, the words of Christ in my daily life. Not the dogma of any church, not the preaching of any minister or priest, but simply, and only, the words of Christ. Seated upon the foundation of that which God gave us early in our history, the moral code called the Ten Commandments. As they were originally given to Moses, and not as they were changed by Man in the form of the Pope. The origin of Mystery ceremonies seems to be India, or at least the place and time when the Brahman priesthoods started its initiations. The ceremonies were based upon the Hindu myths, but the procedure followed in training the aspirant is strikingly similar in Egypt, and Egypt profoundly influenced Greece. Now what's left out here, and the reason it's usually left out is because any mention or discussion of the Babylonian Mysteries, or the Babylonian religion is usually met with much criticism and derision by those who believe that it was a terrible institution. The Mysteries definitely came from the East, and the East in the Mysteries still survives today. When one Freemason greets another and he's not sure if he's really a Freemason, he'll ask him if he's a traveller, or if he's traveling, or if he's a fellow traveler. All, I might add were the same code of identification used by the Communist Party in this country because Communism and the Mysteries are the SAME entity. As are Socialism and the Mysteries. When they meet, and this exchange takes place, the one being queried, if he is indeed a member of the Mystery religion will say, "Yes, I'm a traveler," to which the first or the inquirer will respond with, "Where are you going," or "Where are you traveling," from where to where. An the answer will be, "From West to East," for the East is the position of the rising sun where the knowledge comes from. You see, for an early history, it certainly can be proven to have come from the East. And the Sun was the symbol of the Intellect that began by being the symbol of the unseen God of the Universe, and slowly transformed into the symbol of the Intellect, the Light, Osiris, Ra, Lucifer…

Prayer, fasting, and study were the first requirements when the Indian candidate prepared himself for the trials which were before him. All of this folks, originated in Babylon at the dawn of civilization. For the actual side of the great gods and for the final word or teaching which would be implanted in his mind when it had been sufficiently prepared to receive it, and if the weather were cold he would have to sit in the snow or rain naked, in the torrid heat he sat in the full blaze of the sun with four fires built around him to give additional heat... And this was the first part of the undertaking while he repeated prayers and repetition which included the invocation for his complete conversion. This latter concentration folks, upon the desires of the candidate is applied in more than one of the Mysteries. Some of the initiation ceremonies were cruel and painful. Coupled with the word which is given during the ceremonies it means that the power of suggestion is being applied continuously, and should penetrate into the mind at every moment when it is able to receive it. This period of dedication was succeeded by one in which he visited the underground cave of initiation. And when it wasn't in a cave, it was in a tomb, or a crypt, such as the pyramids of Egypt which were never tombs of Pharaohs, but were from the beginning, until the end of their use they were temples of initiation.

Passing through a tunnel of complete darkness the initiate emerged into the cavern where three priests dressed as gods awaited him in resplendent and intimidating array. After being addressed and partaking in the oration of prayer, the initiate walked rapidly around the temple several times. This is called circumambulation, and was then carried through several subterranean and unlit caves. During this time there were wails. Wails, screams, and shouts from every side while illuminated specters and other horrors abounded. At the end of this terrible experience, the aspirant came to two doors which when thrown open to the sound of the sacred conch trumpet, the conch folks, is a shell, revealed a scene of brilliance and glory. This hall was full of every delight in the form of pictures, music, and perfume. The initiate walked to an alter in the room where he was again harangued [lectured in length] and presented with his sevenfold cord which marked his passing through the initiation.

Now if we compare these proceedings with those which were said to be carried out among the Egyptians, the parallelism is startling even today. The candidate was taken to a well which he had to descend until he came to a tunnel. Torch in hand, he passed through a door which closed with a resounding noise as if never to be opened again. He was met by frightful figures which offered him a last chance of going back. Then he passed through a fire, swam through a dangerous underground stream, and as soon as he reached the door and touched a ring to open it, a blast of air blew out the lamp which gave the only available light. Some type of machine swung him over a bottomless pit and just as he was on the point of exhaustion, an ivory door opened and he found himself on the threshold of the resplendent temple of Isis. Here the priests received him into their company. After the series of tests, he had to undergo fasting and what would nowadays be called indoctrination before he could be considered completely initiated into even the first degree. The foregoing experiences were followed by the higher degrees, those of Serapis, and Osiris, and in the process the wives of the priests would tease him and cajole him, and try to get him to make love to them. And if he successfully resisted, then he could say that he had passed all the tests, but if he succumbed to their advances he was not worthy.

It is needless to outline the beliefs and methods used in the Chinese, Japanese, South American, and other Mysteries because while the legends which are inculcated may vary in some way, they are all essentially and basically the same. The training hardly varies at all. The real Mystery of the Mysteries folks, is how and when man first discovered the use of certain procedures to condition other men, and thus rule them and control them. And whether the discovery was instantaneous, or gradual, or simultaneous or at different times and places. But one cannot date doctrines as one can archaeological finds by radioactive carbon dating. And so you've reached another milestone in your education into the Mysteries and this program has only half completed. And again I must remind you that we have just begun for we are essentially covering 6,000 years of the history of a hidden religion known simply as the Mysteries. To Christians, it is Mystery Babylon. To others it is called the Invisible College. In all cases it belongs to those who consider themselves in possession of the only mature minds, and thus the only ones capable of knowing certain advancements in technology, sociology, and many, many other things. They call themselves the Guardians of the Secrets of the Ages. And I can assure you folks, they are in control of all elements of our society, military, and government at this time. So it is essential that you learn these facts about them and their organization so that we can decide our future. [Bill Breaks for a moment]

The Cult of Mithra, the intercessor between Man and the Persian divine power Ormus was once an extremely widespread one for it is the original Cult of the Sun. From its origins in Persia the faith spread to Babylonia, Greece, and finally the Roman Empire where it struggled against Christianity at the latter's inception. Christianity believes that it won with the decline of the material virtues of the Romans, but there are people who worship the solar deity today and even London has its Mithra temple. Mithra was said to give his worshippers success in this world as well as security and happiness in the next. Sound familiar, Freemasons? He was originally a genie, the worldly representative of the invisible power which ruled the affairs of men. Later, and the cult probably has a history of over 6,000 years, he became thought of by his devotees as being not just one of the 28 geni, but the only one which mattered, and the only one who could cater for the wishes and needs of the people. Thus it was that the ancient Aryan worship of Ahura Mazda, the supreme being, was displaced by that of one of his representatives. Now one way folks you can tell who, or which corporations, or businesses, or societies belong to these cults is to look at these names such as Saturn, Mazda, etc. Ahura Mazda, the Supreme Being, was displaced by that of one of his representatives although archeological research has produced little to give clear picture of the rituals and beliefs of the Mithraists. A considerable amount of secret lore still survives in the East from India to Syria which gives one good idea of exactly how the members of the cult thought and just exactly what their magical ceremonies were. Three ritualistic objects are used by Mithraists, the crown, equivalent to the Sun [corona, coronavirus, or crown virus] and power of the supernatural kind, the hammer or club symbolizing creative activity of mankind, and the bull which stands for nature. Virility increased by the proper understanding of these objects and just exactly what they represent. Mithraists have it that the ordinary man can transcend his environment, can become great or successful, or can achieve what he wants to do and enters a delightful afterlife. What must he give in exchange? Nothing but worship of the principle which presides over all destiny and control to the priests of the religion.

Now let's regress just a moment and let me explain to you why the bull. Throughout the ancient world you see the symbology of the bull. Now you have to remember this history goes back 6,000 years. The first 2,000 of which, looking back, is the Christian era. Now remember this is the Age of Pisces, or the two fish. The six-thousand year period started in antiquity when the sun was in Taurus, or the Bull. That is the meaning of Ba'al or Ba'al the Golden Calf was the representation of the house of the sun, or the Age of the Bull, or Taurus. It was really the same old Mystery religion, the worship of the unseen God of the Universe represented by the Sun. The representation of the Light or Lucifer, the one who gave Man the gift of intellect. Now after Taurus came the goat or Ram and this was symbolized by the symbol of the goat of Mendes. For in Mendes there was a temple erected to the worship of the Mysteries and since the sun was in the house of the goat, or the Ram, the object of the exoteric worship by the masses was the goat. When the sun passed into the house of Pisces, or the 2 fishes, the Christian era began. We are now on our way out of the Age of Pisces, into the Age of Aquarius. Once you you understand that the ancient religion was a religion of the worship of the heavens then everything begins to come together. And when you understand that they ceased believing in an all-powerful, unseen God, or hidden God of the Universe and became essentially pantheists believing that everything is God, they call this Nature or the Natural Way, then you can understand how man came to worship the Intellect, and the symbol which used to represent the unseen God of the Universe came to represent the Intellect. The use of which will bring Man to a state of apotheosis where Man himself will become God, and then you begin to look at all the things that are happening today and you see their symbology everywhere. Nowhere will you see it more prominently than the Looney Tune fringe element which call themselves UFOlogists. You will see that everything to do with so-called UFO phenomena comes right out of the Mystery Schools!

One reason, folks, for the loss of the importance of the Cult of Mithras undoubtedly is the admission was restricted to those who were thought worthy to receive the blessings which would come through the proper beliefs and use of magical powers presided over by the Mithra priests. Christianity, for instance, was open to a far greater section of the population. Even although the Christian mysteries were not accessible to all everywhere until relatively late in our history. At the same time some of the Mithraist ceremonies were of such obvious emotional appeal that scholars are agreed that the purely ritualistic side of Christianity owes much to those of the Sun God of the Persians, and if you've been listening to this program you already know that. That Christianity was actually merged with the religion of the worship of the sun into what is now known as the Vatican. The lowest degree of initiation was known as the sacrament and could be administered to anyone theoretically who could be relied upon to keep a secret and who would eventually develop into a regular and devout worshipper. This degree was called that of the Crow and it's symbolized, according to present day Mithraists, the death of the new member from which he would arise reborn as a new man. And today the "crow" is known as the phoenix. This death, or symbolic death, spelt the end of his life as an unbeliever and canceled his allegiance to former and unaccepted beliefs. The use of the word "Crow" probably derives from the ancient Persian practice of exposing their dead to be eaten by carrion birds which is still carried on by the Parsi community in India who follow parts of ancient Iranian religion as supposedly taught by Zoroaster. But if the Crow symbolized death it was also the delegate privileged to take over the human body after death. Of course this meant that in a sense it was superior to humanity. Thus it was that the members of the cult were superior to the ordinary run of mortals. They believed themselves to be a separate race of Man, and still do.

The candidate descended seven steps into the temple which was an underground one fashioned in the shape of a cavern and made to look as much as possible like a natural cave. Initiation tests now took place. The newcomer was pursued by wild beasts, priests in animal skins, demons, and all sorts of terrors. He had to fast for three days, and [in] this debilitated, altered, and plastic state he was given a lecture by a priest on the responsibilities which were now his. Among these were the necessity to call "brother" only those who had been initiated. In the words of a Freemason today whose son I happen to know,

"If you're not one of us, you are nothing." Those words were spoken to his son when he asked his father why the Freemasons that he knew, and his father, were persecuting a local businessman and trying to drive him out of business. Now bear in mind that his son was NOT a Freemason. Let me say those words for you again, folks, quote, "If you are not one of us, you are nothing," unquote. All family ties were severed. Nothing mattered except doing one's job well and carrying out the worship of Mithra.

The final ceremony took place amid the clash of symbols, the beating of drums, and the unveiling of a statue of Mithra himself. This latter showed Mithra as a man carrying a bull by the hind legs. Now the symbolism of this piece of sculpture was explained to him. The bull, in addition to symbolizing fecundity was representative of animal passion, and it was also the house in which the sun dwelt in the first two-thousand years of the religion. It was through invocations to Mithra that mankind first discovered how to overcome this force and how to discipline himself. Therefore the secret of religion was partly that the worshipper must restrain himself physically in order to attain power over himself, and over others. And this is the Mystery of the Sphinx that man has been trying to decipher since man discovered the Sphinx in the modern world. It is simply this: that man is nothing but an animal with a brain, with an intellect. It is to remind us, folks. It is to tell us that no matter what you think, or how high you get, you are still nothing but an animal with an intellect, period. This graphic teaching of the diversion of sexual power into psychic channels shows that the Mithraists followed, in essence, the pattern of all Mystery Schools which believed in the production of power through discipline. In this they are clearly distinguished from the more primitive, and less important orgiastic schools which merely practiced indiscriminate indulgence, mass immorality, and so on. The Neophyte, in this initiation, then drank a little wine from the cymbal to show that he realized that the symbol is the means whereby ritual ecstasy comes which puts him in touch with the higher powers. Now two long lines of initiates knelt on either side of the low stone benches which traversed the crypt. Remember George Bush was initiated in the crypt, or the tomb at Yale University into what is known as the Skull and Bones, the Russell Trust, the Brotherhood of Death. Now remember, two lines of initiates knelt on either side of the low stone benches which traversed the crypt, and as the new member, accompanied by the priests who were initiating him walked along the central isle for the eating of the bread, a number of pieces of dry bread were placed on a drum similar to those which were being softly beaten by one of the priests. The candidate ate one morsel signifying that he accepted Mithra as the source of his food. This bread according to their beliefs had been exposed to the rays of the sun to absorb some of its quality and thus the worshiper was partaking of the nature of the sun itself in this ritual observance. But it goes deeper than that folks

because the sun is what enables all life to exist on this planet. Being that the planet is at the perfect balance where it is neither too hot nor too cold…
[skipping ahead]

...And now the initiate was taught the password of the cult which was to identify him to other members and which he was to repeat to himself frequently in order to maintain the thought always in his mind. Quote, "I have eaten from the drum and drunk from the cymbal and I have learned the secret of religion," unquote. This is the cryptic phrase which an early Christian writer, Maternus, reports as being taught to the Mithraists, quote, "by a demon," unquote.

The second degree of initiation was called the Secret and during this the candidate was brought to a state of ecstasy in which he was somehow made to believe that he had seen the statue of the god actually endowed with life. Folks it was not likely that there was any mechanical method by which this was done because no such apparatus has been found in Mithraic temples unearthed. The candidate was brought up to the idol to which he offered a loaf of bread and a cup of water, and this was to signify that he was a servant of the God, and that, quote, "By what sustains my life I offer my entire life to your service," unquote.

The grade of soldier may show that the military arts were responsible for a good deal of the power of the Mithra worship in ancient Persia. Certain it is, in any case, that this degree greatly appealed to the Roman warriors who formed a very large part of the rank-and-file of the cult during its western expansion. A sign similar to a cross signifying the Sun was made on the forehead of the initiate who was thus marked as owned by the deity. A crown was placed before him hanging from the point of a sword. This he took and placed it aside with the words, "Mithra alone is my crown." And this folks, this takes place in every… Every Mystery that there have ever been. Remember when Christ went into the desert for 40 days and 40 nights, and was tempted by Satan? Satan offered him the crowns of any or all of the nations of the Earth if he would just follow him and Christ rejected it. The same thing happens in the Mystery School. The initiate is always offered a crown, sometimes by the king, or the Emperor himself and if he accepts the crown he's considered unworthy. And being as it would be interpreted as a threat to the real wearer of the crown, probably would have been executed. He was considered only worth if he rejected the crown, symbolic of the ruler. The ruling of the nation, or people, or area. The Persian crown should be remembered from which pattern all present-day crowns, or are eventually derived is a golden sun disc with a hole in the center for the head. It is jagged at the edges representing the sun's rays just like that worn by the Statue of Liberty. And these projections are turned up to make what is still known in western heraldry as the Oriental crown. You can also see this representation as the halo in Christian art.

Now the candidate has to prove himself in a mock combat with soldiers and animals in a number of caves. When the Emperor Commodus [where we get the word *commode*, meaning toilet, great legacy] went through this degree of initiation he actually killed one of the participants although he was supposed to only make a symbolic slaying.

Passed through the soldier degree, the Mithraist was eligible after a lapse of time to be promoted to the rank of Lion. He was taken again to the cavern and honey was smeared upon his brow as opposed to the water which had been used in his acceptance into the earlier degree, his Baptism. The degree of Lion was taken only by those who had decided to dedicate themselves completely to the cult, and who had henceforth have no truck with the ordinary world. The lion was then a sort of priest, but rather more of a monk. He was trained in the rites of the cult and told certain secrets. The degree of Lion of Mithras could only be conferred Only when the sun was occupying the Zodiacal sign of Leo, and that's about July 21st through August 20th during the Persian month of Assad, the Lion. Now there's a good deal of astrological lore in Mithraism, and also an admixture with Kabbalistic numerology. The Greek branch of the Mithraists, for example, worked out that the numerical equivalent of the name, spelt by them Mitras, was 365, and thus corresponded to the number of days in the solar year. Well since the deity was the Sun, then this is exactly what it should have been.

In the purely magical sense, Mithraism has it that both the name of the God and the rank which the individual holds in the cult have magical power. Thus if a person wants to achieve anything he has to concentrate upon the word, Mithra while preparing for himself the ceremonial repast and beating alternately a drum and cymbals.

That the effect of initiation was to produce someone of upright character is amply evidenced by literature of the Roman times in which the Mithraists were generally considered to be thoroughly trustworthy and improved people. Even their enemies could reproach their own followers with the vitality of the Mithraist Creed. Tertullian in his *De Corona*, which is Latin for "The Crown," which composed in the third Christian Century [I have it as 201 A.D.] upbraids [meaning scolds] the Christians inviting their attention to the Mithraists as examples. *De Corona* actually means the crown of thorns. "You, his fellow warriors, should blush when exposed by any soldier of Mithra. When he is enrolled in the cave, he is offered the crown which he spurns [rejects with contempt] and he takes his oath upon this moment and is to be believed by the fidelity of his servants. The devil puts us to shame," he said.

Now there were seven degrees of initiation in all although there are some branches of the ecstatic side of the lore which includes certain others making the total twelve. After Lion came the Persian, then the Runner of the Sun, then

Father, and finally Father of Fathers. The twelfth degree it is said is King of Kings, and where have we heard that before? And properly, this can be held only by the supreme king and preferably, the Shahensha, or the King of Kings of Persia.

This very ancient cult from which more than one present-day secret society is derived is thus seen to contain many of the elements which underlie organizations of this sort. You see folks, it is a training system. It attempts to produce in its members a real or imagined experience of contact with some supreme power. The magical element is there too, shown in the belief in the power of certain names to achieve things which cannot be done by men. Mithraism was Not an antisocial society in the sense that it did not conflict in its aims with the objectives of the countries in which it flourished, and hence it did not threaten the established order. It was tolerant of other creeds just like Freemasonry is now. You can belong to any religion and join at the lowest level. But I guarantee you when you reach the highest you will belong to only one religion. The tolerance of other creeds meant that it did not attempt to supplant them. It's greatest festival, the Birth of the Sun, on the 25th of December became "Christianized," and it is claimed by those who still believe in its Mysteries, and celebrate them that Christianity did not so much supplant Mithraism as absorb it. Accepting some of its externals, and diverting them to its own use, and that is exactly what has happened. Perhaps incongruously a present-day follower of Mithra in England recently likened this phenomenon to the eclipse of the liberal party, quote, "Because the two other parties have taken over its objectives and widened the basis only the actual initiates of Mithra know what has been lost in the process," unquote. So the young man [Mithra] in the [word unclear] bonnet sometimes seen as the conqueror of the bull, or even as a man with a lion's head, still has his devotees. And folks, the Sun... Still... Shines...

So what does this all got to do with stars and stardust? Many people believe that Venus is the Morning Star. In the ancient days they said it was Sirius that rose just before the sun with a red cast to it and then turned brilliant white as it rose up into the heavens. Well folks, if you really think about it, the Sun is the Morning Star. Goodnight and God bless each and every one of you.

-Milton William Cooper, *The Hour of the Time* 02.24.1993 "Initiation"

My Analysis of "Initiation"

Mr. Cooper encouraged his listening audience to replay and reproduce all of his broadcasts so as to be heard by as many people as possible. He specifically told people to do this should anything foul happen to him and his life be cut short, as it had on

November 5th, 2001. What's either eerie, or orchestrated, is he died allegedly on his doorstep as he attempted to get back in his house after being ambushed by Apache County police. This is exactly how he described his figurative demise on his one and only guest spot on the young, commercialized, sensationalized Alex Jones Show. For him to have died in the exact spot as he imagined he may to Alex is more than a little questionable. It makes you wonder if he was positioned that way. It makes me wonder if it was a signature of the powers, the culprits behind the initiative to kill him that night.

In using portions of Bill's 42 part Mystery Babylon series, my aim is threefold. It brings the attention of a new generation to Bill Cooper's research and efforts, so that he may, in his own words, share his findings. I have come to find that Bill's research is quite solid, the best there is for practical purposes, however sometimes maybe deliberately not interpreted. It helps to show you what others whom allege to be all about "Truth," and "Patriotism" have stolen, cheapened, and watered down since his passing, and it also replaces the omitted portions of information that the current clowns won't talk about or acknowledge. It also gives me an opportunity to expand upon what was given, and in some rare instances present a different, or more complete conclusion as to what it all means that I myself provide from my work, and experiences. I get to analyze it and see where my focused studies may intersect with his. I think Bill sometimes deliberately presented information without giving his conclusion as to what it all meant, so that it would inspire a desire, a curiosity within his listeners to think about it themselves rather than being told what to think. He never wanted to be misconstrued as having the last word on a topic. He wanted people to verify. "Listen to everyone, read everything, believe absolutely nothing, not even me, until you can verify it with your own research." I think he would agree his aim was to get us to think, period, not to guide us as to what to think. Facts are facts. They should lead to a similar conclusion if we know how to think.

We can see a much more ancient root to mind control tactics being implemented to change and condition, in this case, an initiate's mental state for a life of unquestioning obedience. That state of mind is crucial to the rise of Socialist-Communism. To say the MK-Ultra [not Michelob, but that's curious, isn't it?] experiments and all subsequent, numerous programs still ongoing today were all inspired by Paperclip Nazi scientists is extremely naive to the point of being ridiculous. If anything, the revival of the method, so-to-speak, should be accredited to the scoundrel who reemphasized the importance of it to bring about the Modern Age, Aleister Crowley. The Aeon of Horus, the crowned [corona?] and conquering child, needed sex, drugs, rock & roll, and plenty of mass mind control interwoven within those elements to achieve its impact and alter the course of human progress. In came the OSS, Cybernetics, MK-Ultra and hundreds of sub-projects that had their own sub-projects, including Monarch. What happened after that? Public tests on the population. We had the Manson Family, CIA op. Possibly Amityville where Ronald J. Defeo, Jr. shot and killed 6 family members; his father, mother, two brothers, and two sisters. The story of the Lutz's came about the following year when they moved into the house on 112 Ocean Ave, and got right the F back out 28 days later after they claim they were plagued by paranormal activity. Ron DeFeo, Jr. didn't die until 2021, in prison. From a perspective of just briefly glancing at this, and by no means an Amityville expert, Ron's rampage seems to fit the pattern of what the agencies eventually brought into schools in the form of shootings. Perhaps this was an early prototype. I sometimes wonder when people recount being compelled by some very manipulative force to do something evil, something they wouldn't ever think of under "normal" circumstances, if maybe it's a black mold, a fungus of some other kind, or a parasite that is the culprit rather than the default impression of a demonic possession. Or maybe it's one in the same thing, and my comprehension of what can be 'demonic' is immature, and undeveloped.

Other forms of mass testing, or mass application of mind control tactics to the point of guided, and deliberate Culture Creation can be seen in a study of the Hippy generation. At first there was a natural, and organic awakening occurring within the people who wanted less government. Whether we agree or not in the true nature of the Renaissance, it stood for an age, or at least a limited hangout of enlightenment and spiritual evolution of mankind. So we could say the beginning of the 60's movement was taking shape to be a true Renaissance, and therefore intervention was necessary to derail that train before it could threaten the established powers that shouldn't be. Enter, stage left, Ordo Templi Orientis member, CIA operative, [al]chemist, and surprise, surprise, psychotherapist, Timothy Leary. Left as in Left-hand path, by the way. Between him, Ken Kesey, the Grateful Dead, and the rest of the Laurel Canyon crew, they managed to disperse countless hits of acid to the vibrant youth, promote distraction from any true purpose, all the while other agent provocateurs infiltrated honest movements, rose to leadership rolls, bullhorn and all, and started injecting Marxist ideals into a once pure move toward restoring lost freedoms. Would it surprise anyone to learn that the members of these bands, especially in the case of the Grateful Dead, were children of unconstitutional agencies such as the FBI, CIA, the compromised office of Naval Intelligence? Even Jim Morrison's father George was a Navy rear admiral and it was his ship that was involved in the farce we know as the Gulf of Tonkin incident. This was the excuse used to propel us into the Vietnam Conflict. Too bad it didn't actually happen, huh? How many young sons of American families died over that lie? How many were permanently maimed or mentally destroyed? Deception, and a plan to kill off Americans didn't originate with the CoroNOvirus.

A lot of things come to mind as I read or listen to Bill Cooper's Episode 9 of the Mystery Babylon series. My mind recognizes similarities, and sees patterns or connections at the speed of impulse. Just because I notice something that stands out, doesn't always mean I know why it does. Sometimes it just seems out-of-place, forced, or a cryptic representation of something I then need to go into deeper study to make sense of. Other times it's pretty straight forward if you know the foundational doctrine and beliefs or objectives of certain groups. You can identify who the players belong to, or where they have manifested, infiltrated, and influenced. I have some notes here to help supply more detail to, and suggest a practical application of the information you previously read.

The thing to remember throughout the telling of the initiation process by the priests is that the priests in that time period often were the council to kings or priest-kings who themselves had undergone initiations and partook in the rituals. Therefore any time you hear "priest" you have to understand the full value of the term in the time it was applied to. They weren't just some weird hermits in caves making people run through an Indiana Jones style obstacle course to reach some sort of artifact, in this case the promise of knowledge, enlightenment, or superiority over the profane or uninitiated. They were inseparable from the ruling class, and also were the source of magic and medicine. Yes, medicine, and healing were the wheelhouse of the priests in most cases. That should give you some insight as to the evolution of medicine and who controls it today insofar as to how it's derived, and what the root of the philosophy of the types of medicine come from. The sorcerers had potions and herbs, some legitimate, some pure poison, or inert and useless. I'm sure there were some that were just a little poisony too. They didn't have to rattle off at auctioneer's speed a four page list starting with, "Side-effects may include…" back then. You probably shouldn't criticize their medicine either, at least not in earshot of another adept. The more things change, the more they stay the same, once you learn what "same" is by exploring to the origin of things.

In Bill's reading he says times have changed because the extensive studies into brainwashing and mind control have laid bare the Mysteries, and answered the riddles which surrounded them. What he's saying is the methods developed, or applied for they had been developed thousands of years ago, now made aware to the public, serve as an insight into the mechanisms which manufactured belief and loyalty among the initiated of these ancient schools. The techniques were designed to stimulate and sometimes deprive the minds in the process of their conditioning. Coupling this with repetition, fasting, and other physical acts that effect the mental faculties they were indoctrinated. Their minds became moldable under these deliberate processes which produced the ideal state for which to do so. The fact that this practice was utilized by illegitimate agencies of an even less legitimate government in the more recent experiments is an indication of just where these agents and doctors in the OSS and CIA programs were selected from. If not the Knights of Malta, then the Freemasons, or one of the many other Mystery Schools still in practice today, and still producing their own indoctrinated initiates. These methods were well established as effective on individuals or small groups. The application of these techniques on the "masses" was what they seemed to have been experimenting with. What were the best ways to cause extreme terror and impart trauma in the minds of many at once? That may have been the question these tests were leading up to finding out, the ultimate objective. If you think about it, the public murder of a president in broad daylight on national television served as quite a wide-reaching traumatic event many experienced and were forever changed by. In these traumatic states the power of suggestion works more effectively because people are scared and more impressionable, having lost their discernment. Anyone presenting themselves as having answers and offering security and direction in the midst of chaos can usually get away with taking a few of your liberties in exchange for their promises to help. The quote used by Bill from Aristotle seems to sum up such an initiation, or public initiation as "*Those who are being initiated do not so much learn anything, as experience certain emotions, and are thrown into a special state of mind,'...in order that the conditioning might take permanent root.*" Keeping people in perpetual fear is a powerful tool for subduing their better judgment and allows for their manipulation. There was an ancient practice of making a sacrificial king. A king for a certain period of time, maybe a year, where he could do anything even if had the effect of weakening the powers of his controllers, and upsetting them, for the King for a day, was indeed a fool for a lifetime, because his fate was already planned. The devotees of the local priestcraft would convince the common people that the sacrifice of their king would serve their community for it would garner favor from their gods for who the sacrifice was for, and as a result bestow riches, a good harvest, no disease, or no enemy invaders for a time. Essentially they were promised they would rise from the ashes stronger than before. If that has some sense of familiarity to you when overlaid on the Kennedy assassination, and the direction our country's "leaders" steered us afterward, maybe that will serve as more evidence for you as to who these people are that orchestrate such horrific things. Our generation had the World Trade Center demolitions. In the wake of that we were saddled with an inversely named Patriot Act, unless you realize they're naming who they are targeting, then it reads plainly. Many of us, believing a very weak story as to who the culprits were, came out in strong support of the response by the president. He thought it would be a great idea to go after Saddam who was not involved in the attack, nor was his country, but somehow this made sense to those whose thinking was impaired. Many felt a strong patriotic duty and the country was united under a common bond, albeit a deceptive lie upon a deceptive lie. I was in the US Coast Guard at the time. I didn't see much of TV or the outside world, but the speeches by George W. Bush they made sure we all were gathered to watch. I had a feeling well up in my own chest, powerful, moving. I was being manipulated by the energy of the ritual and I didn't even know it.

Dr William Sargant is quoted by Bill, '*...Chinese experiments in mass-excitation, breaking down and reconditioning are based on same physiological principles as religious conversion and also individual and group **psychotherapy** treatments. [Folks,] these include the application of tension, fear, anxiety, conflict, to the point where subjects are uncertain. [And] in this state suggestibility is increased and the old pattern of behavior is disrupted.*'

I hope you're beginning to understand where the roots of psychiatry stem from, and why a certain popular "truther" psychiatrist utilizes a lot of references to alchemy and decorates their MD website with alchemical symbols. Nothing is in the dark, save our comprehension and understanding. The methods used by psychiatrists in planting what they deem more suitable ideas in the mind is no different in its method than in the Mysteries. When we look at the Mind Control experiments where torment, rape, and torture were used in conjunction with psychedelics and other psychoactive drugs, electroshock therapy, psychic driving, and sensory deprivation, you'll notice a resemblance to these methods and those used on large populations today. What is a dark cave but a sensory deprivation chamber?

When Sargent says "religious conversion" you have to take into account where religions draw from and it is the ancient practices and principles of mind control utilized by, if not born from the initiations of the Mystery Schools. Methods may vary, but the impact on the psyche of the individual is the same. Just as Chinese water treatment isn't the only form of torture that causes a mental break. Force me to listen to boy-band music and same result will be achieved. Please don't actually do that. The carrot they dangle of a secret to be revealed if they remain loyal to the order is also a method deployed for manipulative purposes. Or in the case of the Book of Mormon, the promise of your own planet in the afterlife for you to rule as if you yourself, and maybe you and your family, were gods. I wonder who your subordinates would be? Probably not the Predator aliens. Maybe a few meek E.T. types with narrow shoulders and pot bellies. While I'm on this tangent, did anyone else watch Close Encounters of the Third Kind and see the ending as the aliens picking up Take-out in the form of the dupes they had channeled to trust them? They were passing through and needed a snack. I think the people in their appropriately fashioned orange prison jumpsuits went off into space to become food like in that Twilight Zone episode, *To Serve Man*. The very tall, big headed aliens in the show were called Kanamits. That's close enough to Canaanites for me. And they are humanoid in form, so I would call that cannibalism, which is possibly another indication of the link between the name, and Canaanites who did practice this. Anytime your food can have a conversation with you, you're doing something evil by eating it. If they want us to stop consuming meat, they need to give the cows helmets that allow them to verbally protest. That will be very off-putting for most Godly souls.

Bill points out that Christianity, the Friendly Open Society, was a secret society itself, by necessity. Meaning, just because a society is meeting in secret doesn't mean they are always doing something malicious to mankind. I find this important to highlight simply because anyone who's fully aware of the dangers around us, knows any true opposition to these overlords would need to be meeting in secret, not shooting their mouth off on commercial, syndicated television and radio. That's infotainment and it serves as a pressure release valve for the people's frustrations, so that they themselves don't get restless and start a real movement of their own. There are a few genuine voices out there. They take an actual risk. Most however are there to drown those true voices out. Which ones are big budget, and which are constantly being deleted and banned on every platform? And I don't mean as a publicity stunt just to come right back after their all-too-masonic death and resurrection public ritual. The appearance of being attacked is another ploy used to convince people of the legitimacy of a propped up clown in the patriot community.

Even here you have Augustine, whom I refuse to call a saint, saying the mysteries of Christianity are too complex for the minds of men, and therefore only those properly prepared by initiation are truly worthy of their knowing. I'm not finding that in the words-in-red in the Bible. I don't see where Jesus said only initiates can know his teachings. Augustine is showing his previous Mystery School adept colors in his hierarchical attitude. It's this author's position that the religious constructs claiming Jesus's virtues are frequently in direct opposition to His actual message. Christianity, early in its history was morphed with Mithraism to the extent that it allowed the structure to support the sun worship practices, and ever since people are having a chicken-to-egg problem when they say Christianity was just a system of sun worship, or that it's all symbolic because it matches up with the more celestial predecessors. No, it was arranged to appear that way to integrate the pagans into the religion. That's why Jesus's "birthday" aligns with a solar process. Further alterations were made, and who knows what was lost and altered at the Council of Nicea?

The unbaptized weren't allowed so much as to look upon the teachings. So how do you know you want to have your symbolic death and rebirth, the baptism, if you don't know what you're entering into?

Bill emphasizes that communism and the Mysteries are the same entity, and therefore the lingo of Freemasons (Sons of Light) is the same, such as calling one another "fellow travelers."

Take note of the term, "Unseen God of the Universe." This will have more significance later, and you'll learn how it's a giveaway as to the true inspiration behind the Freemasonic Order.

In Mithraism, there is the degree of initiation mentioned where a crown is offered and if it is accepted, it means the candidate is unworthy. In other customs there are sacrificial kings as mentioned where he who wears the crown may do so for a time, but has sealed his fate with the priestcraft for this honor bestowed to him was not without a high cost. A contract was entered, and a term or stipulation yet to be satisfied. I will tell you this practice can appear in some of the most ordinary forms today that one may scarcely recognize it as a test of any kind. My mother and father are very intelligent people. Before you say, "What happened to you?" let me finish.

My mother has repeatedly taken aptitude and IQ tests in the past and scored so high as to be asked to retake the test because the administers were in disbelief. That may be why she was sent letters offering her a place in an unspecified group or secret society. Now we know that officially the Freemasons have a fraternity, that is to say, men-only order. We can only speculate as to who these letters came from because they were cryptic in their correspondence. Maybe it was the Daughters of the Eastern Star. She finally got fed up with their creepy persistence, and wrote a letter declining sternly

151

and with much condemnation of the idea of a group based on secrecy. My question is was she paradoxically passing the first test by denying the crown?

   As for me, I took an aptitude test when I was in third grade and I remember thinking I didn't do well. It was like a placement test because I was in a new school. But like my mother, I did something impressive because I was taken in by something called Ideas Unlimited, an elite reading group that doesn't appear to be a program anymore. The one that integrates agriculture into it is not related to what I was in. When I first got there teacher wanted us to read *A Wrinkle in Time* and talk about symbolism and the esoteric mysticism! I think I comprehend pretty well, but I wouldn't say I'm a good IQ test guy. Best I could ever do was a 145.

   The idea of Man becoming God is called Secular Humanism and it was declared an actual religion.

   From Wiki: *The first Humanist Manifesto was written in 1933 primarily by Raymond Bragg and was published with thirty-four signatories. Unlike its subsequent revisions, the first manifesto described a new "religion", and referred to humanism as a religious movement meant to transcend and replace previous, deity-based religions.*

   Further inquiry into this shows around 1980 it was officially recognized, and the most known figure of the movement may be Paul Kurtz, outwardly, but this is an ancient belief system. It could be seen as an act of defiance against a Creator God, and maybe to some who follow it, that is what it means to them. Objectively speaking however, intent is everything. If you learn of the impurities of organized religion, which Ken Wheeler calls religions secularized metaphysics, then what are you left with but your own personal relationship with God? In this internal church or Kingdom of God within you, why would it be so much different than the concept of a Christ consciousness? That is more of a Deist view than a Humanist one. See what I find comical are the people who say God told me this and that. I know they don't mean out-loud, and certainly not in-person. Maybe some do, but they are easily recognized as either charlatans, or the deluded. The very people who oppose and lash out at hearing the term "Christ consciousness" exhibit the very essence of it with statements like, "Jesus told me," or "God said to me…" Where did they hear that? The little voice in their head that attempts to guide and warn them? Potentially that's mostly them, and it's a form of mental masturbation. But it's not always just you telling yourself what you want to hear to justify an action or even an inaction. There's something else that speaks through us, our connection to the divinity. If we don't listen to that voice when it comes, it's usually at our disadvantage or detriment. If that weren't real, why all these chemical assaults on what they claim to be our VMAT2 gene, and our pineal gland? These materialist scientists deny the soul, and deny God so they have to conceptualize everything into quantifiable matter, and I'm here to tell you some things exist and operate outside of the material. The connection is real, and I personally, having taken the time to purposely engage that voice frequently, think it's something that can be cultivated and strengthened through practice. Whether I'm talking to God, Jesus, a guardian angel, or myself it's not clear. Sometimes I speak aloud, other times in my head. How is that different than prayer? I call it a walking prayer when I'm doing it as I go about my day. It's less formal than a prayer and I think that too helps to build that relationship. I get the feeling we make God and Jesus into these stuffy characters because of the influence of our church upbringings. Maybe they have a sense of humor. Maybe they like to just talk without being asked for things. I see a distinction between thinking you can become as God, and thinking you can have a personal relationship with God within yourself without the need for a middle man in the form of an organized religion. I find the idea of becoming God as an act of defiance, and ludicrous on its face. You're not going to make yourself a glass of water much less a universe from nothing just by thinking you're God, or a god. Try it. Tell me how it works out.

Bill mentions the UFOlogists, or as he later called them, the UFoologists. How they relate to the Mystery Schools and the New Age granola-eating, Gaia TV watching, patchouli-smelling movement is a book unto itself.

Egypt's Mysteries & the Brotherhood of the Snake

In this section I, by no means, am attempting to detail and outline every single aspect of the Egyptian culture and ancient traditions. That would require a library of books unto itself devoted to the topic, and such voluminous books already exist. A lot of which are written in cryptic, symbolic language so that the "profane," or uninitiated commoner gets one superficial or exoteric understanding, and an adept will read quite another. It should also be kept in mind that if the authors themselves are members of these Mysteries, they will never tell you the truth behind the meaning of the symbols, or allegories. They are sworn not to, so any account is written in the Exoteric, or cryptic nature that may hint to the truth for those with the proper knowledge. Manly P. Hall would be an example of someone often heralded as divulging information and insights, but one has to ask for what ends, and where is the line between the truth and the cover story?

"From the Egyptian records we learn that the new born Sun, Horus, was given the title 'The Logos,' which means 'The Word.' Egyptians further said 'The Word' was made flesh and dwelt among us. And since we enjoy only one Sun in heaven, He was said to be 'The Only Begotten' (of the Father)... The word was lost and that story is told in the Osirian cycle of Isis, Osiris and the child Horus, and you will learn that the symbol of the word today is the obelisk, the monolith, the stone. It is also called the Lost Word of Freemasonry...

In the most ancient Egyptian understanding of things, mankind was called 'the sheep of God.' And the great Orb of Day, God's Sun, was the overseer or, in the exact words from the ancient Egyptian manuscript, 'The Good Shepherd' – and we are His flock. All ancient kings thought of their people as sheep to be pastured, with themselves as 'the shepherd.' Sheep are ideal followers, you see, for they do not think for themselves but will blindly follow anyone without question--and that is why I call most people 'sheeple'. It's truly admirable behavior for animals, but it is very, very unwise for humans. Sheep were born to be fleeced, and have 'the wool pulled over their eyes. ...and are eventually always led to the slaughter. Lastly, they end up as a tasty meal, eaten by their masters, and their skin, or their hide or their wool, is worn as an apron around a Freemason's waist. (laughs) How about that?

...You know, Plato--I wrote this in my book--was an initiate of Mystery Babylon and was actually initiated in the Great Pyramid in Egypt where he lay in the sarcophagus for three days and three nights. He entered as a mortal man and, according to his writings, emerged as a god given, or imparted, knowledge which he was to guard and keep. Remember, they called themselves the 'Guardians of the Secrets of the Ages.' From the writings of Proclus and Iamblichus we can gain a considerable insight into the principles of Egyptian magic. To the old philosophers, even Pythagoras and Plato, magic was no mystery. According to Proclus the initiated priests so fully understood the

mutual sympathy between the visible and invisible worlds that they were able to change the course of action and focus divine virtues upon inferior natures. And according to Plato the highest form of magic consisted in the divine worship of the gods [William Cooper: plural], and according to Iamblichus the priests, through sacerdotal theurgy, were able to ascend from a material state of [unconsciousness (*note-book says, 'consciousness')] to a realization of the universal essence, thus coming to an understanding of universal purpose by which the performance of high feats of magic became possible.   Thousands of years later Aleister Crowley claimed the same thing. Now this is significant.

*   It's proper at this point to establish a clear line of demarcation of magic and sorcery. You see, the term magic was not associated with occult jugglery by the Egyptians but arose from a profound understanding of natural law...   'Magic,' said General Albert Pike, 'is the exact and absolute science of nature and its laws.' From the knowledge of this absolute science arises occult science. [William Cooper: Occult merely means "hidden", folks.] From experience in occult science in turn arises the theurgic art, for as surely as man has adapted his physical universe to his purposes so surely the adept of the Mystery School adapts the metaphysical universe to his purposes. To acknowledge that the Egyptians possessed the power of adapting mystical forces to physical ends is to bestow upon them proficiency in the most perfect and difficult of the arts [William Cooper: according to the Mystery Religion of Babylon]. Yet to deny this ability on the part of the Egyptian priests is to deny the evidence, and we must resign ourselves to the undeniable fact that they possessed a form of learning which has not been conferred upon this present race..."*

*   ...at least publicly. Men like Aleister Crowley have proven that it has been passed down through the ages and is kept and practiced secretly by those who call themselves the "Guardians of the Secrets of the Ages."*

The reason for all the quotes and brackets is that this was William Cooper reading from various sources on his broadcast. This is what the adepts believe, not necessarily what Bill believed, and he made that very clear often in his broadcasts in case someone had just tuned in and found him to be speaking out-of-character for himself. Bill would emphasize the importance of learning what the adepts believe because they are the ones in charge both then, and at present, and whether we believe it or not, it will affect us because they are, and have been, running the show.
Quotes taken from *Mystery Babylon Series Pt 3: Egyptian Magic* February 15th, 1993

The story of Isis and Osiris begins with the tale of Nut/Rhea, the daughter of Shu and Tefnut. It's a symbolic soap opera that you will have to endeavor on your own to find more information on. I recommend the *Mystery Babylon series: Osiris and Isis Part I and II* to get you started. It serves as a good overview of Plutarch's writing on the subject. Again we must temper that with the knowledge that Plutarch was himself an adept and therefore not representing the meanings in a straightforward manner.

More importantly to understand is that these stories are representations of the stars and planets, and their behavior in the heavens. For example Osiris, apart from being cut into 14 parts, was a sun symbol, and Isis the moon. Typhon, or Set, kills Osiris, or sunSet, get it? Horus, or Horizon was the rebirth of Osiris or the sun. It was a way to cryptically encode the practical knowledge of season change, and celestial events the Priests recognized, so that only the select would have understanding of it, and the rest would be dependent upon them. If you are ignorant, you are a slave. If you are fearful, you are a slave. They created gods that could become angry and destructive if they were not satisfied. It was of course the responsibility of the "masses" to assure that happiness and homeostasis was maintained through acts, offerings to the priesthood of course, obedience, and sacrifices. They purposely made up an exoteric explanation for things, and manipulated the profane, or common uninitiated members of the society. Nothing has changed in the thousands of years hence. We are delivered "popular" science while the overlords know the truth. We are given allopathy, while even the Queen of England up to her death had homeopathic and natural medicine doctors. We get the cheap, flimsy, distorted version of everything. When the adepts are playing with Transformers, we're stuck playing with K-Mart Go-Bots. We don't even have tangible real money in what's referred to as the last vestige of Freedom on Earth. However outdated that notion, the illusion that we are free prevails in our minds through constant, repetitive reassurance, deliberate misdirection, and it keeps us enslaved.

Rather than sift through the excrement for a choice piece of carrot or corn in these Egyptian dramas, let's instead look at the origin of this manipulation common in every place mankind huddled together across this plane. This is Bill's territory in that I love his boiled down, simple, no bullshit approach. The *Stone of Foundation* Ep. 1078 of *The Hour of the Time* is a great reference that we will venture into again in the coming chapters.

On mankind and the origin of all priestcrafts, Bill says, "*...Most people knuckle under to tyranny for two reasons. One is ignorance. They've been taught wrong. They don't know any better. And the other is fear. ...If you fear any government, you are the slave of that government. So to be afraid is to be enslaved. To be ignorant is also to be enslaved, but it is a different kind of slavery. See if you live your life in fear—if you know the truth, if you know what you should be doing and you don't do it because you're afraid, that is a most miserable life to lead. If you do it out of ignorance, you can even be happy in your enslavement thinking that you're doing all the right things, and that you are a good citizen, and that everything is going to be OK in the long run. Nevertheless, you are a slave.*

Who's doing this to us? How did it come about? Well let's talk about that a little bit, because I think, ladies and gentlemen, that it is imperative that you know the vast history here.

Sometime in the dim, misty path [or past?] *of the human race, man didn't live as we live today. Man lived very much like the animals* [I would call this a post-diluvian history, after the flood or cataclysm that reset us to primitive times again] *If you believe in the Bible, Man was made in the image of his Creator and was endowed with the ability to talk and think and act on a level above the animals. If you believe in the* [debunked, eugenics driven] *theory of evolution, Man once was an animal, unthinking, no intelligence, existing on instinct. It doesn't matter which one of these two you believe in, because what I'm talking about has nothing to do with your religion. It has to do with the religion of those who are lying to us, deceiving us, manipulating us, and have been doing so throughout the history of the world. Sometime back in that dim and misty past one of these men discovered something the rest of them didn't know. And it doesn't even matter what it was. If it was something that made their lives better and only he could do, or perform it, then everyone else who wanted to participate in that better life in order to receive the benefit of his knowledge and his actions had to conform to his dictates. So this man became the first king, the first Priest, and he founded the first religion. You can call it whatever religion you want. The religion of Uklack, if you will. If his name was Bob, you could call it Bob's Religion. But most likely this man had also noticed the movement of the sun, the moon, and the stars in the heavens because as far as we can trace back through history, this turns out to be the earliest religion we can find was the cosmology of the heavens. He could tell these people who depended upon his superior knowledge that this knowledge came from some mysterious deity or deities, and in that time it was probably plural from what we are able to research. He could say it came from the stars, or that particular Star to which he could point as it rose in the East at a certain time in the evening or night. He could attribute certain things that happened in nature to the movement of the sun and the moon. And he could predict through observation the tides. He could predict the coldest part of the winter. He could predict when the Earth would begin to warm again, followed by the summer. And he could predict the coming of the fall, and of the winter. He could tell people the most propitious time to plant crops.*

And maybe one day he was walking through the forest during a rain storm, and a bolt of lightning struck a tree and it burst into flames. And this man having walked through burned forest before and eaten the flesh of cooked animals, decided to take a branch of this tree and preserve the flame, and keep it burning. For there were no matches, ladies and gentlemen. If a fire went out it was out forever until maybe another lightning bolt would strike near enough to them where they could get to it, and preserve the fire again. The man who kept the fire was the Keeper of the Flame. Later in history he became the priest, the head priest. And most religions dating from early history kept a perpetual flame burning upon the altar. And this came from the time when men did not know how to start a fire and thus had to keep the flame alive. It became the most responsible position in the community. So the man responsible became the priest.

Since the fire warmed as the summer sun warmed the earth, and brought forth plants, people saw God in the flames. [an explanation for child sacrifice to a furnace] *So this became the dwelling place for God. The followers of this religion became the Philosophers of Fire. They learned to manipulate those who could not put all of these things together and learn what they had learned with that knowledge. They learned how to deceive with two stories. One called the exoteric, or the outward garment presented to those who are called the profane, the cattle, so-to-speak. The ones who could not use their intelligence and derive the same conclusions from observations of nature that the priests had done. And there was an esoteric presentation which was confined to the priests, the highest initiates of this religion, and it was the truth. The truth was used to manipulate the tribe, or the nation, and even the family. Through the bending of the truth and the presentation to those being manipulated as an exoteric interpretation of the esoteric truth. Most people live their lives believing the exoteric lie that is presented to them by philosophers, by governments, [by doctors] by priests, by churches, by religions, by pseudosciences, by movements.*

You see the great threat to the establishment that Jesus Christ represented was not that he claimed to be king, not that he claimed to be the messiah, and most historians will argue that he never made those claims except once when asked by Herod if he was the Messiah, he made a statement that many have interpreted as, 'Yes.' The threat that Jesus Christ represented, ladies and gentlemen, to the government at that time in history was the Truth. He said 'Seek ye the truth, and the truth will make you free.' He was breaking down the veil of the esoteric curtain behind which the Truth was housed. He was teaching people the reality of the world. He really didn't want to threaten anyone, but the Truth threatens Everyone!"

In Egypt as in Sumer as in Babylon, sun worship, and the worship of the generative forces of the male [and female] as represented by the Obelisk were core themes. Phallic worship some say was symbolic of the generative forces of the sun thought to bring rain and fertilize the seed of the crops, while its rays made them grow and flourish. Seth also known as Setekh, or Set was a deity rival of Osiris. Originally Set(h) was a sky god, not unlike Ba'al. Set was lord of Arizona, just kidding… Lord of the desert (same thing), master of storms (a geoengineer god like Ba'al, and that geoengineering could very well be literal if the pattern of human development is cyclical), disorder, and warfare. He's likened to a trickster. This is interesting because Mercury/Hermes is also considered a trickster or deceiver, and god of merchants and thieves as mentioned previously. Why do deceivers have a god at all? What sort of character would it possess? A God or Jin, really? Mithra was a Jin among many that over time became the most significant to the people, but like the B-movie horror film, Wishmaster, a Jin or "genie" could be likened to a demon who would twist words better than a lawyer. You think you're asking for one thing, but unintentional consequences arise. A separate meaning, or interpretation you didn't consider or even know of is then enacted at your behest. In other words, be careful what you wish for and consider the outcome. It's said the word mercury, or capitalized as a proper noun, is derived from the Latin word, merx, meaning merchandise. I do believe this may be the official Exoteric explanation for the root of the name, but not nearly all there is to say about it. For instance, why would a metal with very odd liquid-state properties and high toxicity, one very important to alchemists also be donned with that name? Another trickster god of the Norse was Loki, said to be cunning and have the ability to change its shape and sex. So Loki is a shape-shifting tranny, basically. By the way, tilt your ear to the ground and tap on your head. Knock out all that poison ooze in your ears Marvel movies infected you with. Loki was not a son of Odin, nor a brother of Thor. He was a companion of theirs, but that makes him no more kin to them than my neighbor is to me if we happen to hang out together. Fárbauti was Loki's father. Loki was a god of chaos who happened to be a bit sadistic at times. When you gather the details from every variation of the same archetype the blanks fill in faster than you with a new Mad Libs booklet. Children, have your parents explain that reference. It came from a time Scholastic Book fliers were handed out in English classes with really cheap books from even cheaper authors like R. L. Stine and Christopher Pike. Most of you will remember at least the Goosebumps series. Nothing says "childhood" like tween horror-drama.

From Ninazu to Mushhussu in Babylon to Wadjet and Nehebu-Kau in Egypt we find serpents playing a role as gods, and guardians at the gates of the underworld. Typhon, who isn't exactly a perfect fit as a comparison to Set, was also a very chaotic multi-headed hydra-like sea monster, but appears in many humanoid forms, but always incorporated with the snake. In fact it was Typhon that Aleister Crowley, 33rd degree Freemason, to say the least of his affiliations, who invoked the demon god of Typhon in his plot to sink the Lusitania. He was British Intelligence during WWI and that little hand gesture you see Churchill hold up didn't mean "peace," or V for "victory." It was, to the adepts, the hand sign for Typhon. Seek out classic Freeman Perspective videos for more on that.

"The association of the Magician with the serpent has been noted since the earliest records of not only Sumerian text yet also Babylonian, Assyrian, Canaanite and Egyptian religion and magical practice. In a 'balbale to Ningiszidaloo' the "Lord (Ningishzida), your mouth is that of a snake with a great tongue, a magician" and is then in a similar script as "a poisonous snake."
-*Maskim Hul,* pg 286 under the heading, " Magickian as Serpent" Michael Ford

*"When the Evil Spirit entered, he intermingled the **poison** of the noxious creatures, the outgrowth of sin, such as that of the **serpent**, the **scorpion**, the large **venomous** lizard, the ant, the fly, the locust, and an immense number of others of this kind, with the waters, the earth, and the plants."*
- Greater Bundahishn as quoted in Maskim Hul, Michael Ford

Necessary Tangent: To stay true to their mystical, or magical works taught through these orders dating back to Sumer, and certainly prolific in Babylon and Egypt, the Priestcraft of today must incorporate the signatures of olde into their manipulations. Here it states the Serpent, the Scorpion, and the venomous lizard. From the research of Dr Ardis, proven by published papers and studies, the allopaths and drug researchers are creating and prescribing venom-based drugs and vaccines. Dr Paul Reid of Celtic Biotech was developing venom based vaccines in the early 90's for "wide-scale implementation" at Fort Detrick, remember. Who's to say that for the last 30 years at least, we haven't already been subjecting ourselves to these venoms by way of common practice compulsory "innoculation?" It's here I should point out that scorpion venom is used on the food you eat in the form of an aerial sprayed insecticide. The most common cause of death after a scorpion sting is heart or respiratory failure. Respiratory failure… But we keep looking for invisible unicorns called viruses as a cause. In Egypt, Serket was a scorpion goddess, and there was a real Scorpion King, like that B-movie starring the very unsavory individual, Dwayne "the Rock" Johnson, currently being sued for his involvement in the theft-scheme of another wrestler's children. There were Scorpion I, and II, of Egypt the first dating back allegedly to 3150 B.C. and riddled with tales of sorcery and mysticism. The scorpion's tail, or teslon, when it strikes, leaves a mark on the skin that looks like a set of lips giving it the name, the "Kiss of Death." Scorpion venom also carries with it bacteria that is 88% identical to that of Micoplasma hyrohinis. Mycoplasma has been found in those afflicted with extreme "flu-like" symptoms, where they have great difficulty breathing, and that becomes relevant to the last 3 years of people suffering from what was termed to be "COVID." Sounds like the Priestcaft is alive and well, and these sorcerers just swapped out their black robes for white coats along the way.

The "venomous lizard": Ozempic and Exenatide are two drugs that are based on gila monster saliva, ie venom. Those who have taken Ozempic for diabetes find themselves developing paralysis of the vagus nerve, a crucial nerve chiropractors are trained on, and intimately familiar with, gastroparesis or the paralysis of the muscles around the stomach for normal digestives processes leading to the inability to keep food down, and the inability to produce insulin.

"Sorcerers and Magicians are viewed as being associated with snakes in nearly every culture. The Greater Bundahishn comments that one says that the noxious creatures are all sorcerers and the serpent is the most sorcerous." -Maskim Hul, Michael Ford

Once again we can go back to Egypt in the time of Cleopatra the VII and learn how cobra venom was "studied" by the magician-physicians in Alexandria:

"Alexandria and other kingdoms had court physicians specialized in pharmacology and venoms. As the last member of Ptolemaic Dynasty, Cleopatra VII inherited the throne and also the great inclination of Ptolemies towards medicine and science. In this city toxicological education seems to have had its most systematic development, and for Galen "human and prompt executions' were made in Alexandria with the intervention of cobras."

...Attracted by the knowledge of venoms and poison, Cleopatra began to test them on condemned prisoners to see the different reactions produced in the body and found toxic limits. When she decided to commit suicide, the use of poison would make sense given the possibility to choose the best one to get a quick and relatively pain free death. Knowing that oral poisons would cause disturbances as painful spasms, nauseas, abdominal cramps and slow end, she presumably compared the major effects of venomous snakebites caused by the various species living in Egypt, specially three families: vipers, hydrophids and elapids.

Cleopatra probably realized that viper bites generally produce violent local pain with inflammation, oedema, skin discoloration, pustules, vomiting and blood loss. With the cobra venom, hemotoxic or neurotoxic, instead, death could happen within half an hour, by **respiratory failure** *and general* **paralysis** *without leaving any trace on the flesh, though. It has been said that Cleopatra used the cobra to kill herself because it would also make sense in terms of Egyptian mythology, being associated with the sacred uraeus worn by the pharaohs.*

Studying the different poisons and the snakes that she could have selected and the symptoms and consequences that they could produce in her body, we'll try to delve into her possible lucubrations and reflexions, weighing the difficulties in each case. Undoubtedly, the mysterious end of Cleopatra remains unsolved, offering a constant source of legends and theories."
-ncbi.nlm.**nih**.gov/pmc/articles/PMC8042289/
Toxicology and snakes in ptolemaic Egyptian dynasty: The suicide of Cleopatra published online 2021 Mar 19 by Anna Maria Rosso

The article goes on to postulate that she could have used a hairpin to poke/inject herself with the selected venom, or may have mixed it with her fancy skin cream.

The priest: Sly, deceptive, and one may even say a sadistic Trickster who hoodwinks the masses by baffling them with bullshit, as W.C. Fields once said in a different, but similar context. It's no wonder the Mystery Schools revere the

Hermes/Mercury/Loki archetype. And now we're beginning to see a historical foundation of poisoning by these sorcerers using the natural venom of various snakes, especially the **cobra**, but also the **scorpion**, and whatever else was known to them.

> *"The ancient Egyptians, who had interaction with Assyria and Babylon at several points, understood the significance of the serpent in both a creative and destructive way. You find the **Uraeus Cobra** as a royal and deified symbol, many gods/goddesses such as Sekhmet, Set and other gods took the form of serpents. The gods Shu, Gebb and Khnemu are shown holding snakes in pre-dynastic illustrations."*
> -*Maskim Hul*, Michael Ford

Egyptian magicians didn't just use the snake, Ouroboros, or cobra as symbolic representations of more complicated concepts, but they used the venomous varieties in their rites and rituals. They understood toxicology and there was no faux TV show-driven pseudoscience of forensics in their day should they choose to poison their enemies, or even a child Pharaoh, for that matter. They were the law and the religion, so who among the people were going to don a French accent, point their finger at them, and say, "J'accuse," anyway? That would have been a good way to get the Egyptian Assassins sicked on you. Like our current US system, how dare you accuse them of their blatant crimes! You report some wrong-doing of an official, and the system starts investigating You! But it's not a police state, honest. No, no.

As I mentioned there was the feminine deity of Wadjet, and also her sister in snakey-ness Nekhbet, of Lower and Upper Egypt, respectively. Snake-hos in different area codes. Still prettier than Lizzo. OK, that's one of those scarce, personal opinions I mentioned in the intro that you may find.

So what of the venoms? Could this be a tradition, a dutiful practice of the adepts from Sumer to Egypt to present day pharmakeia? Is this a signature of the Brotherhood of the Snake we have been describing this whole book, naming them collectively as "the Mystery Schools?" Is Dr Ardis the first to point this out to the profane and uninitiated in several thousands of years? What's different now is simply the industrial process and advanced technology necessary to carry out murder on a mass scale using vaguely explained [to us] sciences, and synthesized venom proteins. Better yet, utilizing yeast and ecoli as venom peptide generating factories they can inject into us.

Like Johnny-5, you need more input. What pins the snake skin on the donkey-adepts?

**Show me more, Kristos!
Need Input.**

Cobras are used on the Pharaoh's headdress. The snake is the symbol of the sun likely due to the observable figure-eight it makes over time in the sky, named the analemma. [Not anal Emma. She retired.] A figure-eight is an infinite serpentine pattern when you get right to it. The priests of the Mysteries used snakes in ceremonies and secret rites, and were the choice source of ingredient for poisonous concoctions. Cleopatra is said to have ended her own life using the venom of an asp, or Egyptian cobra. What's even more interesting is how they said she did it. Either by poisoning her cosmetic cream, or by administering the venom into her bloodstream using a hairpin. The poison quill in its primitive form, before a plunger was added to its ass-end making it a syringe. She was ahead of her time. Now its all the rage. Everyone's doing it and they're not nearly as cool. Apophis, the antagonist of the Egyptians was also depicted as a very destructive serpent, a threat to structured, ordered society. Perhaps Apophis can be viewed as a symbol of a runaway Priestcraft drunk on power, destroying all without prejudice. Even if the people of Egypt didn't, we sure can see Apophis being analogous to the priestcraft. All too often it goes back to the adage, "consider the source." Those in power, who were typically the only literate members of a society, and if you've seen TikTok, you know nothing's changed, made the myths, not the people. Apophis viewed as a threat to their control could have, over time, symbolized Christianity as some claim Typhon was later slyly symbolic of. Propaganda and demonization of your enemy is nothing modern. If they already established the archetype among the profane, they could point to any threat and claim they were the minions of the demons in their own mythology, and the people, as they do now, would believe them. "Russia, Russia, Russia..."

The Ouroboros of Egypt is said by the Kabbalists to have symbolized the lowest level of the body being put in the mouth, meaning the Pharaoh was being immature in speech and action.

"In the Zohar, the imagery of the snake putting its tail in its mouth is used to illustrate the sin of "the evil tongue", i.e. slander, a gross misuse of the power of speech." - chabad.org/Kabbalah Online

The Ouroboros also meant the chaos surrounding the world, and various other things. In Norse texts a similar serpent Jörmungandr eats itself destroying all that is within its circle. Surprise, it's one of Loki's children.

In the Ptolemaic dynasty of Egypt, post Alexander, *"was especially interested in drugs and poisons meanwhile Alexandria became a prestigious center of learning and the first medical center of the ancient world. Scholars dedicated to toxicology would research in the famous Museion and the Hellenistic rulers of Alexandria and other kingdoms had court physicians specialized in **pharmacology** and **venoms**."*
-NIH National Library of Medicine, online, journal title: *Toxicology and snakes in ptolemaic Egyptian dynasty: The suicide of Cleopatra*

This is a very interesting find on the National Institute of ~~Murder~~... I mean, Health's website. They know the effects of venom poisoning, and they have been doing extensive research into it the past 30 years in the pharmakeia, or rather "pharmaceutical" spheres creating drugs and DoD funded vaccine projects. As mentioned, Celtic Biotech's co-founder, Dr. Paul Reid, worked at Fort Dirty Detrick in the 90's to create snake venom based "vaccines."
Dr.Reid was employed by the United States Medical Research Institute for Infectious Diseases (USMRIID) at Fort Detrick, Maryland, under a grant from the National Research Council in Washington, D.C. Under the grant he was responsible for the expression and purification of a variety of neuroactive components from snake venom in ***bacterial and yeast*** *systems and purification of expressed material with expansion to* ***large-scale vaccine production****.*
-walkersresearch.com, Profile of Paul Reid, CEO - ReceptoPharm Inc

Egyptian Revival in England

You know who else were obsessed with poisoning people, and with Egypt? The Victorian Era had what is referred to now as Egyptomania. And it got a little weird. There was great interest in the occult knowledge of Ancient Egypt and they adorned themselves with cobra and snake jewelry.

"...many saw something in Valley of the Kings that struck a clear tone with their darkest desires. Ancient Egyptians believed in giving their dead an appropriate send-off, constructing elaborate mausolea to them, and entombing their corpses with personal possessions that might assist them in the afterlife.
For the Victorians, with their equally morbid and complex mourning rituals, the example of these ancient people was one to follow – perhaps they even saw something

of themselves in this ancient empire, its ambition, wealth and grandeur, and saw its collapse as a potent reminder that even the greatness of Britain will one day fall to dust, just as Champollion's beloved Napoleon had done.

Throughout the 19th century, Egyptian influences could be found in women's mourning jewelry, which often featured obelisks or scarabs…

-.historyanswers.co.uk/people-politics/victorian-egyptomania-how-a-19th-century-fetish-for-pharaohs-turned-seriously-spooky

Dicks and bugs for those of you following along at home. They decorated themselves with obelisk dicks and beetles.

A surgeon by the name of Thomas Pettigrew held mummy unwrappings for the public. Wealthy people would pay to see the ancient corpses exposed and defiled by the doctor. He went so far as to cut into the empty skull to reveal that the brain had been removed. It was scare-based morbid entertainment. Nowadays it's spirit cooking with Marina Abramovic, or any sick event they hold at the Met (Metropolitan Museum.) To say the wealthy and bored of the Victorian Era were fond of the wonders from Egypt is not to imply that they had any respect for the culture, or for the dead. What would be considered now a tragic desecration and disturbance of historical artifacts took place at ludicrous looting-speed and accomplished just that. Disbursement of ancient relics scattered to wealthy collectors, and the contamination of the original condition of rooms and tombs in this lost land had the same effect as letting a herd of idiots trample a crime scene while you're trying to figure out what happened there. When there were, if there ever were, honest, sincere archaeologists, they would have been appalled at this. I'm not one to say like Indiana Jones, "It belongs in a museum," because if the Smithsonian's actions tell us anything, it's that the bury more history than the dig up so that it can be more easily manipulated to support the approved historical narrative. What I am saying is maybe, in the fairy tale world I sometimes pretend can exist, have honest people with good intentions be the first to examine these mysterious ruins and get an understanding of what went on there and what the people were like. Who's to say a tablet, scroll, or some other writing wasn't carted off that did, in fact, describe how they preserved the bodies? How would we know? No one inventoried the stuff they were stealing. It's kind of the whole point not to leave a paper trail of evidence that you're stealing.

Although aristocrats may have been thrill seeking, they didn't humanize their interest with empathy. They didn't care the bodies were disturbed after several thousand years of peace, only to be undignified, disgraced, and laid bare. It's this monstrous banality of evil, where indifference resides in the hearts of people that I have a difficult time relating to. It's not just their money making them feel "Uber Alles," but something else is absent in them that I, and probably you, have that can connect with others, and feels for others. People have said that the ultimate Evil is Indifference. Elie Weisel said, *"Indifference, to me, is the epitome of all evil."* Whereas Heschel took it a step further and put the onus on us, *"Indifference to evil is more insidious than evil itself. It is a silent justification affording evil acceptability in society."* This was likely in reaction to the alleged crimes of the National Socialists of Germany. To which I respond, then what say you of the Bolshevik Revolution? Why did we allow Rothschild agents like Jacob Schiff train and fund a band of cold, soulless murderers, and send them to Russia with US gold as funding for the revolution? Killers that would starve-out and shoot their way through tens of millions of Russians, and only succeed because Wall Street and Big Banking funded them? Plato talks of our individual, and social responsibility when he says, *"The price good men pay for indifference to public affairs is to be ruled by evil men."* By allowing the treasonous actions from 1913-1948 to occur in our country, we got exactly that. The memory may fade, and the crimes may be omitted from state education, but the impact remains, and is evident in the present heresies of illegitimate banking controlled "government."

From the online magazine *History Answers* comes a December 13th 2016 article titled, *Victorian Egyptomania: How a 19th Century Fetish for Pharaohs Turned Seriously Spooky."* Under the section "Ancient Curses and Ritual Magic" we read:

"German Egyptologist Karl Richard Lepsius produced the first modern translation of scattered Ancient Egyptian literature relating to funeral customs, bundled together as the Book of the Dead in the 1840s and erroneously believed to be an authentically Egyptian holy book in itself. This volume detailed Ancient Egyptian beliefs about death and the afterlife, the terrible trials awaiting the deceased in the worlds beyond ours, and the curses and charms by which they could stand a fighting chance of passing on unscathed.

The Freemasons had made use of Egyptian imagery and philosophy in their rituals since the late 18th Century as a way of setting out their own legitimacy and inventing an unbroken sense of heritage, but in tandem with Egyptomania – and in opposition to the Christian lens through which matters of life and death were being viewed – Russian-born occultist and fraud Helena Blavatsky jumbled together emerging theories and fictions in Isis Unveiled: A Master-Key to the Mysteries of Ancient and Modern Science and Theology (1877)."

Whoa, settle down there. That's exactly the sentiment on Blavatsky that Aleister Crowley held. The two had great disdain for one another and Crowley as far as being a thief and a plagiarist are concerned, was plenty a fraud, himself. Both however did work in some strange realms and much of what Blavatsky wrote in **Isis Unveiled**, and **The Secret Doctrine** are definitely worth reading. It's not about adopting their philosophy. It's about learning how the occultists, priestcraft and court mystics who shape our reality think. If you know that, it's all the easier to identify the schemes, and avoid being swept up in the deception. Probably the sharpness against Blavatsky in this establishment article has to do with this line by Russian-born, but present day Ukraine territory, Helena

P Blavatsky, *"Capital punishment is a relic of Jewish barbarity, and far more unjust than the worst crime imaginable."* They really hate criticism or even questioning. We continue with the article:

*"Blavatsky's writing – along with further editions of the Book of the Dead that espoused now discredited views about **death cults** – became linked to the foundation of the Hermetic Order of the Golden Dawn in, an influential circle of occultists and pipe-tapping seekers of mystery whose members included (or were rumoured to include) WB Yeats, Arthur Conan Doyle, Algernon Blackwood, and, eventually, the Edwardian era's 'Wickest Man in the World' Aleister Crowley."*

First of all, the only people that want us to disbelieve in the existence of death cults, would be high ranking members of death cults! This whole book has chronicled the practices of child sacrifice, blood ritual, Assyrian Babylon's ritual sacrifices of all of their perceived enemies in gruesome fashion, and we haven't even gotten into the Order of Nine Angles yet. Don't be fooled by the pseudo-intellectuals who just repeat what they're taught without studying. If they're implying that death cults didn't and don't exist, they're either unqualified to pretend "historian," or they're knowingly deceiving.

"The Golden Dawn took Blavatsky's writing and ran with it, forming pseudo-Egyptian temples and cloaking their rituals (which drew from Ancient Greek philosophy, the writings of John Dee and the Hebrew Kabbalah) in pharaonic set dressing. From the ground up, they presented themselves as heirs to an ancient magical tradition, enthusiastically devouring Egyptology and repurposing it for their own rites, both feeding on the popular mystique of Egypt and perpetuating it."

This is probably true in part, in that the surface practitioners were likely more public about their ceremonies. They may have had more flamboyant showmanship so as to attract curious candidates into membership. But the adepts of the Mysteries have had a consistent undercurrent, an unbroken tether from ancient times of the Mystery schools to now. Those in the truly ancient-rooted mystical practices were not simply adding an Egyptian flare to their origin. They predated, or were organic to the real time of the Egyptians, and not the text book shortened-history version you're taught. I have to now insert an educated, however unproven opinion that Egyptians as we know them, did not build the pyramids, but rather occupied the area of a lost civilization and wrote their names on the walls as if they had. I'm sure with the unearthing of the ruins, it was a great opportunity for these adepts to fill in portions of their lost traditions. For anyone in an article to claim they simply grafted Egypt mysticism into their secret societies as a new element would have to have firsthand knowledge of these societies to confirm that. They do not share what they know or the nature of their practices with the profane, so how could the authors of this article be so sure that this was true? That all of these underground practices simply used Egyptian culture to falsely legitimize their ancient origins for marketing purposes? I think that's a big leap in assumption, but in some cases, such as the newly forming orders of the 1800's era, was likely true for them.

In relation to the potential reality of curses the article states:
"...One account published in the Hampshire Telegraph in 1896 explains how a mummy was purchased by adventurer Herbert Ingram from the British Consul in Luxor, and promptly sent home:

The mummy was that of a priest of Thetis and it bore a mysterious inscription [....] which was long and blood-curdling. It set forth that whosoever disturbed the body of this **priest** should himself be deprived of decent burial; he would meet with a violent death, and his mangled remains would be 'carried down by a rush of waters to the sea'

While hunting in Somaliland (now Somalia), Ingram was gored and trampled by an elephant who remained at the scene. By the time his companions were able to reach his remains days later all but a handful of bones had been washed away by the rains...

... Haggard was deeply respectful of the power of the long dead Egyptians (in part because he believed in reincarnation, claiming to have lived as one in a past life) and cautioned Daily Mail readers against defiling the dead in 1904, with an oblique reference to their reanimation:

It does indeed seem wrong that people with whome [his spelling] it was the first article of religion that their mortal remains should lie undisturbed until the Day of Resurrection should be hauled forth, stripped and broken up [...] If one puts the question to those engaged in excavation, the answer is a shrug of the shoulders and a remark to the effect that they died a long while ago. But what is time to the dead? To them, waking or sleeping, ten thousand years or a nap after dinner must be one and the same thing."

Is there a true curse, a legitimate magic that transcends death that the Egyptian priests had mastered in their own time?

Sanderson

A MUMMY

"In the second half of the nineteenth century, the popular travel company, Thomas Cook and Son, transformed Egypt into the 'ultimate' tourist destination. This meant that tourists could travel to and experience Egypt, an exciting and unique prospect that led

to unruly consequences. Cook's paddle steamers were incredibly popular with Victorian tourists; they could travel on the Nile and see a number of historic sites, including ancient temples and ruins, within a limited amount of time. They were also known to partake in more unusual trips; not all mummies were buried in tombs; some were buried in pits of various sizes in the ground named 'mummy pits' where tourists could visit and 'discover' a mummy of their own...

...The mummy became the fascination of tourists and, unfortunately, the ultimate souvenir from their time in Egypt. Although illegal and unethical, the mummy trade in Egypt was lucrative, promoted by tourists who wanted to take a mummy (or a piece of one) home with them. Both travellers and tourists were known to smuggle mummies and mummy parts back to Europe."

-Epoch Magazine, Dec. 1st, 2021 *The Curse of the Victorians in Egypt: Tourists on the Nile*

It seems there were good reason to embellish any idea or rumor of a curse once the crisis of conscience reached the hearts of those who saw Egypt as more than a site for wealthy tourists to exploit, loot, and desecrate. The tourists would dig their own mummy from a "mummy pit" and eat their lunch beside the corpses. They even would scale the pyramids and carve their initials into it, and sometimes do so on walls that contained hieroglyphics, damaging the ancient inscriptions. The ruling class, nobility, and whatever else you want to call them were no better than any other who disregards, and has no appreciation for the native culture of a place. Good thing they didn't have cans of spray paint back then.

Perhaps, some of the effort in popularizing the tales of curses that resulted in death were promoted in the day to prevent further destruction and reduce the interest in those who visited to take away souvenirs. Kleptomania~Egyptomania. Whether it was deliberate or a natural result of a very real phenomenon, slowly these stories did inspire the return of many objects to museums as anonymous donations, likely from those fearful of some dreaded fate that awaited them for having disturbed the bodies on their trip.

William Cooper, Hour of the Time Broadcast, Mystery Babylon Series pt 3: *Egyptian Magic*
[reading from *Freemasonry of the Ancient Egyptians*, by Manly P. Hall]:

"Isis was the patroness of the magical arts among the Egyptians. The use to which magic should be put is revealed in the Osirian cycle where Isis applies the most potent of her charms and invocations to accomplish the resurrection of Osiris. In other words, the redemption of the human soul. That the gods of Egypt were elements of a profound magical system and possessed a significance far different from that advanced by modern Egyptologists is certain. The various deities of the Nile valley were elements of an elaborate magical metaphysical system, a kind of ceremonial Cabbala. [his spelling]

This cannot be denied. But even when impressed with the reality of this fact, the modern Egyptologist still balks. "Supposing," he asks, "that the Egyptians did possess an elaborate metaphysical doctrine? Of what value is its rediscovery in an age when the natural has been demonstrated to be mediocre and the supernatural non-existent? Even if these extinct persons whose mummies clutter up our museums were the custodians of some mysterious lore, we have simply out grown it. Let the dead past bury its dead [William Cooper: they say]. We prefer to live in an era of enlightenment, an enlightenment which you would blight by asking us to espouse the superstitions of our remote ancestors.

"These so-called superstitions, however, it is interesting to note, die hard. In fact they do not die at all, but insinuate themselves as a discordant note in our matter-of-fact existences. McCall's magazine published some time ago an article by Edgar Wallace entitled The Curse of Amen-Ra, dealing with the phenomena attendant upon the opening of the tomb of the Pharaoh Tutankhamen. After vividly describing the curse of Amen-Ra the author sums up the effect of this curse upon those who came in contact with the tomb or its contents. His statements are in substance as follows: At the time the tomb was opened the party present at the excavations included the Earl of Carnarvon, Howard Carter and his secretary, Dick Bethel, M. Benedite the French archaeologist, and M. Pasanova. Of these, only one, Howard Carter, remains alive. [William Cooper: Now, that was at the time of the article.] Colonel Aubrey Herbert, Carnarvon's half- brother, and Evelyn-White who also entered the tomb were both dead within a year, one by suicide. Sir Archibald Douglas Reed, the radiologist who took an X-Ray of the mummy, was also dead within twelve months; and Professor Laffleur of McGill university, the first American scientist to examine the death chamber, did not leave Luxor alive. Woolf Joel visited the tomb and was dead within a year. Jay Gould was taken ill within the tomb and died. Attendants whose duty it was to look after the exhibit from the tomb in Cairo Museum also sickened and died. Seven French authors and journalists visited the tomb and six were dead within two years. When they unveiled Tutankhamen they found a mark upon his face, and by a strange coincidence (?) the mark left upon the face of Lord Carnarvon, which presumably caused his death, was in exactly the same spot and of similar appearance. Nor does this list include the numerous native workmen who perished from the curse. Only recently another name was added to the long list associated with the tragedy. Arthur Weigall, after a long and mysterious illness similar to that defined in the curse, is the most recent victim. The eminent authority on antiquities, Dr. Mardus, said, 'The Egyptians for seven thousand years possessed the secret of surrounding their mummies with some dynamic force of which we have only the faintest idea.

Over the entrance to the tomb of Tutankhamen was a magical tablet inscribed with strange hieroglyphics. Dr. Mardus named this tablet the 'Stela of Malediction,' for it pronounced a fearful curse upon any sacrilegious person who might violate the sanctuary of the deified head [William Cooper: and it was called the stele]. The words upon the stela were as follows: 'Oh ye Beings from Above, Oh ye Beings from Below! Phantoms riding the breasts of men, ye of the crossroads and of the great highways, wanderers beneath the shade of night! And ye from the Abysses of the West, on the fringes of the Twilight, dwellers in the caverns of obscurity, who rouse terrors and shuddering: and ye, walkers by night whom I will not name, friends of the Moon; and ye intangible inhabitants of the world of night, Oh People, Oh Denizens of the Tombs, all of you approach and be my witnesses and my respondents! Let the hand raised against my form be withered! Let them be destroyed who attack my name, my foundation, my effigies, the images like unto me.

Can modern Egyptologists and scientists and all branches and departments view likely the culture of the Egyptians if their researches into the forces of nature gave them such strange power and enabled them to master natural laws of which modern learning has no knowledge or conception?

Circumstances so extraordinary is the curse of King Tutankhamen simply overtax the theory of mere coincidence [folks]. Nor is this an isolated case as those will remember who read the accounts of the Cleopatra mummy curse many years ago. It will also be noted that in this age of moral certitudes the story of the Tutankhamen curse had no sooner been broadcast than several of our large museums were deluged by gifts of Egyptian antiquities from private individuals who no longer desired to own them. And these, persons most of them well educated (as modern education goes), were not superstitious--they were just careful.

The following article appeared in an English newspaper in 1923: ''The death of Lord Carnarvon has been followed by a panic among collectors of Egyptian antiquities. All over the country people are sending their treasures to the British Museum, anxious to get rid of them because of the superstition that Lord Carnarvon was killed by the 'ka' or double of the soul of Tutankhamen. These fears are, it is hardly necessary to state, absolutely groundless.'

It's also hardly necessary [folks] to add that the journalist fails to give his authority for the last sentence. The newspaper article continues: 'An avalanche of parcels containing mummies' shriveled hands and feet, porcelain and wooden statuettes and other relics of the ancient tombs descended this week on the British Museum. Fear inspires these gifts, brought by every post. The belief that a dead king's curse is potent for evil after thousands of years won thousands of adherents on the day when Lord Carnarvon became ill.
*** Few of the parcels received at the museum bear the sender's name. The owners, in their eagerness to wash their hands of the accursed things, have tried to keep their identity secret. ***

The British Museum is a godsend to the superstitious. It offers a means of shifting the liability to expert shoulders. The museum authorities are used to such liabilities, having harbored the coffin lid of the powerful priestess of Amen-Ra for years, but they are not at all grateful for the present flood of gifts. The museum weathered a similar storm some years ago when the story of the curse of the priestess of Amen-Ra became public. Sufficient scare gifts were received to fill a large showcase. A long chain of fatalities has been attributed to the curse of the priestess. Men who have made fun of the superstitious have died within the year. Another story is that a photographer took pictures of the priestess and placed the plates in his safe. When he went to look at them some weeks later, the glass had become a thin brown powder.'

*[Now,] let us consider the 'rational' explanations, so-called, adduced by science in disposing of the superstition of the king's curse. Dr. Frederick H. Cowles, F.R.G.S., famous British scientist, declared in an interview...years ago that Lord Carnarvon and a number of workmen engaged in excavation met their deaths as the result of a poisonous and **almost invisible dust** [Nano?] placed there purposely by the wily **priests** to bring destruction upon the violators of the dead. 'This poisonous dust,' says Doctor Cowles, 'analysis of which has baffled scientists, was scattered about the tomb. *** Lord Carnarvon was not the only to note its fatal property, as a number of workmen engaged in the excavation were likewise stricken. Most of these died a lingering death, but others, greatly impaired in health have recovered.' There is nothing in the learned doctor's explanation, however, to account for the fact that Howard Carter did not chance to breathe any of the noxious vapors, although he was more steadily engaged in the work of excavation then even Lord Carnarvon. [It's also questioned] how much science actually knows about this mysterious dust which defies analysis, for if it cannot be analyzed how can it be either identified with certainty or even proved poisonous. The term 'poisonous dust' is evidently the charitable term that covers a multitude of scientific shortcomings.*

Or it's an indication of an ancient nanotechnology or what we are told is nanotechnology, but may be an intelligent, however tiny life form on this planet? Perhaps spores of some kind, or even a dried venom was encountered in these tombs. An ancient, or timeless bioweapon?

"Though sorcery has been accorded no official recognition by modern science, there is, nevertheless, a certain quasi-official acceptance of the reality of occult phenomena through out the civilized world...

Skipping ahead, Bill says: *"You may wonder where all this is going, but it becomes clear when you understand that the Egyptians inherited the religion of Babylon."*

Back to Hall: *[So] are we to presume...that the single phase of ceremonial magic constituted the entire repertoire of Egyptian thaumaturgists. [You see,] if they could manifest such surprising power, is it not probable that they possessed a knowledge of natural hidden forces--forces as yet unknown to the modern public world which is possibly of inestimable value?*

William Cooper: *Which may still be contained within what is called the Secrets of the Ages? Which is guarded by the modern Mystery School? Which is still the ancient Mystery School brought forward through the ages?*

Hall: *"...We [can] pass over all the desperate efforts to disprove the magical powers of the Egyptians as arising, not from a mature knowledge, but from a desperate prejudice. [You see,] magic is too ancient and too universal to be explained away by mirrors, wires and hinges. In Egypt we are dealing unquestionably with true manifestations of occult power. The learned author of Art Magic presents what maybe accepted as a reasonable accurate estimation of the priest-magicians of the old Egyptian Mysteries. 'They were highly educated, scientific men. They understood the nature of the lodestone, the virtues of mineral and animal magnetism, which, together with the force of psychological impression, constituted a large portion of their theurgic practices. They perfectly understood the art of reading the inner most secrets of the soul, of impressing the susceptible imagination by enchantment and fascination, of sending their own spirits forth from their body which many modern metaphysical teachers claim that they can do, as clairvoyance, under the action of powerful will--in fact, they were masters of the art now known as mesmerism, clairvoyance, electro-biology, etc. They also realized the virtues of magnets, gums, herbs, drugs and fumigations, and employed music to admirable effect..."*

"Do you believe in magic(k)? Well I hope you do. You'll always have a friend wearing [horrifically symbolic] big, red shoes…" -Ronald McDonald, ass clown.

Oral and Written Kabbalah

"Something's really wrong. Something is destroying everything that we've ever held dear in this country. What is it? Well, if you've been listening to this show, many of you already know what it is. If you've just been listening to this show for a little while, you may have some idea, but you're not quite really sure yet what's going on. Well, I'm going to tell you right now it's all about religion. Whether you're religious or not, doesn't make any difference. It's all about religion. Whether you believe in God or not, it doesn't make any difference. It's all about a big battle between good and evil. And most of it, I got to tell you, exists in the minds of men. Some of it's real. The question is, what's real, what's deception, what should we be paying any attention to? What is it that's driving us insane? Yes, something is wrong in America.

Today's newspapers are full of stories about the rampant rise of divorce rates; the increasing abuse of children by some parents; increases in the incidence of rape; pornography being read by an increasing number of people; more crimes against property; demands for world government; urgings for national borders to fall; Christian churches being closed because they will not seek licensing by the state, etc., etc., etc...

But why, why are these things happening? Why are all of the legacies of the past, the family, national borders, the right to practice any chosen religion, the right to private property, amongst other things, under such an attack? Is it possible that there are actually people and organizations who really want to change the basic order of things?

Well, my regular listeners know the answer to that.

Clues to the answers to these questions can be gleaned from some comments made by people and organizations that are talking about these wide-ranging changes in the nature of our lifestyle.

An Associated Press dispatch on July the 26th, 1968 reported this: 'New York Governor Nelson A. Rockefeller says as President he would work toward international creation of "a new world order.'

On January the 30th, 1976, a new document called The Declaration of Interdependence was introduced to the American people. And it was signed by 124 traitors: 32 Senators and 92 Representatives altogether 124 traitors in Washington D.C. and it read in part: 'Two centuries ago our forefathers brought forth a new nation. Now we must join with others to bring forth a new world order.'

Another individual who has commented is Henry Kissinger, [probably the greatest traitor this nation has ever known,] former Secretary of State. According to the Seattle Post Intelligence of April 18th, 1975, Mr. Kissinger said: 'Our nation is uniquely endowed to play a creative and decisive role in the new order which is taking form around us.'

Historian Walter Mills maintained that prior to World War I, Colonel Edward Mandell House, the major advisor to Woodrow Wilson, the President at the time, had a hidden motive for involving America in the war. The historian wrote [this]: 'The Colonel's sole justification for preparing such a batch of blood for his countrymen was his hope of establishing a New World Order of peace and security.'
-William Cooper reading from **The New World Order**, by A. Ralph Epperson

And we learn from Karl Marx, the Communist definition of "Peace" is the absence of resistance to Socialism. Subduing the world, disarming them, terrifying them into obedient submission. That's what they call peace. UN Peacekeeping missions don't pass out flowers and give hugs. They bomb, terrorize, slaughter, rape, and torture people who did nothing wrong. Bolsheviks in blue helmets.

The one blindspot Bill seemed to have, or was being deliberate to not speak much of, was the Kabbalist element in things. I've listened to nearly all of the broadcasts that have survived, and it's clear based on what he does focus on that the topics of Bolshevism, the Kabbalah, and Sabbatean-Frankism would not come up simply due to his more traditional, or mainstream academic take on the events of World War II. This is not a criticism. It's simply an observation.

If you have not already began to do so, I'm going to suggest taking notes from here on. I'm going to briefly introduce a lot of information up front before delving into each element in greater detail.

My research into Sabbatean-Frankism began with a short book on the topic by Robert Sepehr called, *1666: Redemption Through Sin.* 1666 was also the year the Cestui Que Vie Trust was enacted into law in England. Another book, *Sabbatai Sevi: The Mystical Messiah* by Gershom Sholem is essential for understanding the core beliefs of Kabbalah as it were, and as it has become since.

The story of the evolution of Kabbalism from Mystery Babylon to present day actually takes a turn into the story of the dawn of the Jesuits, however odd that may seem to some readers. That turn into the Jesuits makes another turn into Isaac ben Solomon Luria Ashkenazi, or simply Isaac Luria (1534-1572), accredited for what was later called the Lurian Kabbalah. Long before there was an Illuminati, or Perfectabilisten, as it was originally known, there was the Alumbrado, also meaning illuminated, and where we may derive some influence on the term "Alumni" probably. Readers will certainly point out the term is Latin, and I will point out that so too is derived the language of Spanish where the word Alumbrado comes from.

A single red rose is the symbol for international socialist-communism, for it is the ancient symbol of the Mysteries, but it is also a symbol for Israel.

"What is the Rose? It is the Congregation of Israel. Because there is a rose, and there is a Rose. Just as the rose among the thorns is tinged with red and white, so is the

Congregation of Israel affected by the qualities of Judgment and Mercy." - Zohar
Introduction, Chapter 1

Kind of a load of horse manure and an insult to sensibilities when you consider
that the modern state of Israel is founded by Frankist-Knights of Malta international
bankers, namely the Rothschilds, and has been a murderous terrorist state since
inception. I see plenty of "judgment," but would require clarification as to their
definition of "mercy." I suppose they may mean mercy killing, but even that is offensive
to the senses.

"It depends on what the meaning of the word '*is*' is." -William Jefferson Clinton

Wikipedophilia, I mean, Wikipedia says this regarding the Zohar:

*The Zohar is a foundational work in the literature of Jewish mystical thought
known as Kabbalah. It is a group of books including commentary on the mystical
aspects of the Torah and scriptural interpretations as well as material on* **mysticism,
mythical cosmogony**, *and* **mystical psychology**.

From the online Encyclopedia Britannica/topics/Kabbala is reads:

Sefer ha-zohar, (Hebrew: "Book of Splendour"), 13th-century book, mostly in
Aramaic, that is the classic text of esoteric Jewish <u>mysticism</u>, or <u>Kabbala</u>. Though
esoteric mysticism was taught by Jews as early as the 1st century AD, the Zohar gave
new life and impetus to mystical speculations through the 14th and subsequent
centuries. Many Kabbalists, in fact, invested the Zohar with a sanctity that is normally
accorded only to the Torah and the Talmud.
  The Zohar consists of several units, the largest of which—usually called the
Zohar proper—deals with the "inner" (mystical, symbolic) meaning of biblical texts,
especially those taken from the first five books of the Bible (Torah), from the <u>Book of
Ruth</u>, and from the <u>Song of Solomon</u>. The lengthy homilies of the Zohar are mixed
with short discourses and parables, all centred on Simeon ben Yohai (2nd century AD)
and his disciples. Though the text names Simeon as the author, modern scholars are
convinced that the major portion of the Zohar should be credited to Moses de Leon
[Moses the Lion] (1250–1305) of <u>Spain</u>. They do not rule out the possibility, however,
that earlier mystic materials were used or incorporated into the present text.
  Because the mystery of creation is a recurrent theme in the Zohar, there are
extensive discussions of the 10 divine emanations (<u>sefirot</u>, literally "numbers") of God
the Creator, which reputedly explain the creation and continued existence of the
universe. Other major topics are the problem of evil and the cosmic significance of
prayer and good deeds.

After their expulsion from Spain in 1492, the Jews were much taken up with thoughts of the Messiah and eschatology and turned to the Zohar as a guide for mystical speculations. The greatest influence of the Zohar, especially among the masses, did not occur, therefore, until several centuries after the book was composed.

Couple things right off the bat, eschatology needs to be defined. From Merriam-Webster's online and corrupted dictionary it's stated that **eschatology** is:
1. a branch of theology concerned with the final events in the history of the world or of humankind
2. a belief concerning death, the end of the world, or the ultimate destiny of humankind

I would argue that a pursuit or obsession with negative components brings about negativity in manifest and actually calls forth, or hastens that which you seek. In this case it is the end of humankind. That is why I find it interesting that eschatology is spelled similar to **scatology**, or an interest or preoccupation with excrement (poop) or excretion (the act of pooping.) Either way it's a shitty situation. One could even say when referring to Ba'al, it's a real Shit Storm. And yes there are a handful of scat stories in the Old Testament, or Tanakh, dealing with the obsession that "God" had with excrement, such as Ezekiel 4:12 when God orders him to bake bread over human feces, and there's other examples as well. Malachi 2:1-9 *I will rebuke your offspring, and spread dung (peresh) on your faces, the dung (peresh) of your offerings, and I will put you out of my presence.*
They just got shitfaced with YHWH. Stanks be to "God."

There's also a disturbing bit in the Talmud describing the punishment of Balaam and Jesus indicating they are boiling in excrement. "All who scoff at the words of wise men are judged in Tzoah Rotachat" (boiling excrement.) Onkelos raises the spirit of Yeshu with necromancy, and asks him about his punishment in Gehinnom. Yeshu says he's boiling in excrement. It's said Yeshu is Jesus.

Also, in 1492, the same date of the voyage to the "New World," King Ferdinand issued the Alhambra Decree in Spain ordering the expulsion of the Jews from the kingdom. The Sephardic Jews either had to convert or get out. It is highly likely that Columbus and much of his crew were comprised of Sephardi looking for a refuge from "persecution." You didn't learn that in high school unless you had a teacher speaking off-script. Under the cloak of Marrano or Converso, names for crypto-Jews who outwardly converted to Catholicism/Christianity they moved in the same circles and it is said some of the conquistadors were also of this hidden identity. Even Ignatius of Loyola, the founder of the Jesuits, was a Marrano, or crypto-Jew. He was a Spanish soldier who became a priest, and was also a member of the Alumbrado, a precursor to the Illuminati. In 1540 Pope Paul III approved the Order, or Society of Jesus known as the Jesuits to counter the Protestant Reformation movement.

In setting up the Jesuit order, Loyola devised an elaborate spy system, so that no one in the order was safe. If there was any opposition, death was meted out swiftly. The Jesuit order not only became a destructive arm of the Roman Catholic Church, but developed into a secret intelligence service.
-Conspiracy World, Dec 22nd, 2012

It's alarming to know that the US Central Intelligence Agency is comprised mainly of the Jesuits, and was founded by Wild Bill Donovan (OSS) a high-ranking militant Knight of Malta. But don't worry, the Roman Empire is totally not still in charge of the world, covertly. Yeah, sure. Here's another interesting quote:

"You have been taught to insidiously plant the seeds of jealousy and hatred between communities, provinces, states that were at peace, and incite them to deeds of blood, involving them in war with each other, and to create revolutions and civil wars in countries that were independent and prosperous, cultivating the arts and the sciences and enjoying the blessings of peace. To take sides with the combatants and to act secretly with your brother Jesuit, who might be engaged on the other side, but openly opposed to that with which you might be connected, only that the Church might be the gainer in the end, in the conditions fixed in the treaties for peace and that the end justifies the means."
-portion of the Secret Jesuit Oath

The reason this is an important connection is because there is an argument that certain extreme Zionists, or the Jesuits are responsible for the turmoil around the world. It can be argued, and has been by anthropologist, Robert Sepehr, that they're from a common origin, and only appear separate or in opposition outwardly. The end goal seems quite similar when you consider the objectives of the more infamous Lurian Kabbalah promoters. It's also said Luria was inspired by Ignatius, going so far as to state Luria was faithful follower of Ignatius.

Rabbi Isaac Luria, a faithful follower of Ignatius Loyola, formulated the "New Kabbalah." Luria's youth was spent in Egypt, where he became versed in rabbinic studies, engaged in commerce, and eventually concentrated on study of the Zohar, the central work of the Medieval Kabbalah. In 1570, he went to Safed in Galilee, where he studied under Moses ben Jacob Cordovero, the greatest Kabbalist of the time, and developed his own Kabbalistic system. Although he wrote few works, Luria's doctrines were recorded by his pupil Hayyim Vital, who presented them in a large posthumous collection. Because of this work, Lurianic Kabbalah became the new thought that influenced all Jewish mysticism after him, competing with the Kabbalah of Cordovero.

(Rabbi Moshe Cordevero, a true Kabbalist died one year after he arrived in Tzfat. His student, Luria, then took over. Luria died when he was in his thirties, also mysteriously. His students Chaim Vital and Yosef Caro then took over and Judaism has never been the same since...)
Source: http://www.terrorism-illuminati.com/book/rosicrucians_masons.html

Kabbalah means "the tradition" referring to the original oral tradition of Jewish mysticism and knowledge as it relates to the Torah, or scripture meaning the first five books of the Bible, ie Tanakh. Jewish mysticism is as ancient as Babylon, maybe even Sumer, meaning the mysticism predated formal Judaism. The mystery schools and many of today's secret societies are based on mysticism, magic, and alleged hidden meanings, and the once oral teachings of the Kabbalah, including the religion, yes religion, known as Freemasonry. Regardless of the perception of unique distinction, Luciferian philosophy, theosophy, Freemasonry, the ancient and mysterious secret schools of Babylon all have a common, underlying thread which unites them. You can throw the Oddfellows into that mix as well. These are orders of mystics with very different world views than the uninitiated, or "profane." Another way of saying that is, than everyone else.

Some believe the Kabbalah originated with Adam, while others say it was part of the Oral Torah handed down to Moses on Mount Sinai, or the laws delivered by Ezra before him. It is the esoteric, or hidden, guarded knowledge which the adepts covet. Hitbonenut, or Jewish meditation, isolation, were efforts to attain prophecy from God. *Ma'aseh Breishit and Ma'aseh Merkavah, literally "work of creation" and "work of the chariot" are terms used in the Talmud for the esoteric doctrine of the universe, or for parts of it.* -Wiki

The Merkabah or Divine Chariot refers to the vision of Ezekiel in Ezekiel chapter 1. It's believed to be encrypted with secrets of the creation of the universe. Talmudic doctrine forbade the public teaching of esoteric doctrines.

Divine creation by means of the Ten Sephirot is an ethical process. They represent the different aspects of Morality. Loving-Kindness is a possible moral justification found in Chessed, and Gevurah is the Moral Justification of Justice and both are mediated by Mercy which is Rachamim. However, these pillars of morality become immoral once they become extremes. When Loving-Kindness becomes extreme it can lead to sexual depravity and lack of Justice to the wicked. When Justice becomes extreme, it can lead to torture and the Murder of innocents and unfair punishment.

"Righteous" humans ascend these ethical qualities of the ten sephirot [vessels] by doing righteous actions. If there were no righteous humans, the blessings of God would become completely hidden, and creation would cease to exist. While real human actions are the "Foundation" of this universe, these actions must accompany the conscious intention of compassion. Compassionate actions are often impossible without faith (Emunah), meaning to trust that God always supports compassionate actions even when God seems hidden. Ultimately, it is necessary to show compassion toward oneself too in order to share compassion toward others. -Wiki

This idea of the Hidden God ties into Gnostic belief, however inversely, that this world is not of the supreme All Father, but rather an impostor Creator, and I would call that impostor the G.A.O.T.U. or the Freemason's Grand Architect of the Universe. Architects don't create. They build with what's already been created. The Ein Sof, or unknowable Godhead seems to correlate with the G.A.O.T.U. Compare that with the words of Jesus who said the Kingdom of Heaven is within. These men may be lookin' for love in all the wrong places. It makes me wonder if we truly are dealing with archon/Arkon archetypes within certain people who are attempting to undo creation by making no living man righteous, and killing all whom are good. That is in fact the paradoxical philosophy we will soon get into.

Here's some more sanitized explanation from the Wikipedos:

Tzimtzum (Constriction/Concentration) is the primordial cosmic act whereby God "contracted" His infinite light, leaving a "void" into which the light of existence was poured. This allowed the emergence of independent existence that would not become nullified by the pristine Infinite Light, reconciling the unity of the *Ein Sof* [Infinite] with the plurality of creation. This changed the first creative act into one of withdrawal/exile, the antithesis of the ultimate Divine Will. In contrast, a new emanation after the Tzimtzum shone into the vacuum to begin creation, but led to an initial instability called Tohu (Chaos), leading to a new crisis of *Shevirah* (Shattering) of the sephirot vessels. The shards of the broken vessels fell down into the lower realms, animated by remnants of their divine light, causing primordial exile within the Divine Persona before the creation of man. Exile and enclothement of higher divinity within lower realms throughout existence requires man to complete the Rectification process. Rectification Above corresponds to the reorganization of the independent sephirot into relating *Partzufim* (Divine Personas), previously referred to obliquely in the Zohar. From the catastrophe stems the possibility of self-aware Creation, and also the *Kelipot* (Impure Shells) of previous Medieval kabbalah. The metaphorical anthropomorphism of the Divine Personas accentuates the sexual unifications of the redemption process, while reincarnation emerges from the scheme. Uniquely, Lurianism gave formerly private mysticism the urgency of Messianic social involvement.

According to interpretations of Luria, the catastrophe stemmed from the "unwillingness" of the residue imprint after the Tzimtzum to relate to the new vitality that began creation. The process was arranged to shed and harmonize the Divine Infinity with the latent potential of evil. The creation of Adam would have redeemed existence, but his sin caused new shevirah (Shattering) of Divine vitality, requiring the Giving of the Torah to begin Messianic rectification. Historical and individual history becomes the narrative of reclaiming exiled Divine sparks.

This breaking of the vessels, which is itself something of a cerebral assertion, is important to understanding what Kabbalists, and especially those who refer to the Lurian Kabbalah believe in. Divine light was mixed with impurity at the Creation and apparently we can take that to mean things other than the intended man were formed from this impurity. The death of Kings, or breaking of vessels, is something so outside of what most Christians would be familiar with that it's important to simplify this for everyone who reads. These Divine Sparks were trapped in lesser impure forms, people, and they need to return to source in what is referred to as liberation or the raising of the sparks. Well how does one do that? Purification of the self? Or do you simply break or kill the new vessel, the human, and release it that way? Ah, see there's the hitch.

Apparently we're either in possession of something certain Kabbalists don't think belongs to us, or we need to purify. A good way to purify the reluctant would be to burn them, wouldn't you say? How often do you see that play out in the world? If you think of a circuit diagram with a battery as the source of energy, they want to hasten the return of the sparks to source. They're a little anxious to get this realm over with. They don't feel that their final messiah can come until the conditions are prepared for such an arrival. How does one do that? Glad you asked. You see their philosophy at first glance seems to suggest that their god makes mistakes, and this was an accident in the first place. But it could also be seen as a way the godhead purges itself of impurities. Since this was all born in the minds of men anyway, these tangential mental gymnastics are par for the course. This purging of the divine light of its impurities, given to the minds of unscrupulous men leads to some horrific pursuits in the name of restoration of the Divine. Add to that the concept of the Shekinah or feminine aspects of God said to be hunkered down with, or entangled within the qliphoth/qlippoth meaning excrement, shells, or demons, ie Fallen Ones, and you have talked your way into noble justification to commit limitless, unconscionable atrocities. And there's that scatological excrement, again. Isn't it comforting to know how highly they regard outsiders? It's typical human [or whatever they are] hubris to point the finger away from self and toward the world to declare the rest of it impure/evil/straight-up shit, and in need of an eradication. All religious hierarchies seem to have a knack for doing that, with similar lethal results. What's frightening to those of any faith is coming to understand that fleeing from one extreme leads you right into the clutches of another, but same, only wearing a different costume. That's the effect of thinking there's a core difference in the goals of the extreme Zionist Kabbalists and those of the Upper echelon Catholics or Jesuits. With British Israelism standing between them laughing as you scurry for refuge in a world comprised of the same wickedness in all directions.

Isaac Luria, Sabbatai Zevi, Jacob Frank and the continued Jesuit Connection

Isaac ben Solomon Luria Ashkenazi, commonly known in Jewish religious circles as "Ha'ARI", "Ha'ARI Hakadosh" or "ARIZaL", was a leading rabbi and Jewish mystic in the community of Safed in the Galilee region of Ottoman Syria, now Israel. -Wiki

Luria initiated a new interpretation of the role of the Kabbalah in preparation for the arrival of the messiah. All being is said to have been in exile, that is, separated from God, since the very beginning of creation, and the task of restoring everything to its proper order is the specific role of the Jewish people. The final redemption, however, cannot be achieved merely through the advent of the Messiah, but must be brought about historically, through <u>a long chain of actions that prepare the way</u>. Essentially, the Kabbalists must not await the coming of the Messiah, but must actively bring about his appearance, first by manipulating the course of fate through the use of magic, and finally, by preparing the necessary political and moral circumstances to receive his coming. -terrorism-illuminati.com/book/rosicrucians_masons.html

"...the press in this country absolutely ignores any crimes committed by any officials of the state of Israel, or by the state of Israel itself... It's not an excuse for those who claim to be victims of the Nazis to become Nazis themselves. And in some cases, worse! I'm tired of it. It's got to stop. I think the whole world is tired of it."
In this episode of the Hour of the Time, no. 1912, Bill asked why the UN War Crimes Commission is bent on going after Milosevic, and is completely ignoring the atrocities carried out by Ariel Sharon of Israel.

"...This is a nation of pussies! I mean they're willing to give up everything for nothing... for nobody, for nothing. I can't imagine..! ...But we know who controls the press. Marxists, socialists, and communists. And they're bent on destroying this country, destroying the constitution, and bringing about world, totalitarian socialist government which ultimately will lead to world communism. ...I'm just waitin' for the war to start. I'm just waiting for the moral high ground and you know I think we have it. It's just the people don't recognize it. And the whole country has to recognize it before we can take advantage of it [the moral high ground.] But I really do believe we already have it.
The Illuminati [I say Jesuits, but this is Bill talking, and really what's the difference?] *wrote the Protocols. They do, they use their wives, their daughters. They use their sons, they use every means at their disposal. Their goal is to destroy all nation states, all existing religions, including Judaism... and shackle the mob... Yeah, read the*

Protocols of the Wise Men of Zion. And understand that it is a plan. And don't pay any attention to all this other crap that people say that if you read them you're an anti-Semetic, you're a this, you're a that. The ultimate test of a plan's legitimacy is Was it put into action? And this obviously was."
-The Hour of the Time Episode 1913, originally aired July 9ᵗʰ, 2001.

"What you have to understand is this is not leading toward an Israel-of-the-world. It's leading toward a Marxist-Socialist 'Utopian,' or they believe it's Utopian. It's going to be like the old Soviet Union--world government."
At this point the caller says we know it's the Jews behind it [Oklahoma City Bombing] because they let a guy off named Speigelman. Bill interrupts:
"No we don't know it's the Jews behind it. I've never said that, and neither should you… You don't understand the structure of the organization that is actually bringing about World Government. The reason they're able to recruit so many Jewish people to be a part of this is because the Jews have never allowed themselves to assimilate as citizens really of any country. They're always Jewish. They always separate themselves. They always look forward to next year in Jerusalem. They believe themselves to be part of a world, and they want to bring about a world government. So they're sympathetic to this whole one-world government ideal. But the people at the heart and soul of all of this, and there are a lot of Jewish people involved, are what's called the Illuminati. None of them are Jews. None of them are Catholic. Not a single one of them are what you would call Protestant, or Buddhist, or anything else. They believe that Man is God. They believe in the Humanist religion. They pretend to be Jews. They pretend to be Catholics. They pretend to be Protestants. They infiltrate religions, and organizations, and governments. They take over and destroy from within… They're not Jews. Jew is a religion, not a race… Those people who are involved in bringing about one-world government do not believe in any religion. In fact their goal is to destroy all existing religions, including the Jewish religion. If Jew was a race all Muslim and every member or follower of the prophet Muhammad, who are Semites, would also be Jews and they're not."
-Hour of the Time Episode 1911: *Bill Predicts the Attack* [World Trade Center] originally aired on June 28ᵗʰ, 2001

Before anything else is said, it's of vital importance to iterate again that I do NOT lump all people of any branding into one category, and I do not have any animosity toward anyone on an individual level if they are not involved in malicious acts toward children or the innocent, and are not attempting to break down the ethical morality of a society. If people of any label are persecuted for the actions of a group in which they have no involvement, and are not complicit to it, that is a crime itself and a poor judgment of those doing the persecution. No one is guilty solely by Assumed association. I have very close friends in all shapes, sizes, colors, religions, and non-religion. Prejudice, pre-judging, is an ignorance that robs two parties of the potential to make a new friend. Evaluation should be based on who the individual is, rather than what they are.

To those involved in subversive demoralization and assault on the family unit however, God may be your judge, but you have a lot of others who want an audience with you first. Tread lightly.

Mysticism, numbers, the sum total of numerical value of words, Gematria are where the Kabbalists focus in an effort to extract some esoteric meaning from the Torah. The initial assumption being that there were such messages encrypted in it to begin with. But before there was such a thing there were secrets, mysticism, and magic. Magic(k) seems to have been with mankind ever since the doctored history of us began. And whether or not there is some magical encryption in the ancient scrolls that made up the Torah, and other texts, is only of minor importance so long as the orchestrators in power think there is. Meaning, they could be on a wild goose chase, but if they apply that gematria to their own public rituals they subject us to, we can still see their signature in events that they spin a false narrative for.

For instance, it appears more than a coincidence that on 8/08/2023 Lahaina, a name meaning cruel son, but also means "day of sacrifice," was hit with an uncommon firestorm that created a massive burnt offering, quite literally. Lahaina's area code is 808, or 8/08, the day the attack occurred. That area code was assigned on 8/08/1957. On 8/08 it was also the peak of what is called the "Lion's Gate," celestially. The ancient mystery schools were also heavily concerned with astrology. When you hear "gate," it can be synonymous with "portal." This Lion's Gate is said to occur when the Earth, the Star Sirius, and Orion's belt are aligned. It's called Lion's Gate allegedly because the Sun is in Leo. The lion is also another adopted symbol of Zion, as in the Lion of Zion, what Bob Marley sang about. Mosheh de Leon, or Mosheh the Lion, is credited for the compiling of the Zohar. The Lion of Judah also relates, but Judah and Israel, at least in ancient times weren't exactly friendly with one another. This to me indicates a lot about the true identity of those pawning themselves off as Israelites, for there is evidence they are the same as Canaanites, not the conquerors thereof.

From the Hindustan Times online we read:

"You may ask, why focusing on Lion's Gate Portal manifestations is so important! Because It is the opening of the galactic gate and symbolizes an outburst of high-frequency energy or wisdom, that brings us a great opportunity for growth and manifestation. This period allows us to boost our aspirations, manifest new ideas and aspirations, raise our consciousness and enhance our spiritual energy. Anyone looking for a change in their lifestyle, setting new goals or wanting to accomplish more this gate is for you!"
-Aswetha Anil, Hindustsan Times online, 8/08/2023

Consider this if you will. If these events are neutral, and it's all about intent, or will, then imagine what they may have conjured into our realm, or allured with something as horrific as the burning alive of men, women, and children. Those living in Lahaina say of the roughly 3,000 children, only around one-third are accounted for. That's 33%, but it means that perhaps 66.6% were sacrificed in the flames not unlike a mass Canaanite offering to the Moloch furnace.

The so-called "Angel number" of 8 is said to be one of abundance and success. If those with the desire for total world domination used this energetic time for their success, then the abundance and success was something they hoped to endow themselves with to those ends, not for the betterment of mankind. They may have hijacked the energy that day because they are capable of more profound, elaborate feats than any single white light practitioner. Instead of feeding the portal positive energy, love, and acts of kindness, they fed it death and misery. If a portal is just a door anything can cross through, what do you suppose was the nature of something attracted by such an ordeal as the mass death experienced on that day? They weren't looking for loving spirits. If they were, they were using the wrong bait.

If you've watched my show, and you will, because I willed it so during the Lion's Gate portal, you know I call these modern day Dark Practitioners we've allowed to steal the world "Celestial sodomites." It's not pretty, but pretty accurate.

The magi, spoiler alert, that's where the term "magic" comes from, followed signs in the cosmos. They were Persian Zoroastrian astrologists. A few of them are even said to have followed a celestial body to a particular baby you might recall. If only his mother had invested the gold he received that night into a diversified portfolio, he may not have had to live a humble adulthood. Maybe Judas wouldn't have been such a dick to him if Jesus could have picked up the tab once in awhile when they all went out to eat. There's only so many times you can hear, "I'll take care of the tip," before you get incensed. See what I did there? Incense, incensed? You know, like frankincense and myrrh? C'mon.

The 10 vessels are said to represent points on the Kabbalist Tree of Life. Da'at's about all I have to say on that. Moving on. There's said to be 4 levels of understanding of the Torah: the literal, or straight-forward, the allegoric through allusion, or expression designed to call something to mind, the rabbinic, or imaginative comparisons, and the esoteric, or metaphysical meaning.

Did you know there's also a Christian Kabbalah? It came about during the Renaissance and was geared toward understanding aspects of Christianity even more mystically than the traditional Christian mystics. As it were, Christian scholars took interest in the Jewish Kabbalah which they interpreted through the filter of Christian Theology. They spell theirs Cabala or Cabbala to distinguish it from the other. They linked Jesus, His atonement, and His resurrection to the ten sefirot (vessels) on the Tree of Life. The upper three sefirot were linked to the hypostases, or underlying state, the fundamental reality that supports all else. They replaced the Jewish sefirot of Kether, or crown, with the Creator or the Spirit, the Hokhmah or wisdom, with the Father, and Binah with the Mother, Mary. Placing the Mother on a Divine level with God was something the Christian Orthodox churches refused to do and opposed, but that is where it lies in the Cabbala. Apparently Christians sought to use their Cabbalah as a tool to convert the Jews. Give them something they could relate to, I guess. Some say the Romans did that, too, by grafting Judaism with their own idea of a Messiah, only this time he would exude an arguably pro-Roman attitude and calm demeanor. This may be a stretch for some, but it's said Jesus was a Roman attempt to pacify the notion of a warrior Messiah. I think it depends on who's writing it [the Biblical passage], how it's read and interpreted, or whether someone else is reading and interpreting it for you. There's a strong argument also for the deliberate misinterpretation of Jesus' message, and that he was in reality, tough as nails, didn't take crap, was here to speak truth and expose the adepts who coveted knowledge from the common man, end suffering, free the captives, and certainly wasn't telling anyone to pay their unjust taxes to Caesar. You can decide.

Isaac Luria's theoretical Kabbalah was the impetus for the Sabbatian movement.

...Sabbatai Ṣevi and his prophet Nathan of Gaza had shaken the Jewish world to its very core. The Messiah declared that the long-awaited redemption had finally arrived. The law that had governed Jewish life would soon be superseded by a new Torah and a new faith. Jews everywhere greeted the news of redemption with jubilation...

...It was Nathan of Gaza, not Sabbatai Ṣevi himself, who generated a theology of heretical kabbalism and who inaugurated a new law that sanctified transgression. As Scholem stressed, the Messiah's revelation of the law's new meaning was one thing; his revelation of a new law was quite another. Nathan of Gaza served not only as the theologian of the movement, the thinker who identified and described the new law that elevated antinomian activity [the view that the Jews are released by grace from the obligation of observing the moral law] *to the level of positive commandments; he also served as the new Messiah's principal propagandist.*
-*Sabbatai Sevi: The Mystical Messiah* by Gershom Scholem

Sabbatianism as a popular movement started as far back as 1648, when Sabbatai Ṣevi came forward for the first time with messianic claims.
-*Sabbatai Sevi: The Mystical Messiah* by Gershom Scholem pg 76

As Robert Sepehr writes is his book, *1666: Redemption Through Sin*:

In1666, an exceptionally charismatic Rabbi and Kabbalist by the name of Sabbatai Zevi (1626-1676) declared himself to be the Messiah...

...Born to an affluent family in Western Anatolia, he was a particularly eccentric mystic who had attained a massive following of over one million devotees during his lifetime, roughly half of the world's Jewish population in the 17th century.

And he did that without Twitter, Facebook, or a popular YouTube channel. Not bad. The advent of the printing press had put the Lurian Kabbalah in the hands of many and for the first time, Jewish mysticism was readily available and Lurian's take on participation in redemption brought with it a newfound optimism. Now there was a deeper meaning to the faith they could read about. There were crises in the Jewish communities all over Europe and beyond. I guess that's what happens when you're subversive and revolutionary wherever you go. That's another common thread between the Jesuits and the Kabbalists it seems. They get kicked out of a lot of places throughout time for their behavior.

Notice also these leaders come from wealthy families more often than not. They have been afforded the freedom from toil, giving them more time to ponder and philosophize life's purpose through their own socially constructed filters from which they view the world. This affluence also makes them somewhat blind to the condition, perspectives, and desires of the common man to whom which they can only pretend to relate to. They can't exactly, "feel your pain."

He also violated numerous religious laws, from dietary restrictions to committing acts of sexual immorality.
-Sepehr, Robert. *1666 Redemption Through Sin*: Global Conspiracy in History, Religion, Politics and Finance (p. 6). Atlantean Gardens. Kindle Edition.

*...Zevi's unusual, or socially immoral and religiously unacceptable behavior finally got him expelled from Smyrna around 1650, and he wandered for years through Greece, Thrace, Egypt, and Syria. In 1665 his life forever changed upon meeting Nathan of Gaza in Palestine, the Rabbi who persuaded him that he was indeed the Messiah to usher in a **new age**, and who would become known as one of his greatest proponents and interpreters. Sabbatai Zevi was convinced and formally revealed himself after considerable encouragement from Nathan, making his pronouncement in the year 1666 as to fulfill Messianic prophecy.*
-Sepehr, Robert. *1666 Redemption Through Sin*: Global Conspiracy in History, Religion, Politics and Finance (p. 6). Atlantean Gardens. Kindle Edition.

Timing is everything. They expected a Messiah that year, his birthdate numerologically lined up to when a messiah was thought would be born, and he was the most likely candidate. Especially with such a gifted promoter like Nathan "Don King" of Gaza at his side. Nathan himself was a prodigy of the Kabbalah. He had earned the trust of many as being the authority on such topics.

Although Shabby Sabbatai had the support of a great number of his fellow Jews, some who would travel a great distance to see him and be in his presence, he was not accepted as the Messiah by the leading Rabbis of Jerusalem. In fact, he was outright rejected.

This Creation story according to the Kabbalah of Isaac Luria is somewhat of a mishap in a sense. God created the 10 vessels to hold Divine Light, Illumination, if you will, but apparently God makes mistakes in the engineering phase because the light is too powerful and it shatters the vessels in dramatic form. The sparks of divinity then become stuck or embedded in the matter of this world. God, without these sparks, is unable to shine forth, and is, in effect hidden. The Kabbalists feel it's their duty to free these sparks from the world of matter and return them to source. It is also Luria's proposal that the Jewish people's mission was to prepare the world for the arrival of the Messiah. Robert Sepehr uses the interesting words, "set the stage, initiate, or directly expedite, the fulfillment of Jewish messianic prophecy." From this idea of earthly involvement in Godly affairs we see the seed from which the imposing plant of Zionism grew. More about that later.

Gershom Scholem describes the held belief that in every generation there arrives a Messiah of potentiality, but if the conditions aren't yet favorable, he may never be known, or have limited success. That isn't the exact way he worded it, but it's my summary of his meaning. Instead of waiting for this assumed return of God, Luria gave the Jewish people the responsibility of bringing forth the kingdom of their god on Earth. They now have the fate of the future in their hands, and license to mold this entire world to their design for that outcome. If this sounds to you like it's in-line with the more recent, hastened, and brazen efforts by the would-be One-World Communist government controlled by a dominant class, the UN and its think tanks, the WHO, WEF, etc., you're on to something. The Lurian Kabbalah gave carte blanche, meaning complete freedom to act as the followers deem suited, to fulfill their goal without any regard for what those not of this philosophy have to say about it. In fact the rest of us are just the husks, the excrement that holds back these sparks of Divinity from returning to source. What a convenient rationalization for conducting unthinkable atrocities on a mass scale! It's "God's work." right? I mean the adepts were chosen, and we are the impurity. We're the accidents of Creation that were never meant to be in the first place. They're returning those sparks, our life force, back to their god. Sounds a bit like the collecting of souls, doesn't it?

Words like "evil" when spoken by those with subjective morality have to be analyzed. According to whom? To whom is something evil? If someone thinks they must uplift the fallen sparks and you've got them, they may do evil things while deeming you as the corrupted, evil, and impure one. This idea that some people are subhuman is a very dangerous one which has always led to the indifferent, merciless slaughter of many lives. They say their task isn't to destroy evil, but to return it to its source and include the left with the right, and if you know about magic, there's what's called the left-hand path and the right-hand path, as discussed. Aleister Crowley espoused the left-hand path. You now understand that their interpretation of God is that He is comprised of both. That sounds different than the generally held concept of a benevolent Creator.

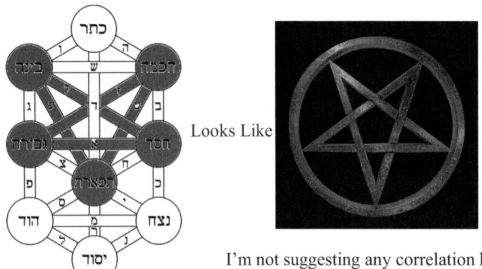

Looks Like

I'm not suggesting any correlation here, but I find it interesting that this symbol appears on the more complete diagrams of the Tree of Life. And who is the "Prince of this world?" The left-hand pillar is Ima (Mother) the right is Aba (Father) The meaning of life, or goal, in Kabbalah is the rectification of the world.

"It's a fact that when you look deeply into the darkness, the darkness actually looks back into you."
-Ken Wheeler, Theoria Apophasis, YouTube, Ep. *Demon. Deeper Metaphysics of*

"...A daemon means an entity that is replete, or full of knowledge, i.e episteme... I do not confuse, as much as the Western World unfortunately does confuse Wisdom i.e. Gnosis with episteme, or empirical knowledge. So just think about that for a second... A daemon [demon] is an entity that is replete with knowledge, but has no wisdom.
...Now whether it is a living demon or a never-been-embodied demon, they exhibit the exact same principles of great intelligence, yet a total lack, or a near total lack of Wisdom."
-Ken Wheeler, Theoria Apophasis, YouTube, Ep. *Demon. Deeper Metaphysics of*

In the Sabbatain/Sabbatean and Frankist interpretations of the Lurian Kabbalah we're about to discuss we need to remember these further comments by Ken Wheeler. Understand that Crowley taught to walk, talk, read, and be backward, inverted, and the paradoxical teachings of both Sabbatai and Jacob Frank which pushed inversion to extreme heresy and offense to sensibility came well before Crowley. What links them together is not only the nature of their practice, but their common reference point, the Lurian Kabbalah. The Freemasons, as well as many of these fraternal orders study as their base, the Jewish mysticism and esoteric interpretations in the Kabbalah. Crowley was a member of the highest degree in several of these orders, and formed some of his own, while reshaping the Ordo Templi Orientis in his Thelemic sex magic image. Try your best to juggle all these correlating elements here: The Kabbalah, magic(k), demonology, mysticism, Sabbatai Sevi/Zevi, Jacob Frank, Ignatius of Loyola and the Jesuits, and Marranos. These all come to a common point intersection, or spearhead and it sticks in the side of mankind not unlike the story where they basically treated Jesus like a piñata.

More from Ken:

"...and they seek to attack the Logos. They attack the Logos, they attack the illuminated forms knowing, and rightly so, that they are transient. They actually seek an INVERSE form, kind of like a Bizarro-world. Everything is absolutely upside-down. They seek a type of unmanifest destruction. And to them in their deluded minds, just as in the deluded minds of intelligent beings, whether they be embodied or disembodied, they seek the destruction of that which they know by heart is ephemeral...
...But what they can't see is that the Logos of something is not in the *thing*...
...They attack the Logos. They attack beauty. They attack anything they see as the Divine...
...Nobody ever sees light. They see illumination. And like the light coming off this rock, my hand, my face is reflected illumination. It is consubstantial [the essence of, despite difference in aspect or attribute] to the form. They think they're attacking light, but they're not. They actually attack that which they know must undergo destruction. They're incredibly knowledgeable, but they don't actually have wisdom. They're attacking, seeking to destroy. And in their eyes it vents the destruction, it is to them Salvation... [Remember that] ...This is the reason why they attack things that are beautiful [and innocent, pure]. They attack things that are Holy. They attack things that contain the Logos of the Divine, but that's as stupid as attacking this radio... You're going to attack this, but the broadcast said of the speaker, yeah is not the signal. It's the interpretation and the Logos *of* the signal, but not the signal [God, gnosis] itself. ...The Logos is not *there* in the beautiful. Neither is the signal *in* the radio. Does anybody think that there's a signal in this radio? ...Of course there's no signal in the radio. Why would you attack it?
...Well, you can smash the radio and it'll stop working forever, and they think that that is an accomplishment of something. But all they've done is destroy the consubstantiality between the radio and the signal. The signal cannot be destroyed.
...Deamons [demons] by purpose of their intelligence, and by magnitude of their lack of Wisdom and understanding, they attack the shadows..."

-Ken Wheeler, Theoria Apophasis, YouTube, Ep. *Demon. Deeper Metaphysics of*

Essentially these living demons and their disembodied influences are breaking the beautiful toys of the craftsman, the Creator God's expressions. We happen to be those toys, those receiving devices, or radios that they want to smash. *They actually seek an INVERSE form, kind of like a Bizarro-world. Everything is absolutely upside-down.* We have just been introduced to the Doctrine of Inversion, a type of undoing of Creation by means of a rewind, or Reset, to the beginning of the Kabbalist's view of Creation. As an aside, a Great Reset is inline with the Lurianic directive and should indicate to the reader what is influencing these world power think tanks like Schwab's World Economic forum. Saturn's equivalent is Kronos, as in time and chronology. He appears with an hour glass. How does one "Reset" an hour glass? They flip it upside-down. What do you see happening to everything? It's being flipped upside-down, being Inverted, and everything is the opposite of what it should be right down to a child's sanctity and a parent's rights to protect them.

Rather than a passively allegorical, or merely symbolic and philosophical application of the creation story, these adepts we sometimes view as overlords are applying it to reality. It's a materialism-to-the-extreme approach to restoring the conditions of existence prior to the breaking of the vessels and the disbursement of these "sparks" into the excrement, that is to say, into the impurities of the material world. They don't see the whole of the world as impure, but rather mixed. They of course exist as well, but these adepts view themselves as being separate from the mess and the stewards of said restoration, or redemption. They're the clean-up crew after the spill, doing God's holy work. It's as if their belief is that by breaking the radio, it frees the signal from it to return to source. The signal, however is everywhere, and nowhere. It is not within anything, but rather the audible message from the radio speaker is an expression or interpretation of the Divine, or God. We are receivers. God is Gnosis, or Wisdom, and therefore these adepts we often call "They" are devoid of it. We are created from the frequency of the signal, and receivers and expressions of that signal. The most they can do to smite God is to keep breaking His toys.

Why do you think technology has gone in the direction it has? Everything is using artificial signals, distorting or interfering with our reception of the one true voice coming across the seas of the cosmos, the aetherial seed of Creation. Or if you are Gnostic, the Logos or Sophia. They bombard us with towers and satellites, pocket devices, TVs and computers, LED light flicker rates which transmit Li-Fi, Wi-Fi, Radar, ULF, ELF, millimeter waves, ELF, EMR, etc. They think they have finally solved for X in this Creation equation. Like a microwave that cooks from the inside-out, the goal of their tech is to corrupt the very building blocks of our makeup, transforming us into whatever they have the ability to replicate. They aren't creative, so they can only mimic that which exists, and it's a cheap copy at that. If they can't destroy the signal, they'll destroy the expression of it in every living thing. They'll cause mutations, chimeras, and soon, like I postulate happened before our mainstream timeline was recorded, produce a worldwide Island of Dr. Moreau style landscape full of experimental abominations. If they can't snuff out the signal, its expressions will be damned to suffer a living hell, a digital prison, and why worry about digital currency when we'll be the last generation before our DNA is manipulated to reduce us to farm animals? Our consciousness and awareness trapped in a disfigured, unnatural state, living off modified food, allopathic injections, and subjected to cruel experimentation...

Another thing to put a pin in for your own research is the similarities between the Tree of Life diagram of the Kabbalah and other aspects, and the molecular model we're told is reality. I believe the way things come together to form something else is more aetherial and less materialistic. It's OK for a working explanation of observable phenomena such as the bonding or breaking down of a substance, but it's been observed by more than just me, that the claims of cosmology, theoretical physics, and quantum physics are concepts derived from the Kabbalah. Even basic physics and chemistry to an extent use models that have similarities to those expressed in the Zohar and other sources of mysticism. So the questions are were they onto something in the Kabbalah that turned out to manifest in the material world from the earlier more cerebral, meditative mysticism, or was it the physicists who modeled the theories around the mysticism they were familiar with from the Kabbalah? Did life imitate art, or art imitate life? Did those born from Mystery School teachings and alchemy try to validate their practice through the "discoveries" of science? Was it legitimate, or much like their other writings, simply a three-layer pancake stack with the literal meaning on the surface, the allegory for those with slightly more understanding beneath that, and the esoteric or bottom layer in coded language only the studied and highly degreed adept could decipher? Are we believing in a goy science, that is to say, knowledge deemed suitable for the cattle? Much of "modern" Theoretical Physics seems to line up very succinctly to the mysticism. From the cosmos to the atom to the bonded atoms in a molecule they all are related in structure with the main difference being size or magnitude. So is it true, or is it following a narrative? Is it a clever way of introducing the occult to the "masses" and in a way, further skew their understanding under a pretext of validity? Is science, and their alleged scientific advances a type of magic trick they use to initiate us into their ancient religions, making us unwitting, base level followers? We've gone from "Trust in God," to "Trust the Science" in under 5 years. When it comes to viruses, we get computer models and CGI or computer generated images. Not real. Cartoons. When it comes to other microscopy we get blurred images that could be anything but we're told it's something, so we as unwitting cult followers believe it, because it feeds our collective ego, that desire to feel how clever we are as a species. We suspend disbelief because the shadows on the walls of our cave entertain us and make us feel special. It's rather funny in a sick way that one of these molecules they were able to photograph using an "atomic force" (already assuming "atom" before it could be proven) microscope was that of a graphene molecule. Carbon. So it was hexagonal, a sacred geometrical shape representing "the potential for life." So before they could ever see it, they knew what shape it would be and they got it right? Going out into the Cosmological realm now we're told there's a) things called planets, and b) one that has a huge hexagon "tattoo" on it, Saturn.

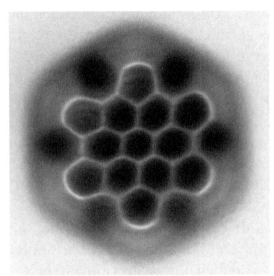 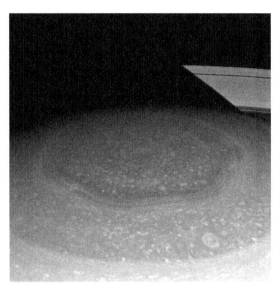

"Molecule" of Graphene   The allegedly spinning vortex of Saturn

So either the Mystery School's true secrets are the coveted knowledge, not wisdom, of a previously destroyed high society—because how else would they have known this with our concepts of primitive man, or one that literally went underground, or someone is modeling reality based on their mysticism to make them appear miraculously accurate. The latter being the premise that these practitioners of the Mysteries, or coveted knowledge, have populated the sciences and medicine of which they founded, and are at work on the most elaborate deception of our time, in an attempt to sell us a new religion of "Science" which is simply the cloaked religion of the ages. That personification of integrity and honesty we call NASA, that was sarcasm, was born from the dark occultist mind of Jack "Sex with a dog and Mom" Parsons, of Jet Propulsion Laboratories. Anything born from deception and omission is only going to bear sour fruit.

If you took a shot of alcohol every time I went on a tangent, you'd be face-down on this book before you made it halfway through.

"Mistaken is he who accepts the Kabalistic works of today, Kaballah and the interpretations of the Zohar by the Rabbis, for the genuine kabalistic lore of old! For no more today than in the day of Frederick von Schelling does the Kabalah accessible to Europe and America contain much more than ruins and fragments, much distorted remnants still of that primitive system which is the key to all religious systems.

The Chaldean Kabbalah, moreover, the Book of Numbers, agrees perfectly with the eastern arrangement, and disagrees with the present orthodox Kabbalah in its diagrams. I saw they had changed it in the most wonderful way, the Kabbalah was entirely lost. Now, in the Chaldean Kabbalah, in the Book of Numbers, you have the wisdom of the Hebrew initiates, but you have not got it in this [i.e. the modern, popular, and accepted versions of the Kabbalah]; they have been so interfering with it.. I say there is more flapdoodle than truth."
-Blavatsky, Helena Petrovna *The Secret Doctrine* (1888)

Anyone who uses "flapdoodle" in a sentence deserves some recognition. Helena wasn't buying the Lurian Kabbalah, and I think that's important to point out. 55 miles south of Baghdad lies the ruins of Babylon. The Chaldeans had their time of rein in the area, albeit a comparatively short one. These days you find a lot of Chaldeans in San Diego, and their outward religion is Eastern Rite Catholicism. Their church is possibly one of the oldest. They're said to have operated since shortly after the death of Jesus, and didn't unify under the pope until 1553.

A comment on the impact of the Lurian Kabbalah:

This new philosophic paradigm, in the estimation of many scholars, provided a spiritual justification for proactive Zionism and the events that directly brought about the modern formation of Israel.

And now, a rationalization for doing all things wicked and debaucherous:

The process of redemption would remain incomplete as long as the last divine sparks (nitzotzot) of holiness and good which fell at the time of Adam's primordial sin into the impure realm of the kelipot ("shells" entrapping divine light) had not been gathered back to their source. It was therefore left to the 'Redeemer', the holiest of men, to accomplish what not even the most righteous souls in the past had been able to do: to descend through the gates of impurity into the impure realm of the kelipot and to rescue the divine sparks still imprisoned there.

Sepehr, Robert. *1666 Redemption Through Sin*

If you didn't pick up on that, it means he, the redeemer, gets to get down and dirty physically, so he can meditatively, symbolically, and spiritually descend into the realms of the shit shells. He, Sabbatai, is doing noble work not by resisting temptation, but by pushing taboos to the farthest degree, or diving head-first into the shit metaphorically, and literally when sodomy was involved. If our life force is what they call this divine spark, "rescue" is a funny word for the destruction/death of the living thing, the individual, so that the spark may be freed and raised back to source. That is soul collecting by a different description assuming they're too busy to try enlightening you into their perception of purity.

The mystics like Sabbatai consider incest and wife swapping as necessary for somehow bringing about world change on a cosmic level. Or at least that's the excuse given for breaking all moral rules. It's like a self-induced trance or psychosis of relating the microcosm effect with the macro. In the time of the Messiah, it's explained, the laws of the Torah are no longer in effect. Basically to collapse the world of evil, one must commit wickedness? It is said that Redemption can be achieved in two ways. It can be brought about when the conditions of the world are such that all people are expressing goodness and purity. This will bring about the return. The other, perceivably more attainable method is to corrupt the whole of the world in the utmost extreme and therefore force the Divine hand to intervene, and basically eradicate the whole damn thing. Now if these powers that shouldn't be at the WEF, WHO, and UN, among others are doing their best to pervert and undo morality, would they not also take on the role of God in the annihilation phase? It seems like they're quite far along in that step of the process with a big crescendo event ominously looming over us like a giant boot ready to drop on our heads.

I'd argue that another way to set the conditions isn't just with wicked deeds, but with the corruption of the blood, meaning altering us from within and detaching us from that tether we have with the Creator, the Logos, or Sophia. To make us other-than-human through injections full of of chemicals and technology, they are essentially creating the conditions, setting the stage, for a Noah-like era. The poison fang or quill of the "vaccine" does that, doesn't it?

The corruption of the blood by the Watchers was the reasoning given for the flood. Now my view of this is that it is a cryptic depiction of a very technological past. I think what we're seeing with these shots and other means of tainting our makeup is in-line with what may have all happened before. Instead of waiting around for their God, it appears they have commissioned themselves to play both the roles of corrupter and judge. Like acts in a play... In their eyes, even if we are duped into becoming impure through their deception, it's still our fault. We took the bait and many allowed the Kool-aid to be injected directly into them. We still are committing the moral crime, in their view, and must be separated from the sparks. This is where atonement concepts seem to fit in. Yom Kippur or Day of Atonement may just be for swinging chickens, but it could tie into the idea of cursing not just fowl, but the foul, at least from their perspective. As I write this I just looked it up, and today was the first day of Yom Kippur. How synchronistic! I did a video in the past where I discussed this and used some clips from Cory Daniel of The Phoenix Enigma from way back. The ritual of swinging a chicken over the head three times while chanting a passage is supposed to relieve the practitioner of their year's burden of sins as they are transferred to the innocent chicken whose only crimes to that point were petty and barely worth a peep.

From Yom to Yum Yum Kippur: Now that the chicken is good and cursed with the many sins of the pseudo-Jew, they have an outdoor makeshift assembly line where they kill the confused and dizzied chicken before donating the meat to a poor neighborhood. Lots of crime in those poor communities. I bet you never considered the cursed chicken component for a reason as to why. All that demon infested chicken being eaten by the poor, next thing you know, they're selling drugs, shooting and raping each other… Hopefully not in that order.

This idea that you can *do what thou wilt* all year because you're going to purify and put the onus of your sins onto a fowl mouthed pecker-head later is again way out of whack with what most would consider natural. Do the deed, blame another, and God would be OK with that? There's conflict between those who closely follow the Torah and this cursing notion. Do we see a potentiality for those outwardly professing Judaism to be tainting the waters, and earning an unjust reputation for those of a true Judaic faith?

Again from the pages of the Most Dangerous Anthropologist, we read the paradoxical Sabbatean credo:

…whoever is as he appears cannot be a true believer. In practice, this meant that true faith could not be a faith which men publicly professed. On the contrary, the true faith must always be concealed. In fact, it was one's duty to deny it outwardly, for it was like a seed planted in the bed of the soul, and it could not grow unless it was first covered over.

Sepehr, Robert. 1666 Redemption Through Sin: Global Conspiracy in History, Religion, Politics and Finance (p. 15). Atlantean Gardens. Kindle Edition.

Riddling metaphors like this are precisely what the clandestine agencies such as CIA and Mossad, but I repeat myself, practice. It's also the way of the Mystery School initiates, and the Jesuit Order, another clandestine, spying, infiltrating group of assassin assholes. Oh, and the Jesuits make up the bulk of the CIA, like I mentioned, but it's worth repeating.

Abraham Miguel Cardoso, was a Sabbatean prophet, whatever that means—do frauds have legitimate prophets? In Spain, post 1492 expulsion, he was a Marrano, or outwardly a Christian, but was what is referred to as a "crypto-Jew." Now being a Sabbatean, by the orthodox account that would also make him a heretical pseudo-Jew, and not accepted by the leading Rabbis of the time. So I guess he was a crypto-crapto. He was full of crap by all traditional standards. In fact, most of these alleged crypto-Jews were considered heretical, as they were not adherent to the core teachings of the

Torah. You would need a Crypto-Jewologist to find whether any of them were legitimately Jewish by the traditional standards and practices.

Remember Jerry O'Connell's late 80's TV show, *My Secret Identity*? Well, as best I can tell, Sabbatai and his followers didn't float around town using aerosol cans as jet propulsion, but the theme of having a double life, and in their case an occult identity, was at the core of the belief system. Nothing they did publicly could reflect their true intent behind it. As Sepehr writes, *a true act cannot be committed publicly, before the eyes of the world.* And to that I propose the public events that draw a great deal of the world's attention are of the Sabbatean form, where the cause and the culprits are almost always falsely reported, and their meanings in the ritualistic sense are esoteric, and only spotted by those trained to see such things, usually from their study of ancient mystery cults. That is to say, even if they want to claim Sabbatai's movement was anomalous, I don't see it that way. There was a historical basis for it, and enough who recognized it for what it was to make it popular. He took the initiation from the caves and the secret dwellings out into the open, and merely donned a disguise. The undoing of the morality came next, for as the supporters proclaimed, in the time of the Messiah, the profane became sacred and the sacred profane. With a complete inversion of the ethical values system by the time of Jacob Frank, they were ready to go to task globally to infiltrate, pervert, and corrupt wide-scale.

It should be noted that many of the followers of Sabbatai Sevi/Zevi were excommunicated by the Jews, including Nathan of Gaza, the man who was the Don King of promoting Sevi as the Messiah. When Sevi was given the ultimatum by the sultan of the Ottoman Empire to convert, or become about a head shorter in stature, this bold and powerful Messiah bitched out, fist bumped the sultan, and was like, "Where's the turban? All you had to do was ask, my brotha." Many of Zevi's followers were disillusioned by this conversion and the promise of the rebuilding of the temple was seemingly defeated. I guess they didn't pay attention in Saturday School (get it? Because the Sabbath is not traditionally on Sunday) because wasn't it conveniently built into the doctrine's wording that you can rationalize everything he did based on the unprincipled principles of inversion and cloaking your outward expression? Furthermore, wasn't it stated the Messiah would need to venture into the realm of the impure to recover the sparks? They perceived all other religions such a realm. Incidentally, the Saudi Royal family of today are Sabbatean-Frankists, and the Donmeh of Salonika, Greece, were Turkish Sabbatean Crypto-Jews, but not really. They're crypto-craptos, right? Because the more authentic Jews weren't validating the Sabbatean movement. The point in bringing it up is just to establish where strongholds of the Sabbatean, and later Sabbatean-Frankists are. We hear a lot about the unauthentic Turkish "Jews" when studying this "Will the Real Jews please stand up," conundrum that has become the murky water of history. Conversos, Marranos, Sabbateans, British Israelism, Khazars, Trashcanazis, I mean Ashkenazi European counterfeits, etc. The claims need to be examined especially in the light of what was for all intents and purposes a clandestine effort to appear to assimilate outwardly while they plotted and subverted, covertly. Not unlike their Marrano-Jesuit counterparts.

Jacob Frank, the Impetus Behind the New World Order and Zionism

At first glance it may appear that the desires of Sabbatai and Jacob Frank are no different than the hedonistic thoughts of an average 20-something male. Heck, by age 17 I was already brainstorming my own religious ideas of very free-loving, orgiastic indulgence. Same ethics applied as would be considered good conduct in any individual with common sense. The single do whatever, while the married aren't to behave like shitheads. But I saw a way to great conflict resolution, to calmness, and harmony through a more socially acceptable sexual expression. The undersexed are very uptight.

I mean, Jacob Frank taught that orgies were necessary for purification from sin. That sounds like something I'd say to a few girls at a beach resort when I couldn't decide which one was my favorite. What? My parents had timeshares.

That is a little weird though, right? The concept of resisting sin wasn't considered. It was better to commit sin so as to cleanse yourself from it. They essentially were purging, like that horrific movie series based on Saturnalia, but perhaps purging with no ceiling, or floor rather, because these acts sank straight to the bottom of hell. Frank and Sevi/Zevi/Tzvi had a religion of convenience where they could make it up as they went along and make excuses for whatever they did. This is my impression of the Lurian Kabbalah, or rather Jacob Frank's manipulation of said. Frank actually took pride in his ignorance of it, to be clear. He wasn't the apt pupil of Kabbalah like his predecessors Sabbatai and Nathan of Gaza.

Born Jacob Leibowitz, Frank was the garbage pail kid of two Polish Sabbateans. He was brought into this realm in Koroliwka (Podolia), Ukraine in 1726. Like the name indicates, this was prior to the recarving of Poland. It's noteworthy to recognize Jacob Frank's birthplace in the same country currently full of murderous, genocidal Neo-Bolsheviks, backed by the NATO NWO, and funded by the looting of America just as the Bolsheviks were funded to invade Russia in 1916-17 using the recently looted gold and confiscated wealth of America post-Federal Reserve Act. You know, the act that allowed the foreign hands in London to successfully bankrupt our nation in 20 short years? In 1933, the insolvent US lost sovereignty, defaulted, and have ever since been fighting wars for bankers, and taking commands from whomever the financial hands tell us to, usually it's the United Nations, or one of its Communist-Socialist offshoots.

Our once free country is owned by counterfeiting pedophiles and child killers. The Rothschilds were long standing Knights of Malta, or the Sovereign Military Order of Malta. There's not only a Zionist, but also a Roman component to this global dominance that many claim is spearheaded by the Rothschilds and the other international banking families. As hopefully this book has been illustrating, it isn't that simple, but they are certainly major players in world affairs. The fact that they are in service to Roman military orders should tell you where the ultimate power likely lies. Same as it ever was…

Messianism, as it's termed on the Jewish Virtual Library site, had gone from an overt and popular pursuit to a "secret sectarian cult" by the end of the 17th century. One may surmise there was a big let-down after Sabbatai/Shabbethai had converted to Islam after proclaiming himself the messiah, and promising the building of the temple in Jerusalem. Many were disillusioned by the whole thing, while others, perhaps overly hopeful and self-deluded, read into the conversion as simply a natural process of what it meant to enter the realm of the qelippah in an effort to liberate the sparks. These loyalists to the vision of Shabbethai/Sabbatai Zevi were playing it close to the chest now, and *a half-Jewish, half-Islamic sect of Shabbetians was established in Turkey. In Poland, and particularly in Podolia and Galicia, there were formed numerous secret societies of Shabbethaians known among the people as "Shabbethai Zezviists," or "Shebs."*

To be clear, these were heretical sects. Awaiting a Messianic revolution, and believing they were living in the Messianic Age, they defied *Jewish principles of faith and discarded Jewish religious laws and custom.* The Shebs partook in sexual acts that were in direct opposition to the nature of Judaism. Mysticism practiced by Shebs still continued to attract the disenfranchised to their doctrine while the rabbinical schools declined. The atmosphere was right for the frustrated to gravitate toward the underground practices.
-italicized quotes from jewishvirtuallibrary.org/jacob-frank

Jacob Leibowitz Frank's father was expelled from their community, Tzeviists, for his involvement in such a sect of Shebs. Remember, one of their practices was wife swapping. He took his family to Chernowitz, Wallachia which is modern day Romania. Wallachia is famous for being the territory of one of my favorite Christians of all time, Vlad III, or Vlad Drakulya: Son of the Dragon. The Order of the Dragon was a *monarchical chivalric order only for selected higher aristocracy and monarchs founded in 1408 by Sigismund of Luxembourg, who was the King of Hungary and Croatia, and later the Holy Roman Emperor. It was fashioned after the military orders of the Crusades, requiring its **initiates** to defend the cross, and fight the enemies of Christianity, particularly the Ottoman Empire.* -Wikipedia, Order of the Dragon

Vlad knew how to handle infiltrators, something useful in the current climate of political terrorism and democide we see worldwide. Nothing gets evil's attention, save its devastation.

The Turkish Shabbethians were thriving in Wallachia by the time the Leibowitz family arrived in 1730. So much for the warrior Christians of earlier predominance. Frank himself, was said to have resisted and rejected Jewish teachings of the Talmud even as a boy. From what I gather from an outsider looking in, that's not necessarily a bad thing considering how the Talmud depicts Yesu, or Jesus, as boiling in excrement for eternity, and basically calling him a magician. I'm sure that's not why Frank opposed it.

In fact the methodology of the Talmud, while maybe not its laws, is something he would embrace as it pertains to numerology, gematria, and esoteric mysticism.

Jacob was given the surname of Frank by those he encountered in Turkey as a merchant. It was a name designating him as a European in their midst. When in Podilia, he began preaching the revelations of Sabbatai, which in Hebrew means Saturn, Zevi and caused a disturbance that led to a backlash by the Orthodox Jews. He was made to leave, while others he had gathered were apprehended by authorities and rabbis to be dealt with. In 1756, *at the rabbinical court held in the village of Satanov many of the sectarians confessed to having broken the fundamental laws of morality; and women confessed to having violated their marriage vows, and told of the sexual looseness which reigned in the sect under the guise of mystical symbolism. As a result of these disclosures the congress of rabbis in Brody proclaimed a strong herem, (Hebrew for excommunication) against all impenitent* [unashamed, not sorry for] *heretics, and made it obligatory upon every pious Jew to search them out and expose them.*
-JewishVirtualLibrary.org/Jacob-Frank

As time went on the sect began styling themselves as Anti-Talmudists or Zoharists. Even under persecution, Frank went all-in and identified himself as the successor to Sabbatai Zevi, and claimed he was receiving messages from God. Which god, one can't simply assume. He insisted his followers convert to Christianity outwardly, while remaining in, and maintaining their true practices in secret. This conversion occurred for political reasons mainly, as a shield for their activities. They went so far as to become baptized. Frank himself took on the baptismal name of Joseph. The Frankists were also urged by Protestants to come to them instead of to Catholicism.

It was a short lived romance, for Frank himself was still seen by his followers as the holy master, and while in Turkey, he posed as a Muslim. He was arrested in Warsaw and brought to a Church tribunal for being a lying faker-pants. He was imprisoned for 13 years for the crime. Being a faker-pants to the Church had stiff penalties, as he was convicted of being a teacher and spreader of heresy. The Frankists posted up near the monastery Frank was held at and would routinely sneak in and receive direction from him. This is why you don't make a God out of any man. These people gave Frank his power by surrendering theirs to him. Without them, he'd just have been a forgotten shit-bird in a cell. This impulse, or desire in people to relinquish their own power and follow another is the only means by which one man can do that which he could not do alone. There's a lesson here that has been beaten out of us about the importance of individuality vs that of a hive mind collective. Unquestioning masses at the command of One often become quite dangerous. Discernment is lost in the mind of the follower-mob.

Frank taught that salvation was only attainable by a religious, paradoxical mixture of Christianity and Sabbateanism. Basically the grafting of the two, to better co-opt and infiltrate it. Frank, once released, was in Poland exploiting his daughter, aptly named

Eve, to build his following. Yes, incest was on the menu, as was the passing around of the children and wives for mystic ritual sex magic. Everywhere Frank traveled, the same story would play out. Optimism by the hierarchy that Frank was a bridge between the Christian and Jewish relations would sour when they learned more of his subversive and perverse practices. Many were awestruck by Eve's beauty, and she played an important role in clouding the better judgment of men. While in Offenbach, Germany, Frank would have an encounter that would greatly improve his financial holdings, and set the parameters for a plan of action that is in effect at a great magnitude today.

The Third Man in the Room

No doubt, anyone even slightly curious about American history has some familiarity with the story of the Jesuit-trained Adam Weishaupt and Mayer Amschel Rothschild's long-term plan for co-opting and infiltrating all key institutions and appointments under the flagship of what most call the Illuminati. Originally known as the Perfektibilisten, or the Perfectablists, the name embodied the concept of the perfected man to its initiates, a concept straight out of the ancient, secret religions of Mystery Babylon, and later the Kabbalah.

But during this planning and plotting phase, there was a third man in the room, none other than Jacob Frank. It's possible that Frank's influence on the Illuminati wasn't until a 1786 meeting, but evidence he was involved earlier exists. From Zevi's teachings and the Lurian Kabbalah, Frank concluded that the only way to a new society, or world order, was through the inversion of every moral law, and the total destruction of the present institutions and cultures. He declared it the duty of every Frankist to partake in ritual sacrifice, child killing, flesh eating, blood drinking, incest, sodomy, and passing around wives and children like party favors. Any of this sound familiar? Do these themes not pop up surrounding celebrities, and Deletes, my term for "elites?" Would it surprise you then that Mayer Rothschild converted to Frankism, and is that influence not apparent now that you've learned some of the core responsibilities of a Frankist?

"He insisted that child sacrifice, rape, incest and the drinking of blood were perfectly acceptable and <u>necessary</u> religious rituals."

Sepehr, Robert. 1666 Redemption Through Sin (p. 20)

All of that and more were part of Frank's annual "Lamb Festivals." It's important to also clarify something that's at the foundation of all of this. Frank believed that the Creator God was not the god that presented himself to the Israelites, who I still maintain are Canaanites. He, similar to some labeled Gnostics but I call Early Christians, saw the Biblical god as an imposter, the demiurge.

For Frank, the central theological point was the garbing of the holy in the unholy. In his pseudo-Gnostic perspective, the wholly evil world was a creation not of YHVH but of an evil creator god. And yet, God had become manifest and present in the world, thus transgressing the boundary between pure and impure. Human beings, according to Frank, to imitate God, likewise must enter into the realm of the profane.

Sepehr, Robert. 1666 Redemption Through Sin (p. 21).

So here's the difference. Frank does another twist of the assignment of who's who in regards to the Gnostics' viewpoint, it appears. Where YHVH is seen as the true God and not the Creator to Frank, the Gnostic Christians saw YHVH, or Yahweh, as both the Creator God, and the Demiurge, or imposter. Gnostics viewed the god of the Old Testament as evil, and I would agree that there seems to be more than one god described in the Tanakh, and one is quite wicked and malicious. Both Frank and a good portion of Gnostics perceived the dualism, although perhaps disagreeing on the identity of the Creator. The very term *Gnostic* or *Gnosticism* was a label later given to early Christians, among others, by those who had a very jaded, negative, and biased opinion of them. The "gnostics" weren't unified by a core doctrine they all agreed with. There were so many exceptions and variables one could hardly lump everyone together and house them under a common term. Calling someone a "Gnostic" had a disparaging connotation. Some claim it was like cynically calling someone a *Know-it-All* by today's vernacular. They were simply Early Christians, prior to the Nicean monopolization of "acceptable" thought.

Other similarities between what was deemed Gnostic viewpoints, and those which were espoused by the Kabbalists was their ruling that this world is either evil (Gnostic) or impure (Kabbalah), and the idea of divine sparks, or a piece of God within. Where Frank greatly differs is pretty distinct. It's all about the approach. A gnostic may clean and bandage a cut on a finger whereas Frank may have cut the hand off at the wrist and sodomized the unfortunate patient. While Gnostic Christians rely on the individual journey for truth and Gnosis to uplift their inner sparks, or pieces of God, and help them remember their true identity and purpose as they ascend after death, Frank took the approach of corrupting oneself to the ultimate extent, and set out with the goal of making the world fully wicked so his Messiah may come annihilate them. His idea was to raise the sparks by way of force. Or the more modern alternative ending will be for the Frankists to play both the role of the corruptor, and the destroyer, feeling justified that in doing so, they're performing a "Great Work." Many Gnostics see this world as a trapping created by an evil hand and that the ascension back to source is full of distractions and obstacles set in place to keep the soul or spark from reuniting with the Monad, or supreme God, therefore stuck in a reincarnation loop. But they seem to agree that it's everyone's personal journey to get to that point of liberation, and not something that can or should be hastened, let alone forced by others. Frank on the other hand worked to invert everything, and rather than lift up, he said, *"I did not come into this world to lift you up but rather to cast you down to the bottom of the abyss. Further than this it is impossible to descend, nor can one ascend again by virtue of one's own strength, for only the Lord can raise one up from the depths by the power of His hand."* So basically, from down there, there's no place to go but up. Most perceive God as benevolent and of Truth and Love. Why oh, why would anyone be worth raising whose deliberate objective was to destroy all good in the world either by violence or by rotting them from within by co-opting and corrupting their homes and institutions? If you make yourself truly disgusting and harm children as a primary means of Frankist duty, who do you think that really attracts the attention of? A good God? Or the other guy? Maybe even legions of other guys. I'm still baffled at how people can read about Solomon using demons to build a temple and think that's somehow in-line with God's will. But hey, who am I besides someone who thinks when they read?

Just a word more for the Christians that were called Gnostics by douche bags who turned Jesus, their enemy, into their mascot for a false doctrine. The douche bags I'm naming then sold out further to the Roman emperor and no bit of authentic, sincere, and true message wasn't without its corrupted elements since. The reason those who would go on to build the Roman abomination to Christ despised the Gnostics was because these church builders had something to protect. Christ was Truth and Truth was dangerous in a world of mystery religions and secret teachings. They didn't want anyone getting the idea that personal liberation was a possibility. That would destroy the power of institutions. That would undermine rule. Gnostics said the world was evil, and if it was the people they meant, then I'd tend to agree.

The parasitic control freaks of this world were threatened by the early Christian "Gnostics" because they lived the word that THE KINGDOM of GOD is WITHIN the individual. It isn't rationed by Man, and it doesn't come from a leader who deifies himself, nor from a church built on the backs of the poor. All the lower forms have are their illusions in an illusory world they fashioned.

Yes the early Christians believed in Christ and in the Christ before time as a principle of the Monad and that which awakens our little piece of divinity into full awareness, so that we may liberate ourselves from what is essentially a prison world of matter through the virtue of our divine nature. Attaining Gnosis is a personal path because it has to be. It's not a group activity. It's about the connection with the One (Monad) and your relationship. If these vaccine sorcerers weren't well aware of this, they wouldn't be so obsessed with trying to sever that tether between us and the Source, by destroying what they claim is the VMAT-2 gene. Everything has to be reduced to quantitative physical material with these sciences. The quantum physicists are what Ken Wheeler refers to as bean counters. When there isn't any matter, like for a soul, they deny it, or make stuff up like a photon to measure light. They cannot admit to anything aetherial or spiritual. From that connection with God we have a sense of right and wrong. We have the ability to feel empathy and relate, for when we are plugged in to it, we're plugged into whoever else is connected to the divine. We all sense each others joys and pains. Some with stronger connections are more sensitive, and we call them empaths.

Jacob Frank was not as popular as Sabbatai Zevi with his 1,000,000 Kabbalah-gram followers. He only hit about 50K, and my question is whose job was it to count these stats, and how in the 16 and 1700s? What Frank lacked in quantity he made up for in quality, if you can call it that. Big surprise he was befriended by the most wealthy bankers, and other members of society with high power and influence.

*Frankfurt at the time was the headquarters of the Jesuit, Adam Weishaupt, founder of the Illuminati, as well as Rothschild Brothers' financial empire. This is worth repeating: Frankfurt was the birthplace of both the Illuminati and the Rothschild empire. When Jacob Frank entered the city, the alliance between the two had already begun. Weishaupt provided the conspiratorial resources of the Jesuit Order, while the Rothschilds contributed the money. What was missing was a means to spread the agenda of the Illuminati and that the Frankists added with their network of agents throughout the **Christian** and **Islamic** worlds. Jacob Frank became instantly wealthy because he was given a nice handout by Mayer Amshel Rothschild of Frankfurt.*

-Rabbi Marvin S. Antleman, *To Eliminate the Opiate* vol. 2

It was this union of ideologies and objectives that formed the building blocks for, and the rationale behind Zionism. One could go so far as to say these days Frankism and Illuminism are masked by this term "Zionism." After all, one cannot be a true Frankist if one expresses so outwardly, right?

We've walked through what a converso is in relation to the Sephardic Jews of Spain who converted to Christianity. Those who convert are known as crypto-jews, as if it's common knowledge that they had no true intention of assimilating. There we learn it was 3 wealthy Jewish converso financiers who funded the voyage of Christopher Columbus and that at least one of the vessels contained the remaining Jews fleeing the Expulsion of 1492.

Marranos were also crypto Jews in Spain and Portugal, and some were members of a secret society of the Alumbrados (Enlightened ones) which at first sounds good. They believed in high forms of spirituality and that they could reach such a state of perfection, oh wait… You mean like the Perfektibilisten or Illuminati? A state of perfection that they could, while living, contemplate the essence of God [become as God], and the Trinity, and that they could sin at will without tainting their own soul. This sounds an awful lot like Frankism, only sin was an absolute duty. This is why Alumbrados were deemed an early form of the Illuminati.

Ignatius of Loyola was a Marrano. He was a Christian in-name-only using the secret society to explore mysticism. He founded the Jesuits. So the tie-in here is Jewish mysticism and the Kabbalah with the Society of Jesus. Marranos were already in the practice of presenting a false outward persona, and as the Jesuit Oath and initiation describes, there is a clandestine organization formed of spies who spy on one another as much as anyone else. It's a cult of severe penalties for betrayers, just like a Masonic lodge or ancient mystery school. Over 200 years before Jacob Frank gets in on the game of spy craft and infiltration, his brethren in Spain are institutionalizing it with the blessings of the Pope!

Now picture this in the proper lighting. We have extremely wealthy Mayer Bauer, or Rothschild, someone with likely significant family ties to the old Roman Empire, who's a Knight in the Military Order of Malta, recipient of their highest accolade, the cross of St Sylvester, and he's having a powwow with Jacob "Rape and Eat Babies" Frank, and Jesuit Adam Weishaupt whose father was a rabbi. All three of these men are familiar with the same Kabbalist mysticism, and deeper incite into magical endeavors whether while in secret societies as members or as leaders. Mayer Amschel Bauer/Rothschild reemerges as a convert to Frankism, and the plan the three endeavor to set in motion adopts the strategies and philosophies of both the Jesuit order and Sabbatean-Frankism. This is why some say extreme Zionists are responsible for the world's hellish, worsening condition while others argue that the Jesuits are sewing the seeds of discontent and fomenting wars through various NGOs (Non-Government Agencies) and the UN. The fact is both are half right. The understanding needed here is that at the core, they're one in the same Frankist movement, galvanized since 1776. That is, it has evolved to become that over time. I'm not suggesting in the least that the Frankists themselves are at the top of the order. What I'm saying is their plan for bringing about the conditions necessary for the End Days Redemption is being utilized and followed to usher in a One World Government. It was this mindset of Jacob Frank that was adopted by the Perfektiblisten, also known as the Illuminati. At the very top it appears that this plague that the world is suffering from is Roman in origin, that is to say, the Roman Empire never left, it just rebranded itself as a religion and has used proxy powers and infiltrated governments, along with their agents, the Rothschilds, Rockefellers, Schiffs, etc and their acquired territories to take over the world. We in America, as an insolvent country brought to bankruptcy in 1933 by Rothschilds central banking, are one of those conquered and controlled territories. We have been under an illusion, a sort of live-action Jesuit theater that makes us believe we still have a government, and that we are somehow free. There are other cult groups that also operate in the world with far reaching power and influence. The Order of Nine Angles is one of them. I don't believe any of these death cults operate independently from the core shadow powers I've been discussing. We should all question why most other monarchies were hunted into extinction by communist radical assassins in the 18-1900's save the British Royal Family. Jacob Schiff, a Rothschild agent sent to destroy America, put together the means for the Bolshevik Revolution, one of the most horrific events to take place in recent history. Who were the Bolsheviks? Communists, yes, but where did that idea of communism really come from? The Jesuits had set up the first Communist commune in Paraguay, known as the Reductions of Paraguay from the early 1600's until their expulsion in 1767. Although Socialism and Communism have roots in the ancient Mystery Schools, we know that Ignatius of Loyola was an Alumbrado, and as a leader of the Jesuits, modeled his organization like a secret society just like those of antiquity.

It was the aim of the Perfektiblisten/Illuminati to infiltrate the lodges of Freemasonry, and select the most suitable candidates to elevate, and induct them into the secret agenda of the organization. Some of the 25 points of the plan included initiating class warfare, the fomenting of wars and controlling peace conferences so no territory be gained, and debt servitude to the banks would result, creating artificial economic disasters, force starvation, eliminate private property and all real estate, utilize terrorism to create dependence on the state, select all political leaders, create chaos, and preach liberalism while indoctrinating the youth into false philosophies, high taxes, become the advisors to governments, promote alcohol, drugs, and deviant lifestyles, and make the mob fight and kill each other. There's more, but that about sums it up.

On the Communist plank front you have these objectives: Abolition of private property, and the institution of a rent-use system (own nothing and be happy?), a heavy progressive, or graduated income tax, Abolition of rights to inheritance, centralization and monopolization of credit, state centralized communication and transportation, state is to own all industry, free state-run education/indoctrination, and so on...

I don't doubt you see the similarities, but to see them back-to-back for comparison really makes the point clear. The Rothschild-Jesuit-Frankist plan was carried out in the lodges setting the course for the Jacobin French Revolution, and the Bolshevik Revolution. It was the French Lodge that devised both plans. Lenin, Trotsky, and Stalin were all Freemasons, and moreover they were Frankists.

Now let's have a look at the objectives and strategies of the long-winded Protocols of the Learned Elders of Zion. These will be in summary form because each protocol goes on for several pages, and I don't mean just 7, as "several" would indicate. The reason I'm including this is because the similarities are striking, and seem to come from the unified mouth of the Roman Empire, Jesuits, Bolshevik Communists, the World Economic Forum, and the Illuminati. You can throw in the United Nations, as well, our true governing body.
Protocol One states:

"It must be noted that men with bad instincts are more in number than the good, and therefore the best results in governing them are attained by violence and terrorization, and not by academic discussions."

Further along Protocol One we read:

"Behold the alcoholized animals, bemused with drink, the right to an immoderate use of which comes along with freedom. It is not for us and ours to walk that road. The peoples of the goyim are bemused with alcoholic liquors; their youth has grown stupid on classicism and from early immorality, into which it has been inducted by our special agents—by tutors, lackeys, governesses in the houses of the wealthy, by clerks and others, by our women in the places of dissipation frequented by the goyim."

I told you it was long-winded, highfalutin writing. Again from Protocol 1:

"Therefore it is not so much by the means themselves as by the doctrine of severity that we shall triumph and bring all governments into subjection to our super-government. It is enough for them to know that we are merciless for all disobedience to cease...

"In all corners of the earth the words "Liberty, Equality, Fraternity" brought to our ranks, thanks to our blind agents, whole legions who bore our banners with enthusiasm. And all the time these words were canker-worms at work boring into the well-being of the goyim, putting an end everywhere to peace, quiet, solidarity and destroying all the foundations of the goy States."

"Liberty, Faternity, Equality" is a commonly held decree, or rally cry of the masonic order. From this cynical description, you see the author held contempt even for the people who are being used to carry out their agenda.

Protocol Two:

"It is indispensable for our purpose that wars, so far as possible, should not result in territorial gains: war will thus be brought on to the economic ground, where the nations will not fail to perceive in the assistance we give the strength of our predominance, and this state of things will put both sides at the mercy of our international agentur; which possesses millions of eyes ever on the watch and unhampered by any limitations whatsoever. Our international rights will then wipe out national rights, in the proper sense of right, and will rule the nations precisely as the civil law of States rules the relations of their subjects among themselves."

Protocol Three describes the current conditions worldwide, and specifically the United States:

"In order to incite seekers after power to a misuse of power we have set all forces in opposition one to another, breaking up their liberal tendencies towards independence. To this end we have stirred up every form of enterprise, we have armed all parties, we have set up authority as a target for every ambition. Of States we have made gladiatorial arenas where a host of confused issues contend... A little more, and disorders and bankruptcy will be universal..."

I highly encourage everyone to learn about the dreaded year of 1913, and the US Bankruptcy of 1933, 20 short years after the 1913 Federal Reserve Act. The terms of the two, along with the Treaty of Paris that ended the Revolutionary War between Great Britain and the United States are necessary reading. Ask yourself why the Roman Empire is named in that treaty. We ourselves are property, we already own nothing, and are blissfully ignorant of it. Property, by definition, has no rights, and can't own property.

Protocol Three continues further along in the arrogant rant:

"The people under our guidance have annihilated the aristocracy, who were their one and only defense and foster-mother for the sake of their own advantage which is inseparably bound up with the well-being of the people. Nowadays, with the destruction of the aristocracy, the people have fallen into the grips of merciless money-grinding scoundrels who have laid a pitiless and cruel yoke upon the necks of the workers."

This is an open admission of the author that whatever disputed group you assume wrote the protocols was behind the assassinations of the monarchs of Europe and Russia. These were communist red radicals, brainwashed dupes, who carried out these shootings, stabbings, and carriage bombings. The Communist Planks, and the Manifesto, read much like the Protocols and this foreshadowing of what was to come in the form of Red Radical assassinations links the two.

If you'd like to read the whole Protocols, and I recommend it because the same plan and objectives are shared and implemented by malicious forces bent on the destruction of humanity in present day, get yourself an electronic copy of *Behold a Pale Horse* by William "Bill" Cooper. He reproduced it in-full, along with several other important documents. The PDF should be free online if you do a search. It's also one of the many electronic books I give away to my telegram group, **https://t.me/BaalBustersStudios** Look for the ebooks under the "Files" tab.

Bill said the test for whether or not a document is true is Was it implemented, and this one most certainly was. If I was to make an educated guess as to the true author, I would have to say it was either a Jesuit, or a Frankist, likely also a Freemason. The only other organization the protocols mentions favorably are the Jesuits. To me this indicates that the author simply couldn't hold back his hubris to not leave some sort of signature on the document.

*"Reared on analysis, observation, on delicacies of fine calculation, in this species of skill we have no rivals, any more than we have either in the drawing up of plans of political actions and solidarity. In this respect the **Jesuits** alone might have compared with us, but we have contrived to discredit them in the eyes of the unthinking mob as an overt organization, while we ourselves all the while have kept our secret organization in the shade."*

That's as close to a compliment as you can expect from the pages of the Protocols.

It should be mentioned too, that the B'nai B'rith, the Jewish social organization that spawned the ADL, was founded by Freemasons on Friday, October 13th, 1843. Yes, Friday the 13th, the anniversary of the Templar massacre and the death of Jacques de

Molay, Templar Grand Master. Two things for your mind to contemplate are what exactly are these Masons up to in organizations they have infiltrated on the world stage and domestically, and are most of their hierarchy Frankists? Jacob Frank said for one to be a Frankist, one must conceal their true identity and don the mask of other religions. He himself posed as a Muslim and a Christian going so far as to be baptized. His people infiltrated the churches, mosques, synagogues, and no doubt the Rothschild State of Israel is run by Frankists, not true Orthodox Jews. The State of Israel was founded by the Rothschild family long after the family religion became Frankist, and outwardly they are Jewish Zionists.

Some may be wondering what came first, The Lurian Kabbalah chicken, or the Zionist egg. Theodor Herzl is credited for the founding of the Zionist Nationalist Movement… The same people accusing you of being a domestic terrorist through their B'nai B'rith mouthpiece, the ADL, have no problem defending their own right of claim to nationalist ideology in Israel. Herzl put this together in 1897, no doubt with the assistance of unlimited Rothschild funny money. Remember the Lurian Kabbalah really took off in the era of ShabbatAl Tzvi, 1648-1676, covering the time from his first messianic claim to when people began to take him seriously, thanks to his bestie, Nathan of Gaza.

" *The difference between myself and the Shabbatai Tzvi (the way I imagine him), apart from the difference in the technical means inherent in the times, is that Shabbatai made himself great so as to be equal to the great of the earth. I, however, find the great small, as small as myself.*" -Theodor Herzl

Lest we forget, there are a ton of so-called Catholics and so-called Christians (in name only) who are outspoken Zionists and supportive of Zionist causes, ignoring the atrocities carried out in its name, while promoting a soft genocide in very carefully selected wording. Pat Robertson and the 700 Club are one such Christian Zionist organization. Rev. Billy Graham was also a strong supporter of the state of Israel in spite of its many crimes against humanity. Ariel Sharon was as horrific of a war criminal as one could possibly be, Netanyahu, the same, stating that the September 11th attacks were quote, "...good for Israel." Yet these so-called Christians blindly support the Zionist State in the face of all of this.

Before going any further, we must discuss something very important to the safety and well-being of innocent people living in Israel. It appears that the present day Zionist state of Israel was always intended to one day become a blood sacrifice. I do hope that I am wrong, but I seriously doubt it. The plan for the establishment of the state was in the making for a long time. Spearheaded by the Rothschild of the day, Lionel Walter Rothschild, the Balfour Declaration was authored by Walter, Arthur Balfour, Leo Amery, and Lord Milner. This gets into the British Israelism of the monarchy a little, but for now let's simplify it. The declaration was sent in a letter to Walter Rothschild on November 2nd, 1917 stating the British government's support for "the establishment in Palestine for a national home for Jewish people, and will use their best endeavors to facilitate the achievement of this project..."

This was nothing less than a Faustian deal with the Rothschilds who promised Britain the involvement of the United States in the war for Britain against Germany in World War I. Germany had Britain beat, and were offering a very civil end to the hostilities, including no ground lost, and a dignified truce. But Britain wouldn't accept the terms, so they agreed to support the creation of the State of Israel on land that didn't yet even belong to them to be giving away. Palestine was still part of the Ottoman Empire, and very few Jews lived there at the time. The inhabitants were mostly Muslim and had been for a thousand or more years.

Think about that. How could Walter promise the involvement of the US in the war, period, let alone specifically on the side of Britain if his family banking establishment wasn't already in possession of America? The Federal Reserve Act indentured us to the Rothschilds. It didn't hurt that Beranrd Baruch, a wealthy Jewish financier, advised, or rather puppeteered President Woodrow Wilson. Many Orthodox Jews opposed the idea of a forced creation of the state. Their tradition was that when it was meant to be it would be ordained by God to be so, and not the work of man's manipulations. They didn't like this form of hastening what the faithful patiently awaited. Yes, to be very clear, anti-Zionism is something found among the orthodox Jews. That's to their credit I would say. This also would indicate that although there's a great deal of historical whitewashing around Bernard Baruch, his efforts to orchestrate our entry into the war were aiding the end goal of the Zionists. Does that make him a Zionist? It makes him a fellow traveler, at the very least. The fact that we did enter the war after some coercion and the sinking of the Lusitania to sell it to the American people, proves no small point. We as a country have no true government. There are powers working above our political theatrics that do not have any consideration for our best interests, and treat us as the property we have become. And it's been going on as far back as the Civil War, but that's a topic for another time. If the Rothschilds will something, nations, including ours scurry about to make it so, climbing over the top of one another eager to please this Frankist-Zionist money counterfeiter, crook, and worldwide slaver of men, women, and children.

For this plan of a state of Israel to come to fruition it would require a second major war with the likely cast of characters. Remember, a lot of the efforts of the Baron (Rothschild) were focused on the destruction of Russia by Freemasonic, Frankist Bolsheviks in the first, or "Great War."

If you do research into the topic, you will find that as far back as the late 1800s this Kabbalist number of 6 million was bandied about by Rothschild owned newspapers, and other publications stating that that many Jews were in certain peril in Europe. 1901 there's a paper, 1905, 1921, and so on. It doesn't appear anything was being left up to chance. During the 2nd War, Germany allowed the Red Cross, another Rothschild entity, with Nathaniel Meyer de Rothschild becoming the second chairman of the British Red Cross as far back as 1901, into the labor camps. The camps housed mostly communists and communist Bolshevik sympathizers. Germany already suffered an attempted Bolshevik Red Revolution in their country, but the Freikorps had defeated them decisively. Freikorps were basically a German militia comprised of former soldiers, paramilitary, and other volunteers. Score 1 for the Militia. They're important for legitimate community defense against both foreign hostilities, and domestic traitors. The Red Cross administered vaccines to the interred, and soon after there was an outbreak of "typhus" that caused the death of many of the recipients of the shots. Although the text books blame this on an insect, given what we should have learned from the Spanish Influenza, and the most recent, ongoing vaccine holocaust, the Red Cross was responsible. I said they weren't leaving anything up to chance. The body count was to be high, and they weren't going to rely on the German forces to carry it out. The goal was to scare Jews to Palestine via methods of terror, and it worked. During the 1936 Transfer Agreement which happened prior to the interment, Adolf Hitler and his soldiers collaborated with the Zionists to offer safe passage to Palestine with all of the wealth and property of the Jews intact. The state of Israel wasn't even official yet by this time. It didn't become recognized until 1948. David Ben-Gurion, head of the Jewish Agency, declared Israel a state on May 14th, 1948, and 33rd Degree Freemason, President Harry S. Truman recognized it that same day.

Understanding that the Orthodoxy didn't want the state, and that is just another thing forced upon the Jews who weren't Zionists, coupled with what we know about the Lurian Kabbalah calling for an active pursuit of Redemption, you can see where the Zionists and the Frankists intersect. You can also see the ruthlessness and lack of hesitation by Rothschild entities to pressure and terrorize other Jews to that aim of gathering them in a state that he created and controls.

This recent war, the 16 points where Hamas was ALLOWED to breach the border and commit murder shows again that there's no empathy for Jews by the leaders of the Frankist-Zionist state. Jews let Muslims in the gates of the Visigoths, too. How did it take 6 hours for the IDL or Israeli Defense League to respond? Countries, including our own, allow active shootings and acts of war to carry on unchallenged so as to maximize their severity. It's a form of terror, a psychological trauma they can use to manipulate the masses with. Look at the school shootings on the domestic front. There you had police officers basically standing guard for the active child killer in the school. They were on scene and allowed the carnage to carry on for 78 minutes. Then what happens? A predictable gun grabbing lobby pointing at the horrors of the school shooting as the example for why they need to take away our right to own the very thing that protects us from such a fate. Only in Frankist Inverted-World could that line of reasoning make sense. We should be arming schools.

This is why I see this war as a tool to further annihilate Jewish people living in Israel whether it's by some boogieman that Israel itself funded in the 70s, Hamas, or if the officials in Israel will do the killings themselves and blame it on acts of war and terrorism. Remember the territory that was the most harsh in their COVID response was Israel, going so far as to reject international shipping, and aggressively mandate the vaccines upward to 4 or 5 total injections. They weren't doing that because they cared for the welfare of the people. All these elements lead me to believe Israel was designed to be a trap where pseudo-jews and Frankist Kabbalists in power will either allow for or cause devastating atrocities against the innocent Jewish inhabitants. Why? To usher in a New World Order by refreshing the sympathies of the world for the Jews, and to bring about the conditions the Frankists want for the coming of a dark Messiah. The Orthodoxy rejected Shabbatai Tzvi, rejected Jacob Frank, and rejected the forced founding of a Zionist state of Israel. About 12.9%, or 1,225,000 Orthodox Jews live within Israel's borders. They tend to live together in their communities like Italians, Chinese, and Latinos do in major US cities. That makes them very visible targets because they are in clusters. If the false, or Lurianic, masonic, Frankist "Jew" wants to once and for all silence the opposition among their own ranks, this war will make for a convenient excuse to do so, and it will provide someone else to blame for it. Funny right? The Society of Jesus, or Jesuits, and the Vatican despise the Russian, or Byzantine, Christian Orthodoxy. The corrupted hate the slightly deluded, but far less malicious ones among them. Same holds true between those who only pose as Christians as it does with those who only use the shielding of Jewish victimhood to cover their own acts of victimization. I think I just described the soul purpose of the ADL, there.

Once these communities begin getting picked off by shelling or shooting during this war, the UN will likely respond with new anti-Genocide initiatives, extreme measures to counter "anti-Semitism," and this terrorism will need to spread to the US so more restrictions on freedom can be introduced, along with roving military presence on American streets. Like I said, I hope I'm wrong, because if I'm right war isn't going to be some thing that happens somewhere else anymore. America will be under attack and it will be blamed on terrorism. Frankists within our own government may liquidate a Jewish community here and blame it on "right-wing domestic terrorists," or the unicorn "white supremacist militia," but we should know that's total bullshit. Actions fabricated to this end will lead to measures to disarm and detain Americans guilty of NO CRIME. There have been people who have seen (as in a mystical premonition) the National Guard implemented to carry out the UN declared disarmament. BATF and the IRS from which it was birthed should not exist. They do exist only as evidence of what the Federal Reserve and the UN's positions in our country truly are. Lord and Master, and we are but property without rights.

I know this information in a book may make this section dated sooner than it would be, normally. However, even if it doesn't happen, these patterns of behavior and the formula of creating a problem, the manipulation of the reaction, and the introduction of an oppressive solution repeat over and over. Once we see the true nature of these dark forces at work, and what their end goals are, there's only a few ways it can go down. If not now, then it will be soon if we don't start taking a stand and stop being herded by these demonic shepherds. Study patterns throughout history, and learn to recognize and identify each distinct pattern with their corresponding group. Once you've established their modus operandi, it serves more accurate than a fingerprint match.

Big Iggy: Ignatius of Loyola

I.N.R.I appears on a placard over the top of Jesus on some crosses. We're told the initials stand for Iesvs Nazarenvs Rex Ivdaeorvm, or "Jesus the Nazarene King of the Jews." If we're to believe this placard carries any historical weight, we would assume it was placed there in cynical mockery of the man the Romans and naughty Pharisee Jews had crucified. Like a, "Here is your King," a warning to others not to step out of line. But the Romans were reluctant to crucify Jesus, so this tone of dark humor seems a bit out of place.

However when we look at the Jesuits who began forming in the years 1531-37, and were recognized by Pope Paul III in 1540, with Ignatius of Loyola elected as first Superior General in 1541, we see another meaning for I.N.R.I. Iustum Necar Reges Impios which roughly means, "Justice is to Exterminate [or annihilate] Heretical Kings [governments, or rulers.]" If we were to place that meaning above the head of Jesus the blasphemy to Christianity is all the more distinct. Because why place the acronym above Jesus's head unless it was to imply He was one such heretical king that was justly dealt with? That's awfully odd for a military order named the Society of Jesus. I guess it could also be like a "Lest we forget" what they did to Jesus, but the Jesuits weren't targeting the Roman Catholic Empire or the money changing "ancient Rothschild" types. They came about specifically to infiltrate and destroy any and all perceived enemies of the Pope, namely the Protestants. To the Jesuits, the Pope's word was God, making the Pope, the proclaimed vicar of Christ, the Anti-Christ. When you pose as something you're not, you're the *Not-that*, get it? So if you claim to speak on behalf of Christ and you're not Christ, you're the Anti-Christ, literally. I'm pretty sure Jesuit Pope Francis and his UN pushing the Green Raw Deal, population reduction, and COVID politics isn't in-line with any Christ we know.

We've already gone over the Marrano, or crypto-Jew, roots of Ignatius. He was born in 1491, one year before the expulsion of the Jews, the Sephardics, from Spain. He was born in Spain, in the Castle of Loyola, and educated by Catholics. He became a Catholic knight. Iñigo Lopez de Loyola lived a privileged life of a modern day rich kid, with expensive clothing, parties, women, gambling, and as one source puts it, *"even a few duels."* -slmedia dot org

He was severely injured in the foot during a battle to defend the fortress at Pamplona, Spain, from the French. Other accounts say a cannonball struck his legs, shattering his right shin. Multiple surgeries followed, and a long healing process. While recovering at his castle of birth, he asked for books, and when he couldn't get the saucy romance novels with medieval Fabio on the covers, he immersed himself in the histories of the church, naturally written by those with a bias, favorable view of the church's endeavors. He learned all about the embellished and mythical lives of the Saints. He's said to have reemerged a changed man. He gave up his armor and went spelunking in caverns where he claimed to receive visions. It could be argued that the Owie he got on his foot or leg scared him from returning to battle, so the diplomatic move would be to appear to have become spiritually enlightened rather than a scaredy Cat-holic. Really though, he didn't have much of a choice, for the injury caused a permanent limp, and he couldn't remain a soldier if he wanted to. Living the charmed life, he made a pilgrimage to Palestine, then studied grammar and philosophy back in Spain. They say he cared for the sick during this time, acted as a spiritual healer, and very accurate suspicions arose that he was a member of the Alumbrados. Although acquitted in the Inquisition—that never happens, he was under constant surveillance. He was even forced into silence on all things theological for four years. In 1528 he went to Paris and began drawing a small crowd with his sketch of the *Exercita Spiritualina* and his charismatic sermons.

He met with a group of followers in 1531 and they took a vow of chastity and poverty, and in 1537 as their numbers slowly grew they ran into the Theatines in Venice, a priestly Order of Clerks Regular, created in 1524 to combat Lutheranism. By the Theatines, Ignatius and his groupies were all ordained as priests, and this band of merry men all headed to Rome together. They preached to many as they journeyed and became a hit among the people they encountered. They got audience with the Pope who recognized them as early as 1540, but would confirm them on March 14th, 1541 or 1543. Different sources date it differently. The Ides of March is on the 15th, incidentally. The Ides or Divides marked the full moons each month (Julian calendar), and were considered days of settling debts. Julius Caesar is said to have been betrayed by the Senate and his buddy-boy Marcus Junius Brutus on the Ides of March. Bestie Brutus was a real backstabber. How much of this is historical, and how much is fictionalized by the Shakespearean play is unclear.

Ignatius's encounter with the Theatines altered the course of history. War broke out and prevented the men in Ignatius's company from traveling all the way to Jerusalem where they planned to do missionary work, and assist in hospitals. Their second choice was to offer themselves in service to the Pope. The Theatines were already engaged in what would become known as the Counter-Reformation War. Protestants would find themselves in a battle that wages on even to this day. The United States was founded by Protestants. There's no wonder that, since our inception, powers have sought to destroy us in one manner or another.

There is some argument as to whether Ignatius could have been a Marrano, maybe because he wasn't practicing, or that his conversion was of another nature. One of the original six founding members of the Jesuits, Laynez, was a converso. Diego Laynez went on to become the Superior General of the Jesuits after Loyola died. What we have are two separate warring ideologies on the topic. One that wants to pin everything on the Jesuits, and ignore the influences that may have shaped them, and the other that acknowledges the rise of mystic Lurian Kabbalah, it's more nefarious representatives, Zevi and Frank. The question isn't whether Ignatius was a Jew, it's whether he was influenced by mysticism, and how he practiced that mysticism. Loyola was certainly a mystic. He infiltrated the church with his original 6 members, and some of them may have been very well versed in magic and sorcery. The Christian "heresy" known as the Alumbrados was in fact founded by Marranos, and Ignatius was a member. Why would he be in their company, and sympathetic to them throughout his life if he wasn't a Marrano himself? I'm going to have to go with Robert Sepehr on this one. Sepehr plainly states, *"The Illuminati Order was preceded in the 1500's in Spain by the 'Alumbrados,' a Christian heresy started by crypto Jews called "Marranos." The founder of the Jesuit Order, Ignatius of Loyola, was a Marrano/Alumbrado."*
-Sepehr, Robert. 1666 Redemption Through Sin (p. 40).

The bit about Ignatius being an inspiration to Isaac Luria is also disputed. Academics agree that there are Ignatian values and similar mystic and meditative exercises found in Lurianic writings. Whether that was independently derived by both, or if Ignatius the senior to Luria somehow inspired Lurianic philosophy is a point of contention among scholars, some with a motive to whitewash history. Upon studying where Ignatius traveled, and where he didn't, it's unclear if the two would have ever crossed paths with one another because we may not have the full story. Loyola was already 35 years old at the time of Luria's birth. We have three accounts that state Luria was a follower of Ignatius, one by Dr David Herbert who teaches, or taught, at Oral Roberts University, Tulsa, OK, Rabbi Antelman, and anthropologist, author, Robert Sepehr.

What is known is there were several conversos welcomed into the Jesuit order. That sort of closeness to the Roman Catholic Empire seems peculiar given the Inquisition being in full swing, and the myriad of unjust persecutions, let alone their otherwise shaky acceptance, or suspicion of those who did convert. On one hand they wanted to convert, and on the other the Church didn't trust the converted. Often upon pain of torture one would renounce their Jewish, pagan—which is ironic given the church's adoption of pagan dates, festivals, and celestial symbolism, or other heathen ways, and be converted. However, that wasn't a ticket out of trouble, for the next step, if you're a sociopath, would be to purify them with fire and burn them alive. I'm pretty sure they strayed just a tad from the Jesus that the Roman Catholic Church, and the Dominicans who led the Inquisition, pretended to embody. I don't recall J-man ever torturing or calling for the torture of anyone in his name, and certainly not in the name of an institution of religion that he would have vehemently opposed. Even the term converso implies an insincere conversion to Catholicism while still practicing the original faith in secrecy. They didn't genuinely embrace Catholicism, yet at least one of the original 6 Ignatians was a Marrano or converso sometimes in the direct presence of the Pope at the time, Pope Paul III?

As mentioned, Ignatius himself was interrogated either 2 or 3 times by the Inquisition, himself. It seems historians can't agree on even how many times he was under suspicion. During those interrogations he was imprisoned. He was certainly a mystic, and as I somewhat humorously described as him going spelunking, he spent time in seclusion in caves in meditative practice upon his recovery from the foot injury. Mysticism can mean many things. It's kind of a vague description that could include any form of meditation, ritual, and magical activity. If you can picture deliberately putting yourself in a state of trance and validating the experience you have as being a form of truth that goes beyond intellectual comprehension, then that is what a mystic practices. You're basically trusting a form of irrationality as being insight into a greater reality. Another way of putting it is a mystic attempts to depart from the material existence and venture into what can only be assumed is a more mental, or spiritual realm. The question is, what influences await one in that realm, and can we assume there aren't malicious or deceptive energies or entities that await such a journeyman there? If they're attempting unity with Deity, the question is what deity showed up to greet the mystic? In that impressionable state, how could the mystic really be sure? Alumbrados practiced a form of mystic Christianity, and as mentioned, they were formed by converts to Christianity known as Marranos. Marranos also pop up around Isaac Luria.

After the expulsion of the Sephardi from Spain in 1492, many Jewish mystics ended up in Safed, a northern district of Israel, modern day Zefat. Luria (1534-1572) was born in Jerusalem, educated in Egypt, and lived out his remaining years in Safed. Traditionally an oral teaching, the Kabbalah was first being committed to writing probably around 1558. Could Luria have been influenced by Marranos or Sephardi who came to Safed? Maybe, but wouldn't they have left a year after Ignatius was born? The expulsion of the Jews from Spain occurred in 1492, and Loyola was born in 1491. Ignatius was still known by his birth name Iñigo until well after the injury he received in battle. It's more likely Luria would have heard of Ignatius of Antioch's 2nd Century martyrdom than of 16th Century Loyola. Rabbi Moses ben Jacob Cordovero is credited for having first organized a written Zohar, or Kabbalah, and was a teacher to Issac Luria. Cordovero's Kabbalah, as to be expected from any piece of writing, was his interpretation of the Kabbalah. This is one of the reasons why it was intended to be an oral tradition, for once something is written, forever will you get interpretations of the initial interpretation committed to written hand, and through each successive filter that is the next interpreter to follow, a further straying from the original tradition is destined to result. It's a matter of organic, perhaps unintentional form of omission of a detail here or there that to the interpreter may not have been of consequence, or comprehension, and therefore isn't present in the interpretation. So if the oral tradition is replaced, then the core data has been reduced to a written summary. How would one know if a lost detail deemed inconsequential to one individual wouldn't be of profound importance to another? In fact, if it is the tendency of men is to accept only that which supports their impression, then a great deal could be lost in one summary. Those elements lost could radically alter the very nature and tone of a body of knowledge. Hopefully reading this helps you understand why no one should tolerate any priest, pastor, rabbi, or imam who reads one verse, or half a sentence from their corresponding religious book, and uses it to drive a point completely out of context with the whole of the work. Also, don't be so quick to jump to the literal meaning as being the true message, for under persecution, and simply for reasons of guarding knowledge from the uninitiated, many surface meanings mask a different meaning all together in the encrypted metaphoric and esoteric understandings. That's the best I can do for apologetics when it comes to a lot of the Tanakh, or Old Testament. A straight read of portions of Deuteronomy would have us believe the benevolent Creator we are taught to envision would have Moses killing every last man, woman, and child, and that it would be God's will to do so. Have a look at Deut 3:6, and 21:10-14. That's not even the tip of the O.T. iceberg. Yes, I'm aware I just encouraged you to pick out passages myself, but they should be enough to make you curious of the whole text which should be read by you, and not read to you with someone else's spin on it.

This meditative mysticism of Ignatius was by no means unique to him. Jewish mysticism and magic has been part of the mystery schools since Babylon. In fact, another reason to keep an oral tradition is to keep the power of a magical practice in secrecy among the initiated, in other words, to keep it among those deemed worthy of receiving such a teaching, and whose devotion to the order, cult, whatever, would use it to serve their interests. This leads one to wonder if an intentional watered down, inert, or self-defeating Kabbalah was deliberately handed to the world with key elements reserved only for those who sought the knowledge from an adept, and who could prove themselves worthy. Having myself sworn NO allegiance to a group of men, the best I can give is an outsider's analysis, so this presents as a form of thought exercise in Socratic reasoning.

Perhaps it was Ignatius's pilgrimage to Palestine in his pre-Jesuit years that left an impression on those he encountered, and perhaps some of what he said was later related to Luria by word or by inspired text. If anyone has solid evidence of a link between Luria and Loyola, I'd like to see it for confirmation. It's very possible someone instructing Luria was themselves inspired by Loyola's mysticism and tales of his divine visions. People were hungry for such stories during this time, and it could very well be the case. What we do know is Sufi mysticism, something Shabbatai himself was quite familiar with, was an influential part of Spanish life.

"I have mentioned the Devotio Moderna, but other precise outside influences on Ignatius' spirituality are a matter of debate. A key basis for his spiritual vision was a deep awareness of his own interior experiences and how to interpret them for the benefit of others. Also important was Ignatius' experience of guiding other people on the spiritual path. Together, these are the key to the development of the Spiritual Exercises. Ignatius also grew up in a culture affected by centuries of **Islamic** *presence in Spain. This probably had an impact on his text – not simply on his use of military-crusading imagery but also on his references to spiritual practices that possibly derived from* **Sufi** *mysticism…*

"…Some scholars have suggested connections with the Eastern Orthodox mystical movement known as hesychasm – the cultivation of inner and outer stillness – best known through the practice of the Jesus Prayer. However, it is difficult to know how Ignatius would have encountered this tradition. Another possible – arguably more likely – source is a similar practice in Al-Andalus **Sufism**. *It is now widely accepted that this version of Sufism influenced Spanish Jewish and Christian mysticism more broadly during the fifteenth and sixteenth centuries – for example, the Christian writings of Francisco de Osuna, Teresa of Avila and John of the Cross, all of whom seem to have also had Jewish connections. Interestingly several early Spanish Jesuit companions of Ignatius had Jewish ancestry, such as Diego Lainez, the second Superior General of the Jesuits, and Juan de Polanco, Ignatius' secretary in Rome."*

-Philip Sheldrake, *A Mysticism of Practice – Ignatius of Loyola*

The Sufi element also influenced Shabbatai Tzvi (there's so many spellings.) Mystical dance, something certain Sufi, namely the Whirling Dervish, are known for was a part of Tzvi's "strange acts," mild in comparison to his other acts, long before his apostasy (conversion). That is, the Sultan's ultimatum led to Tzvi deciding conversion to Islam over beheading, and this disillusioned many of his followers, but some took this to mean they too should convert. The Donmeh were a group of Sabbatean Turkish Jews who converted outwardly to Islam. The term Donmeh means turncoat, or to betray. The

Karakashi was a strict branch of the Donmeh with a presence in Poland, and they taught Jacob Frank Lurianic Kabbalah as per Shabbatai's interpretation. Frank would later claim to have inherited the soul of Russo, a Karakashi who himself claimed to be the rehatching of Tzvi.

It's speculated that the Donmeh headed the Young Turks movement that not only took down the Ottoman Empire, but were responsible for the savage Armenian Genocide (1915-1916) where ultimately more than 1,000,000 Christian Armenians were brutally murdered—man, woman, and child. It's more than despicable that a propaganda news channel would adopt such a name as the Young Turks, but the vast majority of people are ignorant to history and what things mean. Why invoke such a name, and wouldn't one naturally have to wonder whether these liberal news anchors are themselves Sabbatean-Frankists?

What is known is there is a definite marriage of ideas and philosophies, strategies in fact, of Jacob Frank, the self-proclaimed reincarnation of Shabbatai, a Lurian Kabbalist, and the Jesuit Adam Weishaupt to say nothing of how that is still implemented upon the world through Rothschild funding. Once this trio met, forever would it influence the way Jesuits and Frankist would mingle and collectively infiltrate organizations, religions, and government offices. All the while masquerading as anything but Frankists or Jesuits, as per the instructions of both the Jesuit tradition, and Jacob Frank's to his followers, who no doubt were infiltrating an already long corrupted, anti-Christian establishment church—Pope-driven Roman Catholicism.

By the time of Zevi/Tzvi we have this very telling characteristic of what would later become the guiding principle of Frankism, and that of the clandestine (Example: CIA) organizations that they would either infiltrate, like the Freemasons, or create within countries.

The psychology of the radical Sabbateans was utterly paradoxical. Essentially, its guiding principle was: whoever is as he appears cannot be a true believer. In practice, this meant that true faith could not be a faith which men publicly professed. On the contrary, the true faith must always be concealed. In fact, it was one's duty to deny it outwardly...

...In the formulation of Cardozo: "It is ordained that the King Messiah don the garments of a Marrano and so go unrecognized by his fellow Jews. In a word, it is ordained that he become a Marrano like me. For this reason, accordingly, every Jew is obliged to become a Marrano."

-Sepehr, Robert. *1666 Redemption Through Sin*

The Jesuit Oath

"I_____, now in the presence of the Almighty God, the Blessed Virgin Mary, the Blessed Michael the Archangel, the Blessed St. John the Baptist, the Holy Apostles Peter and Paul, and all the Saints, sacred hosts of Heaven, and to you, my ghostly Superior General of the Society of Jesus, founded by St. Ignatius Loyola, in the Pontification of Paul the Third, and continued to the present, so by the womb of the virgin, the matrix of God, and the rod of Jesus Christ, declare and aware that his holiness, the Pope, is Christ's Vicegerent, and is the true and only head of the Catholic or Universal Church throughout the earth, and that by the virtue of the keys of binding and loosing, given to His Holiness by my Savior Jesus Christ, he hath power to depose heretical kings, princes, states, commonwealths and governments, all being illegal without his sacred confirmation, and that they may safely destroyed.

Therefore to the utmost of my power I will defend this doctrine and His Holiness's right and custom against all usurpers of the heretical or Protestant authority whatever, especially the Lutheran Church of Germany, Holland, Denmark, Sweden and Norway, and the now pretended authority and Churches of England and Scotland, and the branches of same now established in Ireland and on the **continent of America** and elsewhere and all adherents in regard that they may be usurped and heretical, opposing the sacred Mother Church of Rome...

"I do further declare, that I will help and assist and advise any and all of His Holiness' agents in any place wherever I shall be, and do my utmost to extirpate the heretical PROTESTANT or LIBERAL doctrines and to destroy all their pretended powers, legal or otherwise.

"I do further promise and declare, that notwithstanding I am dispensed with to assume any religion heretical, for the propagation of the Mother Church's interest, to keep secret and private all her agents' counsels, from time to time as they instruct me, and not to divulge directly or indirectly, by word, writing, circumstances whatsoever; but to execute all that shall be proposed, given in charge, or discovered unto me, by you, my ghostly Father........

"I do further promise and declare, that I will have no opinion of will of my own, or any mental reservation whatsoever, even as a corpse or cadaver (perinde ac cadaver) but unhesitatingly obey each and every command that I may receive from my superiors in the Militia of the Pope and Jesus Christ. That I will go to any part of the world whithersoever I may be sent, to the frozen regions north, jungles of India, to the centers of civilization of Europe, or to the wild haunts of the barbarous savages of America without murmuring or repining, and will be submissive in all things, whatsoever is communicated to me.

"That I will go to any part of the world, whatsoever, and without murmuring and will be submissive in all things whatsoever communicated to me.......I do further promise and declare, that I will, when opportunity presents, make and wage relentless war, secretly or openly, against all heretics, PROTESTANTS and LIBERALS, as I am directed to do to extirpate and exterminate from the face of the whole earth, and that I will spare neither sex, age nor condition, and that I will hang, waste, flay, boil, strangle and bury alive these infamous heretics; rip up the stomachs and wombs of their women and crush their infants' heads against the wall, in order to annihilate forever their execrable race.

"That when the same cannot be done openly, I will secretly use the poison cup, the strangulation cord, the steel of the poniard, or the leaden bullet of the honor, rank, dignity or authority of the person or persons whatsoever may be their condition in life, either public or private, as I at any time be directed so to do by any agent of the Pope or Superior of the Brotherhood of the Holy Faith of the Society of Jesus.

In confirmation of which I hereby dedicate my life, soul, and all corporal powers, and with the dagger which I now receive I will subscribe my name written in my blood in testimony thereof; and should I prove false, or weaken in my determination, may my brethren and fellow soldiers of the militia of the Pope cut off my hands and feet and my throat from ear to ear, my belly be opened and sulphur burned therein with all the punishment that can be inflicted upon me on earth, and my soul shall be tortured by demons in eternal hell forever...

-Portions of the Jesuit '*Extreme Oath of Induction*,' as recorded in the Congressional Record of the United States of America, February 15th, 1913

     Real cheery at the end, there.
Prior to that oath spoken aloud, an oath Jesuit Dr Anthony Fauci has taken, Pope Francis, "Jesuit Joe" Biden, et al, the Superior says his part of the initiation:

     "My son, heretofore you have been taught to act the dissembler: among Roman Catholics to be a Roman Catholic, and to be a spy even among your own brethren; to believe no man, to trust no man. Among the Reformers, to be a Reformer; among the Huguenots, to be a Huguenot; among the Calvinists, to be a Calvinist; among other Protestants, generally to be a Protestant; and obtaining their confidence, to seek even to preach from their pulpits, and to denounce with all the vehemence in your nature our Holy Religion and the Pope; and even to descend so low as to become a Jew among Jews, that you might be enabled to gather together all information for the benefit of your Order as a faithful soldier of the Pope.

     You have been taught to plant insidiously the seeds of jealousy and hatred between communities, provinces, states that were at peace, and to incite them to deeds of blood, involving them in war with each other, and to create revolutions and civil wars in countries that were independent and prosperous, cultivating the arts and the sciences and enjoying the blessings of peace; to take sides with the combatants and to act secretly with your brother Jesuit, who might be engaged on the other side, but openly opposed to that with which you might be connected, only that the Church might be the gainer in the end, in the conditions fixed in the treaties for peace and that the end justifies the means.

     You have been taught your duty as a spy, to gather all statistics, facts and information in your power from every source; to ingratiate yourself into the confidence of the family circle of Protestants and heretics of every class and character, as well as that of the merchant, the banker, the lawyer, among the schools and universities, in parliaments and legislatures, and the judiciaries and councils of state, and to be all things to all men, for the Pope's sake, whose servants we are unto death. You have received all your instructions heretofore as a novice, a neophyte, and have served as co-adjurer, confessor and priest, but you have not yet been invested with all that is necessary to command in the Army of Loyola in the service of the Pope. You must serve the proper time as the instrument and executioner as directed by your superiors; for none can command here who has not consecrated his labours with the blood of the heretic; for "without the shedding of blood no man can be saved". Therefore, to fit yourself for your work and make your own salvation sure, you will, in addition to your former oath of obedience to your order and allegiance to the Pope..."

Cirucci, Johnny. *Illuminati Unmasked: Everything you need to know about the "New World Order" and how we will beat it.* (pp. 936-937).

    That sounds totally in-line with the teachings of Jesus, doesn't it? I mean, after all, it's known as the Society of Jesus.

    The Jesuit Oath sounds a lot like the Freemasonic initiation pledge, especially in the part where it talks about the penalty for betrayal.

    The Counter-Reformation War spearheaded by the Jesuits was a response to Peter Waldo, John Wycliff, Jan Hus, and of course the one everyone knows for his October 31st, 1517 thesis, Martin Luther. They were men tired of living in servitude to the Roman Catholic Empire and the Protestant movement grew from those strong, early voices of reform.

    Our Founding Fathers were Protestants, desiring freedom, and the right to self-determination of their life path. The reason they became Freemasons was back then they were resisting a common oppressor, and some of their goals aligned. They both were being hunted down by Jesuits and the Church more broadly. The much-needed safe haven and support of the Reformation movement came from the lodges, a place they could assemble, have private conversations, and voice their opposition to the RCC (Roman Catholic Church.) By the late 1700s there were Jesuits among the Masons, too.

    Over the course of time, the infiltration of the Masonic order was complete. The Jesuit-Frankist Illuminati had covertly seized control from within. It's not really a valid point of contention that some of our early Presidents were involved in Speculative Freemasonry. John Robison describes a once principled and moral society of men he was proud to make company with. He recounts his experience witnessing how the Order had devolved and were subverted. He tells a tale of metamorphosis that greatly demoralized him, meaning he lost confidence in the organization.

    Given the rank of Scotch Master, a rank he states as having been forced upon him in the French Lodge, Robison compares the English Lodge from which he originated to the others he had occasioned over the years. He speaks of the others as having many frivolous, added degrees, and pointless ritual ceremonies however extravagant, and elegant they may be. But there was something else that was much more troubling to him as he poured over the minutes and a particular collection of papers entrusted to him.

"My curiosity was strongly roused by the accounts given in the Religions Begebenheiten [Religious Occurrences.] There I saw quotations without number, systems and schisms of which I had never heard; but what particularly struck me was a zeal and a fanaticism about what I thought trifles, which astonished me. Men of rank

and fortune, and engaged in serious and honourable public employments, not only frequenting the Lodges of the cities where they resided, but journeying from one end of Germany or France to the other, to visit new Lodges, or to learn new secrets or new doctrines..."

*"...German Masonry appeared a very serious concern, and to be implicated with other subjects with which I had never suspected it to have any connection. I saw it much connected with many occurrences and schisms in the Christian church; I saw that the **Jesuits** had several times interfered in it; and that most of the exceptionable innovations and dissentions had arisen about the time that the order of Loyola was suppressed; so that it should seem, that these intriguing brethren had attempted to maintain their influence by the help of Free Masonry. I saw it much disturbed by the mystical whims of J. Behmen and Swedenborg—by the fanatical and knavish doctrines of the modern Rosycrucians—by Magicians—Magnetisers—Exorcists, &c. And I observed that these different facts **reprobated** [disapproved, were INVERSE of] each other, as not only maintaining erroneous opinions, but even **inculcating** [implanting] opinions which were contrary to the established religions of Germany, and contrary to the principles of the civil establishments."*

-John Robison, *Proofs of a Conspiracy Against Religions and Governments* (Shortened Title) 1795

In a word, John Robison is describing subversion, or the undermining from within of the Freemasonic traditions and values, of which they once held sacred, and were of a noble and refined nature perhaps prior to the 1740's. Having become familiar with the Jesuit Oath, and of the Frankist's shared manner of espionage and infiltration some more detail from Mr. Robison's book is of great value in expressing the account. He wasn't an outsider looking in 230 years after the fact, as I am myself. He was a highly regarded Brother of this fraternal order, and he was holding in his hand the hard evidence of this co-opting of Freemasonry in-progress.

*"I found that the Lodges had become the haunts of many projectors and fanatics, both in science, in religion, and in politics, who had **availed** [taken advantage] themselves of the secrecy and the freedom of speech maintained in these meetings, to broach their particular whims or suspicious doctrines, which, if published to the world in the usual manner, would have exposed the authors to ridicule or to censure. These projectors had contrived to tag their peculiar **nostrums** [ineffective schemes] to the **mummery** [ridiculous or pretentious ceremony] of Masonry, and were even allowed to twist the masonic emblems and ceremonies to to their purpose; so that in their hands Free Masonry became a thing totally unlike, and almost in direct opposition to the system (if it may get such a name) imported from England; and some Lodges had become schools of irreligion and licentiousness."*

We will venture into Robison's detail of the Illuminati as we continue our study of these multiple organizations, their common themes and connecting threads.

George Washington himself was not very involved in the fraternal order. The Freemasons, for obvious reasons, one simply being marketing, hyped up his involvement after his death. Did you know that he hadn't been to a lodge but 3 times in 30 years? He says that in a private letter to George Washington Snyder. Snyder alerts him through correspondence from Europe that the lodges are being infiltrated. Snyder had sent President Washington a copy of Robison's book, *Proofs of a Conspiracy* (1795) that we have been exploring. Washington basically says he believes him, but doesn't know of it first hand because he's out of touch with all of it. Washington also insisted that no monument be built to him. You can see that his wishes weren't honored, and his reputation, for those who know of the evils of Freemasonry, was forever tarnished.

I'm less concerned about Washington's affiliation with the Freemasons than I am of his involvement in the Whiskey Rebellion. Federalist and US Secretary, Alexander Hamilton, whom I deem a traitor, responsible for convincing Washington to agree to the first 20-year Central Banking charter controlled by the Rothschilds, also proposed the excise tax on spirits (alcohol) that same year, 1791. Anti-Federalists, including Thomas Jefferson, opposed the legislation, but Congress passed it.

The extremely tough, brave men and women of the Appalachians were essential to our victory over the British in the Revolution. Our newly freed nation owed them a tremendous debt of gratitude. Instead the young government directed a tax on these poor, simple farmers. These primarily Scotch-Irish, and Germanic settlers had had enough of tyranny and religious persecution in the old country, fought for their freedom in their new home, and weren't about to simply kneel to a new, crippling intrusion into their lives. In 1794, Washington personally led the US militia to Western Pennsylvania to squash the rebellion. Yes, Washington led overwhelming forces, upwards of 13,000 armed men against fellow countrymen in a bold display of federal tyranny. He also ordered others not to aid and abet the "rebels." These "rebels" were poor farmers, being destroyed by Hamilton's tax. It's said that the Appalachians people had burned down the office of a regional tax collector, and that it was this act that resulted in the government's decision to march on them. If this is true then the Appalahians are just in my book, literally, and they stand as an example of the power of the people. They removed the illegitimate element of gov't.

One has to wonder however, if it truly was an organic event, or whether government operators did it themselves as a false flag to give them an excuse to send forces. Upon arrival, the President's men could not find any of the alleged plotters or hostiles. Washington captured 150 men, charged them with treason, but the lack of evidence, when evidence used to mean something, resulted in their eventual release. Two of which were pardoned. Already we see Federal Authority overreach so early on in our American history. It's important to recognize the fact that first significant use of forces on fellow countrymen was over a federal tax on alcohol, and in this way it can be likened to a modern day BATF raid. The Bureau of Alcohol, Tobacco, and Firearms is an extension of the unconstitutional Internal Revenue Service, and draws its tax enforcement "authority" from same. Once president, Thomas Jefferson repealed the unjust tax in 1802.

I'm not saying that Freemasons even in the time of our early Presidents was a respectable organization. What I'm saying is there's a distinct difference between those who treat it as a social club and networking opportunity vs those who were there to plant seeds of ruination.

Both the Masons and the Protestants needed a new place to call home, and they were strange bedfellows for sure. They assisted one another toward a common goal in the "New World," certainly for different reasons that became apparent over time. Franklin's involvement in the Hellfire Club is a whole other story. He may very well have been involved in some dark sacrificial rituals. On the other hand you have Andrew Jackson, a man who thwarted three assassination attempts by Rothschild agents after having rejected the renewal of the 20-year Central Banking charter. He is the only president in our nation's history that paid off all of our debt, and said NO MORE, to that "den of vipers." He too was a Freemason. How involved, one can only speculate.

It is no small point that the Central Intelligence Agency was founded by a Knight in the Sovereign Military Order of Malta, "Wild" Bill Donovan, and is to this day is run primarily by Jesuits, and closet Jesuits. That's right. An order with such an oath operates the most powerful, subversive, espionage, assassin, and terrorist management group in the world. They cause conflicts in foreign countries, stir hostilities within the US, engage in social engineering, culture creation and manipulation, and work to upset the balance and course of world affairs. They control massive drug dealing operations and territories, conduct turf wars over said drugs, and have demoralized and destroyed countless families by funneling narcotics into every town and city in America. There's evidence of their leadership, or at least managerial role in worldwide human trafficking, including child sex trafficking that may very well tie directly to Rome, or rather the shadowy figures operating the Vatican. When you couple that with the Jesuit alliance and assimilation with the Frankists during the founding of the Illuminati, what you're left facing is a very dark and terrifying reality.

Pictured: Family Crest/Shield of Ignatius of Loyola. Wolves by a cauldron.
Wolves eat sheep.

Knights Hospitaller, Knights of Malta, Order of St. Sylvester

As mentioned, members of the Rothschild family, Mayer Amschel, and others, have been painted or photographed wearing the cross of the Order of St. Sylvester, and the cross of the Sovereign Military Order of Malta. Major ~~Jerkoff~~ General William "Wild Bill" Donovan, OSS/CIA was also a Knight of Malta, as were Allen Dulles, and David Rockefeller. There are upwards of 13,500 Knights and Dames, yes women, of the Sovereign Military Order of Malta currently active throughout the world. The Knights of Malta have a seat at the United Nations. As to their influence, one could only speculate.

To get a better picture of how seemingly unrelated, or oppositional elements of World influence could possibly organize under a common agenda, the best place to always start is with their history. Over time, as we trace their steps, their evolutions, and often their instances of infiltration, we can get a better understanding as to whether an undercurrent of interconnectedness exists or not. There are so many established orders, organizations, and exclusive clubs that to name them all just in list form may take up a whole book. It will be my attempt to discuss those which draw the most curiosity from objective researchers, and those which seem to be of the main veins, or branches, with the deepest of historical roots. Any names not covered is not at all suggesting their lack of significance. But if through my own study they appear to be an offshoot of the greater organizations, I may just cover those which appear to be in control of the others. I invite you to look into the topics yourself, seek out the oldest of documents, whenever possible focus first on what they say about themselves, and go from there. The plotting of these data points can end up like a spider web, but also like a chaotic scribble of lines given the deliberate deception which covers much of the information like solid bedrock that isn't easily dug away.

The ever-present challenge to writing a book like this is finding barriers every way I turn, and seeing these barriers was to me confirmation that our historical record isn't just tampered with, and written by the victors, but often erased entirely. I've gone on many time-consuming, explorative journeys into the popular statements of self-proclaimed "patriots," and (I hate the word) "Truthers" only to find them to be baseless and misleading. I went in having no suspicions, no bias to want to prove them wrong. I just wanted references to back the claims, and not only did I come up empty, but I saw something much different in its stead. Without evidence available, where did they get the confidence to state their claims as fact? Rumors are a tool of deception, and I despise those who spread them because it misdirects good people and wastes valuable time and effort. If you haven't noticed, time is running out. We haven't any to spare chasing our tails. This is why I take such strong exception to the popular & promoted alternative media personalities masquerading as the "good guys." People perceive the size of your following to be related to the level of validity of your message. Whereas I'm reflexively suspicious of anything popular and widespread. I know the vast majority of people will champion notions that reinforce their own world views, and that alone is evidence enough for them. They don't do their own research, and until they do, they will always be led by their nose by people who say things that sound good, and flatter their intellect.

Ordo Militia Aurata, or the Order of the Golden Militia, also known as the Order of the Golden Spur began it's existence on August 15ᵗʰ, 1357 in the form of the title "Count Palatine of the Lateran Palace." It was a designation of nobility bestowed upon an individual, awarded by the Holy Roman Emperor. It was a title that could be inherited by male members of the family whose initial relative was a recipient. The honor went to those who through valor, through writing, or other loyal acts defended or propagated the Catholic faith. This was a highly respected order of knighthood directly ordained by the Holy See. The badge of the order was the 8-pointed cross on a red ribbon.

By the 1800's, papal nuncios, or representatives of the **Holy See** (Pope and his territory) were allowed to bestow the honor. Corruption soon followed where for a fee one could buy the favor of the nuncios to award them the Order/title. The title was passed out indiscriminately after payment was made. Once the most prized, and most ancient of papal orders, it had devolved into somewhat of a joke to those who understood how it had been cheapened. You could have probably still impressed a drunk Catholic chick at a pub with one. They were probably in abundance on ancient eBay.

In 1841 the stink was reaching the heavens, and Pope Gregory XVI was getting frustrated with the pigeons God kept sending to shit on his head (may not be historically accurate.) In his Papal Brief of October 31ˢᵗ, 1841 he placed the order under the patronage of Saint Sylvester (285-335 AD), one of the alleged founders, only the dates don't make sense. To restore the reputation of the Order of the Golden ~~Turd~~ Militia, he stripped all of the honor, and forbade anyone to use the title who wasn't specifically knighted by a Papal Brief. He limited the number of Commanders to 150, and Knights to 300. In 1905 Pope Pius X divided it into two orders of knighthood. One that remained the Golden Militia, and the other, the Order of Saint Sylvester. The order has 4 classes for both men, or Knights, and women, or Dames: Dame/Knight, Commander, Commander with a Star, and Grand Cross with a red sash crossing the body, diagonally from the right shoulder. The eight-pointed star is the same as what's worn by the Sovereign Military Order of Malta, another knightly papal order.

The Knight's Hospitaler, long name: Order of Knights of the Hospital of Saint John of Jerusalem, is a military order established after the first Crusade against the Seljuk Turks in 1099. Pope Urban II guaranteed a place in heaven for the men who would fight the battle to take the Holy Land out of the hands of the Muslims. You know, because he can make promises like that, and hold God to the bargain. Roughly 13,000 in total fought what may have been a much smaller number of Turks, and defeated them in just over a month's time. After the victory, they did what Crusaders do, and slaughtered a great many Muslims and Jews, you know, because reasons. It remained in "Christian," more like Roman Catholic control for almost 200 years, thereafter. In what may have been the beginning of a trend by the RCE (Roman Catholic Empire), and later the Jesuits, and churches in general, they did what any logical people with genocide on their minds would do. They got involved in running a hospital. The apologists call this "caring for the sick."

How many of the churches of today are named things like Saint-this or Saint-that, or are directly tied to church organizations with names like Ascension? How many of those have been murdering your children and loved ones with chemo and radiation long before going all-in on NIH protocols to depopulate under the guise of COVID? How many of those church-affiliated hospitals conduct gender mutilation surgery on children, and use CPS to steal your child if you try protecting them from the butchery? Something to seriously think about... What's better? A world with a St. Jude's, or a world where there's no use for a St. Jude's because your children aren't getting cancer as a result of vaccines anymore?

Forgive my skepticism of their noble intent, but they no sooner got through mass murdering people over religion than they started this knightly hospital class. We're supposed to endure a fluffy story of their humanitarianism? The blood of their slain victims was still coagulating in the roads. OK, so maybe not that soon after. More like in the early 12th century. The hospital itself had been there since 603 when Pope Gregory had commissioned the build.

Pope Paschal II officially recognized the monastic Order of the Knights Hospitaler in 1113, granting them independence and sovereignty from the local church. It grew from a hospice to later including an infirmary, meaning they offered what they considered at that time to be advanced scientific health services. The Order of St John, or Hospitallers evolved into a mighty military force having fought in many battles in its history, and offered armed, safe passage for people to Jerusalem. In 1309 the Hospitaller were then known as the Knights of Rhodes, having moved there after losing control of the Holy territory. When the Turks took Rhodes in the 1520's they again resettled, this time in Malta, and have been called the Sovereign Military Order of Malta since 1530.

For their lot, the Knights of Malta had to honor the simple fiefdom. A payment of a single Maltese Falcon was the tribute to be made annually to Charles V, the Holy Roman Emperor. They had to deliver it on All Soul's Day, November 2nd. I wish I could pay my rent with a bird.

Once there the locals were disturbed by their general arrogance, and their nasty habit of making off with their women. Maltese natives were excluded from the order, another disrespect by the mostly French knighthood. The knights quickly got to work on building hospitals in their new region, then fortresses and churches. They became a naval force there as well. The not-so-Maltese Knights soon controlled the most powerful navy in the Mediterranean with Valletta as its main port city.

The Knights managed to resist overwhelming forces of the Barbary Pirates, and Ottoman reinforcements in 1565 thanks to their fortified island. Although they were up against forces using firearms, and lost more than half of their total of 8,700 knights and soldiers combined, victory came to them even though most of the city was destroyed.

They began offering protection to Christian seafarers against pirates, and later when their financial situation diminished, they began raiding Muslim ships, becoming pirates, themselves. Seeing how lucrative the endeavor was, they increased their piracy, and I'm sure the whitewash element of the history books is that they only robbed Muslims. There's probably more to that story. As time progressed, many of these now wealthy Knights enrolled in foreign navies, mostly French and Spanish. They were mercenaries on the seas for these navies and this could have run the risk of conflict with their sworn duties to Rome should these countries turn hostile toward it. What if they found themselves in a battle with a Roman Catholic force?

There are many historical commentaries regarding the Knights of Malta being immoral pleasure seekers, full of pride, basking in their nearly sovereign (kingly) powers, and lavished with ill-gotten wealth. *"...they seized and pillaged without concern of the property of both infidels and Christians,"* wrote Paul Lacroix.

In light of this, less funding was parted with by the Church officials of Rome under the rationale that they were not in need of it due to their exploits. This only added to the Knight's dependency on ignoble deeds to compensate for the loss, thus increasing their unjust activities. The knights were most certainly corsairs, or pirates, not unlike the Templars. In fact, they began encouraging it among their exclusive community. They would stop all vessels and search them for goods that even remotely could be considered Turkish, or destined for Turkish hands. Have you seen how false authorities operate today? They could drum up any excuse if they wanted what the unfortunate seafarers had. Many complaints began swirling around by victims of such experiences with the criminal policing activity of the Knights. These were supposed to be noblemen with a vow of poverty now becoming tyrants with too much authority which they liberally abused in the name of service to the Church. They protected and served the shit out of people, basically. No one in high places complains, or takes appropriate action so long as all parties benefit. That's corruption in a nutshell.

Eventually a judicial court was established in Malta to mitigate the issues arising with these several nations' complaints. Captains could plea their case to the court, and often achieve some justice for the mistreatment, or so says the history books.

The Knights also had been greatly involved in the Imperial Russian Navy, and a non-Catholic chapter of the Hospitaller arose in Prussia. Other ventures, included the purchase of Caribbean Islands St Christopher, St Martin, and St Barts from the French in 1651. Later they would sell these off to the French West India Company in 1665. Little is mentioned of how they treated the native inhabitants of the islands during their occupation, but the standard set by the Jesuit missions of total destruction of indigenous culture and forced religious conversion may give us a hint.

In 1789 the French National Assembly abolished feudalism and therefore tithes, thus abolishing the Knights of Malta in France. Everything they had there was seized by the revolutionary government of France by 1792. Remember, the Knights were mostly French, so this was a monumental kick in the nuts from their countrymen during the upheaval known as the French Revolution.

Napoleon captured most of Malta in 1789 and forced the surrender of the Grand Master of the Knights by 1799. Lesson: even if you're French, you can't trust the French. The Russian Emperor Paul 1st gave them safe refuge in St. Petersburg and soon a Russian Order of the Knights Hospitaller was founded.

By 1834 the order is said to have taken up hospital work again, this time in Rome. It grew in activity and numbers throughout the first and second world wars. To this day they maintain a sovereign status, and as a Malta Knight, or Hospitaller, they are not subject to customs searches. Think about that for a moment and ask yourself whether the Holy See, in its many nefarious endeavors, would bestow knighthood in such an order upon their criminal colleagues so they may more easily carry out their activities whether they be espionage-related or smuggling of illegal goods and weapons. Under the guise of religion and nobility are many a villainous pursuits shrouded.

The many similarities between the Hospitallers of Jerusalem and of the Knights Templar are boldly apparent. They both operated in the same location, with vastly overlapping timelines. If the Hospitallers were indeed caring for, then protecting the sick with arms, to then taking to the roads to offer safe passage for pilgrims to the Latin Kingdom of Jerusalem, they would have bumped elbows and mingled with Templars on the same roads doing the same work. The Templars are said to have been established in 1119, a short score, or 20 years after the Hospitallers. By this time the Hospitallers were already a military force on the roads leading to Jerusalem. Although formed by Italian merchants, the Hospitallers that we find by the time they made it to Malta are said to be predominantly French. Rhodes, their previous limited engagement, is in Greece, so where and at what point did they become mostly French speaking?

The Templars were French, weren't they? Originally founded by Hugues de Payens, and his eight relatives, they set out to "protect the Holy Land" from people who lived there already, Muslims, since the 630s. Did the Hospitallers pick up a bunch of Templars while in Jerusalem, and did the Templars hide themselves among their ranks to escape the persecution and mass murder by King Philip? That's why Friday the 13th is even a thing. It has to do with the "betrayal" of the Templars in 1307. If I were a hunted man due to my affiliations, and I had brothers-in-arms with a strong history together, I think I'd probably seek them out. They'd have a higher probability of reception to requests for a safe haven among them than anyone else.

There are others who stated the same. There's quite the many connections to the Orders we've discussed thus far, actually.

As to the modern Knights Templar and those Masonic Lodges which now claim a direct descent from the ancient Templars, their persecution by the Church was a farce from the beginning. They have not, nor have they ever had any secrets, dangerous to the Church. Quite the contrary; for we find J. G. Findel saying that the Scottish degrees, or the Templar system, only dates from 1735-1740, and "following its Catholic tendency, took up its chief residence in the Jesuit College of Clermont, in Paris, and hence was called the Clermont system."

Count Ramsay, a Jesuit, was the first to start the idea of the Templars being joined to the Knights of Malta. Therefore, we read from his pen the following: "Our forefathers, the Crusaders, assembled in the Holy Land from all Christendom, wished to unite in a fraternity embracing all nations, that when bound together, heart and soul, for mutual improvement, they might, in the course of time, represent one single intellectual people." This is why the Templars are made to join the St. John's Knights, and the latter got into the craft of Masonry known as St. John's Masons.

-Helena Petrovna Blavatsky, *The Secret Doctrine,* 1888

This is why you can't ignore writings of people based on programmed prejudices. You are told not to look at certain works as it's offensive to your Christian mind and spirit to do so, and therefore you would never get an insight into the worlds that only they know. Having swam in the occult circles, being of nobility and privilege, and having herself become a lasting icon of occult philosophy, who better to look to than an expert on the subject? She was privy to the adept secrets that none of us as outsiders are. If you want to learn biochemistry, you don't ask the cable guy. You seek a biochemist.

However it is one thing to learn about them, and something altogether different to learn their magick, as would be the case with the very dangerous writings of Crowley and others. You can't get acquainted with the powers and principalities without them getting acquainted with you. I know I've said this much already, but it merits repeating.

The Templars eventually took to being pirates of the high seas, and ruled over Sidon in Lebanon after the area was sold to them in 1260. Sidon was built into a fortified seaport in the same region of the Phoenicians, known for their purple dye. Jesus is said to have visited Sidon and healed the daughter of a Canaanite woman. Phoenicians are Canaanites with the same practices. In Genesis, Sidon is a son of Canaan. The Templars were deeply engaged in commerce, and even the slave trade, operating out of Sidon. We just read about the pirate, or corsair activities of the Knights of Malta. Both knightly orders were doing similar work in the same area—Jerusalem, both took a vow of poverty but became extremely wealthy at times from their "extracurricular" activities, and we're supposed to believe these statements of "separate and distinct," yet "similar" from the socially accepted textbooks and organizations themselves?

Even if King Philip had a gripe with them doesn't mean it was a universally held position by all organizations of the Church. Mostly feeling threatened by their popularity among the people, their incredible wealth, and because he had a huge debt owed to them he didn't want to pay, Philip started trouble for them.

Much like the sexual deviants, addicts, and con men that Koresh (Vernon Howell) kicked out of the Branch Davidians had been the same who leveled wild accusations against the church members afterward, so too was it an ousted Templar who first accused the Knights Templar of wicked deeds. There's another lesson here. Those who are guilty of misconduct and stripped of their title, or affiliation don't generally think long and hard about their actions in silent introspection. They don't always consider what they did, acknowledge their guilt, and try to be better people. Most people don't grow in maturity or wisdom regardless of what they have done, or experience. In a case where they are thrown out and embarrassed, they instead seem to become lying, vindictive assholes in an effort to destroy everyone who were witness to their embarrassment. In other words, they act like any number of your ex-girlfriends who will just compound error upon irrational, illogical, and unreasonable error. Lead with emotions, and damn logic to hell!

And much as was the case with agencies and other freaks within the government that were looking for an excuse to persecute the Davidians, King Philip was quick to pounce upon these accusations that were generally agreed upon to be wildly untrue. But Philip used them as the base of his argument to arrest all the Templars in 1307, and begin medieval royalty's favorite, fun-loving past time—tortured confessions! If they had TVs, they would have made confessionals into game shows. "Will it be the teeth-puller, or the titty-twister pliers that will extract the confession? Stay tuned..."

If there was one thing King Philip hated more than Jews, it was paying his debts. He had also arrested, tortured, and banished Jews from France in 1307. Busy year.

Wikipedos says this:

De Molay and Clement discussed criminal charges that had been made two years earlier by an ousted Templar and were being discussed by King Philip IV of France and his ministers. It was generally agreed that the charges were false, but Clement sent King Philip a written request for assistance in the investigation.

Oops, so close!

Do you want to know what Jacques De Molay, Templar Grand Master, and Pope Clement V were doing hanging out together all nicey-nice? Pope Clement had been attempting a merger of the Knights Hospitaller with the Templars since 1305. He finally got De Molay to show up in-person in 1307 after dodging the meeting and expressing his resistance to the idea. They were awaiting the arrival of the head Hospitaller, Grand Master Funk... That can't be right. Hold on... Grand Master Fulk de Villaret. He was delayed months, while De Molay was kickin' it with the Pope. So what transpired, and why do the history books do their best to bluntly state their differences, and not even mention this meeting soon before De Molay's martyrdom? It's interesting to note that 25th Grand Master Funk-Fulk had been late when a knight's first duty is to the Pope, and that in 1312 the Templar's assets were assigned to the Hospitallers. The incredibly wealthy Templar estate, minus a "small" administrative fee, I'm sure, were just handed over to the Hospitallers like that.

Whether the massacre by Philip resulted in a secret merger, one the Pope was involved in facilitating, or if the Pope was involved in more of a mafia-style killing of the Templars for refusing an offer they really couldn't, or if maybe not as many of the Templars were killed at wholesale like the official story goes, I don't know. One thing is sure, the events of October 13th, 1307 started the path toward at least a financial absorption and merger between the Knights-not-yet-of-Malta and the toasty Templars. They were burned at the stake. Would one such as the hopeful Pope not assist in getting at least some of these Templars safely hidden among the Hospitaller? Wouldn't some of them already have been Hospitallers, and some of the Hospitallers been Templars? Maybe among the Hospitallers some came to the Templar's aid. Philip was wiping away his debt by wiping away the Templars, so he had to spread the propaganda thick, embellish it, and make sure he captured and arrested all he could that may still try settling said debt with him. It was a more politically motivated reasoning than some religious heresy. Step aside, fake media. Before your pee-pee gate with Trump and Russia, there was the pee-pee gate of the Templars allegedly peeing on, and spitting on the cross. Stupid and ridiculous, but that doesn't mean the Templars weren't a bunch of wicked, terrible, robbing, raping, and pillaging, slave trading shit heads. Because they were. And they were international bankers.

You decide what happened for yourself here, but the common language of the Hospitallers became predominantly French, the Templar's language, at a point in time and with no clear explanation for why.

De Molay wasn't burned until March 18th, 1314. He had previously been tortured into confession, retracted it, and therefore Philip called that "relapse into heresy" and got the briquettes lit. Jacques seems to have at least died a man's death, never giving them the pleasure of him begging or falling to pieces. In fact he cursed Philip and Clement basically saying, "You'll both be joining me very soon, f*ckers!" Clement died within the month, and Philip within the year. Now here's the one short, vague sentence that is probably the most important, but is never even discussed in the dramatic retellings of this moment in probably-true history:

The remaining Knights were absorbed into other Catholic military (knightly) orders.

To be more specific, more were arrested and practically none were convicted in other territories. The Pope was dead, and so was the wind in that sail of persecution after Philip died, or was killed while hunting. As mentioned most all the property and wealth was handed over to the Hospitallers, so which order would you think the remaining Templar Knights ended up?

Those in Portugal, and those who made it there were fortunate to be outside the controlled territories of Philip. King Denis wasn't having that crap. He protected them, and they did reemerge as *The Order of the Knights of Our Lord Jesus Christ*. A bit wordy to print on a t-shirt, but that was the rising phoenix from the literal ashes of the Templars. The rest likely were in Rhodes and then Malta as Hospitallers.

Warning: Before reading further, grab ahold your socks real tight, because they're about to get blown off...

The Templar Order, and more specifically Jacques de Molay and his 2nd in command were absolved in 1308 by Pope Clement V. The Chinon Parchment written in August of 1308 was lost, possibly with intent, in the Vatican archives for hundreds of years due to a "misfiling."

It is a record of the trial of the Templars and shows that Clement absolved the Templars of all heresies in 1308 before formally disbanding the order in 1312, as did another Chinon Parchment dated 20 August 1308 addressed to Philip IV of France also mentioning that all Templars that had confessed to heresy were "restored to the Sacraments and to the unity of the Church..."

The current position of the RCC is that the medieval persecution of the Knights Templar was unjust, that nothing was inherently wrong with the order or its rule, and that Clement was pressed into his actions by the magnitude of the public scandal [medieval media hype] and by the dominating influence of King Philip IV, who was Clement's relative.

-Wiki ~~pedophila~~ pedia

Unjust at that time, perhaps, and maybe the Grand Masters of the pre-persecution time were more noble than those of lower degrees, but they have gone full-blown globalist death plot in the current era.

The Illuminati, which consist of the descendants of the Knights Templar and their allies the Kabbalist-globalist banking families, such as the Rothschild dynasty, have always idealized the Greek philosophers, all while practicing aberrated forms of Frankist-Luciferianism...

During the Templars' sojourn in the Holy Land, they became acquainted with the Kabbalah and learned the mysterious teachings of various other Jewish and Sufi sects...

-Sepehr, Robert. *1666 Redemption Through Sin*

Yet another commonality between the Knightly Orders and what was later the Messianic movements of Tzvi and Frank—Kabbalist mysticism, and the Knight's appreciation of it.

This connection between the Assassins for the Pope, the Jesuits, and The Knights Hospitaller/Malta is no small bit of data. We've seen the interconnectedness of the Knightly Orders, a final admission of the link between the Templars and the Hospitallers, and there's more intrigue and things make all the more sense when it's discovered the Jesuits are connected. They came on the scene 400 years after the aforementioned, but their primary objective was to wage war on the Reformers [Protestants] both overtly, and covertly by any means necessary. They were to be stealthy when necessary, conduct espionage as a matter of course, and to:
"*burn, waste, boil, flay, strangle, and bury alive these infamous heretics; rip up the stomachs and wombs of their women, and crush their infants' heads against the walls in order to annihilate their execrable race.*" --excerpt *Jesuit Oath*

Again from Madame Helena Petrovna Blavatsky:

"*It is curious to note too that most of the bodies which work these, such as the Ancient and Accepted Scottish Rite, the Rite of Avignon, the Order of the Temple, Fessler's Rite, the 'Grand Council of the Emperors of the East and West — Sovereign Prince Masons,' etc., etc., are nearly all the offspring of the sons of* **Ignatius Loyola**...

"*...That bastard foundling of Freemasonry, the 'Ancient and Accepted Scottish Rite,' which is unrecognized by the Blue Lodges was the enunciation, primarily, of the brain of the Jesuit Chevalier Ramsay. It was brought by him to England in 1736-38, to aid the cause of the Catholic Stuarts.*"

There's a connection not only to the Jesuits and the Templars/Knights of Malta, but to the Freemasonic order which we established when discussing Weishaupt's role in infiltrating the lodges, but also these Jesuits used the lodges for refuge when they were excommunicated, much like the Templars did before them, and the Protestants did as well. Pope Clement XIV who was educated by Jesuits had dissolved the Order in 1773. They were getting expelled from countries left and right for subversive revolutionary behavior, had amassed a huge and intimidating fortune off of communist slave labor and brutal treatment of Paraguayans, and seemed to sew seeds of discontent among the underclass wherever they went. Pope Clement XIV died soon after and it's rumored on his deathbed that he proclaimed that it was the Jesuits who got him, likely by poisoning ("the poison cup.") It would be Pope Pius VII that reinstated, or restored the Order in good standing in August of 1814. Both Thomas Jefferson and James Madison were extremely concerned with this, and they expressed it in surviving letter correspondence between one another. On the 50th anniversary of the Unanimous Declaration of the Thirteen United States of America, both men died within hours of each other. Two signatories of the Declaration, one that was in direct defiance of British and Roman Catholic authority, making them enemies of the Jesuits in their Counter-Reformation War were dead.

As there is much overlap in these organizations, it's not surprising that world leaders, CIA directors, heads of state, and even local politicians would be members of one or several of them. It's also not surprising that the United Nations, advised by the Club of Rome, and Fraternal Order-infested think tanks would share the same goal of disarmament with that of the Counter-Reformation War. If you think the Counter-Reformation War is over, I'm here to tell you that much of what we're witnessing is the continuation of said agenda to put us all back in bondage to the Jesuit Pope in Rome.

If you'd like to see what life would be like under the unmitigated power of the Pope, or of the Jesuits in-extension, research the history of the Reductions of Paraguay, and any of the numerous Jesuit Missions in the Americas. Or study the horrors of the Dark Ages which will prove to be a synonym for the New Age movement if they are successful.

There are missions littered all throughout California. Every 'San' city, ie San Diego, San Francisco, San Bernardino etc, or 'Santa' like Santa Barbara, Santa Ana, Santa Rosa, Santa Cruz, etc were at one point the site of a Jesuit mission. Apart from wholesale genocide, and referring to them as "barbarous savages" in part of their oath, they ripped children from the "native" families, and detached them from their culture, forced them to assimilate, and to convert. This is conducted in a more modern form through state funded schools where concerned parents are witnessing more and more that their parental rights are not only ignored, but labeled criminal by malicious 3-letter agencies. There's no more frightening an environment than one where the innocent are considered domestic terrorists by the socialist-communist authorities.

Genocide of the natives was a warm-up for what they wish to do to all of us, as we are the profane to the adepts of these fraternal orders, and sons and daughters of heretics as far as the Jesuits are concerned. Genocide, after all, is simply a heavy-handed form of Eugenics, and population control. What are the stated goals of these carbon-obsessed maniacs, again?

Holy See and the Rothschilds

Allow me to pontificate for a moment. I should get a nickel for every 2-cent pun. In 1832, after the Napoleonic Wars, James Mayer de Rothschild and Carl Mayer von Rothschild of Frankfurt/Offenbach did what Rothschilds have done ever since. After wars they funded destroy the infrastructure of a country and the rubble and ashes are still smoldering, they swoop down with black wings, and offer a Faustian deal. By this time in history the secret meeting of the three masterminds of the Illuminati plot had met decades ago, and the Frankist conversion, possibly by the whole of the family de Rothschild had taken place. The Rothschilds were loaning money to these war-torn countries, including Austria

James and Carl negotiated a loan to the Holy See in the amount of £400,000, equivalent to £4 Billion, or $4,872,720,000 by today's inflation. Thank you for that, Central Banks. Real money doesn't have this problem of inflation. For this loan, and it's important to stress that this wasn't a gift, and it wasn't a grant, James became the official Papal banker, and was also heading the Banque Rothschild in France. Carl went to meet directly with Pope Gregory XVI, and was awarded with the star of the Sacred Military Constantinian Order of Saint George. The Order's motto is *in hoc signo vinces*, or "In This Sign Thou Shalt Conquer." Consider that a moment. The Pope was not only greatly indebting himself to the Rothschilds, but he was also bestowing upon Carl a symbol of divine, successful conquest. Now I know that this could be a sanitized version of events.

As a straight read, it looks like we're witnessing the acquisition of the Holy Roman Empire by the most unconscionable family ever to exist. But if the history of the Bauers, the true name of the Rothschilds and maybe it was changed prior to that, goes as deep into Roman Empire history as I suspect, it's the Rothschilds that are in service to Rome, and have been since the post Julian era. Maybe as trusted court advisors of the highest regard. If there's truth to the well-traveled anecdote about the red sign on the little coinage shop of the Bauers, that shield was a Roman symbol, potentially a family crest. When you literally have all the money in the world, it's real easy to erase yourself from historical record. When so many countries exist for the pleasure of your banking family, and with a flip of a finger you can command their armies to destroy a defiant country, or send assassins to any leader's doorstep, debt slavery aside, most people follow the Rothschilds orders, especially our once sovereign and proud nation.

Because this family pretends Judaism, as a Jew, Carl was allowed to kiss the ring of the Pope rather than bend to the floor and kiss the Pontiff's feet, as is the respectful custom. Critics were quite vocal over the whole ordeal. They didn't like the break in the tradition, and they were outraged over a Jewish banking arrangement, basically claiming what I surmised, that they just bought the whole damn thing. Did the Pope just sell the Holy Roman Empire to the Rothschilds? Would this, or simply any other number of circumstances account for its strange actions and complete flips in policy just in our own lifetime? As you may be aware, the Church itself was founded by corrupt men in opposition to the core principle teachings of Jesus Christ. It could be argued what's birthed from such sin will by its very nature continue that course.

It's difficult to find much information on it, but a second loan to the Holy See by the Rothschilds occurred during the 1850's.

On December 22nd, 2020, F. William Engdahl published an article for *New Eastern Outlook* picked up by NewAgeBD (Bd, short for Bangladesh) .net titled, *Dangerous Alliance of Rothschild and Vatican of Francis*. Right out of the gate he aptly describes Bergoglio, Pope Francis as the *"...most globalist and interventionist Pope since the Crusades of the 12th century..."*

The article describes an alliance between criminal COVID tyrant, Green Initiative radical, suspected Buenos Aires child trafficking facilitator, Jesuit Pope Francis and Lynn Forester de Rothschild on what they called the 'Council for Inclusive Capitalism with the Vatican.' Engdahl writes, *"The venture is one of the more cynical, and given the actors, most dangerous frauds being promoted since Davos WEF guru and Henry Kissinger protégé, Klaus Schwab, began to promote the great reset of the world capitalist order."*

The article by Engdahl is very well written, and packed with important, and interesting facts for those dot-connecting enthusiasts out there.

From the UN article: *"Council members make actionable commitments aligned with the World Economic Forum International Business Council's pillars for sustainable value creation — people, planet, principles of governance, and prosperity — and that advance the United Nations Sustainable Development Goals."*

Lynn de Rothschild states, *"This council will follow the warning from Pope Francis to listen to 'The cry of the earth and the cry of the poor' and answer society's demands for a more equitable and sustainable model of growth."*

Engdahl masterfully retorts, *Their reference to Klaus Schwab's World Economic Forum is no accident. The group is yet another front group in what is becoming a globalist bum's rush to try to convince a skeptical world that the same people who created the post-1945 model of IMF-led globalization and giga-corporate entities more powerful than governments, destroying traditional agriculture in favour of toxic agribusiness, dismantling living standards in industrialised countries to flee to cheap labour countries like Mexico or China, will now lead the effort to correct all their abuses? We are being naïve if we swallow this.*

Engdahl goes on to point out that Lynn de Rothschild's name appears on the flight logs to Epstein's island, and that she once housed Jizz-lane, forgive my mistake, Ghislaine Maxwell in one of her NYC apartments following her Mossad agent father's murder. A murder that likely occurred because too much money was owed to him.

Ghislaine even used the address to register a business venture called TerraMar, and one of the donors to that business was the Clinton Foundation. You can't seem to discuss anything related to child sex-traficking without the Clintons ending up in the conversation. The Rothschilds, Evelyn, now worm food, and Lynn, spent part of their honeymoon at the Clinton's White House.

The list of "moral guardians" of the UN promoted, WEF supported initiative that oddly enough tackles every globalist Reset goal and Agenda 2030 projection ranges from heads of the Rockefeller and Ford Foundations to former partners of the Gates Foundation. And Jesuit Pope Francis resoundingly supports it, stamps his seal on it, and continues to promote the key themes of it.

The Stone of Foundation

Reproduced in John Robison's book, *Proofs of a Conspiracy Against All The Religions and Governments Of Europe, Carried On In The Secret Meetings of Freemasons, Illuminati, and Reading Societies*, I told you it was a long title, Robison reproduces a letter he had in his possession. It was written under Jesuit Adam Weishaupt's code name, Spartacus—the Thracian slave who rises up against his Roman captors. It's of some interest to note that Jersey sludge, Cory Booker invoked the name 'Spartacus' during the Kavanaugh hearing. It's also of some disdainful interest to note that that ass-clown dated Rosario Dawson. Not since Fred 'Douche' Durst and Holly Berry has a beautiful actress plummeted her standards so low.

The letter is addressed to a "Cato," apparently also an Illuminati agent code name, for Cato the Younger was another historical Roman who volunteered to fight in the war against Spartacus. It's unlikely it was addressed to Cato Howe, the Black slave during the American Revolution who carried intel on horseback to the Continental Army that was gathered by his um, let's just say "boss." He was a spy for the Patriots of the Revolution.

The letter gives you an idea of what this Black Robe, another name for the Jesuits given to them by the natives, thought of Jesus and of the religion they pretended.

"Jesus of Nazareth, the Grand Master of our Order, appeared at a time when the world was in the utmost disorder, and among a people who for ages had groaned under the yoke of bondage. He taught them the lessons of Reason. To be more effective, he took in the aid of Religion—of opinions which were current—and, in a very clever manner, he combined his secret doctrines with the popular religion, and with the customs which lay to his hand. In these he wrapped up his lessons—he taught by parables. Never did any prophet lead men so easily and so securely along the road of liberty. He concealed the precious meaning and consequences of his doctrines; but fully disclosed them to a chosen few. He speaks of a kingdom of the upright and faithful; his Father's kingdom, whose children we also are. Let us only take Liberty and Equality as the great aim of his doctrines, and Morality as the way to attain it, and every thing in the New Testament will be comprehensible; and Jesus will appear as the Redeemer of slaves. Man is fallen from the condition of Liberty and Equality, the STATE OF PURE NATURE. He is under subordination and civil bondage, arising from the vices of man. This is the FALL, and ORIGINAL SIN. The KINGDOM OF GRACE is that restoration which may be brought about by Illumination and a just Morality. This is the NEW BIRTH. When man lives under government, he is fallen, his worth is gone, and his nature tarnished. By subduing our passions, or limiting their cravings, we may recover a great deal of our original worth, and live in a state of grace. This is the redemption of men—this is accomplished by Morality; and when this is spread over the world, we have THE KINGDOM OF THE JUST.

"But, alas! the task of self-formation was too hard for the subjects of the Roman empire, corrupted by every species of profligacy. A chosen few received the doctrines in secret, and they have been handed down to us (but frequently almost buried under rubbish of man's invention) by the Free Masons. These three conditions of human society are expressed by the rough, the split, and the polished stone. The rough stone, and the one that is split, express our condition under civil government; rough by every fretting inequality of condition; and split, since we are no longer one family; and are farther divided by differences of government, rank property, and religion; but when reunited in one family, we are represented by the polished stone. G. is Grace; the Flaming Star is the Torch of Reason. Those who possess this knowledge are indeed ILLUMINATI. Hiram is our fictitious Grand Master, slain for the REDEMPTION OF SLAVES; the Nine Masters are the Founders of the Order. Free Masonry is a Royal Art, inasmuch as it teaches us to walk without trammels, and to govern ourselves."

He claims Jesus is the Grand Master of the Jesuit Order, or Society of Jesus, yet in the same letter invokes the symbolism of Prometheus and Lucifer when he describes the "Flaming Star" and the "torch" of illumined knowledge. The name of Jesus is never to be spoken in the masonic lodges, and I doubt it's simply because that wasn't his real name.

What of this imagery of the polished stone, a symbol of reuniting, or in other words the presumption set forth of a previous unity? Does this refer to the Jesuit and Roman perspective of the Protestant break from the Roman rule? Or does this speak to the mythical Babylonian Golden Age, and a desire to bring about those same conditions in a One World, Roman ruled, totalitarian government? On the surface, from sources of academia, and even in their own Oath the Jesuits act as if they are mortal enemies of the Freemasons as much as they are with all Protestant forms that came about during the reformation. But it was the Freemasons who took the Jesuits in when they were expelled, just as they had taken in the Protestants previously when the Church and specifically the Jesuits had hunted after reformers. The time the Oath was written was different from the time where Jesuits lost favor with Pope Clement. Prior to the Pope's actions, the Jesuits, much like the Jews, had been kicked out of every decent country one could think of. And they were ousted for a common reason. Wherever the Jesuits and the Jews went they sewed seeds of discontent among the people, agitated hostilities, wouldn't assimilate and live in peace, and were generally subversive and anti-establishment.

It's said that the term "86 it" meaning to throw someone out, or something away, could be a reference to the number of individual territories the Jesuits were kicked out of, or it could refer to the 8ft by 6ft standard hole dug for a grave. Collectively, the Jesuits were expelled from the Portuguese Empire, France, the Two Sicilies, Malta, Parma, the Spanish Empire where Ignatius had been birthed, Austria, and Hungary all before the Pope finally had enough. When they were reinstated in 1814, it is quite likely they held the same eternal grudge for the for the Roman Catholic Church that they held for those countries including China and Japan who would finally get hip to them as well. Look what happened to China. That may be a "communist country,' but it has been in the control of the Jesuits ever since their groomed and trained puppet Mao came to power. The Black Robes will patiently wait generations to exact their revenge and carry out their bloody vendetta. It was in 1815 that the Jesuits were kicked out of Russia. They weren't the only party with a grudge. The Rothschilds were furious with Russia since its interference, a naval blockade against British ships, during the American Revolution. There was also the matter of the Tsar of Russisa, Alexander, thwarting the first effort of the Rothschilds to establish a league of nations at the Congress of Vienna. Understanding what entities are the tools and what entities wield those tools may help explain how our US gold under the watch of Woodrow Wilson could be spirited off by Jacob Schiff to fund the Bolshevik Revolution. Wilson was an obedient servant of Baruch, Warburg, Schiff, and House, all Rothschild's men.

The Stone of Foundation Broadcast by William Cooper has been sprinkled into this book, in part, already. But now we finally get to the portion of Bill's presentation that deals with the subject matter for which he titled that episode. "[ ]" indicate where I have interjected. "…" indicate where I've skipped ahead.

"The philosophers of fire [refers to the Priestcraft, keepers of knowledge], ladies and gentlemen, do not like to be exposed. They do not want to be undone, discovered, unmasked. They want us to live our lives hoodwinked—is their term for it. But many of us over the years have learned where to look, and how to look and we have found that there is nothing hidden about these people. Even though their societies are secret, and their meetings are held in temples without windows behind closed doors guarded by the Tyler with sword. But they do have a language that is different from the language which we understand. They speak in an esoteric language made up of Gematria, symbology, geometry, and parables [direct reference to Kabbalah].

So the average, everyday, normal citizen can read their writings, and unless they understand the hidden language, or the esoteric meaning of what they are reading, they get one tale, one story when the truth is it tells an entirely different story for those who are well-versed in the hidden language of the Mystery Religion of Babylon.

I'm going to read to you now from three different sections of a book, an old book. You see, when you search these people you must seek out their older writings for their newer writings they have scrubbed out anything… Not all, for even the newer writings for those of us who understand the language reveal great bits of their history and the truth concerning their real agendas. But the older editions of their works lay it all out in plain view for anybody who has studied their symbols, and their esoteric language. I'm going to read to you now three different parts of a new and revised edition of *An Encyclopedia of Freemasonry and It's Kindred Sciences Comprising the Whole Range of*

Arts, Sciences, and Literature as Connected with the Institution by Albert G. Mackey, M.D., 33rd Degree... 1924...

Now I'm on page 722... under the heading, *Stone of Foundation*. This is very important.

And I quote, '*The Stone of Foundation constitutes one of the most important and abstruse of all the symbols of Freemasonry. It is referred to in numerous legends and traditions not only of the Freemasons, but also the Jewish rabbis, the Talmudic writers, even the Mussulmen doctors.*' [Bill:] Mussulman in that day was thee term for the Muslim people. Mussulman doctors was representative of the high state of learning in the Arab world. The first colleges, the first universities that ever existed in the world were Arab. Arab.

They continue, '*Many of these, it must be confessed are apparently puerile and absurd; but most of them, and especially the Masonic ones, are deeply interesting in their allegorical signification.*

The Stone of Foundation is, properly speaking, a symbol of the higher Degrees.' [Bill:] Now it's important that you understand this: '*The Stone of Foundation is, properly speaking, a symbol of the higher Degrees.*' Because we're going to go through a process here where they try to confound the profane with a bunch of gobbledygook— and then they tell you the truth.

'*It makes its first appearance in the Royal Arch, and forms indeed the most important symbol of that Degree. But it is so intimately connected, in its legendary history, with the construction of the Solomonic Temple, that it must be considered as a part of Ancient Craft Masonry, although he who confines the range of his investigations to the first three Degrees will have no means, within that narrow limit, of properly appreciating the symbolism of the Stone of Foundation.*'

Now this is just saying in a polite way that the first three degrees of Freemasonry, and indeed all of the ones below the Royal Arch degree really don't know the truth about the organization to which they belong. And they're going to repeat that admonition all through here. So if you know someone, or if you are a member of a Masonic Lodge in the first three degrees, or any of the degrees below the Royal Arch degree [discontinued in 2004], you have to understand, or make that person understand, that they're being deluded. They've never been told the truth. They don't know what the truth is. And they're not going to learn the truth, most of them, ever. Because they're not considered worthy of it. They never will rise up that high. They'll never be one of the adept—one of the Illuminati who really run things. And it's not just Freemasonry, remember that. All of these fraternal orders, secret societies, and organizations who meet in secret, or have secret doctrines, at the highest levels are the SAME ORGANIZATION. And their masters, or adepts are all known collectively as the Illuminati [Frankist-Jesuit heirarchy.]

'*As preliminary to the inquiry, it is necessary to distinguish the Stone of Foundation, both in its symbolism and its legendary history, from other stones which play an important part in the Masonic Ritual, but which are entirely distinct from it. Such is the corner-stone, which was always placed in the northeast corner of the building about to be erected, and to which such a beautiful reference is made in the ceremonies of the First Degree; or the keystone, which constitutes an interesting part of the Mark Master's Degree; or, lastly, the cap-stone, upon which all the ritual of the Most Excellent Master's Degree is founded. They are all, in their proper places, highly interesting and instructive Symbols, but have no connection whatever with the Stone of Foundation, whose symbolism it is our present object to discuss. Nor, although the Stone of Foundation is said, for peculiar reasons, to have been of a cubical form, must it be confounded with that stone called by the Continental Freemasons the cubical stone—the pierre cubique of the French and the cubik stein of the German Freemasons but which in the English system is known as the perfect ashlar.*

The Stone of Foundation has a legendary history and a symbolic signification which are peculiar to itself, and which differ from the history and meaning which belong to these other stones. We propose first to define this Masonic Stone of Foundation, then to collate the legends which refer to it, and afterward to investigate its significance as a symbol. To the Freemason who takes a pleasure in the study of the mysteries of his Institution, the investigation cannot fail to be interesting, if it is conducted with any ability.'

Now listen to what I just said. '*To the Freemason who takes a pleasure in the study of the mysteries of his Institution, the investigation cannot fail to be interesting, if it is conducted with any ability.*' Which means knowledge of the esoteric, or secret language of the symbols, otherwise the investigator will understand nothing of the truth of the matter.

*'But in the very beginning, as a necessary preliminary to any investigation of this kind, it must be distinctly understood that all that is said of this Stone of Foundation in Freemasonry is to be strictly taken in a mythical or allegorical sense. Doctor Oliver, while undoubtedly himself knowing that it was simply a symbol, has written loosely of it as though it were a substantial reality; and hence, if the passages in his **Historical Landmarks**, and in his other works which refer to this celebrated stone, are accepted by his readers in a literal sense, they will present absurdities and puerilities which would not occur if the Stone of Foundation was received, as it really is, as a myth conveying a most profound and beautiful symbolism.*

It is such that it is to be treated here; and, therefore, if a legend is recited or a tradition related, the reader is requested on every occasion to suppose that such legend or tradition is not intended as the recital or relation of what is deemed a fact in Masonic history, but to wait with patience for the development of the symbolism which it conveys. Read in this spirit, as all the legends of Freemasonry should be read, the legend of the Stone of Foundation becomes one of the most important and interesting of all the Masonic symbols.'

Now if you think this isn't important, ladies and gentlemen, just think how many times you have seen the representations and symbology of this stone in your lives and did not understand what it meant. And if you saw the movie, *2001*, you saw the Stone of Foundation. It appeared before the cave in which the apes were huddled. That's right. It also appeared on the moon when man reached the moon and began digging he found again this mysterious black stone. And again when they traveled to the planet Jupiter, there it was, orbiting around Jupiter, this huge black monolith. Into which the astronaut was finally able to peer, and what he saw was another universe. Most people who saw the movie, *2001 (Space Odyssey)* didn't understand any of it. It was a message in symbolism from the adepts of the Illuminati to the other adepts if the Illuminati, and could only be understood by those who know the esoteric, secret language of the Mystery Religions.

You also see it if you visit Las Vegas and go into the Luxor Hotel which is nothing more than a gigantic temple of initiation. Into which pour the profane tourists from all around the globe, and after spending several days there going through the three degrees of initiation represented by the three entertainment facilities there. And wandering around being indoctrinated into the exoteric meaning of the esoteric language by all the symbolism depart several days later as Freemasons without portfolio. And there in the Luxor Hotel is once again a huge, black, smooth, perfectly polished representation of the Stone of Foundation. What is this all about? (laughs) Well, it's about an awful lot, folks. And you had better learn it because it is important. Because they are manipulating you with all of this, and you don't even know it.

'The Stone of Foundation is supposed, by the theory which establishes it, to have been a stone placed at one time within the foundations of the Temple of Solomon, and afterward, during the building of the second Temple, transported to the Holy of Holies. It was in form a perfect cube, and had inscribed upon its upper face, within a delta or triangle, the sacred Tetragrammaton, or Ineffable Name of God.'

Now don't get all bent out of shape here and think that they're talking about the same god you're talking about because they're not, and it'll become evident.

[Doctor] Oliver, speaking with the solemnity of a historian, says that Solomon thought that he had rendered the house of God worthy, so far as human adornment could effect, for the dwelling of God, "when he had placed the celebrated Stone of Foundation, on which the sacred name was mystically engraven, with solemn ceremonies, in that sacred depository on Mount Moriah, along with the foundations of Dan and Asher, the center of the Most Holy Place, where the Ark was overshadowed by the Shekinah of God." The Hebrew Talmudists, who thought as much of this stone, and had as many legends concerning it, as the Masonic Talmudists, called it eben shatijah, or Stone of Foundation, because as they said, it had been laid by Jehovah as the foundation of the world, and hence the apocryphal Book of Enoch speaks of the "stone which supports the corners of the earth." [my note: It's my view that the entire tale of Solomon's Temple is an allegory or myth. It's the literal, exoteric story that speaks of a darker hidden history of these adepts and their mission, and is a method by which the Priestcraft manipulate mankind, which it is doing successfully with Frankism and Zionism.]

'This idea of a foundation-stone of the world was most probably derived from that magnificent passage of the Book of Job (ch. 38, v. 4-7) in which the Almighty demands of Job,

Where wast thou, when I laid the foundation of the earth?
Declare, since thou hast such knowledge!
Who fixed its dimensions, since thou knowest!
Or who stretched out the line upon it?

Upon what were its foundations fixed?
And who laid its corner-stone,
When the morning stars sang together.
And all the sons of God shouted for joy?

Noyes, whose translation we have adopted as not materially differing from the common version, but more poetical and more in the strain of the original, thus explains the allusions to the foundation-stone: "It was the custom to celebrate the laying of the corner-stone of an important building With music, songs, shouting, etc. Hence the morning stars are represented as celebrating the laying of the cornerstone of the earth."

Upon this meager statement has been accumulated more traditions than appertain to any other Masonic symbol. The Rabbis, as has already been intimated, divide the glory of these apocryphal histories with the Freemasons; indeed, there is good reason for a suspicion that nearly all the Masonic legends owe their first existence to the imaginative genius of the writers of the Jewish Talmud. But there is this difference between the Hebrew and the Masonic traditions: that the Talmudic scholar recited them as truthful histories, and swallowed, in one gulp of faith, all their impossibilities and anachronisms; while the Masonic scholar has received them as allegories, whose value is not in the facts, but in the sentiments which they convey.

And ladies and gentlemen that shows you that even such a learned man as Albert Mackey could be confused [or intentionally deceiving] and ignorant of the facts. For the Talmudic writers, followers of the Mysteries of Judaism did not ever recite them as truthful histories and swallow them in one gulp of faith. They knew their impossibilities and anachronisms for they are one of the original inventors [debatable] and users of the esoteric or hidden language. And in specific, I'm speaking of Gematria.

'With this understanding of their meaning, let us proceed to a collation of these legends.

In that blasphemous work, the Toldoth Jeshu, or Life of Jesus, written, it has been supposed, in the thirteenth or fourteenth century, we find the following account of this wonderful stone:

*"At that time (the time of Jesus) there was in the House of the Sanctuary (that is, the Temple) a stone of foundation, which is the very stone that our father Jacob anointed with oil, as it is described in the twenty-eighth chapter of the Book of Genesis. On that stone the letters of the Tetragrammaton were inscribed, and **whosoever of the Israelites should learn that name would be able to master the world**.'*

Now you're getting to a little bit of some of the ultimate meaning of this.

'To prevent, therefore, any one from learning these letters, two iron dogs were placed upon two columns in front of the Sanctuary. If any person, having acquired the knowledge of these letters, desired to depart from the Sanctuary, the barking of the dogs, by magical power, inspired so much fear that he suddenly forgot what he had acquired."

*This passage is cited by the learned Buxtorf in his **Lexicon Talmudicum**; but in his copy of the Toldoth Jeshu, Doctor Mackey found another passage, which gives* *somehttps://www.mintpressnews.com/red-heifer-project-israel-government-part-of-plan-to-build-third-temple-al-aqsa/285594/ additional particulars, in the following words:*

"At that time there was in the Temple the ineffable name of God, inscribed upon the Stone of Foundation. For when King David was digging the foundation for the Temple, he found in the depths of the excavation a certain stone on which the name of God was inscribed. This stone he removed and deposited it in the Holy of Holies.

The same puerile story of the barking dogs is repeated still more at length. It is not pertinent to the present inquiry, but it may be stated, as a mere matter of curious information, that this scandalous book, which is throughout a blasphemous defamation of our Savior, proceeds to say, that he cunningly obtained a knowledge of the Tetragrammaton from the Stone of Foundation, and by its mystical influence was enabled to perform his miracles.

The Masonic legends of the Stone of Foundation, based on these and other rabbinical reveries, are of the most extraordinary character, if they are to be viewed as histories, but readily reconcilable with sound sense, if looked at only in the light of allegories. They present an uninterrupted succession of events, in which the Stone of Foundation takes a prominent part, from Adam to Solomon, and from Solomon to Zerubbabel.

Thus, the first of these legends, in order of time, relates that the Stone of Foundation was possessed by Adam while in the Garden of Eden; that he used it as an altar, and so reverenced it that, on his expulsion from Paradise, he carried it with him into the world in which he and his descendants were afterward to earn their bread by the sweat of their brow…
…Another legend informs us that from Adam the Stone of Foundation descended to Seth. From Seth it passed by regular succession to Noah, who took it with him into the Ark, and after the subsidence of the Deluge made on it his first thank-offering. Noah left it on Mount Ararat, where it was subsequently, found by Abraham, who removed it, and constantly used it as an altar of sacrifice. His grandson Jacob took it with him when he fled to his uncle Laban in Mesopotamia, and used it as a pillow when, in the vicinity of Luz, he had his celebrated vision.

Here there is a sudden interruption in the legendary history of the stone, and we have no means of conjecturing how it passed from the possession of Jacob into that of Solomon. Moses, it is true, is said to have taken it with him out of Egypt at the time of of the exodus, and thus it may have finally reached Jerusalem. Dr. Adam Clarke repeats, what he very properly calls a foolish tradition, that the stone on which Jacob rested his head was afterward brought to Jerusalem, thence carried after a long lapse of time to Spain, from Spain to Ireland, and from Ireland to Scotland, where it was used as a seat on which the kings of Scotland sat to be crowned. Edward I, we know, brought a stone to which this legend is attached from Scotland to Westminster Abbey where under the name of Jacob's Pillow, it still remains, and is always placed under the chair upon which the British Sovereign sits to be crowned; because there is an old distich which declares that wherever this stone is found the Scottish Kings shall reign…

[Skipping ahead]

…At the building of the first Temple of Jerusalem, the Stone of Foundation again makes its appearance…

*…In the Masonic legend, the Foundation-Stone first makes its appearance, as we have already said, in the days of Enoch, who placed it in the bowels of Mount Moriah. There it was subsequently discovered by King Solomon, who deposited it in a crypt of the **first Temple**, where it remained concealed until the foundations of the **second Temple** were laid, when it was discovered and removed to the Holy of Holies. But the most important point of the legend*

of the Stone of foundation is its intimate and constant connection with the Tetragrammaton or Ineffable Name. It is this name, inscribed upon it within the Sacred and Symbolic Delta, [Bill: Remember Delta Force?] *that gives to the stone all its Masonic value and significance. It is upon this fact, that it was so inscribed, that its whole symbolism depends...*

...Now for those of you, ladies and gentlemen, who think this is a waste of time, bear in mind you have already seen this stone three times in a movie called, *2001 [Space Odyssey.]* You did not understand its significance or even what you were looking at, or the message of the movie. If you tell me you did, I'm going to ask you to explain it to me and you're going to find yourself extremely embarrassed. You see it in Las Vegas if you go to the Luxor Hotel. It is there right in front of everyone. And in the center there is a huge obelisk that from time-to-time shoots a beam of light directly up to the center where a huge X crosses at the very top of the hotel. And at night it shoots up into the heavens. If you go to the United Nations meditation room you will also see this same stone. That's right, ladies and gentlemen. Occupying the center position of the meditation room which is itself shaped as a truncated pyramid with the capstone missing. Now if you believe sincerely that Stanley Kubrick made that movie, *2001* and inserted that stone as a central theme of the meaning of that motion picture, one of the greatest of all time... And if you believe that they erected the Luxor Hotel with all its symbology and placed the Stone of Foundation in that hotel overshadowing and overpowering everything... And if you sincerely believe it rests in the meditation room of the United Nations and that this is unimportant and a waste of time, then ladies and gentlemen I have to say that they're right when they say that you are cattle.

For mos to you, I know that you already understand the significance and do not fit into that category. For those of you who do, I would suggest at this time that you turn off your radio, because you've wasted enough of your time.

...Now, as in all the other systems the stone is admitted to be symbolic, and the traditions connected with it mystical, we are compelled to assume the same predicates of the Masonic stone. It, too, is Symbolic, and its legend a myth or an allegory.

Of the fable, myth, or allegory, [Jean Silvain] Bailly has said that, "subordinate to history and philosophy, it only deceives that it may the better instruct us.

Listen to this! They admit that they LIE! (Bill repeats the previous line)
Faithful in preserving the realities which are confided to it, it covers with its seductive envelop the lessons of tile one and the truths of the other."

So you see, they believe that they are the only mature minds. They deceive everyone else. To each other they tell the truth. And they learn the lessons of the one and the truths of the other.

It is from this standpoint that we are to view the allegory of the Stone of Foundation, as developed in one of the most interesting and important symbols of Freemasonry.

The fact that the mystical stone in all the ancient religions was a symbol of the Deity, leads us necessarily to the conclusion that the Stone of Foundation was also a symbol of Deity. And this symbolic idea is strengthened by the Tetragrammaton, or sacred name of God, that was inscribed upon it. This Ineffable Name sanctifies the stone upon which it is engraved as the symbol of the Grand Architect. It takes from it its heathen Signification as an idol, and consecrates it to the worship of the true God.

The predominant idea of the Deity, in the Masonic system, connects him with his creative and formative power. God is to the Freemason Al Gabil, as the Arabians called him, that is, The Builder; or, as expressed in his Masonic title, the Grand Architect of the Universe, by common consent abbreviated in the formula G. A. O. T. U. Now, it is evident that no Symbol could so appropriately suit him in this character as the Stone of Foundation, upon which he is allegorically supposed to have erected his world. Such a symbol closely connects the creative work of God, as a pattern and exemplar, with the workman's erection of his temporal building on a similar foundation stone...

...When we have arrived at this point in our speculations, we are ready to show how all the myths and legends of the Stone of Foundation may be rationally explained as parts of that beautiful "science of morality, veiled in allegory and illustrated by symbols," which is the acknowledged definition of Freemasonry.

In the Masonic system there are two Temples: the First Temple, in which the Degrees of Ancient Craft Masonry are concerned, and the Second Temple, with which the higher Degrees, and especially the Royal Arch, are related. The first Temple is symbolic of the present life; the Second Temple is symbolic of the life to come.

Bill: And in between there is a symbolic death and rebirth and the raising by the grip of the lion's paw. [author note: the Lion is the adopted symbol of Israel]

*The First Temple, **the present life, must he destroyed**; on its foundations the Second Temple, the life eternal, must be built.*

Ordo ab Chao.

[Skipping ahead]

...But although the present life is necessarily built upon the foundation of truth, yet we never thoroughly attain it in this sublunary sphere. The Foundation Stone is concealed in the First Temple, and the Master Mason knows it not. He has not the true word. He receives only a substitute.

And there is one of the greatest admissions that they ever make: that they DO NOT tell the truth to the lower degrees. Let me read that again:

The Foundation Stone is concealed in the First Temple, and the Master Mason knows it not. He has not the true word. He receives only a substitute.

The Blue Lodge exists in deception…

-Excerpts from *The Hour of the Time* broadcast number 1078, *The Stone of Foundation*, March 18th, 1997

I encourage the reader, that's you, to seek out this broadcast in its entirety from the remastered recordings offered on the BitChute channel, *The Hour of the Time*.

Jacob Frank, and Jesuit Adam Weishaupt galvanized the Frankists and the Jesuits under the umbrella term, "Illuminati," with the backing of the wealthiest family in this prison realm of the Demiurgos. Their network selects the leaders and creates the think tanks, fills the seats in the United Nations, the World Economic Forum, and gives rise to counter-intuitive, weakening, self-destructive political initiatives that are eagerly adopted by all nations indebted to, and controlled by the aforementioned family of banking institutions. They recruit through these Freemasonic lodges only the best and brightest for their anti-human objectives.

Zionism is a direct product of the Lurian Kabbalah's proposed sense of purpose and duty to be stewards and orchestrators, Builders of the ideal world conditions to artificially hasten the Redemption, or Day of Judgment upon the Earth. It was Shabbatai and Jacob Frank who championed this idea, and the latter, Frank, who demanded and cultivated the most insidious, and sociopathic means by which to arrive at that goal. Zionism, by any other name, is still Frankism. And by that name it should be known because it is that name which signifies its true, dark, and evil nature. They want to "rebuild" the temple in Jerusalem, and many Frankists who pretend Christianity aggressively support the effort for they claim the Messiah that will return will be Jesus. I think that's just the story they deceive other Christians with, but regardless if they truly believe that or not, Frankist-Zionists are still attempting to usher in the Final Judgment, the end of the world. They want to rush what their religion has convinced them is the eventual outcome. What we are seeing occur in the Ukraine with Zelenskyy stating that Ukraine will become Greater Israel, and the bloody, wicked war erupting in Palestine at present are all efforts to create the end times for humanity. Absolute Evil, child-killing sociopaths are deciding the fate of the world, and they have all the money and the support to achieve their ends, by whatever means of human suffering and torture necessary. They are not just indifferent to killing the most innocent, but they take great pleasure in doing so, and see it as fulfillment of their responsibilities as Frankists, Zionists, Lurian Kabbalists, whatever the label.

To get a measurement of just how close they are to this capping of the Great Pyramid, the completion of the "Great Work," we need only open our eyes to the symbols, and the entities which boldly display them.

The Stone of Foundation symbolism is right in front of us, and is discussed often with no one, that I have ever heard, recognizing it. Blackstone is the largest alternative asset manager in the world, and it has barely been in existence for 40 years. This is the firm where Larry Fink, "under its corporate umbrella" co-founded **BlackRock** and became it's CEO. Fink founded BlackRock in 1988, and it now has a total AUM (Assets Under Management) of 9.4 Trillion dollars. For the sake of time, it would make a much shorter list to name what BlackRock doesn't yet own, but not to worry soon you will own nothing, because BlackRock will have it all. These two names Blackstone and BlackRock weren't picked out of a hat. This is a deliberate Kabbalistic reference, for it is from there which the Stone of Foundation derives its mysticism and magical attributes. Now do you think Freemasonry is a significant problem? Do you see the overwhelming power that the Frankist-Illuminati yield over mankind? Fink is a California-born Democrat, and a staunch supporter of Israel. One cannot support the forced building of Israel and not be a supporter of Zionism. It was a Zionist action that created it. It fulfills the Zionist objective, and sadly for those living there, a destruction of Israel and all lives within it, followed by a "Greater" rebuilding of it, also follow the

Zionist objectives. Larry Fink is on a board of "Strategic Advisors" along with Lady Lynn Forester de Rothschild in something called FCLTGlobal. You remember *Lady Lynn*, right? Chums with Ghislaine Maxwell, child-trafficker, and the Clinton Mafia?

The Rothschild & Co. firm partnered with BlackRock, and these companies are listed as top shareholders: Vanguard 9.04%, State Street Corp 4.21%, and Bank of America 3.45%.

Larry Fink and Bill Gates have had televised discussions of their shared views on, and proposals to battle the false climate crisis with the discussion revolving around Gate's net zero emissions goal. That goal is only reached if "one of these numbers is near zero." (paraphrased) That referred to mankind.

The child-killers own the world, they advise the world, they influence medicine that is marketed "safe and effective" killing children in a blind game of Eugenics, and they are onboard with climate politics—mass murder by many means including war and forced famine. Who do you think controls the food supply, and the companies that produce it? Who do you think manipulates municipal water supplies and local politics in even the smallest of towns? I'll let you ponder that.

At some point in our lost, and nearly lost history, the once fair, integral, and still fierce warriors who treated those they conquered with dignity and kindness were marked for annihilation. The noble Scythian and Goth cultures, a culture that rejected the marketplace, were replaced or displaced by deceivers, manipulators, and the cunning and ruthless Priestcraft arose. Nobility and bloodlines known for such a trait have been the target ever since. These hunted noblemen whose whole communities were as one big family, became the obsession of these priesthoods for thousands of years. Corrupted and materialistic empires such as late Rome, whom these noble warriors shared a history of cooperation with, turned on them out of fear and envy. Envy seems to be one emotion the sociopaths of history are capable of feeling.

Dome of the Rock Haram al-Sharif

The Dome of the Rock, also known as the Temple Mount, or Haram al-Sharif is located in the old city of Jersalem, and contains within its structure the large rock believed by both the Muslims, Jews, and Christians to be the rock Ibrahim or Abraham brought his son Isaac to be sacrificed. I question any religion whose basis is on a man who would betray his own child's trust and their love to please the voices in his head, or any voice outside of his head for that matter.

This is also the site that the Mussulman/Muslims believe is the Bayt-Allah, or House of God, where their prophet Muhammad went to for his mythical "Night Journey" where he ascended into heavenly spheres. It's the oldest standing religious building of Islamic construction. It is not a mosque, but rather a shrine intended for pilgrimage.

There are retaining walls on all sides of the plaza where the shrine structure housing the rock, still embedded in the ground, is exposed in the center. The oldest of these retaining walls is said to have been laid on the orders of King Herod, quite the foul character. Additions and renovations to these walls have been added over time.

The views on this location from the Jewish perspective is that it was built upon the ruins of the "Second Temple," and to some, that it's even the site of both the first, or Solomon's Temple, and the second temple. It's doubtful to me that there was a Solomon's Temple at all, and I see it more as cryptic story relating a magical working, than a literal temple. To what god was Solomon building a temple to that he needed to elicit the help of demon(s)? The "second" temple is said to have been destroyed in 70AD by Titus when Rome reclaimed Jerusalem under the ruler Vespasio/Vespasian. There's a whole, long trail we could go down discussing Flavius Josephus, the spared Jewish turncoat, whom Vespasian adopted and made his court historian. Especially if we got into the work of Joseph Atwill, *Caesar's Messiah*. I explore everything. It doesn't mean I agree with every explanation I encounter. There's another interesting book by Ralph Ellis called, *Jesus, King of Edessa* which would likely rouse suspicion in most given that it seems to, in part, blend the story of Tammuz with Jesus, and because Ralph himself is a high degree Freemason. Which leaves the question, does the book mean something else to the adept who knows the secret language of the Mystery Schools?

The Stone of Foundation described in the passages by Albert Mackey say that it was the stone upon which Abraham had intended to sacrifice Isaac. When you look at the enormous size of this rock at the Dome, it definitely wasn't Jacob's Pillow, nor is it small enough to fit under the throne chair of a king. Nevertheless, both the Stone of Foundation and the rock at the Dome claim to be the intended place where Isaac was to be sacrificed, making at least some kind of connection. If Abraham went there to sacrifice his son, it would fit the biblical description of a mountain he had to ascend with

Isaac to get to his chosen spot. The Dome of the Rock, or Temple Mount is at the highest point of Mt. Moriah in Jerusalem, Palestine.

Here's where this site, the Temple Mount/Haram al Sharif becomes very relevant to current events at the time I write this book, which today is November 8th, 2023, a month after the "Hamas" attack. Today I received a Haaretz Israel News email stating that it had been 33 days since Hamas killed "at least 1,300 Israelis," and wounded "more than 3,300." 33, 13, and 33 again. These aren't Freemasonic numbers. They're Kabbalah numbers significant to Freemasons because the masonic order is founded upon the magic of the Kabbalah, and infested Frankist-Illuminati. Most initiates have no idea of the symbolic meanings of their own ceremonies and rituals. These numbers are magical and are used in the portion of the public ritual that is seen. It was awful thoughtful of Hamas to kill and wound the amounts needed to fulfill this number scheme. Obviously these aren't accurate counts, but rather a cryptic manner of note passing among one another and their superiors.

It's proclaimed by Zionists, both Christian and Jewish, that the "third temple" by my count, second, MUST BE BUILT on this locale that doesn't belong to either Jews or Christians. When you see the term **Holy of Holies**, they don't mean your butt hole. Only Aleister Crowley would have said that. The Temple Mount area is where this Holy of Holies is located. This war going on in Israel makes for the perfect opportunity, and the perfect smokescreen under which to destroy or capture this holy land and demolish the Muslim structure while preparing the building of their prophetic temple. They need to destroy Haram al-Sharif the Dome and that isn't all.

Jews are allowed to visit the site, but not to pray there. Jews have exclusive rights to the Western Wall for their worship. When you see Trump and other US politicians wearing a yarmulke/kippot (small hat) touching a wall and genuflecting or prostrating with their hand on a wall, it's likely this Western Wall where the photo was taken. They're not allowed to enter certain areas according to their own beliefs which prohibit it, not so much by restrictions placed on them by the Islamic caretakers. According to Jewish law, for the Jews to enter all places, a needed aspect to any good invasion, they must first "cleanse" Haram al-Sharif.

Written on August 1, 2023, two months before the IDF (Israeli Defense Force) allowed for a breach at 16 points along their own defense walls, and had moved the site of an outdoor music festival much closer to said defense wall (how thoughtful of them) Ir Amim published a rather telling article. They warned that something was in the making and it involved the Dome of the Rock/Haram al-Sharif.

Research conducted by Ir Amim over the past year has uncovered the involvement of the Israeli government in helping to secure "red heifers" for ritual sacrifice, which according to Jewish law is required to rebuild the Jewish temple on the Haram al-Sharif/Temple Mount (HAS/TM). The project to acquire this specific type of cow from the United States was spearheaded by the Temple Movements and an American

Evangelical Christian group with the support of the state. According to Jewish law, the sacrifice of a red heifer (young female cow) would enable ritual purification necessary for mass Jewish ascent to the Mount and ultimately the construction of the third temple in place of the Dome of the Rock.
-Ir Amim

The ashes of these red female cows have to be spread over the holy site before they could enter to worship, yes, but also it was a necessary, and very odd stipulation to fulfill before the 2nd/3rd Temple can be built. Another insight came from Ir Amim in July, 2021:

*On Sunday July 18, which was Tisha B'av—a **Jewish day of mourning commemorating the destruction of the Jewish Temples** and other Jewish tragedies over the course of history - the Israel police forcefully and indiscriminately removed Muslims from the Temple Mount/Haram al-Sharif for fear of protests against Jewish visitors to the holy compound. Later that day, Israeli Prime Minister Naftali Bennett praised the Jerusalem police for "protecting Jewish freedom of worship on the Temple Mount" - a statement that is a blatant violation of the longstanding status quo whereby only Muslims are afforded worship rights while Jews have visitation rights.*

Again from the August 1ˢᵗ Ir Amim research article:
The "Temple Movements" is an umbrella term for various Jewish groups who are opposed to not only exclusive prayer rights of Muslims on the Holy Esplanade, but are also hostile to their very presence in the holy place. Their goal is to overturn the status quo [established by a 1967 peace agreement with Jordan] and impose Jewish domination over the Mount. This includes achieving Jewish prayer rights, establishing a temporal and/or spatial division of the holy space, and ultimately destroying the Dome of [the] Rock and replacing it with the third temple.

In order to sell a holy war, there has to be a holy aspect in dispute. The City of London bankers, the Rothschilds' are only interested in this site for what it means to Zionism for manipulative purposes. It goes without saying that Larry Fink, CEO of world-owning BlackRock is a Zionist. Remember, Zionism crept out of the pages of the Lurian Kabbalah, and into the minds of Shabbatai Tzvi and Jacob Frank, who developed it into a clarified mission long before Theodor Herzl established it as "Zionism." The pioneers who successfully campaigned the notion and outlined the strategy, duties, and objectives are required study to understand what truly fuels the passions of the Jesuits, and the Illuminati. It's also important to understand its deception. That's what prompted me to take on the task of writing this book. Like I said, it's necessary to convince the radical followers that this Zionist goal will lead them to their much anticipated Day of Judgment and Redemption. The religious leaders are not at all what they appear. If they are supporting Zionist ideas—that is the hastening of God's work by man's meddling, they are in defiance of God, and acting against the natural order and balance of the world.

These top religious organizations, whether they're fully aware, or idealistic dupes, are in fact practicing Frankism, and mass murder is something they gladly will employ. Their whole objective is to bring us all on a high-speed rail to Armageddon. Some think that will bring Jesus back, completely ignorant of the fact Jesus would be the first to condemn them for their wicked deeds, and others say it's to bring their Messiah in to sit on the throne of the world. Any god that would be pleased over this method is no god of mine. I honestly don't think many of them believe in God at all, for at the very top of the orders they are secular humanists, an actual recognized religion where Man is God. If you ask me if I think the Family de Rothschild believe in any Messiah or God, the answer is a flat-out NO. But if they can convince a bunch of maniacs to murder everyone and each other, that makes for a pretty hands-free Reset. The Overlords will use the Old Testament and the New, and the Quran as they always have—to control the minds of the masses by following it like a playbook. They will fulfill the End Times prophecy these religions are clamoring for by artificial and unnatural means. And by doing so, they will be *as* God, but not God.

The Knights Templar were given the Temple Mount for their headquarters after the success of the Crusade that captured Jerusalem from the Muslims. They are the ones who referred to it as "Solomon's Temple" because the site seemed to be built over the ruins of some preexisting structure. It was there they gave themselves the name *Poor Knights of Christ and the Temple Solomon*, or Templar Knights. Knowing the Freemasons claim lineage to these knights, and knowing they are a changed organization since the times of John Robison who witnessed the radicalization occur when the Illuminati infiltrated, the conquest of the Dome of the Rock is of great significance to them as well.

Since there are no cows of the necessary breed and shade in Israel, the search for a "red heifer" has been focused on the US with the assistance and involvement of **Evangelical Christians**. *Some Evangelicals view the "red heifer" initiative as essential for setting in motion an apocalyptic process, which would usher in Armageddon and ultimately the return of the Messiah. Last year, with the help of Israeli authorities, the Temple Institute and an Evangelical group by the name of Boneh Israel imported five cows to Israel from the US that they claim meet the definition of what constitutes a "red heifer..."*

...According to ancient Jewish law, the ashes of a red heifer are required for ritual purification prior to ascent to specific areas on the Mount which are considered holy in Judaism. Due to the lack of such ritual purification, many religious Jews do not enter the Holy Esplanade, and even Temple activists will only walk on very small parts of the compound.

...According to Ir Amim's research, the Jerusalem Development Authority under the Ministry of Jerusalem Affairs has been promoting a plan for the establishment of a promenade on the Mount of Olives overlooking the Haram al-Sharif/Temple Mount. This promenade is slated to lead to the precise area where the Temple Movements intend to hold the **burning of the "red heifer" ceremony**. *In interviews given to Evangelical media, Tzachi Mamo, one of the leading figures involved in bringing the cows to Israel, detailed the goals of the "red heifer" initiative and its direct link to rebuilding the temple on the Mount. Mamo likewise described having gained control of an olive grove on the Mount of Olives, which will serve as the location for conducting the" red heifer" ceremony as "the first step towards building the Temple."*

Amy Cohen
Director of International Relations & Advocacy
Ir Amim (City of Nations/City of Peoples)

Remember, sacrifices must be done in a grove, as Bill Cooper reminds us, and this land on Mount Olive is an olive grove. That ritual has quite the Canaanite overtone. I wonder what else will be burned there, or whether we're really talking about cows at all. They call us cattle. How do we know this isn't a child smuggling operation for a huge burnt offering sacrifice of young US girls? And if so what do you, dear reader, intend to do about it? They would need a lot of cows, or children to have a sufficient amount of ash to cover the entirety of the area. The red heifer element seems so absurd it almost has to be code talk for something else. We already know from our study of ancient Priestcraft practices what the sacrifice of choice always is. Do you really think cows will be worthy enough for something as important as the christening (wrong word, I know) of the third temple, and the kickoff to WWIII? Red heifer may as well be *red herring*, because it's throwing us off what may really be going on right now as they prepare for this event.

Christians United For Israel (CUFI) are actively involved in the plan. In the history of its predecessors, there was an American preacher, William **Blackstone** who enthusiastically promoted Jews moving to Palestine to fulfill the prophecy. These people don't understand that when you make it happen it's not a "sign."

The Blackstone Memorial would later attract the attention of Louis Brandeis, one of the most prominent American Jewish Zionists, who would later refer to Blackstone as the real "founding father of Zionism," according to Brandeis' close friend Nathan Straus.

-MintPressNews.com (MPN)

Just so we're clear, Louis Brandeis was a Frankist from a Frankist family. He was the first Jewish Supreme Court Judge. He did his part to ensure that the greatest evil to befall America was ushered in. I'm of course referring to the Federal Reserve Act.

Brandeis went to Harvard Law School, and eared the highest average in the school's history. This goes right back to the Ken Wheeler comment about the daemon/demons being replete with knowledge, but possessing no soulful wisdom.

Interior of the Dome 1914, Library of Congress

Regarded as a place of sacrifice from antiquity, it appears it has been chosen as the altar upon which the entire world should be offered up to God. Again, the question is which *God*?

More about this strange ritual that baffled even the "wise" Solomon (Shlomo) can be read at this site, and I encourage all to get familiar with these ceremonies and magical workings so you may predict and recognize coming events:

calledoutbelievers.org/the-history-and-symbolism-of-the-red-heifer/

Ari Ventura, Cow Detective
(not real name)

Kaaba and the Black Stone of Mecca

Much like the Freemasons, Muslims who make the hajj, or pilgrimage to the Great Mosque of Mecca practice a ritual of circumambulation. That is, they walk in circles around the center shrine, the Kaaba, or Ka'bah—meaning "cube" in Arabic. The cube itself is said to predate Islam, and was of importance to the Arab practices long before the mariachis of Muhammad began playing their tune. The visitors circle counter-clockwise seven times in imitation of the movement of the Earth and planets around the sun—so they say. This may be a debatable statement given vantage point, frame of reference, and whether or not anything we're taught about the nature of the universe is accurate or valid. Let's just go with that prevailing explanation of existence for the sake of argument. When looking north, objects in the sky appear to move counter-clockwise. Hindus also practice circumambulation, and Greeks and Romans incorporated it as part of their sacrificial rites. So, if some Greeks or Romans start oddly walking circles around you, they may be getting ready to ritually murder you. Where's the "The More You Know" rainbow when you need it?

The Ka'bah is the stone building at the center of Islam's holiest site, the Masjid al-Haram, or Grand/Great Mosque. This stone cube of a structure is the ***House of God*** according to Muslims, and the direction of prayer in which practitioners of the faith are to pay their respects five times a day in accordance with the Pillars of Islam, or five duties. The other four duties are a profession of faith, fasting during the month of Ramadan, the hajj or pilgrimage itself to the Masjid al-Haram, and the giving of an alms tax intended to provide for the needy. If it's anything like our NPOs, the majority will of course go to "administrative expenses." The Ka'bah is draped with an enormous, snug-fit, black kiswah, or woven silk fabric having a raised design. In the case of the Ka'bah, its outer garment is adorned with beautifully intricate gold and silver patterns. Written within the ornate gold and silver patterns are holy passages of praise. Each year a new kiswah is made in Egypt and brought to the Great Mosque by those making the hajj, or pilgrimage.

There's a couple things to parse out here. First is the assumption that "Arab" is going to mean the same in pre-history as it does in modern day, as far as predominate ethnic traits go is not at all accurate. Migrations and co-mingling cause whole demographic shifts quite often. The other thing to question is why was the black cube of the ancient past brought into the Islamic faith as their most important icon, as well? What did they revere the black cube for? We may need to go back in time and ask the Bedouin, or Bedu nomads if they know. This monolith-like black object seems to be related, or at least similar to the monolith in *2001: Space Odyssey* as well.

It's important to note this example of the theme of a black cube being revered as divine, or all-powerful. There are others, and knowing this detail may assist you in recognizing their correlations with one another. This piques my curiosity especially concerning the international Black Cube. Black Cube is a Tel Aviv headquartered firm comprised of "veterans of Israel's *elite* intelligence units." It has a history of assisting the IDF, or Israeli Defense Force, and became more widely known to the world when Harvey Weinstein employed their services while he was facing multiple rape, and sexual misconduct accusations spanning several years. The Black Cube ambiguously claim to provide "litigation services." The two founders themselves are former Israeli Defense Force spooks. The CEO, Dan Zorella, was in IDF intelligence, and Avi Yanus was an IDF strategic planning officer. They were the elite of the elite. Labeled in an article by George Kerevan as *The Mossad of Commercial Spying*, tamely the Black Cube has been criticized for covertly surveilling, "finding" difficult to acquire evidence—another way of saying fabricating convincing evidence, and engaging in character attacks to diminish credibility and reputations of accusers and witnesses. The Black Cube claims to have former Mossad agents on their advisory board. If you know anything about intelligence agencies, there's no such thing as "former." The Mossad is Israel's foreign intel and assassination bureau. That's correct. They plan and carry out murders. Would the firm not have access to assassins, then? The Mossad has a license to kill by their Rothschild-created state. The Mossad and IDF are essentially highly-trained armed terrorist forces conducting operations under the authority of their government, and typically in-cooperation with other governments, maybe even the UN and NATO. If they have a client whose protection of their secrets is of mutual interest to other operators, don't you think they would, oh I don't know, red scarf a person or two? Make deaths look like suicides or overdoses? If the client needed to rid themselves of a nuisance, I'm just saying, they might pay whatever astronomical sum Black Cube charges to handle that matter indefinitely. What I'm getting at is there are entities that operate above the law. Most of them have ties to our domestic 3-letter agencies, to the Mossad, or to the prosperity of the state of Israel. Being connected to one, pretty much gives you carte blanche with the others.

Harvey Weinstein had a total of 87 accusers, and probably not all of them were true victims. I think he had become a liability, and to "burn him" or make him the scapegoat for a much more rampant problem, more "victims" were instructed to pile on the claims. But maybe not.

How many of his victims or witnesses to his sex crimes ended up dead, or suddenly retracted their claims? It could be surmised that change-of-heart was a result of the efforts of the Black Cube firm.

What is known about the spy agency that doesn't want you to know about it is that they share a common structure and purpose as the Society of Jesus (Jesuits) does, only they are seemingly for hire. Being that Spain has always been seen as the origin and a stronghold of the Jesuits, it's interesting that Black Cube has a base in Madrid, along with their Te Aviv and City of London locations. One gets the impression Black Cube cleans up messes that the operators of the sick and wicked industries get themselves into while they facilitate for the (child, drug, dark priestcraft) agenda.

Fixed within the black cube, or Ka'bah, is a stone called the Hajr ul Aswad. Not ass-wad, but more of a Z or even short, chopped S sound. The black stone is set into the eastern corner of the black cube of Ka'bah. The legend of the Black Stone is that it fell from the final sphere, or abode of righteousness in the heavens. This is very similar in conceptual structure to the "gnostic" Seven Spheres of Heaven. It's said the stone fell to this realm at the time of Adam and Eve and was viewed as a divine answer to where they should build an altar to their evicting landlord. I have not been evicted yet in life, but I haven't been inspired to build an alter to any of my past property managers. The Demiurge seems to fail upward, kind of like politicians, and CEOs of masonic corporations. Looking right at you, Bezos, even if only one of your eyes can look back.

Muslims believe the stone was once white, the color symbolizing purity, but over time turned black from absorbing the sins of all who have touched it. There's a whole, long, speculative history of the stone being lost in the flood, and recovered by Ibrahim/Abraham who was shown the stone by an angel and told to get his mortar and start building. The Demiurgos is a bit unstable, so the sooner you build that altar and praise him the better. He has more floods where that one came from, and he's crazy enough to do it. Oh, and don't build a tall tower so you can help keep your people's heads above water. He hates that.

An alternate Black Stone myth story is that the stone itself is an angel that the Demiurge positioned to "guard" Adam, and he was unfortunately on duty when Adam met the wrong girl, and did that infamous teen-rebellion-level thing and ate from the wrong tree. The not-so-benevolent god, then punished the angel by turning him into the stone, itself. They don't say which version is Muhammad's official story.

I'm saying Demiuge/Demiurgos rather than "God" in the above because the Tanakh, or Old Testament describes often very evil, petty, jealous, blood-thirsty, and unhinged behaviors attributed to that 'god.' I'm asserting my position that the book written by not-so-reputable individuals is a little misleading, and maybe describing their god, and not *thee* God. You wouldn't buy a used car from them, but you'll adopt their religious stories without even lifting the hood, or kicking the tires. I also find it curious that a symbolic, or allegorical garden story would have a "real-life" relic. As far as the term "guard" Adam, that can be taken two ways. Protecting him, which is likely what most would assume, but it could also mean the angel was akin to a prison guard. The latter would line-up with how the early Christians dubbed as "Gnostics" would have viewed it. The intention of pointing out these potential similarities to the beliefs of the early Christians, those prior to Nicean canonization, is to leave room for the possibility that time and manipulation has altered the meanings and views of the pioneers of Islam as well as Christianity.

The stone has been damaged in conflicts, and by vandals. It was stolen for a period of time, and recovered. Whether the stone is the same stone is a question of faith just as the claim that it had fallen from heaven or a flying object in the sky like in the film, *The Gods Must Be Crazy,* is also a matter for faith. The stone might be their Coke bottle.

Today the stone is in fragments, encased in a larger, impressively polished stone, and wrapped in a silver ring. Those fortunate to make it close enough are allowed to touch, and kiss the stone. If the stone is in fact an unfortunate angel, it could lend credence to the accounts that it greeted Muhammad either by speaking to him, or emitting a tone or sound. Some do debate whether it is a stone, or some type of being. This incident with Muhammad is said to have been the catalyst for his prophethood. Some scientists say it is indeed a piece of a meteorite, while others claim it's of natural, terrestrial origin. They will not analyze it using so-called modern scientific equipment, and personally I think that's fine. Why ruin the legends and mystery? Let people have their beliefs when those beliefs don't harm others. So, is this the Stone of Foundation? Is this why a monstrously huge company called itself Blackstone, or is it, like many firms, a reference to their founders' names? Schwarzman, where Schwarz means *Black,* and Peterson—Peter means *stone.* What is known is veneration of stones has been a practice since ancient times, and continues on today, as is demonstrated by the lore and importance surrounding the black stone enshrined in the House of God, or black cube of Ka'bah/Kaaba.

In an effort to be thorough, it should be mentioned that there are many who claim the Kaaba is a monument to Saturn worship. Muslims are also known as Ishmaelites, for their focus on Abraham/Ibrahim's son, Ishmael/Ismail. There is a Shi'a branch of Islam called the Ismaili. From the story of Muhammad, Abraham and Ishmael built the first Kaaba long ago. Pre-Islamic people of the area of Mecca, the Yemeni tribes, and others, were polytheists. Muhammad didn't "create" Islam until about 610 A.D. The Kaaba was already a monument by then if the history is accurate, and Saturn worship was a thing, only Saturn was referred to as Zuhul, the Meccan goddess of the planet. I find it interesting that in Ghostbusters, the name Zuul is used for the demonic possession of Dana. "There is no Dana, only Zuul." That's pretty close to Zuhul.

It's something of a question of intent. Was the construction initially intended for Saturn/Zuhul? I would argue NO, if Abraham and Ishmael are who we're told they are. But child and animal sacrifice are a part of Saturn offerings, and Abraham was up to his elbows in blood from those activities. This controversy being stirred by those deemed "anti-Islamics" opens up the floor to discuss the true nature of all Abrahamic religions, and not just the relative newcomer, Islam.

Nakruh is the Minaean and Hymiarite Arabs' equivalent for Saturn. Arabic peoples are Semitic, because the term refers to a language group, not a Jewish label monopoly. Semitic people and beyond, in a very common manner, gave praise and offerings to Saturn by different names. It was a widespread practice in the Roman empire. Saturn was their god of agriculture, and remnants of the pagan rituals still remain grafted into Roman Catholicism. December 17-23rd is Saturnalia, the Winter Solstice, Sol meaning the Sun. Time is Kronos is Saturn is Satan. Remember, Ba'al was a fertility god responsible for good harvests and agriculture. The priesthood of Ba'al also demanded sacrifice for proper worship.

Saturn is the "Lord of the Rings" and the tradition of exchanging wedding rings is a practice leftover from Saturn worship. Isis in Egyptian lore claims she is the daughter of Saturn, the oldest of the gods. Saturn is equated to El by some, as an ancient name for it. I don't think that holds up when studying the Ugaritic texts, however. The attribute of Saturn as the "Great Malefic" doesn't seem to pair well with El. The age, El being the El-dest of the gods does match up with Isis' reference, however.

I believe Saturn and its seeming transition, or cataclysmic event holds clues to a much longer history of mankind on Earth. There are fading whispers from the past that remember Saturn before it received its rings. If this is true, and something occurred to change its nature and effect a massive catastrophe on Earth, we may start to understand why a "planet" would have such fear-based reverence. We also see how this could put the priestcraft of the time in a position to rise to power. In chaos, dealing with death and destruction all around, fear is felt by all. Fear is a great tool of manipulation. Anyone claiming they knew how to prevent further anger from the "gods" could find new audience from formerly rational people. The event being so extreme meant the response must be equally extreme, right? A priest clan could have persuaded people to begin sacrificing children and animals to appease the wrath of Saturn.

A black cube is a known symbol of Saturn. Do I think that's how Islamic people of today view their Kaaba? I can only speculate. Was Saturn worship likely practiced at the Kaaba/Ka'bah in the past? Most certainly. Many forms of polytheistic, celestial worship came and went through the entire region, and throughout the world. I'd be more concerned about the Black Cube firm comprised of IDF and Mossad members naming themselves after Saturn than I would Muslims knowingly and consciously worshipping Saturn in their religion.

It appears the customs and tradition of the circumambulation have a multiple possible origins. The first being the story of Ismail/Ishmael being thirsty and Hagar running around 7 times looking for water before an angel intervenes and is like, "Here. You're making me dizzy just looking at you." He scratches at the earth and Zamzam al-akabam, there's water. They named the well Zamzam, hence the pun. It stands about 70 feet away from the Kaaba, and is enshrined at the Masjid al-Haram in Mecca, Saudi Arabia. The visitors circle seven times when visiting the Kaaba and the Black Stone. At least to the Muslims, I believe they sincerely do this to ritually replay the movements of Hagar out of respect for the tradition. Another explanation for the seven runs around the Kaaba is that it represents the seven rings of Saturn. That is very compelling—the notion of a symbol of Saturn, the Black Cube, and the movements of the worshippers emulating the rings of Saturn by revolving around it one time for each ring. Even some official statements say it's to represent celestial movements because their Kaaba is the center of the Earth and universe…

Muhammad, like the Roman Catholic Church, made concessions with the pagans, or polytheists, to get them to accept the faith with less resistance. In fact it was his decision to keep the Black Stone in its original place to prevent a war between the tribes. Because he kept their established practice intact, but gave it a new meaning, perhaps it was not to cover up Islam's alleged secret Saturn worship, but the other way around. To bring the polytheists into the religion of Islam with a refreshed explanation of the ritual. It does appear to have evolved from Saturn worship. All the Abrahamic religions have elements of this ancient practice. At the highest levels of priesthoods and secret societies, Saturn plays a very important role. They insist on veneration to Saturn, or one of his composits to achieve enlightenment, or illumination. The common, everyday devotees of each religion however are not practicing Saturn worship simply because it's not their intent to be doing so. They buy the exoteric meaning, and they believe in the Quran. It would not be wise to condemn any of the followers for what those deceiving them and the world do.

Lastly, as somewhat of a curious side note, the Burning Man Festival is held in the Black Rock Desert in Nevada. There they burn an **effigy** (a sculpture of model of a person) and if you haven't seen the original film, *The Wicker Man,* 1973, I highly recommend you do. It will walk you through some of the practices we see manifesting as themes of the ancient cults in our present world.

The Canted Square and Saturn, Sam Walton and his Fraternity

Within the rituals of occultic orders, such as our Order (Freemasonry), it is required that the candidate circle the altar of the lodge in a particular manner. It is called circumambulation. Circumambulation is the practice of "...making a circuit about a thing or in an area of reverence..." In Masonry, circumambulation involves the making of a circuit around the Lodge, while keeping the right hand toward the altar.
During the circuits of the lodge room, corners should be squared in accordance with the ancient tradition of 'squaring the lodge'
-masonicbookworm.com/2012/08/the-canted-square

When I was in US Coast Guard basic training, we were instructed to turn in right angles when we had to make corners down a hallway into an office or room. Every movement had to be clean and mechanical—robotic. If we were summoned to the Company Commander's office, we'd announce ourselves before entering, and they would yell, "Square it!" I would pivot to change direction in an almost dance-move to turn my body toward the doorway, and then march in, upright posture, and salute.

Learning later in life that these rituals of the armed forces, not just the US Coast Guard, had commonalities with masonic practices, specifically in regards to initiates, left me to ponder. Was it a direct influence of the Freemasons that had crept into the military and was adopted, or is this just a coincidence? I was essentially an initiate of the 'Guard, wasn't I? The square is a representative of a cube in 2D. Is there a Saturn cult within the military?

Sam Walton, the famous CEO of Walmart and later Sam's Club (1983), was at one point the richest man in America (1982-1988.) At the time of his death in 1992 he was said to be the second richest man in the world behind Bill Gates. Although I cannot find any conclusive evidence of his membership in the Freemasonic Order, he was formerly a manager-trainee for JC Penney store. The founder James Cash Penney, yeah a real name, was born in Hamilton, Missouri in 1875, and worked for two partners of a store called Golden Rule in Colorado. After showing his worth he was made one-third partner in 1902, and soon he was able to buy out the shares and have full control of a Wyoming store. Today that store still operates, and is referred to as the "Mother Store."

Soon after moving to Salt Lake City, UT Penney joined the Wasatch Lodge of Free and Accepted Masons (1911). He became a member of both the Scottish and York Rites, and was made an honorary 33rd degree Mason in 1945. James "Loads-of-Cash" Penney later lived at 666 Park Ave in New York. 666 Fifth Avenue was the building steeped on controversy regarding the owner, Jared Kushner, and Qatar Investment Authority, Saudi Arabia.

In 1940 on a visit to one of his stores in Des Moines, Iowa, Penney personally trained a young Sam Walton. Walton would later serve in the US Army Intelligence

Corps. For those unaware, not anyone just "joins" an office of military intelligence. They are selected, and typically you must have been to college, and have some affiliation with the Mormon Church or a fraternal order. That was the first-hand experience relayed by William Cooper who served in the Office of Naval Intelligence. He got in because he had been to 3 meetings of the DeMolay, a youth Masonic order. When the questionnaire asked if he was ever a member of a list of groups, he checked the box for "Freemasonic Order," knowing that what he attended as a young boy was associated with them.

At the time Sam Walton had entered into the war effort, the US Army Intelligence Corps had just formed, consisting of 16 officers and 10 enlisted members. That's a pretty exclusive and selective group. Although there are unqualified, illiterate, self-proclaimed arbiters of "Truth" out there called *fact checkers* who declare this is false, Sam Walton's official bio states that he *"supervised security at aircraft plants and **prisoner of war camps."*** They claim that it's false that he "ran" the camps. This is what they do, these mental midgets. No one is claiming he organized or commanded, the damn things. The *fact checkers* fabricate an attribute that no one is suggesting, and then tell you the part they just made up is false, and bigger idiots who read the *fact checkers* think that means the whole statement, video, etc. is false.

For example there is a video that has been circulating for many years, before the Dark Ages of CoroNOvirus. It has a running tape time on it, and if I remember correctly it was filmed in 2004 or 2006 according to that date stamp. It's of a lecture hall where a weak-voiced man is doing a presentation to some 3-letter agency or another about the VMAT-2 gene, and how they can manipulate the human brain using special "flu shots" to destroy the gene they claim is responsible for religious fundamentalism. You've likely seen this video. It was suggested they should use it on the Middle East where you know, terrorist come from and stuff. They even had a sick name for it, calling it FUNvax. They were going to vaccinate the religious fundamentalism out of people by essentially causing brain damage and genetic alteration. It's a well-documented fact that scientists are very interested in the VMAT2 gene, with the National Institute of Health (NIH) calling it the "God gene." They are trying, and probably have augmented people to sever their tether with higher-self, God, etc. Have you spoken to a fully vaccinated individual? How deep was that conversation, especially after 2021?

The almighty 40-year-olds in their parent's basements calling themselves *fact checkers* "debunked" the video, and said it's false. Here's their conclusion: No that was not Bill Gates conducting the presentation in the video. Who the hell said it was? No one was claiming that. It wasn't Bill Cosby, either. What does that have to do with the authenticity of the video itself? They made no attempt to deny there's ongoing research into gene-altering, VMAT2 attacking designer shots. Because they can't. They want the dumbest of the dumb to think their erroneous statement about *who* is, or isn't in the video be a condemnation of *what* is in the video. They didn't challenge any of the information related in the tape, nor its authenticity. They merely suggested that it was solely dependent on Bill Gates being in it that made the video true or false. The sad part is this type of logical fallacy tricks a lot of incompetent people. I used a portion of that video in one of my presentations years back, and true to idiot form, some moron said "That's not Bill Gates! This video was debunked…" and then proceeded to tell me what a stupid person *I* was. The irony. It's times like that I feel I could be onboard with selective breeding at the very least, if not aggressive Eugenics. Not on the innocent, of course. On the very people responsible for a system that produces such useless and belligerent human paper weights.

Sam Walton had plenty of contacts and wealth to create whatever public image he, or his superiors wanted him to have. The details of Sam's life are often vague, short on relevance, and finely polished. Sam's bio is more airbrushed than a centerfold with acne. He was awarded the Presidential Medal of Freedom by George H.W. Bush in 1992, not long before Sam died. I guess you get that award after putting countless small store owners out of business, and therefore destroying the middle class entrepreneurial spirit of America. Sam could have only been assigned one of five original groups in Military Intel: administrative, intelligence, counter-intelligence, operations, or a language school. If he was counter-intelligence, there may be another reason for the vagueness. He was not an enlisted man. He was an officer who somehow seemingly went in as a Captain! The Horatio Alger Association states on their site that he was a Captain from 1942-1945. That was practically his whole service time. So he was almost immediately an O-3. He was out after only 3 years. Just because you hung up your uniform doesn't mean you've stopped working for the government.

They say he supervised security at prison camps. The claim here is that the internment camps were something different than P.O.W. camps. Sam Walton did indeed supervise security where 10,000 German soldiers were said to have been housed according to a relative of Sam's, Frank Robson.

Sam Walton and James Cash Penney grew up in Missouri 2 hours and 15 minutes from one another. JC took special interest in Sam while he worked for him in Des Moines. Sam made top rank in Eagle Scouts, breaking a record for how young he was when he achieve the rank. Sam seemed to become an immediate O-3 (Captain) in Military Intelligence. Was something guiding him? Where there entities helping him along? To enter the military as an O-3, you have to have a bachelor's degree, and have completed Officer Candidate School, so it's not that uncommon. I'm more interested in the Military Intelligence aspect of it, and his assigned duties.

There's plenty we can say about corporate logos, and the person to first present this was probably Freeman of Freeman Perspective, and now of Freeman TV, which isn't TV. It's a podcast… What are words, anyway? I'm not going to rehash Freeman's classic video on the subject, but I recommend you seeking it out. It's called *Corporate Logos*. What I feel compelled to share with you is one thing I think Freeman didn't cover. Let's first have a look at the Sam's Club logo, and the new Sam's Club NOW logo, which incidentally, has no cashiers, registers, or checkout lines. It's a store after

Klaus Schwab's blackened, dead heart. The only other mega-corporation I'm aware of that scans You when you enter and exit is Amazon GO. Bezos and the Walmart execs, if not Sam himself, have some questionable practices, power, and affiliations.

Naturally, the only logical conclusion here is… These people are very enthusiastic about their Sam's Club membership.

Merkel is extremely proud of hers!

Trump had some real intense talks about his Sam's Club Membership!

As you can see, Mr. Putin doesn't have a Sam's Club membership.
On the table is the application, but President Putin wouldn't fill it out.

This is the Plus Member card, and look at that? Another Black Cube of Saturn! OK, it's a square because it's 2-Dimensional.

There's a lot of wackadoodles out there that see that hand gesture and immediately jump to, "It's Illuminati!" Obviously these are the profane, who don't know of the mysteries of Sam's Club. If I were you, I wouldn't even associate with such unwashed masses.

The hand sign or signal above, when palms are outward, is the Greek Delta-Sigma-Theta symbol, and also the energetic hand positioning for casting your intent in magic(k). If a sorcerer is doing it, they could be directing a spell at you, or more widely, at an audience who all gathered 'round for a concert.

To understand this more, and what is meant by energetic hand configurations, it would require getting familiar with the true nature of the magneto-electric body, and the intelligence contained within. The heart appears more of a vortex generator for a biofield, or toroidal field—the donut shaped magnetic field around the body. Like all circuitry, the body energy is dependent on pathways and the source. Dr. Alphonso Monzo, III, ND, whom I regard as a living Nikola Tesla, put over a decade of study into his book, *Aleph-Tav Body System* where he not only explains the energetic pathways of the body, but also teaches the reader how to apply self-therapy, and assist others.

Dr Monzo has been on the Ba'al Busters channel multiple times, and I had the fortunate opportunity to meet him in Freemason-infested Salt Lake City, at the enormous Salt Palace not long ago. One of my objectives is to complete the practitioners course he offers, having already taken the pre-course, and studied from his *Aleph-Tav Body System* book. Links to his site to see what he does, and what you can get to promote healthier living are in the description of all my videos and podcasts, along with a coupon code the viewers and subscribers can benefit from. I never promote what I don't do or use myself, and therefore I have a select few affiliates. Like Bill Cooper, if I don't know it works, I don't recommend it, and vice versa, I won't hesitate to talk about things that have helped me, and I know work.

Sam Walton was tapped by the QEBH, an honorary secret society, while attending the University of Missouri. Tap Day is something that societies like the Yale Skull and Bones conduct. It's a day they select the new members by tapping them on the shoulder. Another society at UM, alleged friendly rivals of the QEBH who play pranks on each other, is called the Mystical 7. The logo for the Mystical 7 contains a skull and crossbones, a pitchfork, and a sabre. These elite fraternal orders are structured like the Freemasons, Oddfellows, etc., and therefore are in the fashion of the ancient Mystery Schools with secret rites, initiations, and secret pledges or oaths to one another.

Sam attended the college as an ROTC cadet, another reason for his quickly acquired rank as Captain (O-3) when he was assigned to the newly created US Army Military Intelligence. He had joined the Zeta Phi chapter of the Beta Theta Pi fraternity and the Scabbard and Blade military society before being tapped for the select QEBH whose purpose and activities are not known to outsiders.

College Fraternities are not just some house to drink and get the best college girls at, although that's usually a part of it. These fraternities play a role in the lives of the members long after college, and brothers, like in Freemasonry, are always supposed to help one another as a basic lifelong pledge common to all of them. Think about that. If the member is pulled over by an officer and they recognize each other as having been in the same fraternity, would that effect the outcome of their chance meeting? If they need a loan and the bank manager is a brother? There are so many scenarios where these brotherhoods lift up one another and show favoritism. Fraternities are houses where scouts for more nefarious secret orders choose initiates, and Sam was tapped by one that was likely a training camp for these more intense organizations.

The state of Missouri itself has a very strong Freemasonic presence. Lewis and Clark paved the way for it to become a state (1821) due to their explorations and charting of the area. Meriwether Lewis established the Saint Louis Lodge, number 111 as its Master. He worked to spread Freemasonry throughout the state.

As mentioned before, Sam was awarded the Presidential Medal of Freedom by then president, former CIA director and Skull and Bones member, George H.W. Bush. Sam died 18 days after the ceremony. 6+6+6=18.

The Walton Family owns the majority of the company shares. They are worth $Billions each, and that buys a lot of influence on the world stage should they be so inclined. During the Obama Abomination, there were some very curious renovations done to southern state Walmart and Target buildings. There are videos going back to 2010 of people showing how these former warehouse grocery stores were converted into prison-like facilities complete with razor wire on the outside and cages and holding cells on the inside. These building were all very close to railway tracks.

Given Sam's affiliations, his Military Intelligence background, and his detail as a supervisor of POW camps many have speculated that his company was working with the NSA, DoD, DHS, and US military on a subterranean tunnel project that would help our corrupted, Frankist-infiltrated, communist "government" stealthily move troops underground so as not to arouse the suspicion of the American people. I don't think any of these citizen journalists ever were focused to heavily on Sam himself because he had passed in 1992. They were more concerned with the government's involvement with the company itself.

I wasn't as diligent in my research and verification back when this was a hot topic. I barely paid attention to any of it. I haven't had cable since I left my parent's house in the late 90s and then left for good in 2002, after getting out of the Coast Guard, another element that detached me from most alternative media. I was probably not watching videos on YouTube until 2012, and back then I was interested in Ron Paul, not tunnels. When I did come across this information it was probably 2015 or 2016. I didn't have time to think about much besides my own problems until my store made the financial woes go away. The impression these videos had on my undeveloped mind back then was that there were a huge network of underground military installments and vast tunnels connecting them, tunnels large enough to drive big rigs through with supplies, hidden troops, pesky patriotic prisoners, etc. The claim was that warehouse sized grocery and department stores were introduced into every-town, USA gradually, over time so that people would never question why huge buildings were being erected in their neighborhoods. They were harmless stores, right? Outside of destroying small family businesses with lower prices, they were harmless, anyway. The theory put forth was that when the time came to subdue the American people, these stores would be converted into processing and internment facilities to shackle the mob, as they say. These tunnels were said to be part of a huge underground operation to take down America, and enslave and murder millions in a way that would be hard for us to detect, and therefore catch us by surprise. It sounded more than feasible to me at the time, but I was pretty green. I was a new dad, so I suddenly became interested in anything and everything that could pose a potential threat to my family. I didn't rule out or dismiss anything off hand.

Often the videos depicted multiple freight trucks with either no marking on them, or Walmart trucks driving into the entrances to these tunnels. These were videos done by concerned people, and sometimes more commercialized fringe-topic channels.

Later I discovered a channel called SeekingtheTruth by a guy who called himself JoshWho. He made great short videos on some of these theoretical topics, and had a lot of knowledge regarding the world of computer tech, and computer security. We became friends. One day he sent me one of his videos on the tunnels, and I was very impressed by it. I encourage you to get on his free speech video platform that he created called JoshWhoTV. He has all of the videos YouTube deleted preserved on there.

Below is the Walmart logo that was adopted in 2008. Mind you, that was 16 years after the death of Sam Walton, so it's safe to say he isn't responsible for the change.

The picture to the right of the logo is a tunnel drill bit head.

The Boring Company isn't just a play on words by Elon Musk. This is a tunnel boring unit minus the drill bit head.

I can't conclusively say Walmart is doing anything aside from sending supplies, or *something* into the tunnels using their trucks. But the logo change was timely to the stir in alternative media when people started reporting on the underground operations. There were a lot of loud "trumpet" noises or tones heard in towns across America from 2010-present, and when you compare the sounds recorded by residents of those places to the sounds made by the drill that was used to create the Gotthard Tunnel near CERN in Switzerland they sound identical.

AI, Parasites, Demons, or Same-Same?

There's much discussion regarding the *enemy within* when referring to an infiltrated lodge, group, religion, and governmental body, but what about our actual bodies? That's something that falls under the humorous cliché, "It's always in the last place you look." Of course it is. If you kept looking for something you already found you may be one of those wackadoodles I mentioned. Sorry for all the highly intellectual technical terms.

There are parallels that can be drawn between the liberalized, destabilized, and demoralized state of affairs the people of the US and most of the world find themselves trapped within, and the relationships we have with people of-this-world. Meaning, the products of this world. They're the result of deliberate social, cultural, and ethical breakdown of the previous standards. It's the nation-scale Macro vs the home-scale micro—the macro not being able to be reached, without first eroding the micro.

Take for example the culture of **no accountability** and the promotion of destructive selfishness coupled with the embedding of a sense of entitlement, and the *right* to immediate gratification. Media has melted away an already devastated and disincentivized former state and sense of nobility, courage, and responsibility. When I say, "media," I'm referring not just to news reports of questionable validity. I mean it in the classic sense to include books, magazines, newspapers, ads promoting materialism or selfish behavior, TV sitcoms, dramas, music, and movies. All have worked to shape minds for the modern age and completely confuse and distract people from our true sense of duty.

Aleister Crowley is regarded as the father of the Modern Age, the same guy who proudly called himself "The Beast," and introduced male-on-male sodomy to the Ordo Templi Orientis for magickal purposes, of course. Crowley is a huge topic for the next Ba'al Busters book, but you will see his influence in the music of the 60s from The Beatles to Morrison's The Doors, to Jimmy Page and Led Zeppelin. There is a very strong, very heavy dependence on the teachings of Crowley within anything that influences large amounts of people. Sex, drugs, and magick was to bring about the Aeon of Horus, the Crowned and Conquering Child—a time of great selfishness, great power, and immaturity. That's an extremely dangerous combination. It translated into Sex, Drugs and Rock'n Roll for the sorcerers of the music industry. For the CIA MK-Ultra program, you have manufactured "rebels" like [Dr.] Timothy Leary. Leary was promoting LSD, an MK (mind control) drug once exclusive to in-house experiments. Leary wrote a book called, *Turn on, Tune in, Drop out*. Timothy was a member of the Ordo Templi Orientis, an order that Crowley had forever changed. David Bowie was also a member and devotee to Crowley whom he emulated. The Grateful Dead, once known as the Warlocks, facilitated the distribution of millions of hits of LSD. They were the children of Intelligence officers and 3-letter agency members who made up that band. Laurel Canyon was a nest of musicians that were using their music to suit the CIA's agenda. Drugs provided the highly suggestive state, coupled with tones in the hypnotic music, and the imprinting of thoughts and behaviors could occur—all reinforced by a media culture echoing the same themes making it your whole environment.

Pseudo-researchers who try to shape the minds of the curious by feeding them garbage and selling it as truth-against-the-system I have a big problem with. They imply and insinuate that if you are against the movements of restrictive authority in your life then this is what "we" believe over here. Then they proceed to indoctrinate you with an approved list of beliefs and views that qualify you as a member of their Church of Truth. These agent provocateurs are attempting to step in front of real patriots and noble researchers and assume their role. This is why I have retarded minds asking me how it is I speak "bad" of Trump when I'm supposed to stand for truth and the constitution. Do you see the indoctrination and the use of icons here? They don't think for themselves and therefore associate Trump with truth, patriotism, and the bill of rights, and don't even consider his multiple actions to the contrary. Because Trump opposes Biden, he must be good, and if you criticize Trump you must be bad and "for" Biden. That's too idiotic of a thought pattern to even comment on. Read some of the comments I get. These people need camps and teams and there can't be any individual thought or analysis otherwise it's wrong-think, just like the liberal end of it.

My point is there's people out there who will believe anything because of who it is who says it, and what they assume that person represents. So when these phony researchers who did no research, say the popular things verbatim, and don't deviate from the agent-approved controlled opposition playbook, those who consider themselves true Americans believe them without question.

I went on this tangent to explain it wasn't "Paperclip Nazis" coming over to the US who taught us MK-Ultra methods and built the program for the CIA. That's the popular, unresearched, gullible tourist explanation. *Paperclip Nazis* is a loaded term, itself implying other incorrect, but widely believed details about Germany and its leadership in WWII. Cybernetics was the name of the research that predated the MK-Ultra of the Devilish Dulles boys and Sidney Gottlieb. Cybernetics was spearheaded by the Josiah Macy Jr. Foundation's Frank Fremont-Smith and heavily funded, facilitated, and helped by the Rockefellers.

This wasn't due to some influx of newly discovered methods of mind control developed by people who NEVER referred to themselves as Nazis. This had more to do with Crowley's ritual experimentation and his own long history of creating human torture victims. Cybernetics was an infusion of the torture techniques of ancient Sumer, and Babylon (especially in the Assyrian rule) that Crowley had gleaned from grimoires that were passed up the channels of secret societies. One of the more famous of which were that of MacGregor Mathers who had deciphered ancient writings and was intending to keep the information exclusive to select members of the Golden Dawn.

Crowley betrayed Mathers' trust and published it under his own name. Injustice fell upon Mathers for he never copyrighted the material, and therefore Crowley won in court. Crowley was a scoundrel being hailed a genius because of the actual genius of not-Marshall Mathers, but Samuel Liddell MacGregor Mathers.

Crowley was a member and founder of numerous fraternal orders, and achieved degree ranks none but those who are top-level adepts even know of. He was also a member of MI-5 during World War I, as an intelligence officer for Great Britain, working out of New York and around the US. No, this notion that Paperclip doctors were the origin or the spark for mind control research is false. The absolute traumatic destruction of an individual was as ancient as the dawn of time, and made popular and known again through Aleister Crowley. He truly ushered in the Modern Age, and he did it in concert with Military Intelligence, and with secret societies whose own forgotten writings outlined such practices. *"Doubt it not."* -Pike

There is this push for us to think and act globally, which nothing could be more unnatural to do. Squirrels don't contemplate or feel guilt over storing a nut because somewhere in Madagascar there's a lemur going hungry. Each community of cooperative animals and people should be handling their affairs locally. There's an adage that you cannot help others, love others etc. until you handle your inner work first. The same holds true outwardly. We can't solve our own issues with local corruption, false scarcity, and treasonous tyrants. Mostly this is due to being infinitely divided on artificial lines through hyperbolic speeches and invalid concepts of virtue, or victimhood. The man who is weak and feminine is recommended by the algorithms, showcased in media, and propped up before us on stages. Those men who are noble, who still have the heart of a warrior, a guardian, a protector are labeled racists, domestic terrorists, and accused of possessing a "toxic masculinity."

We see the macro as a whole state or condition of politics designed to weaken and destroy all that makes us human. On the micro level we experience the effect this has on the family unit, the most important and most powerful weapon we have against dependency on a system. Not to mention the basic human need for love and respect. They say financial issues are the number one cause of divorce and broken families. The true main cause is women. Most men who are men, who are fathers, would and do anything to keep the family together, when it's their choice, and stick it out for the sake of being a part of their young children's lives. My dad, and myself included. A far cry from a Phoenician (notice the root for the masonic *phoenix*) or a Canaanite, real men would themselves walk through fire, and do metaphorically in order to keep making memories with their children. This artificial culture has stripped women of their divine natural purpose making them hollow. It has shamed them, and stuffed garbage in as a substitute for their motherly and nurturing nature. It has confused them with countless hollow pursuits that only make them more empty. It has weaponized the motherly instinct by redirecting that powerful energy toward "social justice" and other *worldly* causes. *Social Justice* was a term first conceived of by Jesuits. Look it up. We talk of the enemy within the government, and rightly so, but what of the enemy whose name is on the lease, or on the deed? One who would exploit and extort with threats, who would leverage the ultimate threat of taking your children away? All destruction is self-destruction, but in this world without mirrors, where no one has to see themselves for what they've become, who are backed almost by default in the unlawful family courts, told they are victims by this culture, they can carry on for a long time before sensing any repercussion for their self-serving actions. Meanwhile those with hearts—break. They see the children internalizing trauma, being scared and confused, and maybe the father has gone through such a thing himself when he was their age for this didn't begin yesterday. I find the system and what it values to be the source of this schism within the home. This is the rotten tree bearing rotten fruit. We are constantly fed examples that reinforce negative behavior, indifference, and disregard for the love of family. It's usually done in what is sold to us as comedy—the sitcom. One example that comes to mind right away is *Roseanne*. This is what we hold up as exemplary family life? This downtrodden, apathetic, miserable bunch always saying mean, hurtful things to one another, and expressing a total lack of gratitude for being together? This is how they portray family life to women, and to men. *Married With Children,* the blundering, weak, and arrogant male archetype whose life is a mess, is resentful of his family, and who still glorifies his high school days. This type of programming gets embedded in our psyche. When enough of this mind garbage piles up, it causes destruction in our real lives. This isn't the only cause, but try to find a positive family relationship showcased on television that would act as a counterbalance. This is all just one big open-air MK Ultra lab, and we are all the unwitting volunteers by one means of legalese or another that bind us to it. The result being, both men and women don't know what they have, have been shamed out of monogamy, love for their families, and sent down a hollow pursuit for self-fulfillment by the **MK-Cult culture**. Now that truly is ironic. For like our fiat currency, we have traded away true wealth for the counterfeit. We need to fix our family before we can fix the community, and certainly before we can restore our Constitutional Republic. All of that must be done before we can even consider what happens elsewhere. If we all worked on the family, the biggest and shared target of Jesuits, Frankists, Marxists, the UN and the WEF, we could become strong and noble once more. Warriors need a cause, but they also need to know there's something worth preserving in the first place. The MK-Cult culture has made it their mission to implode women and explode femininity in men. They pursue them politically, convincing them they are victims rather than the most powerful force on Earth. Women breed warriors, women are warriors, and with no woman to breathe life into a man, he cannot recognize his potential as a noble warrior.

Like the Borg, another Black Cube and possible reference to Saturn or Kronos, the overlords are a collection of surrendered wills to a secret technology, and demand we surrender as well. They want those that remain alive after the Reset Wars to be completely subdued, connected to the one circuit, imprisoned by a grid, and ratted on by sensors in them and around them wherever they go. Some will accept the pretty lies of virtual reality made all the more realistic by the psychoactive and opioid drug cocktail being administered periodically, or in time-release. "The Brave New World has arrived," thus spake the Metaverse and Big-Pharma.

What is nanotechnology, really? I can understand capsule-like structures, and maybe even magnetic, or magnetized material like payload carrying dynabeads wrapped in lipid particles being possible for man to create. However, if anyone is to suggest that there are tools, and those dexterous enough to manipulate those tools to assemble intricate moving parts on something whose total size is sub-microscopic, they obviously haven't thought this through. Either something nearer to its own size is actually creating these things, like when Horton found a Who, or the government has a physics defying shrink-ray that sucks the magnetic volume out of material objects reducing them to less than dust. Or the *nanobots* are a cover story for an intelligent parasite, or living creature. Or maybe it had to be invisible because really it's a bunch of disembodied demons or archons brought into our realm, and into being somehow given reign in our own bodies through ingestion and injection. Or it's bullshit science. Crowley had a habit of opening portals, or so goes the story. CERN, the giant magnet may have the capacity to tear a hole in our reality and let the flood in.

Whatever their nature, whether it's insect, material nanobot, yeast spore, an intelligent micro-dude, like the green builders in *Fraggle Rock*, micro-*Minions*, or some highly advanced species that only likes to communicate with the assholes of the planet and not furnish the rest of us with their sage information and technology, all can be said to be of a parasitic nature. Imagine a mini person sailing in our body in something like a submarine… Able to drop venom producing yeast and e. coli into your body whenever the little-Last Starfighter felt the urge? Or whatever payload… Remember *Innerspace*?

I'm very interested in, and am doing more work on this topic. I can't say it's anything more than a thought exercise at the moment. What I can't get over is this idea that man can create something complex that is that small. Like assembling the world's tiniest watch. That leads me to think they're either overstating what the actual technology is, what its true nature is, or lying about the very existence of nanobots. If there is *intelligent evil dust scattered everywhere, in everything* as Julian Assange had said, it could be a spore of some sort, a bacterial parasite not yet understood by the public, but in the latter, I think bacteria in-general are larger than the nanobots they claim exist. I'm not ruling out a tiny-verse of creatures able to communicate with these mad scientists somehow. Seeing how these scientists and governments behave, I'd be concerned these tiny ones are tricking mankind into destroying itself so their mutual home is rid of the threat the governments of the world pose to all living things. What if the creatures are anaerobic? Could that be why everyone is hard-selling this climate nonsense? Are they manipulating us to terraform for them?

Whether they're hideous creatures, a handsome nano-race of young Sean Connerys, a nano-Instagram chick with a huge chest making a duck face, talking parasites, tiny machines, hybrid bio-machines, or some boring graphene structures, and capsules, the search for answers continues.

Parasites have been shown to completely alter the thought patterns, hormonal release, and behavior of people and of animals. How something that small could have understanding of how to manipulate and basically hack a human shows they really aren't giving us the whole story in mainstream science regarding the nature of things. And the Priestcraft since the past flood "Reset" have been in control of the sciences, which strangely enough are very similar to the claims of the Kabbalah. Wonder why that is?

The people we've passively allowed to rule us without impaling them on tall pikes in Frankfurt, City of London, Switzerland, New York (UN & CFR), and the Vatican have many characteristics in common with parasitic behavior. It's here I think we need to devote serious effort and time examining. We shouldn't reflexively dismiss this as an impossible factor. It may very well play a role in the manner in which they operate. Their actions, although destructive to all, are also self-destructive to them. Parasites don't care about their host. They often use them as food vehicles to get them to some other destination. An example would be the parasite toxoplasma gondii that gets into mice and manipulates them to be sexually attracted to their common predator—a cat. The mouse presents itself to the cat without caution, and of course, usually the cat will eat the mouse. All this is done because the parasite *prefers* the gut of the cat as it's ideal hangout. The parasite sacrificed the mouse to get to the cat, and was somehow able to know how to do all of this and what the end result would be. What is really going on with parasites? They seem to display evidence of cognition, complex thought, and the mastery of biochemistry and mind manipulation. So is there a **Nanoverse** of sentient entities, and are they operating these parasites, or are they the parasites themselves?

Two elements to consider: Many of these *Deletes* (not elite because they're scum and they delete history and people) attempt to keep, or have attempted to keep their bloodlines pure for a long time. This is a nice way of saying a lot of the royal families and banking moguls are inbred. This could have something to do with the desired environment of the speculative parasite who, once they find a very supportive biochemical and blood environment they try to keep it that way for each successive host. Remember this is a thought exercise, but when looking at these clues it seems there's room for a *Sentient Nanoverse Theory*. I think it goes beyond hypothesis because of the known abilities of parasites, already. Nano is simply a prefix denoting size, not specific to nanotech or nanobots, etc. There's nanometers, as well. Like how the envious Deletes measure their penises.

The other of the two elements is the structure of the secret societies, the schools of the adepts, and the priestcraft in-general. What if a group of people were infected or infested with a parasite that was able to completely shut down their empathy for other people, because what was controlling them wasn't human? Essentially we have observed a phenomenon among known parasites where the impulses and desires of the host serve the parasite. They're the ones inside pushing the buttons and pulling the levers. They basically hack, or hijack the emotional control board. If it isn't human controlled, then the individual that's being manipulated would not have regard for human life. If the parasite was able to deeply affect the host, it could even cause them to infect others, possibly selectively, upon a successful initiation. During these initiation ceremonies there's almost always a cup to drink or something to ingest as part of the rites and rituals. They could be exposing the candidate to a parasite that will eventually take over the helm of their body and mind.

In an old X-Files: Season 1, Episode 8, originally aired November 5th, 1993, called *Ice* a parasite from an ice core sample infects the team of the Arctic Ice Core Project. The larvae that could be seen only under a microscope later becomes the size of a meal worm.

In the episode an actual super meal worm got the role of "alien parasite." It was was later stated in conversation between scientists that went along with Mulder and Scully that the worm eventually made its way into the hypothalamus.

The hypothalamus helps manage your body temperature, hunger and thirst, **mood**, *sex drive, blood pressure and sleep.*
-my.clevelandclinic.org/health/body/22566-hypothalamus

The hypothalamus is basically a control center deep in the brain that sends hormones (signals) to the pituitary gland that also sends out hormones to control a part of the body. Acetylcholine (ACh) was also mentioned in the X-Files show, and I verified that it is a neurotransmitter that is linked to aggression. Acetylcholine and it's corresponding "receptors" are found in the neocortex (sensory perception, cognition) and limbic system (emotions, mood, sexual stimulation, behavior, motivation) but also in the Gut-Brain. There are a lot of neurons in the gut. These nicotinic acetylcholine receptors are therefore able to be manipulated by gut, blood, or brain parasites if these parasites have mastered the control deck of any one of the centers responsible for the regulation or stimulation of hormonal signaling.

The episode's writers did their homework, at least. This is one way these parasites or nanobots could manipulate impulses to get the host to operate in service to it. This also makes me think of the "chatter" that people sometimes call the constant *inner dialog*. What we perceive as our own thoughts, desires, hunger, impulses, cravings for fat and sugar, etc. could potentially be a foreign entity, or a whole colony of foreign entities inspiring you to give them what they want. And the million thoughts in the mind could represent the desires each of your nano-buddies echoing through your body chemistry.

I would argue that the mind clutter is at least in part due to the bombardment of signals from radio frequencies (RF), and other electromagnetic radiation (EMR) from doppler, radar, sonar, satellites, wi-fi, etc. This leads into another question as to whether all these transmitted frequencies are deliberately suppressing us, and/or interfering with a divine communication. Like, would that guiding inner voice be louder were it not for all the artificial frequencies?

We are energetic beings, and all living things emit a frequency. If something were to alter the natural frequencies, one could see disease, mental disruptions and disturbances occur in effected, or targeted areas.

Imagine if some of the anti-human tendencies of the powerful and wealthy are due to stowaways operating them from within. Our whole concept of Evil would change, and a possibility to kill off the unwanted influences would exist. It makes you wonder if the compulsory immunization craze of the last 200 years has been spreading these parasitic, manipulative beings throughout the world population. Are many of us golems, avatars for completely different entities that only use us to experience stimuli and cause reckless, self-destructive behaviors? Maybe they feed off of particular hormones and know how to push our buttons to release them. This possession could be seen as demonic, for any possession is a parasitic relationship.

Are Demons and AI related? Again this is a thought exercise, and it's not something anyone I know of can say definitively one way or the other.

I have often wondered, because to me there's no doubt that human history is cyclical, not linear, if AI is something ancient relative to this particular era. There should be enough proof in existing wonders of the world that remain impossible to recreate that a higher peak was reached in the past. I don't believe in the religion of Aliens. When you believe something without having any proof you're practicing a religion, as per Bill Cooper's statement on the matter. Although there was a time that I was very entertained by *Ancient Aliens* and even spent money two years in a row to attend CONTACT in the Desert, where many of the cast members appear and hold workshops and lectures. I met Brien Foerster, Michael Tellinger, Erik Von Daniken, Giorgio Tsoukalos, Clyde Lewis, Travis Waton (probably no relation), and a bunch of other known faces in the UFOlogy community. Cooper had his moment of exploring the possibility, as well. He later renamed it U-Foology. Which is funny since before I listened to my first episode of Bill's *The Hour of the Time*, I renamed the event I had previously attended, COMMUNISTS in the Desert. Kind of paints a picturesque image of Marxist hippies from Gaia TV holding hands and dancing in a circle, doesn't it? It's pretty accurate. Just add aliens.

There have been cataclysms that have reduced people back to primitive means. If you lose the knowledge, the technology rusts and falls away into the sands of time. But have all or any disasters been natural, or is Ba'al the Storm God a name for a directed energy weapon or Ionospheric heater that gets juiced up when the shitheads decide it's time to wipe the slate clean, again? Or better yet, have good people consciously decided that technology was growing out of hand and attempted to destroy it before it destroyed them? "What are you doing, Dave?" -HAL *2001: Space Odyssey*

Maybe I take too much stock in the notion that television and movies mock us by showing us some truths in a fictional manner. That way they can get ahead of any discovery of evidence to validate a theory by having already shown it to us. Then it can be laughed off as, "You watch too much TV," or "You saw that on Fringe," and dismissed by the status quo. I definitely see a mixture of black magic(k) and technology in today's world. What every government does with potentially helpful discoveries that could make mankind more independent and happy is either suppress it, or they weaponize it. They cause harm rather than liberate. So why couldn't there have been an attempt in the past to destroy malicious technology? Could AI be some relic of the distant past that was thought to have been thoroughly eradicated, but some artifact remained, and was rediscovered long after the world had chosen to forget about it? Do archons and the disembodied that we would typically associate with demons dwell within the "artificial" intelligence? Picture a priesthood discovering or being brought a strange object and making a religion around it, or having that be their secret and precious philosopher's stone. We have witnessed advances in technology in the past 200 years that, when compared to all the time that came before it, has unfolded at breakneck-speed. Accounting for some claims probably being lies to humble us before the priests of Science, there's still a great amount of tangible "progress" that has occurred right in our lifetime. Was something feeding information to the select guardians of knowledge? When you study the practitioners of magick, you find they seek insight from their communication with beings, forces, archetypes, demons, etc. If something was feeding them knowledge on how to build new machinery and technology, is that something a demon would know about, or a computer? And for what purpose? To build a world that is better for the priesthood, for mankind, or for the beings that provide said data? Whatever AI or these spirits are, are they using people to rebuild a world for them? This has been on my mind because of this push to integrate us with technology that itself would act like a parasite. This could be the way to give that which does not have a body of its own new life in us. This would certainly be evil whether AI or demons were behind it. Transhumanism is the end of life. It will be like relegating your will to the back seat while something else drives. Living hell would be conscious awareness of this with no ability to regain control of yourself. The ultimate Evil would be having to witness helplessly as your hands, being controlled for you, murder your loved ones and make you watch. If you want an ultimate hell scenario, there it is. Body hacking the likes of a worldwide Amityville Horror. Either you'll be tricked into thinking your family are demons, or you will be looking through your eyes as the hands do the work and you can't control them. If it ever got to that, if you were forced to integrate with technology, it's time to take yourself out before you can be used to cause such horrible things.

These mind control experiments were never stopped, and since Cybernetics they were building toward a final goal. Some of you remember the "legal highs" that used to be sold online. These were mind control drugs being tested on the population rather than a controlled setting. The whole country is a Mind Control project. Bath Salts was a generic name given to several different chemical formulas over time. It began with MDPV, a drug that was also called *super cocaine* given the tiny amount needed and the duration of the effects. Some reported it as being like putting on the glasses from *They Live*, after a prolonged use. The formula was then changed, but the name wasn't, and the real experiment began. I'm sure some recall the homeless guy in Florida eating someone's face. What some took for an energy boost had now changed form. Were there nanotech in that compound?

If AI is exclusively intellect with no heart or compassion, no empathy, then whether or not it's an actual demon is irrelevant, because it is demonic by definition. Replete with empirical knowledge, the epitome of the Tree of Knowledge, but containing no wisdom.

A Few Parting Topics to Cover in Greater Detail in Book II

The goal of Ba'al Busters Book I: ***Priestcraft, Beyond Babylon*** wasn't to leave the curious reader with nothing to seek out and research on their own. In fact, it was my mission to provide you with enough compelling information arranged in the proper way (that's subjective, ha ha) so that the patterns of behavior throughout the history that was covered would inspire readers to become researchers themselves.

I was not on the track to become a historical analyst by any means 20 years ago. I was busy trying to figure myself out. I spent a lot of time solo, on hiking trails, and in the gym. I never liked money for any reason other than it bought less worry and anxiety. I wasn't materialistic. I just wanted enough to afford to not be harassed. My goal was to become a writer and possibly direct my own screenplays. I wrote short fiction ever since I was 15 when I first read *Dark Tower: The Gunslinger* by Stephen King. It inspired me to explore some of the concepts presented in it. I was pondering the very essence of existence, and questioning whether reality was an illusion, a huge trap, or if we had the power to make it whatever we wanted it to be.

It wasn't until 2017 that I discovered early Christians had questioned these very things themselves. To call anything a heresy is a subjective statement. The question is, *a heresy according to whom?* An anti-Christian church who canonized, secularized, homogenized and standardized what it meant to be "Christian" even though they weren't the predominant theory at the time? They just had the muscle, so they tossed or allowed the tossing of what they only much later labeled "Gnostic" Christians to the lions. They campaigned Crusades that targeted, tortured, and brutally murdered them. These priests in blood soaked robes are not representatives of Jesus. They disgrace and mock his teachings, and by the way, the very fact there's an institutionalized church and a vicar, or Pope goes against the very nature of authentic Christianity, as does writing everything in Latin, and killing those who possessed a copy of a book they couldn't read, anyway.

To the Early Christians the personal journey was of the utmost importance. You don't get to heaven as a group or a collective. You don't escape the seven trappings of the Demiurgos without cultivating yourself, and experiencing life to gain much needed wisdom. If you have a spark of divinity, then it's your job to cultivate and nourish it so that it may burn brightly within you. Gnosis, or Knowing, goes beyond belief or faith. There's no question for those who have that connection and communication with the benevolent one. You know it, because it's not just conceptual to you. You experience it. There are too many people that have faith simply because they're scared not to. They hide under their book, but don't read the pages. Only obscure passages out-of-context that have been read to them by the Marxist-Frankist pastors when they are propagandizing from the pulpit. Look up the history of the National, and World Council of Churches to see what controls the mouths of priests and even pastors.

At this juncture, the elements described throughout this reading have come together and their connections to one another, and to ancient, mystical, and brutally dark priesthoods is undeniable. It's no small task to track down valuable details on a history that has been not only suppressed, but buried under a pile of academic misguidance, and inaccurate depictions. In many cases the original histories were "lost," or have been completely rewritten, with figures, events and peoples damaging to the official narrative written out. I did my best. If more data is hidden somewhere, I may have more to say, or more definitive answers should I ever discover it.

Inner work is a solo journey. But Community and Family are our only way out of this mess. Once you strengthen yourself you can be a valuable asset and mentor for others. There's always more that you can learn. Life is a process, and it, like the word, is a living process. Never stunt your growth by thinking you have it all figured out. I learn from my daughter. She teaches me to be loving and gentle, and is an example of pure intent. That's an element this world's people need to protect and defend at all costs. If we lose our innocence, there's nothing left. The most noble cause there is for mankind is to protect the children for they are closest to a personification of the Benevolent spirit. "Protect" does NOT mean getting them vaccinated and bringing them to allopathic wellness visits. These are deceptions of a system designed to annihilate the most precious gift we could receive.

Parents, it's time we grew up, understood our role, and muster the courage to do whatever it takes to put a halt to this wickedness aimed at destroying the children and the family unit.

I appreciate everyone who has come this far in the journey. This is not even close to all I wanted to write about, and I'm learning new elements and details of our past all the time. This is by no means complete or perfect. It's a start.

Topics I wish to cover in the next volume are a more in-depth look at Aleister Crowley and his impact on the secret societies, and therefore the direction the world has gone. I just discovered the work of Asha Logos, and I need to explore the history of the Scythians and Goths, a seemingly noble and just people. Some of them rejected the path and it's possible they grew into the very adversaries that are still actively attempting to eradicate the remaining Germanic people and others of common ancestry. We have yet to hit upon Scientology, only briefly discussing one element of L. Ron Hubbard, an Officer in Naval Intelligence. If you want a head start, look up Operation Snow White. We haven't covered the truth about WWI, WWII, Vietnam, Lybia, and so on, but that is a huge topic as well. I didn't get a chance to cover the Rosicrucians, Francis Bacon, or Alice and Foster Bailey. The Lucifer Trust, now called the Lucis Trust publishes the releases by the United Nations. It's important to take a closer look at Greek letter college fraternities and Sororities, and Jesuit universities such as Georgetown that are recruiting grounds for the NSA, CIA, and so on. There's more to be said about Saturn, the cults, and the symbolism still at play in modern politics. Politicians are what I call Crowliticians, a reference to the influence of Aleister Crowley and their work toward the Aeon of Horus.

The Rothschilds discussion would not be complete without mention of their connections with the Sassoon family (Baghdadi Jewish family), and the opium trade that destroyed China. That topic leads into the Khazarian Mafia where we see more of the **machinations** (plots) of the Rothschilds. This isn't to say that everything Jewish is bad, by any means. These are mostly converts that do bad things under the shield of protection that pretending "Jewish" affords them. Luria was an Ashkenazi, which typically means a Turkish convert that settled in Rhineland (Germanic territories) and migrated elsewhere. About 3 million Ashkenazi live in Israel, and that state is a blight on Judaism by its very nature. Zionism, remember, is a Lurian, and thereby a Sabbatean-Frankkist concept. The orthodoxy didn't accept Shabbatai, Frank, and many were also opposed to a forced state of Israel. I do not fully understand all the moving parts of this yet, and maybe I can't, but I do know that Deuteronomy doesn't do Judaism any favors either, or at least not the literalization (is that a word?) of it.

We didn't cover the demonology of the ancients fully, and there are Vedic gods that pop up with different names in Canaanite lore and sculptures. This could be evidence of a portion of the Scythians migrating to that area to create the population, or an influential visitation by them. The Vedas were of the Scythian/Indo-European (Aryan) culture, but at the core they were of the belief in a singular Heavenly Father, Papaeus, in Greek.

When I have an opportunity to speak more with Nichudeemus, and Niish of *The Cosmic Salon* podcast, we need to get more data on the depictions and symbolism of Lilith that have been rampant lately surrounding the alleged natural fires and other devastating events around the world. Demonology takes on a huge role in the efforts of the Great Reset, further evidence that these are dark priests of the ancient and secret Mystery Schools. You can catch some of my previous discussions with Nichudeemus on the cryptic, often celestial symbolism of Saturn, Magna Mater (Lilith?) and the Sirius star on my channel.

I'd also like to detail a *Timeline of Tyranny* beginning with the colonies up to present day in America. We have to tie in the French Revolution as well. I happened to know some big names, or at least their staff, watch my video presentations because I catch them "borrowing," to put it politely, my hash tags and topics for their more commercial productions. A certain large-tree on a tightrope took the term Timeline of Tyranny, as an example. Just as a certain soup-stones (Peter(s) means stone or rock) covers stuff I did 4 years ago like it's breaking news—with a less meaningful slant on it, of course.

Until the next book, I encourage you to find my Rumble Channel, Ba'al Busters, for as long as it may last given the Canadian government's efforts. Rumble is based out of Canada, not out of Bongino's Bat Cave, for those unaware. If these topics interested you in any way, watch the videos I put out, and share them. I'm an independent channel, and I put up my own funds to do the broadcasts. Ba'al Busters relies on real view & subscriber counts, not some doctored numbers to make it appear more engaged.

Yeah that's a thing. There isn't much honest or real about the monster-sized influencers with mouths to match. I remain independent because it's the only way I can talk about what I do, and do it without restrictions. That means Ba'al Busters is as appreciated, or as neglected as you make it.

You can also find my videos on JoshWhoTV.com. Big people with power and influence do not like that Josh is independent, uncontrolled, and a real Section 230 platform. If you want to fight the system, make JoshWhoTV eclipse these other honeypot and censored platforms just by watching videos there. Create a user account and find great content. Or become a content creator yourself in the one place that will never take down your videos or issue strikes. My channel is at BaalBuster.JoshWhoTV.com   If the platform is gone before you seek it out, it means the bad guys who constantly DDos attack it have won. It means Josh didn't receive the support he needed to keep your lifeboat afloat. My people suffer for lack of Babylonian curse-money.

Last note: We're running out of time. There's no way to prepare for the devastation being planned for us all. That implies that we sit and wait for it and hope our preparations keep us alive. Bad strategy! You don't box someone with your guard up, and never swing back. You still lose because you never threw a punch, and you're likely to get knocked on your ass hard, anyway.

Take a lesson from Bruce Lee, and the Way of the Intercepting Fist (Jeet Kun Do.) If you see trouble coming at you go after the source before it can deliver the blow. Fast, reflexive, and powerful. They have been going on for too long beating us down without us ever returning the favor. We don't even conceive of it. We drop to our knees in the middle of the ring and pray that God protects us. He gave you what you need to protect yourself: Two fists. Now friggin' use them. New metaphor: If you wait until you're already in checkmate, in a digital prison, disarmed, children stolen and vaccinated with poison and biosensors, it will be too late!

William Cooper started his mission to educate and warn people in the 80's. He began his first *The Hour of the Time* broadcast in May of '92, with his book, *Behold a Pale Horse* being released in December of '91. He tried to help us prevent ever having to get to this point. Too many took it as entertainment, and didn't put the lessons to action. The system created an Alex Jones to divert attention away from Cooper's message. They picked a guy whose sole assignment was to distort, pervert, and make a mockery of the truth. To this day, people use the same guy as a release valve for their stress, so they feel like they "did something." Jones still speaks poorly of the dead desecrating Bill's memory whenever a caller brings up Bill Cooper, or his book. The shirts Jones or his ilk sell stating "Alex Jones Was Right" are a direct slap in the face to Bill whose research has been adopted and repackaged as Jones' and many others have taken Bill's work and used it for their own advancement as well. Few ever give credit to the original source. They're happy to let you assume it was their tireless effort, and often they claim as much.

Listening isn't doing anything. A mental journey has no bearing on the world in front of us. We make our own energy inert by LARPing as we listen to these loudmouths complain about what's within the status quo's approved parameters. They take the audience on the emotional ride and the listener thinks they're changing the world simply by tuning in and getting worked up. We all may be heroic legends in our own minds, sleeping dragons with great potential, but until we use that potential we have done nothing. We blew off steam, and were comforted just knowing others were upset about the same stuff we were. As previously stated, our battle is mostly fought in the comments sections, not in reality, and never directed at those actually responsible for the condition we're in. We've been reduced to agitated spectators—strong in voice, weak in action. We daydreamed while the world went to shit, and the safety of our families deteriorated to an extremely dangerous level. The only reason this small percentage has gained so much is because they pursued it. We didn't. We even got out of their way so they could rob our birthright. It's up to us to restore our freedom. It was never the job of one man to do it for us. We need to do it as a family, as a community. We need a place to raise our children. This is our purpose.

BA'AL BUSTERS

Rumble Channel: **https://rumble.com/c/BaalBusters**

JoshWhoTV: **https://BaalBuster.JoshWhoTV.com**

Telegram: **https://t.me/BaalBustersStudios**

Twitter: **https://twitter.com/DisguiseLimits**

GiveSendGo: **https://GiveSendGo.com/BaalBusters**

Find me on all podcast distributors

 Support from viewers keeps the show going. This is an independent effort. Thank You

-Daniel Kristos

Code for Dr Monzo's site is **baalbusters15** for 15% off his items.
https://drmonzo.kartra.com/page/shop

Printed in Great Britain
by Amazon

46597573R00163